A History of
Music Education in
the United States

A History of
Music Education in
the United States

JAMES A. KEENE

UNIVERSITY PRESS OF NEW ENGLAND
Hanover and London

Illustration credits: Shinichi Suzuki photo by Arthur Montzka.
All other illustrations courtesy of Music Educators National
Conference Historical Center, University of Maryland.

Copyright © 1982 by Trustees Dartmouth College

Printed in the United States of America

LIBRARY OF CONGRESS CATALOGING IN PUBLICATION DATA

Keene, James A., 1932–
    A history of music education in the United States.

    Includes index.
    I. Music—Instruction and study—United States—History. I. Title.
MT3.U5K3   780'.7'2973   81-51610
ISBN 0–87451–212–3   AACR2
ISBN 0–87451–405–3 (pbk)

5   4   3

Contents

Preface

THE HISTORY of music education in the United States has been, generally speaking, one of reform. Our early settlers, as well as the Founding Fathers, considered their efforts to be rooted in an idealism whether it be expressed in terms of religious or political liberty, and from such beginnings Americans have tended to regard themselves as reformers from that day to the present. It is less important to approve or disapprove of each reform than it is to observe the consistent efforts of Americans to cast aside the old way and adopt that which is new and different. This national trait prevailed throughout the history of music education in America, resulting in our music educators changing methods and philosophies sometimes capriciously, sometimes thoughtfully.

The history of music education in the United States cannot have an independent existence, just as the history of art, the history of music, and the history of education all relate to and feed upon the social history of a people. America's music education cannot be divorced from the history of music both in this country and in Europe. The American white man is, after all, only a displaced European, while the American black man's contributions to American music, particularly in the field of jazz, have been considerable, though his role in music education has only begun to be explored.

The white man's folk art was an important force which began to develop after the landing of the Pilgrims in 1620. Generally taken for granted by its practitioners, folk art is close to the people and is considered an everyday necessity. It is mentioned by early writers and observers only in times of controversy but otherwise blends into the culture of the people. As the first formal attempts at music education came in reaction against the folklorization of church music in the colonies, this music will be examined in some detail in order to understand what processes were involved, not only in the folklorization but in the so-called reform that followed.

The folk culture in America has always been a source of embar-

rassment to those who looked toward Europe as their artistic
Mecca, and the polarity between America's indigenous music and
its European counterpart has not been resolved to this day. The
earliest reforms of the eighteenth century have much in common
with the average sentiments of music educators of the twentieth
century. Both groups fought against and were critical of American
folk art.

It is usual to think of the development of music education in
terms of music and music teachers. But such an approach is limiting and omits certain trends in the general history of education,
trends that affected the development and direction of the profession. To give this idea substance, parts of this volume deal forthrightly with various historical and philosophical tendencies, with
an attempt made to relate them to the prevailing thoughts and
movements in music education. It would have been much more
difficult for our music teachers to promote the concept of teaching
their art in the public schools if society were not ready to endorse a
general expansion of the school curriculum. It is necessary to observe these changes in our educational expectations in order to
gain a broader understanding of the role of music education as it
relates to the public school.

The subject of the history of music education in the United
States is broad. A one volume study can never hope to be definitive, and this work is no exception. Our informal educational
practices, instruction in the home and in the streets, are a part of
our sociology and influence our formal educational practices even
when the two areas are in contention. The formal introduction of
music education into the public school curriculum was repeated
again and again in various cities and towns throughout the country. Lowell Mason's efforts, being the first, have been more fully
chronicled, but many hard-working and politically active music
teachers repeated his work in their own cities, but one could never
hope to mention them all. Even the many influential music educators who made contributions on a national scale must await due
recognition in another volume whose point of view would be more
receptive to such an account.

It would have been impossible to write this volume had it not
been for the increase in interest in the history of music education
on the campuses of our colleges and universities in recent years.

The number of doctoral dissertations in this field has multiplied dramatically, and I am indebted to these scholars who have done the difficult and time-consuming spadework of identifying the primary sources and pointing out trends. But the field is still in its infancy with much work remaining to be done. Music teachers deserve to know where they have been in relation to where they are at the present. Without a secure knowledge of our past, music educators reinvent methods and philosophies believing sincerely in the universal efficacy of that which they espouse. Insights based upon an historical prospective will make our profession more mature (more thoughtful when presented with older methodologies masquerading as new) and more understanding of the complex interrelationships between our profession, the problems of general education, and the changing values of our society.

I would be remiss if I did not take the opportunity to express my appreciation to Allen P. Britton who was kind enough to read this manuscript and make many valuable suggestions, to Charles Leonhard whose interest and enthusiasm helped to make publication a reality, and to Cynthia Barry whose diligent work with the manuscript contributed much to the organization and clarity of this volume.

A History of
Music Education in
the United States

CHAPTER I

Colonial New England

THE AMERICAN musical folk art took some years to develop.
After the unsuccessful attempt at forming a colony at Jamestown in 1607, the Pilgrim separatists established their more successful enterprise at Plymouth, Massachusetts, in 1620, followed
ten years later by the Puritans in the Massachusetts Bay area. The
Mayflower's passengers were on the whole landed gentry, crafts-
men, tradesmen, and artisans. They had emigrated from England
to Holland to escape religious persecution. Fearful that their children would be assimilated into the Dutch world, they left the relative security of their refuge to start life anew.

The Pilgrims had an essential musicality as evidenced by the famous statement of Edward Winslow in his *Hypocrisie Unmasked*
of 1646. Winslow describes the large Leyden congregation in Holland bidding farewell to those setting out on their long and per-
ilous journey.

They that stayed at Leyden feasted us that were to go at our pastor's
house. it being large; where we refreshed ourselves, after tears, with singing of Psalms, making joyful melody in our hearts as well as with the
voice, there being many of our congregation very expert in music; and
indeed it was the sweetest melody that ever mine ears hears.[1]

Despite hardships, the small band maintained a unity based upon
religious and social homogeneity. But the Plymouth colony had little support from outside sources and no influential friends. In
1630, the larger and more prosperous Massachusetts Bay area,
colonized by the Puritans, began to eclipse the Plymouth colony.

Both the Pilgrims and the Puritans were English separatists, followers of the religious tenets of John Calvin, and expressed their religious sentiments through the singing of psalms. The Pilgrims brought with them the *Ainsworth Psalter*, prepared especially for the separatists by Henry Ainsworth in Holland and first printed in Amsterdam in 1612.*

The thirty-nine different tunes were written for one voice only, with diamond notes and without bar lines. Ainsworth borrowed French and Dutch psalm-tunes as well as some from the older *Sternhold and Hopkins Psalter*. Many tunes in the latter psalter were also borrowed from the *French Psalter* of the sixteenth century, pointing to a common source for both the *Sternhold and Hopkins* and the *Ainsworth* psalters. The music of the *Genevan* or *French Psalter* was either composed or arranged by Louis Bourgeois, who made good use of French *popular songs* of the sixteenth century. The music of *Ainsworth* had much rhythmic variety; the rigid regularity so often associated with psalmody was absent. Waldo Pratt observed forty-five different line-rhythms, typical of the folk-song style.[2] Stanzas of five, six, eight, and twelve lines as well as eight different rhythms used for one six-syllable line were frequently incorporated.[3] The melodies, both in minor and in modes typical of the day, were meant to be sung in unison with the men's voices leading. Apparently the Pilgrims did little part singing, although harmonized versions of some of the psalms appeared in England during the latter part of the sixteenth century.[†] What part singing there was tended toward the contrapuntal, which is understandable considering the nature of music in the late sixteenth century. As modality was only on the verge of giving

* Ainsworth was born near Norwich about 1570. He studied four years at Cambridge and then became active in the separatist movement, probably in London. Religious persecution caused him to go to Amsterdam in 1593 where he worked for a time as a porter in a Dutch book shop. By 1610, he became a recognized leader and teacher of the principal congregation in Amsterdam. He was a biblical scholar and learned in Hebrew. His commentaries on the Old Testament were collected in 1627 and often republished. He died in 1623.

† Day in 1563; Damon in 1579; Estes in 1592; and Ellison in 1599. William Brewster, one of the original Pilgrim fathers, brought with him his personal library of three hundred volumes. Among these volumes was the *Psalms of David*, by Richard Allison, London, 1599, a harmonized version of the psalms. Allison's psalms were in four parts accompanied for "lute, orpharyen, citterne, or bass violl." This was one of the first psalm books to give the melody to the soprano. It was intended for domestic use, set out in "table music" fashion. It is conceivable that these harmonized versions of the psalms were sung in America by those settlers who remembered them. Unfortunately the evidence is not clear.

way completely to the system of tonality in the early seventeenth century, the few offerings of a modal designation in *Ainsworth* were in keeping with the period.

The *Ainsworth Psalter* was an octavo volume of 342 pages. It represented the first real competition to the *Sternhold and Hopkins Psalter*.* The book circulated mainly in Holland and England. Pratt believes there are about ten copies in America: one each at the Boston Public Library, Boston University, Congregational Library of Boston, the American Antiquarian Society, and the Hartford Theological Seminary. The remainder are privately owned.[4] *Ainsworth* constituted a completely new translation of the psalms in prose. Each psalm was accompanied by notes and comments on the text. Beside the prose are metrical arrangements for use in song. This translation from prose to metered verse is shown in the two versions of the Twenty-third Psalm:

Jehovah feedeth me; I shall not lack. In folds of budding grass He maketh me lie down; He easily leadeth me by the waters of rests. He returneth my soul; He leadeth me in the beaten paths of justice for his name sake.

Metered version:

> Jehovah feedeth me, I shall not lack;
> In grassy folds He down dooth make my lye;
> He gently leads me quiet waters by.
> He dooth return my soul; for His name sake
> In paths of justice leads me quietly.[5]

The versification in all early English metrical psalters is uniformly iambic. In *Ainsworth* only a few psalms have feminine endings.

The metrical versions of the psalms had considerable influence on the musical renditions. Verses and music were interdependent. The various types of verse were joined to the available kinds of melody. As many of the melodies were interchangeable—that is different melodies could be used for the same metrical patterns—the genre had the potential to minimize the number of different tunes that were used when the settlers, for diverse reasons, forgot many of the more complex melodies and retained and passed on to their children the less complex tunes.

But in the *Ainsworth Psalter* a preference for long stanzas predominated. The four-line pattern, so popular at a later time, was

---

* Later editions of *Ainsworth* came out in 1617, 1626, 1639, 1644, and 1690.

only used in one psalm in ten. One-half the psalms were in eight-line stanzas, while thirty-four had six lines and eleven had five lines.

The complex melodies in the *Ainsworth Psalter* became increasingly difficult for the colonists to remember. During the seventeenth century, the thirty-nine tunes were reduced to about a dozen. The shorter tunes were easier to remember and sing to common meter, a trend which aligned with the increasing simplification of the psalm tunes. This trend toward greater simplicity was as evident in England as in the colonies and is an example of the gradual change in stylistic expectation.

The *Ainsworth* tunes were not original but were borrowed from Dutch, English, and French sources.

Tunes for the Psalms I find none set of God; so that each people is to use the most grave, decent and comfortable manner of singing that they know. . . . The singing-notes, therefore, I have most taken from our former Englished Psalms, when they will fit the measure of the verse, and for the other long verses I have also taken (for the most part) the gravest and easiest tunes of the French and Dutch Psalters.[6]

The many, varied melodies represented the Late Renaissance style, incorporating a more or less free and irregularly accented melodic line whether that be a single melody or several contrapuntally conceived parts. The emergence of a regularly accented meter caused profound changes in the singing habits of American congregations. These changes, attributed by many to a musical illiteracy in the colonies, may very likely reflect a dramatic change in the musical expectations of the seventeenth century. While these changes were observed on the Continent and have been well-documented, similar changes also occurred in Protestant church music in America and will be discussed later.

In 1630, the Puritans landed in Salem carrying with them the *Sternhold and Hopkins Psalter*, first printed without music around 1548. This psalter was begun before 1550 by Thomas Sternhold and was finally edited by a committee chaired by John Hopkins. The combined effort was first published in 1562. Sternhold's psalms were originally intended for court circles but were of poorer quality to those of Marot in the *Genevan Psalter*, which was first printed with music at Geneva in 1556. It expanded through other editions until 1561 when it reached its final edition of eighty-seven psalms set to sixty tunes. This psalter was heavily indebted to the *French Psalter* but the preparer of the music is unknown.[7]

The Puritans then were a modestly musical people. It had long been considered that the Puritans were antimusical, an idea beautifully put to rest by Percy Scholes.[8] The Puritans loved their psalm singing both in church and in the home. There were no laws prohibiting music though there were some statutes that attempted to control it. An English ordinance tried to regulate street and tavern music, but such an effort only points to the universality of the practice. In 1644 another English ordinance cautioned against organs and elaborate music in the churches. We do not know exactly what the church fathers considered "elaborate"; quite possibly any renditions of the psalms that violated the simple, grave, and unison treatment dictated by the divines.

At the Conference of Baptists in Bridgewater, England, in 1655, the question was asked "Whether a believing man or woman, being head of a family, in this day of the gospell, may keepe in his or her house an instrument of musicke, playing on them or admitting others to play thereon." The question was answered:

It is the duty of the saintes to abstaine from all appearance of evil, and not to make provision for the flesh, to fulfill ye lusts thereof, to redeem the time, and to do all they do to the glory of God; and though we cannot conclude the use of such instruments to be unlawful, yet we desire the saints to be very cautious lest they transgress the aforesaid rules in the use of it, and do what may not be of good report, and so give offence to their tender brethren.[9]

And so the Puritan divines approved music, with qualifications. Admitting that the practice of music was not unlawful, the church most self-consciously and with much reserve gave its permission if not its blessing. Today our task is to try to understand the relative power and influence of psalm singing upon the Puritans themselves and their institutions.

The leaders of the Puritans at Salem felt too many liberties had been taken with the original Hebrew in the *Sternhold and Hopkins Psalter* and sought to improve it. A committee of thirty was charged with the responsibility of making a more literal translation. In 1640, a small press at Cambridge, Massachusetts published 1,700 copies of *The Whole Booke of Psalmes Faithfully*

Translated into English Metre. Because the new psalter was immediately accepted almost everywhere in the Massachusetts Bay
colony it became known as the *Bay Psalm Book.* No music was
included in the first edition of the first book-length publication in
the American colonies.[10] The tunes at first were well-known to the
Puritans, and there was no readily available music printing at this
early time. The number of meters, however, was reduced from that
of the *Sternhold and Hopkins Psalter,* demonstrating that even at
this date, Puritan psalmody was in the gradual process of simplification. The more difficult tunes were either being ignored or
had been forgotten by the early settlers. Fully three-quarters of the
psalms in the *Bay Psalm Book* were in common meter. Although
tunes for these psalms could easily be found in Ravenscroft's
Whole Book of Psalms, not all the tunes in Ravenscroft were familiar to the Puritans in 1640. This first attempt by the Puritan
divines to save psalm singing by reducing the number and complexity of the tunes was destined to fail. The scarcity of music and
the gradual decline in congregational participation in the church
services lead to an increasing musical illiteracy in the colonies.

The old *Sternhold and Hopkins Psalter* employed seventeen
metrical schemes, and it was a Puritan ordinance to sing the entire
book of psalms through in sequence. The early settlers apparently
had this repertoire, but by 1640 the *Bay Psalm Book* with its six
metrical patterns presented sufficient difficulties for the Puritan
congregations. This simplifying trend started in England and
therefore could not be attributed exclusively to the difficult frontier life of the settlers and their isolation from Europe. It corresponded instead with the trend away from the late Renaissance
melodic complexity toward a more straightforward, rhythmic
style that was to fuse in America with certain indigenous folk
tendencies into a unique genre of religious folk music.

The second edition of the *Bay Psalm Book* was the same as
the first, but the third edition in 1651 incorporated considerable
changes. This later edition, of which two thousand copies were
printed, reflected growing dissatisfaction with the original text.
The psalm-tune repertory diminished again with increasing reliance on a common-meter text, a state of affairs prevalent in England also during this time. Thirty-six new songs were added in
this edition, and its name was changed to *The Psalm Hymns and*

Spiritual Songs of the Old and New Testament faithfully translated into English metre for the use, edification, and comfort of the saints in publick and private, especially in New England. This was the definitive edition until 1758.[11] As a testament to the popularity of this version, forty editions were printed in both England and Scotland.

The ninth edition is of special interest as it was the first edition known to us to include music.[12] Thirteen psalm tunes in two parts were included in addition to a few instructions for "their proper performance."[13] The thirteen tunes were copied from the 1679 editions of John Playford's *Brief Introduction to the Skill of Music*, a standard treatise of the latter part of the seventeenth century.

The following from the ninth edition was taken verbatim from Playford's *Brief Introduction*:

First observe of how many *Notes* compass the *Tune* is. Next, the place of your first *Note*, and how many *Notes* above and below that: so as you may begin the *Tune* of your first *Note* as the rest may be sung in the compass of your and the peoples voices, without Squeaking above, or Grumbling below.[14]

Such rudimentary instruction is significant. We see an initial attempt at instruction in music, an effort that will be repeated in American tune books hundreds of times in the eighteenth century in an effort to improve the quality of church singing in the colonies. The *Sternhold and Hopkins Psalter* had a discourse on the theory of reading music from its 1562 edition. This effort in the colonies in a sense paralleled similar attempts at improvement and reform in England as well.

The four note gamut was recommended in the ninth edition of the *Bay Psalm Book*, and again this system appears in the 1672 edition of *Brief Introduction*. This system of syllable notation became fashionable in Elizabethan England and came into use in the colonies. Only four syllables were used: fa, sol, la, and mi. Only mi was not repeated in the scale and was used to identify the leading tone and hence the key. A major scale would appear thus:

Fa sol la fa sol la mi fa

The fasola system was to retain its popularity into the nineteenth century, and the story of its gradual removal—first from the urban centers and later from rural New England to the Southwest—is closely tied to the changes in music and music education during the first half of the nineteenth century. In the ninth edition of the *Bay Psalm Book* the fasola letters were placed directly under the musical notes.* The use of notation and syllable indicates that there was some musical literacy in the colonies. No institutions existed at this time to perpetuate music instruction in the colonies, but the singing of psalmody was transmitted mostly through an oral tradition from one generation to another. Although the trend was toward simplification between the time of the *Ainsworth* and *Sternhold and Hopkins* psalters and the *Bay Psalm Book*, the institution of psalmody was indeed vigorous and close to the hearts of Puritan colonists.

Secular music also existed in the colonies, but there was little official enthusiasm for this art. Its practice was tolerated by some and enjoyed by others, but this music was uncomfortably close to the devil to be a necessary and vital part of Puritan culture. That it appears to be condemned in the literature of the times tells us of its prevalence. Cotton Mather, a leading Puritan, noted in a "Discourse on the Good Education of Children"[†] that teachers are worthy of honor "that convey Wisdom unto our children."

Their stipends are generally far short of their Deserts. . . . I can't but observe with a just indignation; to feed our children, to Cloath our Children, to do any thing for the Bodies of our Children, or perhaps to teach them some trifle at a Dancing School, scarcely worth their learning, we account no expense too much; at the same time to have the Minds of our Children Enriched with the most valuable Knowledge, here. To what purpose? is the cry; a little Expense, how heavily it goes off! *My Brethren, These things ought not so to be.*[15]

In church, the Puritan settlers in America probably sang their psalm tunes in unison and unaccompanied. But at home these same tunes would have been sung in harmony and accompanied by instruments. While harmonized versions of the psalms did oc-

* Probably the source of John Tufts's notation in the *Introduction to the Singing of Psalm Tunes* of 1721.
† Delivered at the funeral of Ezekial Cheever, principal of the Latin School in Boston, "who died August, 1708, in the ninety-fourth year of his age, with an Elegy and Epistle by one that was once a Scholar to him."

casionally find their way into the Puritan churches in the eighteenth century, generally speaking, the use of instruments was considered the work of the devil until the early years of the nineteenth
century. Both Thomas Ravenscroft's *Whole Book of Psalms* in
1621 and Richard Allison's *Psalms of David* in 1599 were in four
parts and the use of instruments was suggested for both. As there
was a social and economic intercourse between the Puritans in England and those in America, it is reasonable to suppose, as Percy
Scholes does, that this situation existed in America also.

Instruments appeared early in colonial New England. Judge
Sewell "was at Mr. Hiller's to enquire for [his] wife's virginal" on
December 1, 1699.[16] In England Cromwell himself maintained a
body of ten vocal and instrumental performers, and Milton believed that music should have a suitable place in education in his
Tractate of Education. So instrumental music and dancing were
tolerated by the Puritans, both in England and in America. In
1647, John Cotton offered some advice about the performance of
music outside the church.

We also grant that any private Christian who hath a gift to frame a spir-
ituall song may both frame it and sing it privately for his own private
comfort and remembrance of some speciall benefit or deliverance. Nor
doe we forbid the use of any instrument therewithall: so that attention to
the instrument does not divert the heart from attention to the matter of
song.[17]

It is likely that the above was a liberal reaction to criticism of a
prevailing practice. From 1700, however, we see a rather spirited
business in musical instruments, which points to a growing interest in the several aspects of music. Instruments were imported
from London for a population increasingly willing and able to
play them. In an advertisement in the Boston *News* of 1716, the
following arrived from London: "Flageolets, Flutes, Haut-boys,
Bass-viols, Violins, bows, strings, reeds for hautboys, books of instruction, books of ruled paper." The statements also indicate that
a greater number of instruments existed in colonial New England
than has been accounted for by current scholars. Tolerance, however, is a long way from enthusiastic cultivation. At no time were
the Puritans officially enthusiastic about any form of music other
than psalm singing. This point is of special interest because the
first organized institution to teach singing—the singing school—

came about in response to the need to "reform" psalm singing in New England.

An important custom that prepared the way for the singing school was known as "lining out." Begun in England, "lining out" was officially inaugurated and sanctioned by the Puritan Assembly of Divines at Westminster in 1644. Called "deaconing" in America, it required the deacon of the church to recite a line of the psalm (as distinguished from intoning) which the congregation would then sing. The purpose of the custom was to help those who had not learned to read to participate happily in the singing. Lining out was introduced in the colonies in 1681 in Plymouth but it was not in general use until about the middle of the eighteenth century. Though it is possible that a meeting in Worcester, Massachusetts, decided to abandon the practice, it continued in some places for nearly a hundred years.[18] The practice began to die out in America near the end of the eighteenth century, but in England and Scotland the practice was rather common for another hundred years.[19] From John Cotton's *Singing of Psalms: a Gospel-Ordinance*,[20] we learn about the motives of the Puritans regarding the use of lining out.

The last scruple remaining in the manner of singing, *Concernith the order of singing after* the Reading of the Psalm. . . . We for our parts easily grant, that where all have books and can read, or else can say the *Psalm* by heart, it were needless there to read each line of the *Psalm* before hand in order to [sing it] . . . it will be a necessary, that the words of the *Psalm* be openly read before hand, line after line, or two lines together, that so they who want either books or skill to read, may know what is to be sung, and join with the rest in the duty of singing.[21]

Perhaps one cannot read too much into the use of the word "duty," but the choice of such a word hardly indicates enthusiasm for such singing. In 1707 Isaac Watts wrote that he was disgusted "to see the dull indifference, the neglect and the thoughtless air that sits upon the faces of a whole assembly while the Psalm is on their lips." But lining out was accepted with enthusiasm in most places and died slowly in the eighteenth century even after it had become unnecessary.

"Deaconing the hymn" led to breaking up the musical rendition of a psalm by the deacon reciting the words every line or two. In 1730 Leman complained in his *New Method of Learning Psalm*

Tunes that the congregation's thoughts are so intent on what the clerk "is going next to deliver that they in great measure forget the preceeding part of the tune, and doing this one line after another may be one reason why the whole tune is remembered in but a very imperfect manner."[22] Though singing of the line by the precentor did occur occasionally in America, most precentors merely spoke the text.

There was a continuing interest in psalm singing in the colonies, although we cannot be sure of its quality. Gilbert Chase makes a good case for the growing folklorization of psalm singing in the colonies with an increasing use of ornamentation. The art of note reading was preserved in only a few intellectual centers such as Harvard College, and we must assume that the ability to read music was rare. The psalm tunes were sung "by ear," from memory, and probably were embellished freely until the relationship between the original tune and its performed version was marginal at best. In time, however, the Reverend Thomas Symmes and Nathaniel Chauncey's admonitions concerning the abysmal state of psalm singing set the stage for the appearance of the singing school, the first formal institution in English colonial America whose purpose was to teach music.

The reformers advocated "regular singing" or singing by note, pointing to the usual manner of singing as being a corruption. Symmes speculated that regular singing would divert young people "from learning idle, foolish, yea, pernicious songs and ballads, and banish all such trash from their minds."[23] He wrote that music was studied and approved "in our college [Harvard] for many years after its first founding. This is evident from the Musical Theses which were formerly printed, and from some writings containing some tunes, with directions for singing by note, as they are now sung; and these are yet in being, though of more than sixty years standing; besides no man that studied music, as it is treated of by Alstead, Playford and Others, could be ignorant of it."[24]

The tradition of ornamentation is long, and the embellishment of the tunes was commonplace both in Europe and in America. This tradition was perpetuated even after "singing by rule" became the norm, and singing schools taught the more common varieties of ornamentation. If Symmes, Chauncey, Thomas Walter, and other reformers were interested in doing away with ornamentation, they did not succeed. Their significance lies in their efforts to reintroduce the art of singing by note, paving the way for our nation's first music teachers—those early singing masters who moved from town to town in New England practicing their trade in homes, meetinghouses, and even saloons. And in 1723 Symmes strongly urged the expansion of the singing school.

Would it not greatly tend to promote singing of psalms if singing schools were promoted? Would not this be conforming to the *scripture pattern*? Have we not as much need of them as God's people of old? Have we any reason to expect to be inspired with the gift of singing any more than of reading? Or to attain it without suitable means, any more than they of old, when *miracles*, *inspirations*, etc., were common. Where would be the *difficulty* or what the disadvantage, if people who want skill in singing would procure a skillful person to instruct them, and meet two or three evenings in the week, from *five* or *six* to *eight*, and spend the time in learning to sing? Would it not be proper for *school masters* in *country parishes* to teach their scholars? Would it not be very sensible in ministers to encourage their people to learn to sing? Are they not under some obligation by virtue of their office to do so?[25]

The institution of the singing school was gaining in popularity. But before describing these schools in detail, we should meet two men whose contributions to the singing school were important.

CHAPTER II

The Singing School

JOHN TUFTS

IN JANUARY 1721 an advertisement appeared in the Boston
News Letter proclaiming that a new book had been published
by Samuel Garish, bookseller near the Brick Church in Cornhill.

A Small Book containing 20 Psalm Tunes, with Directions how to Sing
them, contrived in the most easy Method ever yet Invented, for the ease
of Learners, whereby even Children, or People of the meanist Capacities,
may come to Sing them by Rule, may serve as an Introduction to a more
compleat Treatise of Singing, which will speedily be published.

John Tufts, a little-known, forty-two-year-old minister compiled
a small volume of psalm tunes (published unharmonized in the
first edition) in which a new system of note reading was introduced.[1] The letters F S L M appeared on the staff each signifying a
syllable of the four note gamut fa, sol, la, and mi. The lengths of
notes were indicated by various signs of punctuation following
one of the above letters: a period represented a half note; a colon
represented a whole note; and no punctuation mark at all indicated a quarter note.[2] Tufts's book included thirty-seven tunes
printed on twelve pages, and it was the first book of music instruction to appear in Britain's North American colonies. The author's
name was not given in the advertisements for the earlier editions
perhaps because he was not widely enough known to have helped
sales.

He was born in Medford, Massachusetts, on either February 26, or May 5, 1689, the son of Captain Peter Tufts and his second wife, Mercy. Tufts's mother, Mercy Cotton, was a direct descendant of the Reverend Seaborn Cotton and the Reverend John Cotton. His maternal grandmother was Dorothy Bradstreet, oldest daughter of Simon and Anne Bradstreet (the first female poet in America).[3] The first record of his life was as a Harvard freshman.[4] After his graduation in 1708, he spent a year as a schoolmaster in Woburn, Massachusetts, and then served as temporary pastor of the church at Medford. One year later he was offered a permanent position, but his response was evasive and the post was given to an Aaron Porter. In 1713 he was a candidate for the post of associate pastor of a church in Charlestown, Massachusetts. Of the three candidates Tufts received the least number of votes.[5]

One year later he accepted the position of pastor of the Church of Newbury, Massachusetts. The post more nearly approximated that of assistant pastor as he was to receive the sum of eighty pounds while the old pastor was still living, but that amount was to be increased to eighty-four pounds with the death of the older man. Perhaps Tufts had complete responsibility for the church, but this is unclear. On June 30, 1714, Tufts was ordained at "Newbury's second parish" and that year he married Sarah Bradstreet, daughter of the town physician.

He remained in Newbury for over twenty years. On February 26, 1738, Tufts was charged by the council of ten ministers and twenty delegates with "indecent carriage" and "abusive and unchristian behavior" toward one or more women of West Newbury, and on March 2nd the church acted not to recommend Tufts as minister. Tufts had refused to cooperate with the council or to question witnesses called to testify against him. He had asked only that he be released from his duties as pastor, and his public pronouncements had alluded to the "consequence of the unhappy differences prevailing in the parish." He moved to Amesbury, Massachusetts, where he set himself up as a shopkeeper, and he died there twelve years later on August 17, 1750.

John Tufts will be remembered for his *Introduction to the Singing of Psalm Tunes*. The book was popular from the beginning, and Samuel Garish, his publisher, did include Tufts's name in later advertisements for the book when the author's name could be recognized by a public which was more and more enthusiastic about learning to sing by rule and which showed an increasing affinity for the rigors and pleasures of the singing school. Copies of Tufts's book were used as late as 1881. As one church after another painfully gave up the old way of singing and adopted the new singing by rule, perhaps the little volume by Tufts not only helped to show that the accurate reading of notation could be learned, was not to be confused with popery, and was not a machination of the devil. The people's music was not yet to be taken from them. Another hundred years would pass before such an alienation prevailed. Instead, a golden age of church singing came of age as new singers with music reading skills took their places in the choir lofts of New England churches. But before examining this phase of America's music, we should review the life of another person active in the early reform period, the Reverend Thomas Walter.

THOMAS WALTER

One of the most influential figures of this period was the author of *Grounds and Rules of Musick Explained*. Thomas Walter's volume appeared the same year as Tufts's but Walter, although a young man, was already widely known and in the forefront of efforts to encourage the New England congregations to sing by rule. His powerful pen gave full expression to an incisive intellect that knew the benefits that the reading of notes would provide, a knowledge that had been preserved at Harvard College. In a published sermon, *The Sweet Psalmist of Israel*, Walter explains to the neophyte the values of singing by note and describes a method by which such a skill may be attained. "They will instruct us in the right and true singing of the Tunes that are already in use in our Churches; which, when they first came out of the hands of the Composers of them, were sung according to the *Scale of Musick*, but are now miserably tortured and twisted, and quavered, in some Churches, into an horrid Medley of confused and disorderly voices."[6] Oral tradition had resulted in a decrease of the number of tunes known to New England congregations. Both complex and stylistic factors played a part in this loss, and reformers of the times could not reasonably be expected to understand causes. Even today, the complex interplay of factors is open to interpretation by modern scholars.

Walter makes the point that singing by rule will help add more tunes to psalm singing. "For the present we are confined to *eight or ten tunes*, and in some Congregations to little more than half that Number, which being so often sung over, are too apt if not to create a distaste, yet at least mightily to lessen the Relish of them."[7] The number of tunes decreased, but the old and too familiar pieces were embellished, creating new versions with each performance. The result, to Walter, was discord but to the congregation this was music! "For much time is taken up in making these Turns and Quavers, and besides, no two Men in the Congregation quaver alike, or together; which sounds in the Ears of a good judge, like *Five Hundred* different Tunes roared out at the same time, where perpetual interferings with one another, perplexed, jars, and unmeasured Periods, would make a man wonder at the false Pleasure which then conceive in that which good Judges of Musick and Sounds cannot bear to hear."[8]

Walter was born in Boston, December 7, 1696, the son of Nehemiah Walter and Sarah Mather. He was the grandson of Increase Mather and Maria Cotton and the great-grandson of John Cotton who also had much to say about the singing of psalms. Walter was graduated from Harvard at the age of seventeen, evidently possessing a "retentive memory" and having learned much from conversations with his uncle Cotton Mather.[9]

He was called to the Roxbury Church in 1717 when the church fathers agreed enthusiastically to having the younger Walter join his father as an assistant pastor. On May 13, 1717, "the town met to consider of a settlement of Mr. Walter. . . . [It] voted that there should be five hundred pounds raised for Mr. Walter, as encouragement for his settling among us."[10] The call was accepted and Walter was ordained October 29, 1718. On Christmas day of the same year he married Rebecca Belcher, daughter of the Reverend Joseph Belcher, of Dedham. Of those recommending his book we find the names of Joseph Belcher, his father-in-law; the Reverend Nehemiah Walter, his father; as well as Cotton and Increase Mather.

In a letter from the Reverend Dr. Chauncey to a Dr. Styles in 1768, forty-three years after Walter's untimely death (he died before he reached thirty), the abilities and talents of Thomas Walter were remembered in unusually glowing terms.

Dr. Jeremiah Dummer, Mr. John Bulkley, and Mr. Thomas Walter I reckon the first three clergymen for extent and strength of genius and powers New England has yet produced. I was acquainted with the latter, and often had occasion to admire the superlative excellence of his natural and acquired accomplishments. His genius was universal, yet surprisingly strong. He seemed to have almost an intuitive knowledge of everything. There was no subject but he was acquainted with, and such was the power he had over his thoughts and words that he could readily and without any pains write or speak just what he would. [11]

There can be no doubt that Walter was a young man of considerable talent.

In *The Sweet Psalmist of Israel* we learn much of the ideas and philosophy of this first reform period in American music. The sermon was preached at a "Lecture held in Boston, by the Society for promoting Regular & Good Singing, And for Reforming the Depravations and Debasements our Psalmody labors under, in order to introduce the proper and the Old Way of Singing." [12] Walter avers that America was not alone in the gradual deterioration of psalm singing. Most likely referring to England, Walter writes in his dedication,

I am glad to hear of the attempts made in another Country in prosecution of the same noble Design, and that the Reverend Mr. Brown of Reading has Justified and put Respect upon their Undertaking, by preaching a Sermon at a *Singing Lecture* there. [13]

MUSIC IN THE CHURCHES OF ENGLAND

Singing in the churches of England during this period was in a similar state as that of New England. Around the middle of the sixteenth century, institutions for the instruction in vocal music appeared in England. At Windsor, the "Grandsire of the Choristers" taught schoolboys ordinary subjects such as writing, reading, behavior, and religion from 6:00 to 8:00 A.M. and again from noon to 2:00 P.M. The music taught there was singing, pricksong, descant, and "such as be apt to the instruments." [*]

The early seventeenth-century parish churches, however, seem to have had little music. Organs had been commonplace in the fif-

---

[*] Pricksong was learning to perform from written or printed music while the study of descant was learning to improvise vocally and the rules of composition.

teenth and sixteenth centuries in the churches of England, but in Elizabeth's reign there were fewer of them. The old organs had been destroyed and new instruments were not built to replace them. In Lancashire "all the orders of the church go down the wind, for they call the surplices the rap of Rome; they do it at Preston and at Manchester, and will suffer no organs, nor sign no children with the cross when they are christened." [14]

Not only was there little use of instruments, but singing suffered as choristers also worked at outside employment. In the Bristol cathedral, singing-men had extra employment as parish clerks or organists, and their extra responsibilities were such that the singing had to be given up altogether at the ten o'clock prayers on Sunday mornings. The Archbishop Laud wrote to the "dean and chapter of the Norwich cathedral to point out the poverty of their choir," and articles of the 1630s pointed out that "choristers and singing men were chosen for friendship, rewards, or money, rather than for their "aptness, voices, and towardness in singing." [15] Thomas Morley wrote that as

to the expressing of the ditty, the matter is now come to that state that though a song be never so well made and never so aptly applied to the words yet shall you hardly find singers to express it as it ought to be, for most of our church men . . . will never study to sing better than they did the first day of their preferment. . . . [It] should seem that having attained the living which they sought for, they have little or no care at all either of their own credit, or with discharging of that duty whereby they have their maintenance. [16]

It is no wonder that in the colonies—where the fundamental Puritan beliefs forbade the use of instruments, where no professional singers were ever employed, and where congregations sang the Psalms as they were passed down in the families—the art of note reading had become unpracticed and singing became linked to the growing folk tradition. It is to this audience and tradition that Thomas Walter addressed himself, as did the other so-called reformers of the day.

At the turn of the nineteenth century there were many signs of vital and active music participation throughout New England. Timothy Dwight observed that "people of wealth, and many in moderate circumstances, have their children taught music; particularly on the piano-forte; and many of the young men play on the

German Flute; violin, clarionet, etc. and that serenading is not infrequent."[17] At this time evidence of the universality of church choirs and of a growing interest in instrumental music existed throughout New England. The instrument most commonly used in the New England churches was the cello—often called the "bass-viol." Later the flute, clarinet, trombone, and the violin were introduced, but not without controversy.

The church singers were taught at the now-ubiquitous singing schools. The function of the school was to supply the church choirs with an ever-increasing supply of singers who were well-versed in the vagaries of voice production and in the intricacies of reading according to the four note gamut. The singing school could meet almost anywhere: a room at the meeting house, a private home, a barn, even the local saloon. The usual place, however, was in an extra room in the meeting house. Wherever the schools were held, the singers brought their own candles and those who had them brought books. They often sat in semicircles around the singing master who taught them the clefs, syllables, keys, and note lengths. They also learned some of the niceties of voice production and the "proper" pronunciation of the vowels according to the custom of the day.

Few singing schools ran for more than twenty four evenings. But two meetings per week for three months was not a short term by eighteenth-century standards as the common schools of the period were not ordinarily in session for longer periods. Following the term of the singing school, a "demonstration" or "singing lecture" took place. Such neutral names covered a host of public exhibitions of singing by choirs formed from the participants of the singing schools. The performed selections were often taken from the master's own tune book, sold to the singing school students for the musical edification of the school and for the financial remuneration of the singing master. The tune books themselves, being the first texts used in American music education, are interesting and important source material for understanding the techniques of the singing school.

As our early Americans learned to sing primarily for the purpose of singing in church, the singing school and early religious customs cannot easily be separated. Like the church, the singing school was important in the social fabric of the towns and villages.

In Bennington, Vermont, for example, between 1829 and 1837 at the Mt. Anthony Seminary

only the lower room of the old academy was used for school purposes, and in the upper room were held the prayer-meetings of the First Church. . . . Singing-schools and choir rehearsals were also held here, and how enjoyable they were; for the genial chorister, John Fay, had a happy way of diversifying his instruction with witty remarks, and an evening with him always passed quickly.[18]

John Fay's voice was described as "no great marvel of range, no wonderful high notes, but was what is called sympathetic, or as the French say, *pleurs des Larmes*—full of tears." A writer in the *Bennington Banner* describes his voice as one "to be remembered long after being heard. Few voices unite, as did his, such volume and power, with such richness and sweetness, and such adeptness for musical expression and eloquence."[19]

Records of the First Church of Christ at New London, Connecticut, in 1797 show "To one Quarter's Tuition of Singing School beginning 17th of July and ending 17th of October as per agreement with the Singing Committee £3 5s." The sum was paid to George Harris, who taught for three years. During the same period it was voted that certain funds collected that year be appropriated "to the use of the Encouragement and supporting of Singing."[20]

One of the most widely known singing masters was Moses Cheney, one of a large family of singing masters and musicians in New England. He was born in Haverhill, Massachusetts, December 15, 1776, and his family moved to Sanbornton, New Hampshire, when he was five years old. Though sickly in his youth, Cheney was able to apply himself to his library and his music. By the age of seventeen his health had improved sufficiently so that he was able to work on a farm. At twenty he learned a joiner's trade, and the next year, he attended a school during the winter

kept by the Elder John Drew, as also to a singing school, by Mr. William Tenney of Gaffstown, New Hampshire. At the close of these two schools, his teachers gave him the credit of having done *very well*; and the latter, as was his custom, to his best scholar, at the close of a winter's school, gave Moses Cheney his pitch-pipe and singing book.[21]

His voice was described as "pure tenor, and whether you heard him sing or preach, you could but feel that he possessed great vitality, and capability of most protracted vocal effort."[22] Cheney married and had five sons and four daughters, all of whom could sing when quite young. Four of the sons and one of the daughters became teachers of music. In time the loss of two children and the return of ill health influenced his decision to become a minister, but he never lost interest in music. Cheney moved to Derby, Vermont, in 1823 remaining there temporarily but returning to Sanbornton. But in 1843 he again moved to Vermont—this time to Sheffield, where he lived until his death on August 9, 1856.

Cheney's musical education was typical of his time in New England. Many in rural sections of New England found it difficult to provide themselves with a standard tune book. As a substitute, small books were used with blank pages on which various favorite tunes were carefully copied. Occasionally, these manuscript books included a printed theoretical introduction of several pages after which blank pages were provided for copying the tunes.

Cheney describes his first experiences at a singing school and indirectly comments on the state of common school education in rural New England in 1788. His observation concerning the use of a manuscript tune book by his teacher is also of interest as such books dating from this period are found more rarely today than the more common tune books.

And it came to pass when I was about twelve years of age, that a singing school was got up about two miles from my father's house. In much fear and trembling I went down with the rest of the boys in our town. I was told on the way to the first school that the master would try every voice alone to see if it was good. The thought of having my voice tried in that way, by a singing-master too, brought a heavy damp on my spirits. I said nothing, but traveled on to the place to see what a singing school might be.

When we came to the house, quite a number of young ladies and gentlemen had come, and were coming to the school. This was the first school which I attended of any kind, with very little exception. I did not pay much attention to the scholars, but I watched the master closely. We were soon paraded all around the room, standing up to the boards supported by old fashioned kitchen chairs. I being the youngest of the company managed to get the lowest seat, hoping thereby to be the last to have my voice tried. The master took his place inside the circle, took out of his pocket a paper manuscript, with rules and tunes all written with pen and ink, read to us the rules, and then said we must attend to the raising and falling of the notes.[23]

Scholars attending singing school at this period read music by means of the four note gamut: mi, fa, sol, and la. The only note which was not repeated in the octave was the syllable mi.* In order to understand the proper use of the syllables, the scholars had to find the position of mi on the staff. The rules recollected by Cheney are typical of the period and can be found in the theoretical introductions of numerous tune books from the early eighteenth to the mid-nineteenth century.[24]

I shall take the liberty now to call ladies and gentlemen, and things, just as they were called in that school. And I begin with the rules as they were called, first:

RULES

FLATS

The natural place for mi is in B
But if B be flat mi is in E
If B and E be flat mi is in A
If B, E, A, and D be flat mi
   is in G

SHARPS

But if F be sharp mi is in F
If F and C be sharp mi is in C
If F, C, and G be sharp mi is in G
If F, C, G, and D be sharp mi is
   in D.

The books in the hands of the scholars were somewhat unusual as most tune books of the period included all four parts. As Cheney's singing school teacher had a manuscript tune book, it was likely that the scholars themselves had books in this form and to copy one part would have been easier than four:

These rules, as then called were all that was presented in that school. The books contained only one part each, bass books, tenor books, counter books, and treble books. Such as sung bass had a bass book; he that sung

---

* A key could be quickly established by singing the seventh and the following tonic. If mi represented the seventh tone of the scale and was used only to determine the tonic, any given key could be quickly ascertained.

tenor had a tenor book; he who sung counter, had a counter book and the gals, as then called, had treble books, I had no book.[25]

Manuscript tune books were common during this period. Perhaps a revealing insight into the cultural habits of eighteenth-century America can be found in Joseph Tenny's manuscript tune book which was complete with a theoretical introduction. Tenny called his book *The Gamut or Scale of Music*. He advertised it as a "concise and comprehensive Gamut Or Scale of Music Together with about 20 pages of blank lines for writing in tunes, all bound together—the design of it is to supply schools, without the cost of buying books which contain a large number of tunes, and but few of them such as they want to learn. And also, those who have books may have blank lines ready at their hand, to write in such tunes as they wish to collect from other books, Windor, June 1st, 1795."[26] Even in Thomas Atwill's *New York and Vermont Collection of Sacred Harmony*, five manuscript pages were reserved in the front of the book, presumably for the above purposes.

Pennsylvania singing schools made good use of such copybooks. Such books were oblong, about five-by-seven inches, and filled with blank pages. Students would draw their own lines with quill and ink, mixed by the teacher, and then copy material given by the "master." Examples in the Bucks County Historical Society begin with the gamut showing the letter names for the lines and spaces using either a great or single staff.

The scholars in Moses Cheney's school were accustomed to the appearance of manuscript tune books. After the class was started with a theoretical introduction to the reading of music, Cheney's teacher was quick to test the voices and to proceed with the singing of a tune.

With all these things before the school, the good master began "Come boys, you must rise and fall the notes first and then the gals must try." So he began with the oldest, who stood at the head, "Now follow me right up and down; sound." So he sounded; then the boy sounded, and followed the master up and down as it was called. Some more than one half could follow the master. Others would go up two or three notes, and then fall back lower than the first note. My feelings grew acute. To see some of the large boys, full twenty years old, make such dreadful work, what could I do! Great fits of laughing, both with boys and gals, would often occur. This scared me, and I was at my wit's end. Now my eyes were fixed on the Master's mouth, if possible to learn the names of the notes before he came to me. I saw all that was needed was to make just the same sound that he made; and it came to my mind that I could mimic every beast, and bird, and thing, that I had ever heard make any noise, and it was no more to mimic my master than it was anything else. And then I had a firm belief I could do it. And I had only time to draw a long breath, and blow out the flutter of my heart, when the master came to me. "Well my lad, will you try?" "Yes sir." I looked him in the mouth, and as he spoke a note, so did I, both up and down. I did not wait for him to call the note First; I spoke with him. Now by watching him so closely, and observing how he spoke the notes, but would come so as to speak with him. The master turned away, saying, "this boy will make a singer." I felt well enough.

Then the gals had their turn to rise and fall the notes. "Come gals, now see if you can't beat the boys." So when he had gone through the gals' side of the school, he seemed to think the gals had done rather the best.

Now the rules were left for tunes. Old "Russia" was brought on first. The master sang it over several times, first with the bass, then with the tenor, then with the counter, and then with the treble. Such as had notes looked on, such as had none, listened to the rest. In this way, the school went on through the winter. A good number of tunes were learned in this school, and were sung well as we thought; but as to the science of music very little was gained.[27]

There is some controversy in the literature regarding the efficacy of the singing school education and the degree of skill acquired by the teaching methods employed and the use of the four note gamut. The theoretical introductions to the tune books of the period are concerned with the rudiments of the staff and notation, strongly suggesting that the scholars memorize the keys, staff, and note values before they begin to sing. Cheney's singing master only gave lip-service to this long-held pedagogy. As detailed descriptions of procedures followed in singing schools are rare, one can only conjecture whether the techniques that Cheney describes represent a typical approach for his time. One might suspect that American eclecticism and pragmatic outlook took precedence over any one theory of teaching, just as they do today. Cheney's singing master saw a need to encourage his class to sing. Cheney attended other singing schools with other teachers and reported that the theoretical gaps in his musical education were made up in other schools. His observations show a reasonable variation in procedure and not a clear indication of a common method.

Modern writers seem quick to pass judgment on the efficacy of the singing school and the four note gamut then in vogue. Used in England about the time of Queen Elizabeth, the four note gamut remained popular through the eighteenth century and was displaced only during the first third of the nineteenth century. George Pullen Jackson reports that the syllables were sung "part by part and time after time" until the parts were thoroughly learned. The scholars were then allowed to sing the words. Allen Britton observes that any apparent success that eighteenth-century vocal teachers had was not exclusively based on the universal use of the solmization system. Alan Buechner notes that Hans Gram, as early as 1793, recommended no particular system believing none to be very effective. And Hamilton C. MacDougall reports, no doubt with exaggeration, that the four note gamut "must have muddled weak brains and done the singing master's business no harm."[28]

It would appear that the music reading of that day was at least as good as that of the present time. It seems reasonable to suppose that scholars with a good ear could and did learn pieces by rote instead of mastering the syllables. At the same time the four note gamut was indeed a workable system, and some apparently gained much skill through its use.

At the close of the school, and after singing the last night, we made a settlement with the master. He agreed to keep, as then called, for one shilling and sixpence a night, and to take his pay in Indian corn at three shillings a bushel. A true dividend was made of the cost among the boys (the gals found candles for their part), and it amounted to thirteen quarts and one pint of corn apiece. After the master had made some good wishes on us all, we were dismissed, and all went hence in harmony and good union.

In the eyes of singers at this time, with the advance of the science of music for half a century past, this school must appear very insignificant indeed. But suffer me to try to express some of my feelings at that time. To me the whole movement of the school was of the brightest cast. Carrying with it, all through, from first to last, the most striking and affecting realities that I had ever been made witness before, and I expected it was all that could be done in regard to the glorious work of singing for ages to come. A school! A Singing School! O those words! Every other word vanished at the sound.

Think for a moment. A little boy of twelve years of age, growing up in the shade of the deep and condensed forests of the mountains of N. H., seldom out of sight of his mother, or the hearing of her voice, never saw a singing master or musical note, seldom ever heard the voice of any human being except his own domestic circle, by the fireside of his Father's humble hearth.

Think again; now he is a member of a school; more, a Singing School! Singing tunes by note! Singing the "We Live Above!" Carrying any part all in the same high boy's voice. O, that Winter's work! The Foundation of many many happy days for more than fifty years past. The bright blue sparkling eyes, his sweet angelic voice, his manifest care and love to his pupils, everything combined to make him one of a thousand.[29]

Sixty-seven years after the publication of the first instruction books in this country by Tufts and by Walter, rural New England was only beginning to sing by rule.

Not long after this school was closed, I heard there were plenty of printed singing books in Boston; and that our storekeeper would have some to sell before the next winter. It was my whole concern to be ready by the time they came up to buy one. I would persuade my father to give me a stint, to hoe by myself, to gain time to peal red oak bark, burn it, and save the ashes for the purpose of buying a printed singing book. When the books came I was ready to pay in ashes. This I did, and then I owned a singing book.

I looked at the rules with astonishment. I do not remember the name of the book, or the author's name; but this I perfectly remember, it was a Singing Book. In my new book, I had possessed myself of not far from a hundred new tunes. This was more than I ever expected to see. Now I could read but very poorly indeed, must spell all large words, and had it not been for singing, I should not have been able to read at all. Singing did more for me by far, in learning me to read than every other way of teaching. So on I went, studying my new book, and when I came to a hard name, or word, I would go to my mother, and in this way I made some progress.

In my book I found that notes had another name, Semibreve, Minim, Crotchet, Quaver, Semiquaver, and Demisemiquaver. I learned also that the semibreve was the longest note in singing and that it was as long as two minims, four crotchets, eight quavers, sixteen semiquavers, or thirty-two demisemiquavers. This put one link more into the chain of my understanding.

My new book taught me likewise more modes of time than one. In my school without a book, I had only learned to beat up and down; but now I saw different ways, some two down beats and one up, another two down and two up. Some were slow, and some fast. This swelled my mind a little larger still. So I went on, committing from memory all that came in my way, until I had eaten that book up.[30]

It was impossible to learn to read music by any system after only three months in a singing school. If progress was to be made, the scholar had to attend several schools, as did Moses Cheney.

I attended some kind of singing school every winter but two until I was twenty-one year old. Forty-three years ago, or the winter after I was twenty-one, I followed Mr. Wm. Tenney, the best instructor that I had ever found. He taught every afternoon and evening in the week, Sunday excepted. When he left us, he gave me his singing book and wooden pitchpipe, and told me to believe I was the best singer in the world, and then I should never be afraid to sing anywhere. He and myself could take any singing book that we met with and sing through as easily as we could read many other books. That was something then, and no small thing at this day.

After this school, from the time of my age twenty-one, I have taught singing until I became fifty, that is, more or less from time to time.[31]

The scenes described by Moses Cheney were acted out in almost all communities in rural New England. One such town was Woodstock, Vermont, which possesses a rich and well chronicled history of the early singing school. One of the earliest singers to come to Woodstock was Elisha West. Though he called himself a housewright when he arrived in 1791, he quickly became the "unquestioned musical leader of the town." He was considered to be a fine teacher and was recognized by his contemporaries as being a composer of singular merit. Singing masters were drawn from the society which they served. In musical taste and education they were only a short step ahead of that society. The teachers learned music themselves from a singing school, whose instruction was popular and whose subject was taught for immediate social usefulness. The town employed him as a singing teacher as the townspeople regarded good singing highly and as an indispensable part of the church service. West was to "regulate harmony in the religious societies in this town . . . and to encourage youth and others who [wished] to gain knowledge in the pleasing Art of Psalm singing." He formed an agreement for his services with a "committee of subscribers" in 1794. West continued as the leading music teacher in Woodstock for about twelve years, opening singing schools in different places during the winter months and providing a well-drilled choir for any emergency.[32]

The singing schools in Woodstock were attended by most of the townspeople. The younger pupils met in the afternoon, while the evenings were reserved for the older students. Some former students of Elisha West recorded their impressions of their singing master.

As a teacher West was a careful drill-master. He gave most patient attention to the rudiments, and those who still remember his instructions speak of him in this particular with high respect. Above all things there was in his school the most rigid observance of the laws of time, and even certain bad habits of his were not allowed to interfere with the order and discipline he considered needful to have the school a success.[33]

About the year 1801 he published a collection of tunes and anthems containing many original pieces. The collection was printed at Northampton, Massachusetts, by Andrew Wright, for Elisha West and Benjamin Billings, Jr.

Woodstock had the advantage of several singing masters who followed West. Captain John Durkee presided over the musical affairs of his town in 1806. His church choir numbered forty or fifty, most of whom were treble and bass singers. Following Captain Durkee, came James Cutler, a law student in the village who conducted his choir and singing school in a peculiarly idiosyncratic manner; he marked the time with a "downward left foot." But one day his scholars were to have their revenge.

As he was thus zealously occupied one evening, a mischievous boy named Curtis came behind him and caught his foot while suspended in air, causing him to fall forward on the floor. The joke, though a rough one, only produced general merriment in the school, in which Cutler himself heartily joined.[34]

As was the case with so many singing school teachers for whom music was supposed to be an avocation, Cutler regarded music as more important to him than law. His classes must have been popular as his pupils were said to have numbered ninety in his combined classes. In addition to his singing school activities, he organized a six-piece band, which appeared in public regularly.

1800 AND REFORM

Around the turn of the nineteenth century the style of the hymn tune in New England was again undergoing a reform. The old fuge-tune was falling from favor, and the folk-harmonizations which were popular in the eighteenth century gradually gave way to a harmonic practice consistent with the European tradition. The old "fuges," which were popularized by William Billings and which delighted New Englanders, were nothing more than imitative sections usually in the middle of the old tunes. But all enjoyed singing them, and contemporary records abound with reports of congregations lifting their voices to the old fuges.

This unique American folk music was originally derived from an English sacred choir tradition of the eighteenth century. It was allied with certain native folk idioms, such as a natural affinity for the minor mode, an irregularity of phrase, and a pronounced rhythmic vitality. The style can be traced from William Tans'ur's *A New Musical Grammar*, and "New Introduction to the Grounds of Music," or *American Chorister*.[35] Tans'ur opened the door to parallel fifths and octaves in the harmonization of psalm tunes, and William Billings carried on the tradition and set an example to be followed by other composers and compilers of sacred music of the time. Tans'ur decreed that "two *Fifths*, or two *Eights* (when it cannot be well avoided) be used rather than spoil the air."[36] As a result of such a modest admonition, Billings's compositions are heavily endowed with parallels.

Music in the latter part of the eighteenth century was contrapuntally conceived, and chords often lacked a third, particularly the opening and closing chords. Billings, himself, admonished that all parts should conform to the tenor. The style was based on the folk song of the day, and the harmonic idiom seemed to demonstrate an ignorance of the conventional European part-writing procedures. Charles Seeger believes that the conception of three voices sounding simultaneously was not necessarily thought of as being a chord. Each added voice was independent. Thus the pieces show a definite contrapuntal style.[37]

During the last third of the eighteenth century, certain changes in style slowly appeared with the importation of William Tans'ur's *Royal Melody Compleat** and Aaron Williams's *Universal Psalmist*.† These collections were reprinted in America between 1767 and 1774 by Daniel Bayley of Newburyport, Massachusetts. Bayley issued them in a composite edition entitled *The American Harmony*. The work provided New England with its first introduction to canons, fuging tunes, anthems, and occasional pieces. Among

---

* London: 1775, 1760, 1764, 1766
† London: 1763, 1764, 1765, 1770

its many influences the collection tended to stimulate the development of choirs in American churches.

The fuge-tune was adapted from English sources, and it was probably Joseph Stephenson who gave New England one of its first fuging tunes around 1755. Irving Lowens believes it likely that Stephenson's "fuging psalm tunes" acted as prototypes for Billings's work and perhaps as that of other American composers as well.[38] Fuging music evidently became immediately popular among the congregations of New England, a phenomenon that was first noticed by Jocelyn and Doolittle in 1782.

It is very obvious that Psalmody hath undergone a considerable revolution, in most of our religious assemblies, within the course of a few years, not only the tunes formerly in common use are now generally laid aside, instead of which, those of the more lively and airy turn are substituted. And though many improvements have been made in Church Music, yet there appears a danger of erring, by introducing, in public worship, light and trifling airs, more becoming the theatre or Shepherd's Pipe; a liberty (as we apprehend) by no means admissable in the solemnities of Devine Service.[39]

Harriet Beecher Stowe described the singing of fuging music as "a grand wild freedom, an energy of motion, . . . that well expressed the heart of a people courageous in combat and unshaken in endurance." Governor Frederick Holbrook of Vermont described this early fuge music and his church choir "composed of thirty or forty members." He remembered that the music was rendered "with unction." Holbrook also suggested that "the congregation quite generally joined in singing the old fuge-tunes in their pews to the hymns announced."[40] The governor himself was the leader of a church choir, a fact which lends more credence to his descriptions.

In an article by the Reverend E. H. Sears in *Dwight's Journal of Music*, Sears describes the sounds created by the fuging tune and hints that acoustical idiosyncracies of some of the old churches could create some interesting and unusual effects.

To those who were seated downstairs facing the pulpit the sound appeared to come from three different directions: from behind, from the right, and from the left.[41]

And in Pawlet, Vermont, Hiel Hollister vividly describes the power of the "fugue" on the villagers of his day:

The revolution which stirred the souls of men developed a new style of music, which was styled fugue music. This was in sympathy with the clash and excitement of the day. . . . The parts falling in one after another, each part singing different words at the same time, are thought to represent the clanger and confusion of the battle field.[42]

Composer Asahel Benham gave sound directions for singing the fuge in the theoretical introduction to his *Federal Harmony*.

A solo should generally be sung soft; and peculiarly graceful. When the music fuges the strength of voice should increase on the engaged part or parts, which the others are falling in with spirit; In which case the pronunciation ought to be peculiarly distinct and emphatic. When words or music are repeated the sound should increase together with the emphasis.[43]

Around the turn of the nineteenth century, musical styles in the churches of New England were beginning to change. The growing influence of European-trained musicians stimulated the dissolution of the fuge tune, the reliance on the minor mode, and the melody in the tenor voice. But before we can observe the compositional practices that are familiar to musicians of today, we will look at some of the practices used in this folk art of the eighteenth century.

CHAPTER III

Tune Books and
Performance Practice

T HE ONLY text available to the singing school teacher was the
tune book. A theoretical introduction to the reading and performance of music occupied the first few pages of the hundreds of
tune books that swept the country between 1721 and the middle
of the nineteenth century. Were these suggestions followed by the
singing masters? We must guess that, for the most part, they were.
The authors of the tune books were themselves singing school
masters, and a brisk sale of their books helped reinforce a pre-
carious livelihood. A similar approach is evidenced in the various
books showing a common acquaintance with a musical culture.
But as the theoretical introductions are studied, the modern reader
must always assume that the teachers, then as now, bent orthodox
procedures to accommmodate a particular class.

The basic rules for "finding mi"—as indicated previously in
Cheney's memoir—are universally in evidence. Most masters followed this scheme for finding mi. Others, such as Jacob Kimball,
substituted complete charts showing the actual transpositions of
mi on the staves.[1] But the excessive difficulties of the charts apparently discouraged beginners, and the charts were abandoned.

The four note gamut mitigated against finding the key note or
"do" according to the seven note solmization. Fa represented two
scale tones, both the first and fourth notes of a major scale. Only
mi appeared once in the scale representing the leading tone; hence
such an identification could determine the key.

32

Eighteenth-century tune books supplied little material for practice. The examples used were for intellectual purposes and were abstract. Thomas Walter used the following scale in his theoretical introduction:[2]

| Sol | la | fa | sol | la | mi | fa | sol | la | fa | sol |

| la | mi | fa | sol | la | fa | sol | la | mi | fa | sol |

No attempt was made to write a major scale. Walter and others like him were only writing notes on a staff to be considered intellectually. With no sharps or flats in the key signature, the "natural place of mi is B." When this had been determined, the remaining syllables could easily have been supplied. Walter's book was the first book in America to use regular notes. It was the sole American-made book of this type in use in the American colonies for forty years after its publication. The diamond-shaped notes were typical of those used in Europe during the eighteenth century.

There appeared to be no concern whether the student understood the concept, only whether the rules could be correctly recited. The concept would have to come later. Andrew Law, one of America's most influential music masters in the early years of the eighteenth century, demonstrated a confusion over the purpose of syllables believing their function to be the beautification of the vowel sounds when singing syllables. The singing master complains about the seven note system of Andrew Adgate and defends the four note gamut.

Syllables, in music, are not the signs of particular sounds. . . . A single syllable is sufficient to express the whole variety of musical sounds. Does it then become a question why *four* syllables are used instead of one? The answer is easy. To consult conveniency by means of variety. Were it not tiresome to repeat one syllable continually, there would be no need of more than one. But constant experience proves, that it is tiresome, and that more than one *are* necessary. By the use of four syllables, mi, faw, sol, law, the variety is found to be sufficient; and these syllables sung according to the directions, which I have given, are admirably calculated for the purpose to which they are appropriated. For tho, they cannot as-

sist us in attaining sounds, yet, they *may*, and *do* assist in forming the
organs of sound into a position for making more open and smooth
sounds.[3]

Such a state of affairs helps to demonstrate that the singing master's success was not based entirely upon the universal success of
the solmization system.

Minor scales were sung using the same syllables as those of the
major scale. Only toward the end of the eighteenth century were
the sixth and seventh scale steps revised. Correctly sung harmonic
or melodic minor scales could be navigated only by ear, as the syllables were useless for that purpose. Rarely could there be found
any mention of the revised organization of syllables for treatment
of chromatic alterations. Andrew Adgate demonstrated such a
concern in his *Rudiments of Music*. He admonishes the scholars
that

if a sharp comes before any particular note, that is not found in the cliff,
we change its vowel into E, and give it the sound of E in me, as long as the
sound is affected by the accidental sharp: The same alteration takes place
when a note that is flat at the cliff has a natural set before it. Sometimes
after the beginning of a tune, and when me has an accidental flat or natural set before it, we may change E into A, sounded as in hall. [For
example:]

fe   se   be   de

fa   so   la ba   do   &c.[4]

Chromatic alterations were rare, modulations scarce, and chromatic nonharmonic tones were almost nonexistent, causing most
compilers of eighteenth-century tune books to ignore the problems
of chromaticism.

Andrew Adgate introduced the function of syllables when he introduced a seven note gamut in 1788. Adgate's solution was the
following: fa, so, la, ba, do, ma, me. This singing master recognized the value of not repeating syllables within a scale. Hans
Gram criticized the fasola system and explained the French, German, and Italian systems but endorsed none of them.[5]

No well-developed system emphasizing a feeling for the tonic
was in evidence. The four note gamut provided no unambiguous
syllable for the first note of the scale. The seventh note or leading tone was sought as the "key." Whether the scholars either

imagined or actually sang the tonic after finding mi can only be conjectured.

Walter's rules for identifying major and minor were typical. "If the Two Notes above the last note of your Tune be whole Notes [steps], it is upon a *sharp* Key; [major key] but if the Two Notes above, be one an *whole* Note, and the other an *half Note*, then it is a *flat Key* [minor key]." But Walter does suggest that listening and hearing do, after all, have a place in learning to sing. "And when you have learned to raise and fall the Notes, the Difference of the Sound will be perceptable by the Ear."[6]

Does Walter really mean what he implies, that *after* the student has learned to "raise and fall" the notes he will *then* be able to perceive the "difference of sounds"? Perhaps he means that an improvement in the student's perception will take place. The theoretical introduction discusses scale-like intervals. Perhaps Walter means that the accuracy of the scale-like intervals will be improved with practice. Or does he imply that students were unable to perceive intervalic differences of half-steps in the early years of the eighteenth century? If the latter was indeed the case, then the harsh judgment of the early reformers was well founded.

PERFORMANCE PRACTICES

From bits and pieces of evidence it is possible to reconstruct certain aspects of performance practice as it existed in New England in the eighteenth century. Contemporary European practices can be seriously considered in such a discussion as American singing and instruction did not occur in isolation. Cultural and economic intercourse thrived between America and Europe as sailing ships crossed the Atlantic bringing musical instruments, books, and people from England. Travelers brought with them the gradually changing styles and performance practices which transformed the notes and rules into a living, breathing art. A few were professionals, but most were amateurs quavering variously and pursuing Terpsichore with a happy but serious abandon.

The theoretical introductions to the eighteenth-century tune books give us some evidence that, true to the eighteenth-century European performance tradition, the notes on the page were expected to be used only as a starting place. The custom of including a theoretical introduction in the tune books began in 1708 in the sixth edition of W. L. Already *A Supplement to the New Version of the Psalms*.[7] Many writers of tune books were critical of the mistaken zeal of church singers, many of whom became excessively enamored with their powers of embellishing a line of music, and continually importuned dilettantes to cease and desist. More often, however, the writers simply admonished the singers to allow the singing master to give instruction, as such enterprises as improvisation and embellishment required examples and a good ear. The postulations of the printed page did have limitations.

But the modern reader must look to the theoretical introductions for guidance. A careful reading, perhaps some judicious jumping to conclusions, and a little reading between the lines should bring us closer not only to some performance practices of eighteenth-century psalmody and hymnody but also to the instructional practices of the ubiquitous New England singing school.

Jeremiah Ingalls tantalizes us with the "conclusion" to his theoretical introduction to *Christian Harmony*. "The Trills, Transitions and Accents, have not been attended to in the preceeding rules, they are learnt principally from their teachers and had better be omitted than attempted by young singers." As a musician of taste, at least in the rural and frontier community of Newbury, Vermont, Ingalls preferred to encourage his younger, less experienced scholars to recognize that "the best graces and ornaments in music, are to sing with ease and freedom not very loud nor very soft, (except when directed) but sing with animation, pronouncing the words distinctly, so that the audience be edified, the glory of God, and the praise of our redeemer exalted."[8]

Ingalls is quite clear when he discusses the proper tempo indications for his music. A pendulum can be made using a small tight cord and connected to a leaden ball. As it swings, so the tempi of the various meters may be determined. A pendulum of forty inches allowed to swing freely will establish the tempo for 6/4 time.

The Second Mode has likewise two beats in a bar, which contains six Quavers, or other notes to that amount, and is beat in the same meter as

the first mode, only one quarter faster—marked thus 6/8. The pendulum
for this mode is 22¹/₁₀ inches.⁹

RHYTHM

The beating of time assumed an importance in the instruction and
performance of music during this period. Asahel Benham describes the appropriate manner of beating time in the 1790s.

A perfect understanding of this is of so much importance, that without it,
'tis impossible to perform accurately especially in a concert; hence arises
the necessity of a motion of the hand (called the beating of time) in order
to give every particular note and rest their due measure. The two first
modes of common time have four beats in each bar and may be beat in
the following manner, viz. First strike the ends of the fingers on the thing
beat upon; secondly, bring down the heal of the hand; thirdly, raise the
hand a little and fourthly; raise it still higher, which completes the bar.
Let it be observed that the hand is not to rest in any position while beating time but to be constantly in motion.¹⁰

Thomas Atwill suggested that "young singers should be indus-
trious in acquiring a graceful manner of standing and beating
time." He admonished that "beating time with the feet is highly
unbecoming in church music, and ought to be carefully avoided."
Joel Harmon also proclaimed, in 1809, that "in all moods of time,
the hand must fall at the beginning, and rise at the close of every
single bar." Though Harmon opines that pendulum lengths be
used to determine tempo, he carefully counsels disregard for a
strict interpretation of rule of weight and string. "Many teachers
have been governed by the Pendulum, notwithstanding the variety
of the subjects. But this [is] a gross error, and discovers want of
taste. Whatever the operating of time may be, the subject ought to
govern the time."¹¹

Meter signatures not only indicated the number of beats in a
measure but foretold the tempo of the performance. The well-
known meter signature of "C" proclaimed four beats per measure
as well as four seconds of time. The *alla breve* designation meant
not only two beats per measure but that those two beats should be
performed in three seconds. The less familiar symbol Ɔ indicated

one semibreve (𝅝) and two beats to a measure but at a speed of two seconds for the measure. The following chart explains the remaining signatures:

2/4 contained   𝅗𝅥   and each measure performed in 1½ seconds
3/2 contained   𝅝·   and each measure performed in 3 seconds
3/4 contained   𝅗𝅥·   and each measure performed in 2 seconds
3/8 contained   ♩·   and each measure performed in 1½ seconds
6/4 contained ♩♩♩♩♩♩ and each measure performed in 2 seconds
6/8 contained ♪♪♪♪♪♪ and each measure performed in 1½ seconds

Allen Britton gives the following modern metronome equivalents: [12]

C ♩ = M. M. 60   2/4 ♩ = M. M. 120   3/8 ♪ = M. M. 120

₵ ♩ = M. M. 90   3/2 𝅗𝅥 = M. M. 60   6/4 ♩· = M. M. 60

𐤃 ♩ = M. M. 120   3/4 ♩ = M. M. 90   6/8 ♩· = M. M. 90

Terms such as *breve*, *semibreve*, and *minum* were used in this country until the nineteenth century. Gram was the first to use numerical terms based upon proportional relationships.[13] The introduction is believed to have been written by Gram. The numerical terms were of German origin.

In the time before instruments were accepted into the New England churches, the setting of the pitch often lead to unsettling problems for the church choirs and congregations. An early pitchpipe was often used before the invention of the tuning fork (in 1711). The pitchpipe came equipped with an adjustable stopper which by pushing in or pulling out the notes could be raised or lowered. Graduated marks on the pipe gave some indication to the singing master of the position of the correct pitch. But these artificially produced degrees were inordinately inaccurate. Temperature, moisture of breath, and force of blowing affected the pitch. It is not surprising that around the turn of the nineteenth century instruments (usually the bass-viol) began to be introduced gradually into the choirlofts of rural New England.

PITCH AND KEY NOTE

Information concerning the manner in which a key note was sounded is difficult to uncover. Few tune books touch upon this subject. But in

William Norman's *Federal Harmony* of 1794, there are "directions for pitching the tune by a concert pitch pipe." The pitch was to be given to each part separately. Frequently the singers would use the phrase "Praise Ye the Lord," as each took his pitch. Billings is often credited with having introduced the pitchpipe to America.[14] In his *New England Psalm Singer* of 1770 he included a diagram of a pitchpipe, but a diagram cannot be said to have been responsible for the introduction of that instrument. Judging by the paucity of documentary evidence, the correct pitching of a tune seems not to have been a matter of overriding urgency. Only here and there a comment calls the problem to our attention. Samuel Sewell wrote on October 25, 1691, that at an evening exercise the singer "was not sure he had the tune till 2d line." Again, in 1705, he wrote of going "into a Key much too high and of wandering from Wisdom into High Dutch."[15]

THE ASSIGNMENT OF VOICE PARTS

Voice parts were classified as bass, tenor, counter, and treble. The bass part was supposed to have been sung "grave and majestic," the tenor "steady and engaging," the counter "soft and delicate," and the treble "shrill and melodious."[16] Samuel Holyoke admonished the singing classes to assign the deepest men's voices to the bass and the highest men's voices to the tenor, the voices of boys to the counter, and the highest voices of women to the treble.[17] The tune-book compilers were divided in suggesting that the counter may be sung either by women with lower voices or by boys with unchanged voices. Solomon Howe suggested that the counter be sung by the unchanged voices of children of both sexes.[18]

THEORETICAL INTRODUCTIONS

Although it is difficult to know with certainty how closely the actual practice of instruction in a singing school corresponded with the instructions in the theoretical introductions, it is still necessary to examine these instructions for hints. It was customary before Lowell Mason to recommend that the rudiments be learned before any singing was done. We have evidence from Moses Cheney that this was not done universally. The rules were many and long, and teachers must have done some singing rather early in the three-month course of instruction. It must be assumed that, although some students learned to read effectively, others were obliged to learn the music by rote in the time-honored fashion of those who are never quite able to decipher the apparent intricacies of the demi- and semiquavers.

With the emphasis on the reading of notes, the singing masters were still concerned with the sanctity and intelligibility of the words. Andrew Law suggests that "the music ought to lend to the words, not the words to the musick."[19] And in J. W. Moore's *Vocal and Instrumental Self-Instructor*, we find the admonition that the "words should not be lost."[20]

Instruction was atomistic. Little provision was made for review, and each part in the instruction was required to be learned before the next was begun. Instruction began with the gamut followed by proportional note values and rests. Rules were given pertaining to the finding of mi. The scholars were taught to identify the last note in the bass to find the tonic or key. It was either major or minor depending on the key signature. There was almost no variation in the content or order of presentation.

The earlier tune books had a longer, more elaborate theoretical introduction. These elaborations could have been directed toward the less well-trained singing master as well as toward the students. The later tune book included less instructional material, depending more upon the singing master's more complete training and skill.

The styles of the tunes themselves were varied, but the harmonies were kept to a small selection of chords. There was little inversion, and modulation was at a minimum. The harmonic practices came from William Tans'ur who influenced Billings. Tans'ur decreed that "two *Fifths*, or two *Eighths* (when it cannot be well avoided) may be used rather than spoil the Air." From these vaporous declarations, Billings produced 257 psalm tunes and 47 anthems with the greatest measure containing parallel fifths and octaves.

Billings dealt somewhat with the rules of composition. He believed that the tenor should be written first followed by the remaining parts which must conform to that of the tenor. The parts show a contrapuntal arrangement, a style consistent with the folk song idiom of the day and ignorant of the European harmonic practices of the latter part of the eighteenth century. Suspensions were not written, but the effect may have been exercised in the ubiquitous ornamentation of the period. Thirds were not regularly included in every chord while the fourth could be either a consonance or dissonance depending upon one's point of view.

Such was the folk style of New England until around 1800 when, again, reformers would make their influence felt. Another painful musical convulsion would ensue, leaving the votaries of good taste firmly in charge and the singing school masters packing their wagons and moving west and south.

In the last years of the eighteenth century, the beginnings of reform were glimpsed in the contributions of Andrew Law, Samuel Holyoke, and others. Admonitions against the use of parallel fifths and octaves appeared as well as the stricture against giving the melody to the tenor part.

Unison, fifth, octave 'perfect cords' fifths and eighths are not allowed to move together, ascending or descending.[21]

ORNAMENTATION IN THE TUNE BOOKS

The ornamentation of the psalms and hymns was common practice in eighteenth-century America and Europe. The mention of ornamentation is all but universal in eighteenth-century tune books, although most compilers leave the details to the individual singing masters. As a result, what little we know of these details must be gleaned from a few sources, who amplified the general remarks with details.

Most writers cautioned the student to be chary of ornaments and were concerned that the untrained singer would indulge in an excess of embellishment. The available evidence shows that the practice was widespread and many writers chose simply not to comment upon it. But we of the modern era, where all intricate and detailed markings on the page are surrounded by a sanctity of a holy writ, must attempt to return to the day when cadences were instinctively embellished and slow melodic skips of consecutive thirds were quavered with passing quarter notes (grace of transition).

The major influence on American practices was British. Secondary to this was the influence of American writers on each other. We have already noted that the more rhythmically and melodically complex tunes of the early psalters were replaced by simpler and slower melodies. With the expanded note values New England congregations supplied what must have been a free and improvisatory kind of ornamentation. The reformers of the early eighteenth century succeeded in inhibiting the congregations from these excesses as the singing schools developed more and more the singing by rule. Congregational singing gave way to the church choir whose members were graduates of the singing school. Often fifty or sixty strong, the choirs no doubt added quality as well as an increased quantity of tunes to the repertory.

But ornamentation did not die. The practice was too well entrenched in standard European practice, and its execution was only modified to conform to what was considered good taste.

Robert Donnington tells us of difficulties in trying to understand the performance of ornamentation in the eighteenth century. While Donnington was discussing European practices, it seems reasonable to assume that his sentiments would also apply to the ornamentation of psalms and hymns.

The consistency on which the chief utility of this system should have depended never remotely approached being realized in practice. With the exception of certain conscientious Frenchmen, and a few imitators of whom C. P. E. Bach was the most influential, confusion reigned virtually universal. . . . one sign may serve for a half dozen ornaments; one ornament may be served by a half a dozen signs, but we cannot rely on them.[22]

Only recorded examples would be reliable, an avenue unfortunately closed to us. We can only investigate the written instruction for the best answers, try to imagine what the music sounded like, and attempt an appreciation of the enthusiasm that enveloped the singers in both the singing schools and choir lofts.

Ornamentation was an integral part of music during the late colonial period, 1760 to 1800, first appearing in American tune books in 1761. It is reasonable to suspect, however, that ornamentation existed long before this in the colonies.[23] Thomas Atwill tells us that "many notes may be varied from their true sounds, with very great advantage, but it must be done with judgment." He criticized the gracing of tunes by fixed rules complaining that such a condition "is frequently attended with very evil consequences."[24] Jeremiah Ingalls admonished the readers of his *Christian Harmony* that the "Trills, Transitions and Accents, have not been attended to in the preceeding rules; they are learnt principally from their teachers."

Ornamentation came to colonial America from British sources, and all American tune books were indebted to these sources in one way or another. Except for the manner of presentation none of the ornaments presented in American tune books was original. American ornamentation, a mixture of English and Continental practices, was about fifty years behind Europe. The ornamentation described by Leopold Mozart, K. P. E. Bach, and Johann Quantz between 1760 and 1800 was not reflected in American tune books until the works of Gram (1795), Holyoke (1802), and Kimball (1793).

William Tans'ur's work, *A Compleat Melody* (1738), had more information on ornamentation than any other British or American tune book.[25] But we can assume that the practice of ornamentation must have been popular in English churches during the early eighteenth century not only because of the above sources but also because of the satires that appeared in British humor magazines of the day.*

The American tradition had its roots in the American oral or folk tradition as well as in the British tradition. American tune books gave more attention to expressive means than did the British, and the Americans had a greater variety of ornaments, particularly the "ornaments of expressions." American writers made much of the *swell, hold, accent, propriety of expression*, and the *mark of distinction*. But the only English source to include all these ornaments was Aaron Williams's *Universal Psalmist*. American graces represented a variety of styles and methods including the *accent, mark of distinction, staccato, swell*, and *hold* which at the time were considered ornaments but now are not. Other ornaments included the *turned shake*, the *trill*, the *forefall* (synonymous with *backfall* and *appogiatura*), the *grace of transition*, the *turn*, and the *beat*.

In general, accents were described in a manner with which we are already familiar, that is, accents appeared naturally on the first beat of a measure and the first and third beats in 4/4 time. Only Samuel Holyoke suggested something different and that was an accent on the first and third beats in triple meter.[26] As this practice was decried by Billings[27] and Holyoke's counsel is repeated by no

---

*The influences on British ornamentation were Continental in general and Italian in particular.

other compiler, one can only guess at Holyoke's reasons for his suggestion. But Tans'ur's description of the *accent* varies somewhat from our own and places it clearly within the province of ornamentation. The *accent* was "a Sort of wavering or quavering of the Voice, or Instrument, on certain Notes, with a Stronger or weaker Tone than the rest, and to express the Passion thereof: which renders Musick (especially vocal) so very agreeable to the Ear, it being chiefly intended to move and affect."[28] Tans'ur was obviously concerned with the aesthetic renditions and expressions of music which not only are subtle principles in themselves but relate in vocal music to textual considerations as well. Important words and accented syllables of the text always received the accent. While composers tried to make this agree with the music, conflicts were usually resolved in favor of the words. Andrew Law was concerned about this principle, however, and admonished the singers to accent the strong beat. Holyoke suggested no variation in strength between accented and unaccented notes. The accent, believed Holyoke, must come through pronunciation of accented and unaccented syllables giving a far more subtle nature to the concept of ornamentation.[29]

The *mark of distinction* was synonymous with *staccato* with the former term used almost exclusively until near the end of the eighteenth century. Its use differed little from one tune book to another and was indicated by marks over the notes denoting a "distinct and emphatic" rendition.[30]

But a "distinct and emphatic" rendition did not necessarily result in a shorter note as does the concept of *staccato*. One may assume, however, that the usual result was a shorter note. Holyoke did make a distinction between *staccato* and the *mark of distinction* indicating that the latter be performed short and the *staccato* be performed somewhat smoother. Hans Engelke tells us that this concept is in keeping with Continental practices of the latter eighteenth century. Billings was concerned lest we combine the *grace of transition* (passing tones) with the *mark of transition* leading toward an unintended triplet pattern.[31]

The *swell* became popular in America during the first decade of the nineteenth century. From Stephen Jenks we learn that the *swell* "should be applied by striking the note soft and gradually increasing the sound to the centre, then diminishing in the same proportion." Daniel Read suggested that its use be associated with sounds of considerable length, while Jocelyn believed that a *hold* was the appropriate place.[32] Engelke informs us that almost all information on the *swell* appeared around the turn of the nineteenth century. The exceptions were the *Chorister's Companion* and Williams's *Universal Psalmist*. Williams was the only English tune book writer to mention the *swell*, indicating that either the ornament was not widely favored in England or, conversely, that its use was so commonplace that contemporary writers saw no need to comment. Law tells us that the *swell* should be practiced almost universally. "The swell is in one sense applicable to all music," believed Law. "There is something of it upon every note."[33] Law describes a typically European baroque practice, but at an interestingly late date. Its universal acceptance and use would account for its infrequency in the theoretical introduction to American tune books.

The *hold* (also called *pause*, *cadence*, or *mark of suspension*) is found in only a few works. While it is discussed in *Royal Melody Compleat*, it was ignored by most American writers. Holyoke enlightens us. The *hold* is "an unmeasured pause, or suspension, that room may be given for a peculiar expression, or for introducing voluntary graces, as may suit taste and fancy." This, of course, is another way of telling his readers that a cadenza may be improvised by the performer. To make that especially clear, Holyoke gives us a delightful example:[34]

Again the absence of much discussion of the function of the *hold* may indicate that much choral music of this period did not lend itself to improvised cadenzas of this type. Yet in those few American sources where the *hold* is discussed we are led to believe that its use was common. Oliver Holden gives us a more conventional description of the *hold* in his *Union Harmony*. The *hold*

"gives the performer liberty to continue the sound of the note, to which it refers, beyond its common length. . . . Whenever it occurs, the school or choir should discontinue beating time, dwelling sweetly on the sound, until the master resumes the time in its proper order."[35] Obviously no cadenza is implied here, and we can now balance our interpretation of this practice: first, that cadenzas were occasionally improvised at appropriate places, second, that the *swell* was undoubtedly used in such situations, and third, that the held note was merely held with or without a swell depending upon the fancy of the performer.

Simon Jocelyn considered the *trill* or *shake* to be the most difficult to execute properly and describes its performance in some detail.

The trill, or common Shake: which is the shaking of two distinct notes upon one syllable as long as the time allows, always beginning with the upper, and ending on the lower note; and may be used on descending pointed crotchets, and before a close;—also on descending sharp'd notes, and semi-tones, but none shorter than a crotchet. Of this there are two sorts, called open, or close; if the next note above the note to be shaken be a whole tone, it is an open shake. N.B. This is reckoned the capital Grace; and requires considerable practice to gain the perfection of it.[36]

Many authors give examples. Daniel Read in his *New Haven Collection of Sacred Music* gives the following:[37]

Jacob Kimball gives his readers the following:

And he describes it as "a quick and alternate repetition of the note over which it is placed, and the note immediately above it (from which the trill begins), so long as the time will allow." As beginners or less-experienced singers would have trouble with this ornament, Kimball suggested a simpler version. "The trill is a very beautiful grace, but as it is difficult to be acquired, it may not be amiss to propose the following substitute for it, till it can be perfectly learned."[38]

There appears to be a rather universal understanding of the conventional practice of trilling since few compilers thought to describe its application. Of Italian origin, the *trill* was introduced to the New World in about 1750 via the English tune books and soon became the most frequently used ornament.

The terms *trill* and *turn* were often used interchangeably. Billings and Read both show the following examples of the *trill*: [39]

But Engelke tells us that only William Norman's *Federal Harmony* and *Boston Collection* utilize these graces.

As the most popular ornament, the *trill* was abused. Billings particularly complained that singers took "great license from these Trills, and without confining themselves to any rule, they shake all notes promiscuously." Notes should be trilled only when so marked, believed Billings, and only then according to rule "which may be easily learned under a good master." [40] That few tune books included trill markings forces us to conclude that trills were performed by rule, and the rules were learned in the singing schools. In Howe's *Worshipper's Assistant* the author advises his students not to trill at random and "without the mark," [41] yet Howe's work had no trill sign. Josiah Flagg in *A Collection of the Best Psalm Tunes* includes many trill signs, a rarity in these New England collections, but, paradoxically, he violates the usual rules for his time. An examination of Flagg's book reveals that trills were sung primarily in tenor and treble parts, less often in the counter, and almost never in the bass.

It was perhaps no wonder that the usual rules were noted more for their violations than for their acceptance. If Flagg made exceptions to the rules, so may have others. One can logically assume that the rules were generally used as a point of departure rather than as fixed law. But what were these rules for the tasteful performance of trills? Jocelyn supplies them in his theoretical introduction to his *Chorister's Companion*. Here is where the *trill* may be appropriate: [42]

Daniel Bayley describes the use of the *trill* similarly:

The trilloe, or shake, may be used in all descending Pricked Notes, and always before a Close; also on all descending sharp'd Notes, and all descending Semitones; but none shorter than Crotchets.[43]

The *turn* enjoyed a degree of flexibility in its performance. Often used interchangeably with the *trill*, it invited a variety of interpretations, as the contemporary examples show. James Lyon's *Urania* gives several examples of possible performance practices while Daniel Read shows a new version of the *trill*, but the result is merely a *turn*.[44]

Lyon's suggestions concerning the *turn* are as follows:

The Turn may be used on a Note that sinks a Semitone below two notes on the same Line or Space, always beginning with the first; and also at the End of the Strain, when the last note is grac'd.[45]

A later interesting example of a *turned shake* appears in Holyoke's *Columbian Repository*:

It is obvious that to sing these graces, no little skill was required to achieve the desired musical effect. It is no wonder that Billings and others were reluctant to hear the average singer indulge himself in the *trills* and *turns* that might have sounded like an eighteenth-century musical rollercoaster. But such a carnival was a source of popular enjoyment that unfortunately became stunted when the styles began to change.

The *beat*, whose sign approximates that of a *mordant*, was variously interpreted in the New England tune books. It can be found in Christopher Simpson's *Division Violist or an Introduction to the Playing upon a Ground*:[46]

It reappeared in Aaron Williams's *Universal Psalmist* and was later reproduced in Jocelyn and Doolittle's *Chorister's Companion*. Only James Lyon and Samuel Holyoke mentioned the *beat*, and Jocelyn and Doolittle saw no difference between the *beat* and the *shake*. Holyoke believed the *beat* and the *turn* to be an ornament of the same nature, but his illustration is similar to that of Jocelyn and Doolittle.[47]

The *grace of transition* was the second most popular ornament. There was no designated sign in the music making, its practical reconstruction a challenge. We know that all melodic intervals of thirds and fourths could be so ornamented as most American writers have agreed to the concept. In practice this grace was seldom used in intervals of a fourth. Jocelyn and Doolittle allow it on descending fourths if "in a flat key," but nothing mentioned in relation to an ascending fourth. Read gives an example of the *grace of transition* used in an interval of an ascending fourth:[48]

But Kimball's interpretation of this grace shows confusion. One cannot help but notice the lack of precision in the use of the terminology. Kimball's examples are obviously not *graces of transition* or *passing tones* in the modern vernacular.[49]

Billings gives us good examples of the proper execution of the *Grace of Transition.*[50]

Billings tells us that only half notes should be so graced, but Engelke says that such an admonition appears only in Billings. Billings attempted to clarify the interpretation. "You must not . . . lean on the intermediate Note in thirds, where the notes are but a half beat in length; for that makes them sound like notes tied together in threes; but you must strike such notes as distinctly and emphatically as possible."[51] Billings believed that the *grace of transition* added an increased vigor to his tunes as well as acting to keep the singers on pitch during skips in the vocal line.

Toward the end of the eighteenth century, ornamentation gradually came under criticism. The proponents of "better taste" were always those people of New England coastal cities who were closer to the accepted European practices. Trends then entered the rural areas, grating against the well-rooted sensibilities of the populace. Always in touch with the best European practice, Benjamin Franklin scoffed at the process of ornamentation in his description of Scotch tunes. "Scotch tunes have lived so long and will probably live forever (if they escape being stifled in modern affected ornament)."[52] Times were changing and Franklin had difficulty appreciating the contrapuntally complex writings of no less than a George Frederick Handel! Baroque and classical practices were not as well delineated in the practice of church music as in the mainstream of European secular music. And the staid simplicity of church hymns which came to be accepted during the nineteenth century was resisted fiercely by those whose comfort and security were challenged by the new way.

SHAPED NOTES

Books with unorthodox notation occurred from the beginning of music texts in America with John Tufts's *Introduction to the Singing of Psalm Tunes*. Each innovator sought to simplify the reading of notation in the hope that the learner could find a shortcut to the difficult art of reading music by note and that the author would sell large quantities of books. The use of unorthodox notation, beginning early in the nineteenth century, was clearly aimed at the singing-school market. But as these singing schools were replaced by other institutions for music teaching, only the then-current European practices were used.

By far the most popular of the various systems of notation was the shape note system. An individual character for each note identifies the syllable. While modulatory systems require that the shapes be placed in different positions on the staff, the interpretation of the syllable by the singer mitigates against difficulties of performance.

There were several systems of four-character notation in the early nineteenth century, but the most important were by William Little and William Smith in *The Easy Instructor*, and by Andrew Law in his *The Art of Singing*.[53]

The Easy Instructor, published in 1798, was probably the first book to use shape notes; its system was perfectly orthodox except for the shape note heads. Fa was represented by a triangular shaped note, sol by a regular round note, la by a square note, and mi by a diamond shaped note. The reception of this volume and of the system of music reading that it espoused was immediate and enthusiastic. A flood of editions poured from the printers between 1805 and 1831 and tens of thousands of copies were sold. While the earlier editions adhered firmly to concepts and tenants of hymnody that made parallel intervals and fuge singing a hallmark of New England folk culture, later editions were nonetheless indistinguishable from the reform collections.

So popular did the shape notes become that even Timothy Mason, Lowell's brother, had to publish his *Ohio Sacred Harp* in shape note version as those west of the Alleghenies were reported in 1834 as not being able to read the round notes.[54] The *Ohio Sacred Harp* sold fifty thousand copies using the shape note format before it was then introduced in a round note edition.

As the so-called better music people drove the singing school masters southward and westward from their positions in the churches and meeting-houses of New England, the shape note adherents formed their own encampments in those regions and remained there even into the present century. Between 1815 and 1855, southern tune books appeared using the shape note system and aimed at the revival market; the *Kentucky Harmony* in Harrisonburg, Virginia; the *Columbian Harmony* from Wilson County, Tennessee; the *Missouri Harmony* from Saint Louis, Missouri, and many, many more. The Civil War marked the end of the expansion of shape notation and the famous fasola system, and no new compilations came out after 1865. But William Walker's famous *Southern Harmony*, published in 1835, continued in use for over fifty years after its appearance.[55]

About the same time that Little and Smith were inventing their shape note system, Andrew Law was pursuing a similar system, but with the shapes in a somewhat different order. In Law's system the diamond is mi; the square is faw; and round note is sol; and the quarter of a diamond is law. The two systems differ in the representation of faw and law. Also Law's system did not put the notes on the staff.

In 1780 the first edition of Law's *Musical Primer* was published in New Haven, Connecticut. This edition was printed in round notes, but in Law's fourth edition, printed in 1803 in Cambridge, Massachusetts, by W. Hillard, there appears for the first time in his works the introduction of shape notes.[56] Law had been a teacher of music for over twenty years. Like so many teachers, Law strongly felt the need to develop a system whereby the student might learn the art of music reading more easily. There is every evidence that Law was influenced by the work of Little and Smith since the latter's work was published four years in advance of the *Musical Primer*. But Law's system never did achieve the popularity of *The Easy Instructor*.

Law's early years were spent with an uncertainty as to whether he would go into the ministry or embrace music as a career. He enrolled in Rhode Island College (renamed Brown in 1804) when the student population was less than forty. He seemed to settle for a religious vocation. His sacerdotal piety earned him the name of "Domine" among his fellow students. He came under the influence of William Billings as the composer and singing master taught a singing school at Providence in 1774. Crawford tells us that there is no record that Law and Billings met.[57] But six tunes by Billings appear in Law's *Select Harmony* of 1779.

Law was a practicing musician during his four years at college and acted as a singing master. In 1776 the New London Association of Ministers granted him a license to preach the gospel. While his formal education was directed toward a ministerial career, his love and practice of music soon convinced Law to devote his time exclusively to music. The year 1777 represented Law's earliest appearance in the pulpit and also the beginning of his career as a compiler of tune books. As no further references can be found concerning his career as a minister, Law's choice is self-evident. His musical career spanned fifty years. He established singing schools in eleven states, devised an original notation, became the first American musician to become actively interested in copyright legislation, and was the most prolific compiler of tune books of his generation.

The standards and tastes in music had begun to change. Good taste meant correct composition and in this, Samuel Holyoke, Oliver Holden, and Andrew Law were in the forefront in the decade before the nineteenth century. In 1793 Andrew Law wrote in his *The Art of Singing*, Part I, that "correct composers of modern date for the most part make use of the Treble, as the leading part, or air." After this date Law scored his melodies on the top staff. In addition reformers used more major tunes than the compilers writing in the folk tradition.[58]

In an analysis of the works of Oliver Holden, Daniel Wilfred McCormick succinctly outlines the theoretical and stylistic traits of this composer and, by so doing, acquaints the reader with the basic tenets of "reform" or of what came to be known as "good taste" in music. Holden wrote 236 hymn tunes and anthem-like pieces. In these works duets occur twice as often as fuges, which occurred twice as often in the composer's earlier pieces. Three voice tunes account for one-third of the total. Two-thirds are in major keys while the "third mood of common time" is used in 70 percent of his pieces. Holden's melodic characteristics incorporate triadic construction and long scale lines.[59]

Samuel Gilman's vivid and often humorous description of pressures and controversies that arose over the changes from fuge music to the slower style admirably describes this significant period in our cultural history. The understandably ambivalent reaction of the congregation and the singing gallery to the change in style must have taken place again and again in the churches of New England:

On the very first Sabbath that he joined us, he startled me a little by requesting that *Old Hundred* might be sung to a psalm which the minister had just begun to read. I told him that I should be very glad to oblige him by announcing that tune to the choir, but the truth was, it had not been performed in our meeting-house probably for thirty years;—that there were but four or five singers who were acquainted with it, being such only as had chanced to hear it sung at home by their fathers or grandfathers, and that these few had practised it once or twice together and in private, from mere curiosity to ascertain how so celebrated a piece of musical antiquity would sound.

My prevailing disposition to oblige, and the great quantity of time already consumed in our conversation, imposed upon me now the necessity of pronouncing aloud, as was usual just before beginning to sing, the name of this venerable air. No sooner had the word proceeded from my mouth, than there appeared to be a motion of keen curiosity among the congregation below, but in the choir around me there reigned the stillness of incredulity and surprise. All the elder members of the flock, I could observe, looked upwards to the gallery, with the gleams of pleasurable expectation in their countenances. Of our well-filled orchestra, only eight individuals arose, for there were no more among us, who possessed the least acquaintance with Old Hundred. And even three out of that number were as ignorant of it as those who continued seated, but ventured to expose themselves, trusting to assistance they might derive from the voices of the other performers, and from the score of the tune itself, contained in some, though I think not in all of the copies of the Village Harmony which were present.

The psalm was sung with tolerable correctness; but accompanied with *such* a fanning on the part of the females, who were all sitting, and *such* awhispering among those of the correlative sex who were unemployed, that I could note nothing but disturbance and unhappiness for a long time to come in our choral circle.

At the close of the morning service, I had the promised interview and explanation with my new acquaintance. It seems that since leaving college he had been reading law for a year in an office at one of our seaport towns, and while there, had occasionally assisted in the choir of some congregation, into which had been introduced a new and purer taste for sacred music than generally prevailed through the rest of the country. In that choir, as he informed me, no tunes of American origin were ever permitted to entrance. Fuges there were a loathing and detestation. None but the slow, grand, and simple airs which our forefathers sang, found any indulgence. Mr. Forehead assured me that no other music was worth hearing, and what seemed to weigh particularly with him was the circumstance that the slow music in question was beginning to be in the fashion.

In the course of a month, Mr. Forehead's argument, persuasion, and example, wrought in a large portion of the choir a very considerable change of taste on this subject. There were some, who loved novelty; there were others, who yielded to the stranger's assurances respecting the fashionableness of the thing; and there was a third description, who were really convinced of the better adaption of the ancient tunes to the purposes of worship, and had a taste to enjoy their solemn and beautiful strains. All these classes composed perhaps about a moiety of the choir, and were eager for the introduction of the good old music. The other half were extremely obstinate and almost bigoted in their opposition to this measure, and in their attachment to the existing catalogue of tunes. Most of us took sides on the question with an inexcusable warmth, and without any attempt at compromise. . . .

And now for several weeks was the full-breathing triumph of the lovers of crotchets and quavers over the votaries of minims and semibreves. The latter faction sullenly absented themselves from the singing pew, and generally from worship, while the former revelled amid the labyrinths of fuges, believing to their own happiness, certainly, the order of consecutive parts to be the sweetest of melodies, and the recurrence of consecutive fifths the most delightful of harmonies. . . .

The terms of reconciliation and reunion were settled in the following manner. As our performances were required regularly five times on a Sabbath, it was agreed that the arrangement of tunes throughout the day should be two fuges, two of the slow ancient airs, and one of a different description from either. Neither party could well object to airs of a rapid and animated movement, in which all the parts continued uninterruptedly to the close, as in the case with Wells, Windham, Virginia, and many others.[60]

THE DECLINE OF THE SINGING SCHOOL

The days of the singing school were numbered. During the first two decades of the nineteenth century a change in life-style was

brought about by easier modes of transportation, a newly rekindled interest in the improvement of the common school systems, and the wider dissemination of traveling entertainers. The
Boston Handel and Haydn Society, founded in 1815, always
aimed toward the improvement of taste in music. The publications
of the society extended its influence. Many people came to Boston
to hear concerts of the society and would, in turn, try these works
at home with their choirs. So the word was carried. In time, the
various societies turned people from their own folk traditions and
toward the correctly harmonized European renditions. The *Boston Musical Gazette*, a reform publication edited by Bartholomew
Brown, one of the founders of the Boston Handel and Haydn Society, took every opportunity to ridicule the ancient psalmody.[61] *

The barrier of Puritanism was breached by the theatre which
brought a concert life that flourished after the War of 1812. The
reformed sacred music was virtually indistinguishable from the
secular songs of the day. Immediately after the turn of the century
the writers seemed to have found "good taste" in earnest. It meant
correctly harmonized compositions (according to the best European practices) but it also represented a reaction to the fuge-tune.
European secular song became acceptable to Americans and with
this acceptance came European-trained musicians. With some notable exceptions, most American musicians who were trained in
singing schools could not conform to the dictates of the changing
tastes and values. When Lowell Mason came on the scene in the
second decade of the century, the stage had already been set by
such men as Holyoke, Law, and Holden, along with Read and
Gram. In Holden's *Union Harmony* of 1793, twelve anthems were
composed conspicuously without fuging passages. Representing a
reaction to the baroque polyphony that had already moved into
the classical period in Europe, Holden, in his *Union Harmony*,
was concerned lest the words be unintelligible in fuge passages. In
1790 the problem of stylistic transitions was disclosed to the
American public.

In the present age we are many times more surprised at the attempts and
extravagance of execution, than pleased by neatness; the simplicity of air
has often spoiled, by the redundance of variations and graces; nature is

---

* Other editors of the Boston Musical Gazette were Lowell Mason, G. J. Webb, Thomas
Comer, John Rowe Packer (former editor of *Euterpeiad*) and John Sullivan Dwight.

outraged, in imitations, and the ear is perplexed, if not lost, in a crowd of harmony, or tired with everlasting repetitions of the subject.[62]

Slowly the minor tunes which were so prominent in the early collections give way to an emphasis on major. The fourth edition of Daniel Read's *American Singing Book*, published in 1793, included 29 major tunes and 18 minor, while Elias Mann's *Massachusetts's Collection* of 1807 includes 110 major tunes but only 52 minor. Hans Gram, along with George K. Jackson, that memorable musician from England who settled in Boston, deprecated the native American school and were joined eventually by Andrew Law and Samuel Holyoke who, though products of the American singing school, took exception to it. Andrew Law delivered his attacks upon American music in 1793 recommending its replacement with European music. The reform was slowly taken up by other musicians and clergymen. Twenty years later the reform was an accomplished fact in New England. Daniel Read lived to repudiate in old age that style which he had helped develop. Even the better American composers seemed self-conscious about their own compositions. As early as the 1790s American composers looked toward Europe for guidance. Anthem collections after 1812 showed an increasingly European orientation in such collections as *A Volume of Sacred Musick Containing Thirty Anthems Selected from the Works of Handel, Purcel (sic), Croft and other eminent European Authors* (Newburyport: E. Little & Co., 1814) and the *Old Colony Collection*, Vol. I (1818), which included pieces by Mozart and Beethoven.[63]

The Musical Fund Society of Philadelphia was organized in 1820 with the help of the fine English musicians Raynor Taylor and Benjamin Carr. A rapid development of American instrument manufacturing, especially pianos, took place in the first half of the nineteenth century. Serious American students of music began their pilgrimages to Europe to study, a trend that has diminished only in recent years. European teachers were coming to America and plying the only trade they knew, not the rudiments of a singing school but the best European tradition. The study of instrumental music became increasingly popular about this time, particularly of the piano and the cabinet organ.

The use of organs in churches increased dramatically during these years, and in the words of George Pullen Jackson, "became monarchs, reducing to musical serfdom all attempts at vocal harmonizing."[64] There was much to disturb the status quo, and mass immigrations of comparatively urban Germans into almost all areas of the country brought their more advanced practices of instrumental and vocal music. Family concertizers poured through urban and rural America, singing, bell-ringing, and creating audiences for secular music which would not have been countenanced a generation earlier.

The early nineteenth century saw a significant improvement in the country's systems of transportation. Fulton's *Clermont* proved the value of the steamboat in 1807. In 1825 the Erie Canal opened, which was to reduce travel between Albany and Buffalo from twenty to ten days. Other canals were planned. The first railroad tracks were laid in 1830.

Singing schools were less and less required. Americans could learn their songs by ear without the trouble of a singing school and without the required diligence. The best European practices required that the melody be placed in the top voice. No longer were fuge-tunes tolerated as creative embellishment, and in the churches ornamentation was now considered poor taste. The people saw their own music taken from them, with a corresponding diminution in the size and quality of church choirs and the exodus of the singing school master to the west and to the south.

By the time Lowell Mason had published his enormously successful *Boston Handel and Haydn Collection of Church Music* in 1822, there was a public ready and eager to embrace the standards of good taste preached by Mason, Isaac Woodbury, William Bradbury, and so many others. As so often happens in America, the arbiters of good taste looked across the Atlantic for their models and scorned that which was home-grown. And such was their influence, then as now, that an uncertain population, striving for cultural respectability, embraced the common practice of European art music. Those who studied in Europe or in the European mold cultivated a social superiority. The democratic tradition of the singing school began its decline. But these arbiters of taste from Boston did not represent the mean of the population. Their influence left the congregation without a music to which they could identify. An interest in church singing waned, giving way to the quartet choir. New England would not again hear the stimulating strains of the fuge-tune coming from all parts of the sanctuary.

CHAPTER IV

Colonial Education:
Public Attitudes of the
North and South

PUBLIC EDUCATION IN COLONIAL TIMES

COLONIAL ATTITUDES reflected religious differences that resulted in marked contrasts between the New England colonists and those in the South. The Puritan contributions in the New World were remarkable, especially since great advancements are not to be expected of colonial peoples soon after their departure from the mother country.

New England communities were compact, with a growing interest in mercantile pursuits. Timber was more than adequate for shipbuilding; bays and harbors were numerous, and the water teemed with fish. In 1675, there were 6,000 vessels in New England with 4,000 men engaged in the fishing industry. There was also a lively interest in the fur trade and textiles.[1] Such a people had a predisposition toward the establishment of public schools.

The Englishmen in Virginia were dispersed. Nothing resembling a town existed in Virginia until the eighteenth century; Jamestown was the only village.[2] Like New England, Virginia derived many of its social and educational customs from England. Unlike New England, however, people in the southern colonies regarded education as a luxury and as a privilege of the wealthy. In the South the parish or the county, not the town, developed as the nucleus of social and cultural activities, and the plantation was the primary sociocultural unit. The foremost political, economic, and social fact of the eighteenth-century southern parish was the rule by class. This class structure was derived from the manorial society of Europe, specifically England.[3] Richmond was the seat of this cultural inheritance, and its attitude toward public education was in marked contrast to that of New England. John Peyton Little's comments on the state of education in Virginia were perhaps typical of many in the southern ruling classes.

It is better to place education under church influence, than under that of the State. . . . The government cannot, itself, educate the communities; it can only act by a cloud of irresponsible and ignorant school masters; nor would it be right for it to exercise the power, if it possessed the ability of imparting a good education. . . . Schools originated and sustained by private, or denominational enterprise, are best; of such kinds are the schools of Richmond.[4]

Yet early class distinctions in New England were about as sharp as in the southern colonies. Puritans were seated in church according to their social status, and, until 1722, the Harvard catalogue arranged their students by social class.

The early records of education in New England are few. Boston hired a schoolmaster in 1635, and one year later Charlestown voted to hire an English university graduate "to keepe a school for a twelve monthe," voted him forty pounds a year out of town rates, and appointed a school committee.[5] The early Puritan community, like most societies, was most interested in serving and preserving the existing system. Their pupils were educated to accept passively the Puritan creed.

The first educational law in the colonies was the Massachusetts Act of 1642. This act required the selectmen of the town "to inquire into the literacy of the children and to fine those parents and apprentices' masters who refused to account for their children's ability to read and understand the principles of religion and the capital laws of the country."[6]

The first school law that required the establishment and support of schools was the "Old Deluder Satan" Act of 1647. Towns of fifty householders were to appoint someone to instruct "all such children as shall resort to him to write and read." The teachers were to be paid either by the parents or by the "masters of such children" or by "the inhabitants in general." At the same time every town of one hundred families or householders was to establish a Latin grammar school to prepare youth for Harvard College. Failure to comply with the law was punishable by a fine of five pounds.[7] Such was the first legal basis in Massachusetts for a public school system, a basis for popular support of education which the South was not to develop until after the Civil War.

But this was only the beginning of publicly supported education in Massachusetts, and many difficulties had to be overcome before universal educational opportunity was achieved. The uneducated were not always enthusiastic about the notion of universal schooling. Almost a century would pass before the ideal of universal education was implanted firmly in New England. Even then many people considered that the private school offered more prestige and often better education.

Town records of the seventeenth century are fragmentary; only those of Essex County, Massachusetts, and a ten-year sequence of the records of Suffolk County have been printed. The data on literacy are incomplete. In Suffolk County in the years 1653 to 1656, 89 percent of the men but only 42 percent of the women could sign their names, although from 1681 to 1697 the number of women literates grew to 62 percent of the female population.[8] In the seventeenth century, there were no reliable population statistics to tell which towns had over fifty or over one hundred families. Consequently, the provisions of the 1647 act were all but unenforceable.[9]

The 1670s saw a decline in education in New England. Ministers complained "that the schools languish, and are in a low Condition in the Country." Grammar instruction lapsed in New Haven and Hartford, Connecticut, in 1673 as well as in Watertown, Massachusetts, in 1675. Harvard, too, came close to extinction, with no graduating class of 1672. But trade was booming during these years, and Morison carefully describes the likely lads as preferring "a berth in the forecastle or cabin of a yankee vessel to spending seven years in grammar school and four more in college."[10] But schools advanced in New England, following this short period of decline, right up to the end of the century.

An education at Harvard was not expensive in the seventeenth century. A quarter's tuition could have been covered by a bushel and a half of wheat and a "Gershom Bulkeley was kept in college an entire year by a side of beef, a small side of backen, five bushels of wheat, fourteen of corn, fifteen and a half of apples, and a cask of butter."[11] The aim of the college was to provide a broad education, not only to train ministers.[12] The formal curriculum included six of the seven liberal arts: grammar, rhetoric, logic, arithmetic, geometry, astronomy. Music was not mentioned. Other subjects included metaphysics, ethics, natural science, Greek, Hebrew, and ancient history. The language of instruction was Latin, which was supposed to have been learned in the grammar schools. Texts were, for the most part, in Latin.[13]

The Puritans believed that they were God's elect, and such a belief bred a sense of responsibility to God. The Puritan ideal encouraged ethical business transactions believing that the hard-working businessman was just as noble in the sight of God as the celibate living a monastic life. Such a movement had its roots in the middle class and appealed largely to the rising middle class of the seventeenth century. Puritanism had nothing against music, as such. In England Cromwell employed an orchestra, and during this time the first Italian opera was performed there. The pioneer spirit in the New England colonies did not prevent a burgeoning intellectual activity soon after the Plymouth landing, though a musical awakening was not to take place until the early years of the eighteenth century.

MUSIC EDUCATION IN COLONIAL VIRGINIA

In the South, as in New England, the accumulation of material wealth was respected. In the North, however, there was no patronage of the arts, while in the South a transplanted baroque manorial society was beginning to flourish. Such a society easily assimilated European-trained music, and dancing masters traveled from plantation to plantation instructing the planter's children and their friends and often providing music for balls and dances.

While the Puritans were uniquely sympathetic to public education, the Anglicans of the South enjoyed their music but held their musicians in a baroque servile capacity. Music in the southern manorial culture was a class privilege; music in New England was a music of the people. Although New Englanders were also conscious of class, this English attitude did not appear to affect their practice of music. Nevertheless, concerts and entertainment flourished in Charleston and Virginia but were frowned upon in New England.

In colonial Virginia a musician would earn his livelihood in three ways: by playing and singing in the theatre; by playing and singing at the "court" or plantation seats; or by playing the organ in the Anglican churches. Of course, the playing or singing at the plantations almost always went hand in hand with instructional activities.[14]

Only the owners of the larger plantations could afford to indulge their taste for music. With the breakup of the larger plantations after the Revolutionary War, the sources of patronage for the itinerant music and dancing masters began to dissolve. The patronage system was dying in Europe, also, and the theories of the natural rights of man meant that musicians, both in Europe and in the New World, would have to search elsewhere for their livelihoods. The areas of public performance and teaching presented the best possibilities. The itinerant music master was a transitional element between the older, strictly patronage-oriented musician and the musicians who served the public. While the itinerant musician had to serve several patrons on widely scattered plantations, later musicians often taught music in the private schools.

In the mid-eighteenth century, in Williamsburg, Virginia, was an actor-musican named Singleton. Between acts he played the violin for dances. In the June 12, 1752, issue of the *Virginia Gazette*, he advertised the following:

Mr. Singleton takes the Opportunity of informing Gentlemen and others, That he proposes to Teach the Violin in this city and places adjacent, at a Pistole [$2.50 each per month] and a Pistole Entrance, provided a Sufficient Number of Scholars can be engaged (not less than six in any one place). He will give attendance at York, Hampton, and Norfolk, on the aforesaid terms.[15]

John Victor, another itinerant music master, made his home at Port Royal from 1775 to 1789. He was a teacher of the harpsichord, "forte-piano," guitar, and spinet and was seemingly able to tune and repair these instruments.[16] In a letter from John Caster to Thomas Jefferson, dated July 27, 1778, Victor's varied talents are reported.

You are pleased to say that the practical part of musick afforded you much Entertainment, that you wanted an organ. I have two daughters who practice upon keyed instruments. Their music master did enter the continental Service who lately resigned his commission. The girls and Mrs. Caster are in expectation of Mr. Victors returning to his former calling.

John Stadler's teaching circuit in Virginia included the families of Fayloe, Lee, Custis, Washington, Carter, Fairfax, and Fitzhugh. He had attempted initially to earn his livelihood as a music teacher in Philadelphia, and in 1764 had appeared in concerts with Francis Hopkinson, John Schneider, James Bremmer, Stephen Farragan, and Governor John Penn. Stadler left Philadelphia sometime between 1764 and 1766. He appeared at Mount Vernon at least once a month and stayed for three or four days. In addition to his teaching duties, he more than likely furnished music for balls and dances held at the various plantations. Stadler played the organ, harpsichord, spinet, "forte-piano," harmonica, flute, and the violin. In 1774, the diarist Philip Fithian wrote about Stadler, "I love this good German. He used to teach in New York and Philadelphia. He has much simplicity and goodness of heart—He performs extremely well." [17]

German music masters made up the greater number of itinerant dancing and music masters in Virginia. (Their presence represented an extension of the alliance of England with the Hanoverian kings.) And German musicians are to prove important and influential in the middle colonies and in New England as the story of music and music education unfolds.

Cuthbert Ogle was another important musician in mid-eighteenth-century Williamsburg. Ogel was an Englishman and was known as a concert manager and harpsichordist in London. When he arrived in Williamsburg in 1754, he endeavored to earn his livelihood in a similar manner. He immediately established himself as the foremost musician in Williamsburg, furnishing harpsichord and spinet music for theatrical performances. After his death the inventory of his music showed a most unusual collection for this time and place. [18]

Norman Arthur Benson believes that Ogle was playing Handel almost twenty-five years before such performances took place in Philadelphia and Boston. But Oscar Sonneck reports of the existence of an "unparalleled Musical Clock" in Philadelphia in 1774, fully ten years before Ogle arrived in Virginia. This interesting clock, made by David Lockwood, was described as excelling all others in the Beauty of its Structure and plays the choicest Airs from the most celebrated Operas with the greatest Nicety and Exactness. It performs with beautiful graces, ingeniously and variously, intermixed, the French Horn Pieces, performed upon the Organ, German and Common Flute, Flageolet etc. Sonatas, Concertos, marches, minuets, jiggs and Scots Airs, composed by Corelli, Albinoni, Mr. Handel, and other great and eminent Masters of Musick.[19]

Of course it is possible that such a clock represented the only "performances" of the works of Handel, but that is doubtful. If such an advertisement appeared, it is reasonable to suppose that such music and composers were probably well known to Philadelphians at this time.

MUSIC EDUCATION IN CHARLESTON, SOUTH CAROLINA

Music in Charleston, South Carolina, flourished during the colonial period, and as a consequence music education was required. The earliest concerts in the colonies took place in Charleston, a center of culture and manners reminiscent of the contemporary European capitals. Secular music was practiced enthusiastically in the middle and southern colonies and outstripped religious music in these regions. The Anglican church in the South exerted little influence compared with the Puritan influence in the North.

Charleston was established in 1670 by planters from Jamaica and Barbados. Plantation families moved from the environs of Charleston to the sea coast in an effort to make the hot summers more bearable. The plantation families therefore became urbanites for almost five months of the year. They maintained private houses in town and supported musical and theatrical performances. As a result, itinerant dancing and music masters were attracted from Europe, the West Indies, and the northern colonies. The result was an interesting interchange between musical styles and culture. A thriving commerce in Charleston supported a leisure class. Theatres played a significant role along with concerts, balls, dancing assemblies, and private societies—a situation not too different from that of London.[20] The population mix virtually guaranteed a cosmopolitan outlook. English, Irish, Welsh, Scots, West Indians, Huguenots, Germans, Dutch, Jews, Swiss, and Quakers contributed their own unique life-styles to their adopted community. The Charleston ladies were described by Dr. Milligan in 1763 as being "fond of dancing, and exercise their perform very gracefully; and many sing well, and play upon the harpsichord and guitar with great skill."

The artistic life of Jamaica and Barbados was especially rich. As early as 1721, at a time when New England witnessed the first tune books written to improve singing in church, an announcement in the weekly *Jamaican Courant* indicated that a choice collection of the newest songs with notes were available, and violins, harpsichords, and flutes were offered for sale. There were concerts in Jamaica as early as 1726, a remarkably early date in as much as public and private concerts were rare even in London at this time. These concerts were probably held in the two principal taverns, the Ranelagh and the Vauxhall. Both had large and long rooms for concerts, balls, and public entertainments.

Foreign travelers reacted to Charleston as if it were a European metropolis. The Marquis de Chastellux reported that Charleston was a "commercial town in which strangers abound as in Marseilles and Amsterdam." He believed it was "more European in its manners than any in America." Edmund Burke thought that people in Charleston were "showy and expensive in their dress and way of living; so that everything conspires to make this by much the liveliest and politest place, as it is one of the richest too in all America."[21] And all this in a community whose white inhabitants in 1763 numbered only four thousand with an equal number of negro servants for a total population of eight thousand.

The South Carolina *Gazette* of April 15, 1732, announced the sale of *Musical Miscellany, being a Collection of Choice Songs set to the Violin and Flute by the most eminent masters.*[22] And in 1735, Charleston residents could see Cibber's ballad opera *Flora* or *Hob in the Well*. It had been given its first performance in Lincoln Inn Fields, London, in 1729.

Charleston's theatres flourished during the eighteenth century at a time when those of the North were involved in intense religious and political upheavals. In the 1773–1774 season alone, seventy-nine major performances were given. In 1794 two theatres competed to give the local population 270 plays with performances presented three nights a week.[23]

The permanent orchestras supported in Charleston attracted itinerant musicians from Europe, the West Indies, and the inhospitable northern colonies. Musical societies, of which the St. Cecilia Society was the most famous, contracted musicians by the year. Northern papers held advertisements for musicians needed in the orchestras of the society. The most talented of the northern musicians were drawn to Charleston by the prospect of work not only in the orchestra of the St. Cecilia Society but also in the theatre orchestras where ballad operas were extremely popular and where popular songs were performed between the acts.

The rich and abundant musical activities of Charleston stimulated the teaching of music and, consequently, helped the upper class to become sensitive and sympathetic to the arts. One music teacher was Peter Valton, an English musician. A student of William Boyce and James Nares, Valton was organist at St. Phillips Church in Charleston from 1764 to 1781. He was initially engaged for only three years at fifty pounds, paid for by the parishioners by subscription. He had been known in London as a composer of catches and glees, and he came to Charleston highly recommended. While at St. Phillips, he composed eleven psalm and hymn tunes, gave private lessons on the harpsichord, sold spinets and harpsichords, gave concerts, and played with the orchestra of the St. Cecilia Society. He also composed incidental music for the theatre, six sonatas for harpsichord, and music for the organ and violin.

Charles Theodore Pachelbel, son of the great Johann Pachelbel, advertised on March 1, 1749, that he would open a singing school for young ladies, one of the first singing schools in Charleston. The school was kept on Wednesdays and Saturdays throughout the year, in summer from four to six in the evening and in winter from two to four in the afternoon. As was the custom of itinerant musicians of the South, he traveled to surrounding plantations and gave harpsichord and spinet instruction to the daughters of the wealthy planters. It can be assumed that the singing schools taught by the highly trained and sophisticated European musicians were rather different from their northern Puritan counterparts. The New England tunesmiths, with a limited musical literature of psalms and hymns, taught a largely folk tradition which undoubtedly contrasted with the singing school of Charles Theodore Pachelbel, his European contrapuntal tradition, and strict part-writing rules. But the South was less democratic, and the music instruction in this region was aimed at the sons and daughters of the upper classes.

In 1751, Pachelbel became ill and could no longer serve as organist. The vestry of St. Phillips wrote to London for a well-qualified replacement. Edmund Larkin answered the call. In 1751 Larkin was giving private lessons on the harpsichord and spinet and also teaching the art of "singing with instruments." In an advertisement in the *South Carolina Gazette* of November 8, 1751, Larkin notes that "each pupil who chooses to be taught at home, to pay 12 pounds at Entrance, and the same Sum per Month, which will be eight Lessons at twice a Week, and an Hours Attendance each lesson. Such as are willing to take their Lessons at his own House, 8 pounds Entrance and the same per Month."

Larkin died within a short time and was replaced at St. Phillips by Benjamin Yarnold. He was paid fifty pounds a year and was given permission to seek pupils from the aristocratic families of the area. Upon arriving in Charleston in 1753 he announced that he would teach harpsichord at the usual rates, eight pounds entrance and twenty shillings a lesson. Yarnold was trained in the tradition of English cathedral music and also composed. In 1762 he opened a school of music for "no more than twelve ladies." He boasted that he could teach the science and theory of music so that the ladies could attain a proficiency in twelve to eighteen months. Each student had to pay twenty-five pounds and engaged to study at least one year.

Yarnold remained at St. Phillips from October, 1753, until January 23, 1764. In October of that year he became organist at St. Michaels Church. In May 1768, Yarnold left Charleston and remained abroad throughout the revolutionary war. In 1784 he returned to Charleston as organist at St. Michaels where he remained until his death on June 16, 1787.*

But the best in European music was not the only kind of music taught in Charleston. Jonathan Badger was one of the early New England psalmodists who made his way south and plied his trade,

---

* Instructions to the organist at St. Michaels included the following admonitions: He was required to perform on the organ at all required times, to chant the *Venite exultemus* and the *te deum* on alternate Sundays, to perform at all funerals to which invited, to instruct the youth "that choose to attend (who shall be particularly placed under his charge) in the Rules and Practice of Psalmody; and he shall command and require them, a serious and decent Deportment, during the Time of divine service."

presumably in the manner of the New England singing school. Badger established his school in Charleston in 1752. He had just published a collection of "the best psalm and hymn tunes, the first collection of its kind in the province." One year later he opened an evening school for teaching young persons in plain psalmody. Badger and the European-trained Pachelbel seem to have been acquainted as the former appears as a witness to Pachelbel's will. Both styles of church music appeared able to survive in a city that was infused by the crosscurrents of musical America in the eighteenth century.

MUSIC EDUCATION IN PHILADELPHIA, PENNSYLVANIA

Philadelphia began to flower musically about the middle of the eighteenth century. By 1780 it ranked first in music in the cities of America. The teaching of various instruments accompanied the gradual awakening of interest in the theatre. Any analysis of early secular music must include a discussion of early theatre. Drama and opera were introduced in Philadelphia in 1749.[24] Between acts or between plays (several dramas were often performed), singing and dancing took place, furnishing additional entertainment and employing many musicians newly arrived from Europe. Accompanying the singing and dancing between the acts was probably the harpsichord.

The first music teacher in Philadelphia to be identified was a Miss Ball. An advertisement in the *Pennsylvania Gazette*, March 5–13, 1730, announced that a Mr. Ball taught

writing, Arithmetic with the true Grounds of the French Tongue at Twenty Shillings per Quarter, and His Wife teaches writing and French. Likewise Singing, Playing on the Spinet, Dancing, and all sorts of Needle Work are taught by his sister lately arrived from London.[25]

Music was taught before this time in Philadelphia, but it is difficult to identify the persons and the circumstances surrounding the instruction. Sonneck draws attention to a reprint of "Chambers Dictionary" published in the *Pennsylvania Gazette*, January 20, July 25, 1729, to the effect that an "*Accent* in Musick, is a Modulation of the Voice to express Musical Composition, and an *Air* in Musick signifies the Melody, or the Inflection of a Musical Composition." If nothing more, we must expect that "musick" was considered of interest and importance before it became acceptable to pursue instruction. But 1729 is eight years after the publication of the Tufts and Walter texts in New England, where there was a ready market for such texts in the developing New England singing school.

The teaching of instruments seemed to be directed at the young ladies. Music was considered one of the polite branches of education, seemingly more popular with women but not limited exclusively to them. From an advertisment in the *Pennsylvania Gazette* of March 21, 1749, we find that a

John Beals, Musick Master from London at his House in Fourth Street, near Chestnut Street, joining to Mr. Linton's, collar maker, teaches the Violin, Hautboy, German Flute, Common Flute and Dulcimer by note.

Said Beals will likewise attend young ladies, or others, that may desire it, at their houses. He likewise provides musick for balls and other entertainments.

The early Quaker philosophy was similar to that of the Puritans. A rising middle class required a degree of social stability, and law and order was held in high regard. If a democratization was to take place in eighteenth-century society, then it would have to be through the ideals of "order, civility, and contracts." Crowds were synonymous with riots and other disturbances endangering private property. As theatres drew crowds, they became subject to this condemnation. The immoral plays, of course, did nothing to endear themselves to a righteous Quaker spirituality. But although theatrical entertainments were not allowed, lectures were—and soon no difference could be perceived between the two.

Opera galleries in eighteenth-century America were not those of today, and riots and disturbances regularly accompanied the theatrical diversions. Indignant at the practical jokes of the gallery, a David Douglas inserted the following in the New York *Mercury*, May 3, 1773. "The repeated insults which some mischievous persons in the gallery have given, not only to the stage and orchestra, but to the other parts of the house, call loudly for reprehension." He threatened to "point the culprits out to the constables."

On November 27, 1700, the Quakers passed a law against "Riots, Rioters, and Riotous Sports, Plays and Games." That such a law was honored by its breach can be shown by the haste of the Quakers to pass additional laws repeating in substance the first law. Again on January 12, 1705, another "Act against Riotous Sports, Plays, and Games" was passed reluctantly by Governor Logan. The second "stronger" law was deemed necessary because of the inadequacy of the first.

The official Quaker attitude toward music was not enthusiastic. In the writings of William Priest in his *Travels in the United States of America from 1793–97*, Priest quotes a Quaker:

It is a judgement on the inhabitants for their sins, in so much that they sent to England for a number of play-actors, singers, and musicians, who were *actually arrived*; and as a just judgement on the Philadelphians for encouraging these *children of iniquity*, for they were now afflicted with yellow fever.[26]

But professional theatrical performances came to Philadelphia in 1749 regardless of the laws against them. The prohibitions were only partly successful. Years later in an effort to preserve the forcefulness and revolutionary discipline of the American Revolution, Congress passed a law prohibiting "Theatrical Entertainments, horse-racing, gaming, and other diversions, which are only productive of Idleness, dissipation, and a general depravity of principles and Manners." These were also ignored. Plays were performed even at Valley Forge, according to several accounts, and the last attempt by the Quakers to suppress theatres was in 1788.

In 1789 some 1,900 citizens petitioned the General Assembly to repeal the antitheatre law. A Committee of Dramatic Association believed the law to have been an interference with the natural rights of people to make judgments; they believed it was the "right of every freeman to dispose of his time and money, according to his own taste and disposition, when not obnoxious to the real interest of society."[27] In 1791, a theatre was finally built within the city of Philadelphia.[28]

But official pronouncements to the contrary, musicians and dancing masters appeared to do a brisk business almost from the beginning of the eighteenth century. We know only the name of Mr. Staples, who was a dancing master in Philadelphia around the year 1710. In the fashionable boarding schools of Philadelphia in the eighteenth century, dancing, singing, and the playing of instruments constituted in part the elegant education of the young ladies.

At George Whitefield's "Revivals," the *Pennsylvania Gazette* reported that his preaching caused the closing of the "Dancing Assembly and Concert Room" because they were "inconsistent with the doctrine of the Gospel." [29] Actually, however, the rooms were closed as a courtesy to Whitefield when the two activities fell on the same night.

The Dancing Assembly dates in Philadelphia from 1748.* In 1748–1749 nine assemblies were given for fifty-nine subscribers, each of whom paid a subscription fee. [30] The assemblies began at six o'clock and never ran beyond midnight. The second season showed an increase of six members and a subscription rate that rose to $7.50. Interestingly enough, the governor was usually a member of this organization.

The Marquis de Chastellux draws a clear picture for us.

A manager, a master of ceremonies presides over these methodical amusements: he presents to the gentlemen and ladies, dancers, billets folded up containing each a number; thus fate decides the male or female partner for the whole evening. All the dances are previously arranged, and the dances are called in their turns. [31]

Quakerism did not stifle this amusement completely, but these assemblies were for members only.

Although Philadelphia did not come into its own in musical matters until later in the eighteenth century, the pages of the *Pennsylvania Gazette* show the awakening of interest in the musical life of the city. Musicians from Europe advertised their services, and we must presume a reasonable response from those colonists wanting to study instruments. We note that John Beals taught the violin, oboe, German and common flute, and the dulcimer. At the same time he announced that he would provide "musick" for balls and other entertainments. As the dancing assemblies had their origin about this time, it is reasonable to suppose that Beals provided music for these events as well. But it is also obvious that Beals could not support himself exclusively with music as he placed an advertisement in the *New York Weekly Post Boy*, June 20, 1757, presenting himself as a maker of nets "to keep the flys off horses." That music was not completely forgotten can be seen in his additional advertisement that he would play the violin and "Hautboy" for assemblies "at private balls, or any other entertainments." (In

---

*The term "assembly" was a common one in the eighteenth century and meant "society."

1764 the wanderer is in Maryland advertising himself as a manufacturer of stockings, according to the New York *Gazette* of August 30, 1764.)

A John Kramer proposed opening a music school in 1755. In addition to music Kramer intended to teach French, Italian, and German. He would teach the violin "after the Italian manner" and also offered drawing and miniature painting.

One of the last itinerant musicians in Philadelphia before the revolutionary war was H. B. Victor. Leaving Germany for London in 1759, Victor was in Philadelphia in 1774. He advertised instruction in harpsichord, "forte-piano," violin, German flute, and thorough bass. He was active in music publishing, supplying the four-volume *The Compleat Instructor* for violin, flute, harpsichord, and guitar. A dictionary of musical terms was advertised in the Pennsylvania *Ledger*, January 31, 1778.

William Priest, an itinerant music master in the late eighteenth century and who announced his intention to go into publishing, was a member of an orchestra playing a benefit concert for Raynor Taylor in 1796. He wrote in his *Travels in the United States of America* (1793–1797)[32] an interesting account of a concert.

At our first concert, three clownish-looking fellows came into the room, and, after sitting a few minutes, (the weather being *warm*, not to say *hot*), very composedly took off their coats: they were in the usual summer dress of farmer's servants in this part of the country; that is to say, without either stockings or breeches, a loose pair of trousers being the only *succedaneum*. As we fixed our admission at a dollar each (here seven shillings and six pence), we expect this circumstance would be sufficient to exclude such characters; but on inquiry, I found (to my great surprise!) our three *sans culottes* were German *gentlemen* of considerable property in the neighborhood.

Even at this late date, concerts of this kind were restricted affairs aimed only at the wealthy. Without a titled aristocracy, musicians from Europe tried to substitute a suitable audience in the New World. But the age of the common man was at hand, and the luxury of patronage was about over.

CHAPTER V

Educational Reform
of the Eighteenth and
Nineteenth Centuries

IT IS IMPOSSIBLE to separate the problems of educational reform of the eighteenth and nineteenth centuries from the gradual emergence of music education as a part of the curriculum of
the common schools in America. Education in the Enlightenment
was based on the scientific findings of Copernicus, Kepler, and
Galileo whose radical views precipitated a strong reaction by
those who embraced the more traditional idealistic views. A new
philosophy of materialism was born led by Thomas Hobbes and
Pierre Gassendi. The materialistic philosophy emphasized that the
universe could be explained in terms of mechanical laws. Reli-
gionists fought back, with both Protestants and Catholics believing in the dualism of man's nature. As man's spiritual nature was
paramount, it was the function of education to emphasize man's
spirituality.

Science relied on sense experience and reason, concepts that
were treated with suspicion by the churchmen. Would education
have to choose between reason and faith? René Descartes offered a
compromise. The mind being "free of matter" was divine and
hence relegated to the theological sphere. Matter, subject of physical laws, became suitable material for science. But such an arbitrary distinction could not last. Francis Bacon attacked the uni-

versities for their Scholasticism or formalized religious dogma. A more suitable curriculum should be the study of facts. Such thoughts contributed to the educational changes that were to have profound effects upon content and method through the eighteenth century in Europe and into the nineteenth century in America.

The beginnings of modern educational philosophy developed when Comenius, Wolfgang van Ratke, and John Milton, among others, supported a broader and more practical curriculum. John Locke maintained that man was not born with his nature completely predetermined at birth. Environment was important as knowledge reached man through his senses. Locke recommended the use of the English vernacular in schools as well as additions of dancing, history, fine arts, geography, and practical arts to the curriculum.

Locke's reading of Descartes led to a revolt against the Scholasticism of Oxford and against the narrow Puritan theology. Locke devoted himself to experimental work in medicine, but in 1690 published his *Essay Concerning Human Understanding*, after seventeen years of work. Three years later in his *Some Thoughts Concerning Education* his criticism of education was bitter and pointed. The disadvantages of the schools outweigh their advantages, said Locke. A master should "look after the manners of his scholars," rather than "forming their tongues to the learned languages." Locke believed that what ordinarily passed for education in the schools could be eliminated with no disservice to the student. He believed that a man should be able to "manage his affairs wisely" rather than speak Greek and Latin.

Locke did not consider the learning that was done at schools to be education at all. He believed that each "boy" must be dealt with as an individual. As a philosopher, Locke was interested in the theoretical and did not think of forming a school. He gave little help in regard to the actual teaching. Locke's program of studies would include reading, writing, drawing, French, Latin, English, geography, arithmetic (astronomy, geometry), history, ethics, art of speaking and writing English, dancing, fencing and riding, and one or two manual occupations. He deliberately omitted Greek, rhetoric and logic, music and painting, and natural philosophy and related sciences.

European education of the eighteenth century was one of almost

universal decadence. Only in Scotland and parts of Germany did
common people get some education. Teachers were often ignorant,
unfit for other occupations. There was no grading of children according to advancement, and many schoolrooms consisted of the
living rooms and workshops of the teachers. The "three R's" were
taught—reading, writing, and religion. But arithmetic was often
too difficult for the teacher! The ordinary child's education was
over at age ten or eleven.

Grammar schools did little better. With the beggarly remuneration for the teachers, it was surprising when occasionally a teacher
of quality was found. Once a power and an inspiration, the classical curriculum had fallen out of touch with the times. Latin was no
longer spoken and written; its instructions seemed obscure and
irrelevant.

There were complaints of the barrenness of the Jesuit schools in
France around 1762. Lord Chief Justice Kenyon condemned the
grammar schools of England in 1795 as "empty walls without
scholars and everything neglected but the receipt of salaries and
endowments."[1] The universities at Paris and Oxford declined
profoundly.

But there were some oases in this educational desert. Many realized the dismal state of the educational institutions and seemed eager for the reform that was about to take place. In 1682 there were
"Christian schools" in France to instruct children in religion, reading, and writing. There were charity schools in England established for the same purpose.

In Germany, August Hermann Francke realized the need for elementary schooling for all citizens and worked to carry out this
ideal. While a professor of Oriental languages at the University at
Halle, he started a small school for the poor in 1695. Public contributions enabled him to add several other institutions. Frederick
William I, King of Prussia, became interested in Francke's work,
and in 1716–1717, attendance in elementary schools was made
compulsory. The king's interest in education passed to his son
Frederick the Great who agreed on the necessity of universal education in 1763 and strengthened the compulsory attendance laws
by mandating schooling for children from age five through fourteen. The financial responsibility rested on the landowners and
tenants, while the clergy had the duty for the supervision and inspection of the schools.

The efforts at reform in higher education were less common, but at the University of Halle the principle of academic freedom was advanced, a conviction that was to become a cornerstone of modern university life.

The influence of Jean Jacques Rousseau on the later reform in education both in Europe and in America must be understood. Without the influence of Rousseau and of the philosophers of the revolution, the curricular reforms—which reflect the sociology and culture of a people—would not have occurred in the time and manner that they did. Rousseau blended French and English influences through his reading of Montaigne, Fenelon, Addison, Pope, and Locke. His *Émile* was immediately condemned by Catholic Paris and Protestant Geneva because of its Deistic, or atheistic, treatise (The Savoyard Vicar's "Confession of Faith") which it included. Rousseau could not endure the materialistic philosophy, where the human soul was reduced to a product of mere sense experience. He believed in a "free self-active principle inborn in the soul."

Education begins by studying the child, believed Rousseau. Men and women are not alike and should not have the same education. "Each age and condition of life has a perfection and maturity of its own."[2]

In spite of its weaknesses by modern standards, *Émile* was the most considerable book written on education during its time. Its impression was such that society women began to nurse their own babies, and fathers and mothers attempted to bring up their own children as "Émiles and Sophies" (Rousseau devoted a few pages of his book to the raising of Sophie). For the first time, a child's life was not viewed as an inferior counterpart of adulthood. Children were no longer forced to dress as miniature adults. Nobles, especially in Germany, installed workshops in their homes to give their sons training in some craft. As a result of this book, statesmen and educators began to realize the importance of education, and new schemes for educational improvement were entertained. There was now general agreement that the nature of the child was of paramount importance and must be taken into account in any educational program. Rousseau stressed naturalism in education and laid the foundation for a new curriculum.

THE ENLIGHTENMENT AND AMERICA

The Enlightenment, or Age of Reason, refers to the intellectual revolution that occurred during the latter part of the seventeenth century and into the eighteenth century. Theology was rejected as the final authority in all earthly matters and the effort was on interpreting the universe in terms of logical analysis. Faith in science and human reason gradually replaced an exclusive dependence upon religious belief and supernatural revelation. Replacing dogma with mathematics, men built new worlds on mechanical approaches to their environment. Philosophers embraced logic and human reason which, along with mathematics, would lead to momentous and fundamental changes in human thought. Centuries of myth and dogma would be swept away, preparing for conceptual changes affecting men's lives, thoughts, and education.

An altered view of the scientific nature of the universe was accompanied by a new view of religion known as Deism. Newton theorized that the Deity, although possibly having designed the world, did not interfere with the natural processes of the universe. If human thought and behavior were thought of as superior to those earthly matters, then man may enjoy a primacy in his analysis of his religious beliefs. For those embracing this point of view, the emphasis shifted from the Scripture to nature. In colonial America, Thomas Paine in his *Age of Reason* argued that only science could reveal the true essence of Christianity and that man finds religious faith through rational thought. Nature was to be the source of God's revelation. These thoughts were shared by Thomas Jefferson and Benjamin Franklin. Calvinism in America was truly dying.

The Enlightenment came to America slowly. With the influx of new ideas, Puritanism's control gradually loosened. Controversies emerged within the churches as many favored a more democratic control. Men now had the ability to prevail upon their own destinies. This was a natural philosophy for a free, rising middle class of tradesmen in search of material success.

In 1743, Franklin founded the American Philosophical Society whose aim was to promote political discussion and to exchange scientific knowledge. The society helped to create a deepening interest not only in education but in other social problems of the day. In 1795 it offered a prize for the best essay on a "system of liberal education and literary instruction, adapted to the genius of the government of the United States; comprehending also a plan for instituting and conducting public schools in the country, on principles of the most extensive utility."

Before the end of the eighteenth century every prominent leader had given some attention to the building of an educational system in the republic. All seemed aware of educational deficiencies such as the poorly qualified teachers, inadequate schools, and poor equipment. There seemed to be an almost universal interest at the time for developing a tax-supported system of popular education from the elementary school through the university. Advertisements can be seen in newspapers during the eighteenth century advertising private schools for evening instruction in useful subjects concerned with commerce and trade.

HEINRICH PESTALOZZI

One of the most important influences on educational thought and practice of the late eighteenth and early nineteenth centuries was Heinrich Pestalozzi. His work indirectly created an educational climate that encouraged the expansion of the curriculum and, at the same time, affected the methods of teaching music. The Pestalozzian movement was complex and revolutionary, having its roots in the amelioration of poverty and the equalization of opportunity among the masses. His educational theories lay in the concepts of the natural rights of man, the germinal ideas of the great revolutionary period at the end of the eighteenth century. The old system of learning was "wordy foolishness," as Pestalozzi referred to it, and demanded of the student unquestioning obedience in the face of severe discipline.

The annihilation of all real power in our country by this unnatural monkish instruction and all the misery of its unconnected teaching, is incredible. . . .

The mass of our public schools not only give us nothing, but, on the contrary, they *quench* all that is in us which humanity has without schools, that which every savage possesses, to the degree of which we can form no conception. . . . A man who is instructed with monkish art in this wordy foolishness, is, so far, less susceptible to truth than a savage, and more unfit than he to make use of the guidance of Nature, and of what she does herself to make our ideas clear.[3]

Pestalozzi was born in Zurich, Switzerland, in 1746. His father was a surgeon who died when the boy was only five years old. Brought up by his mother and maidservant, he was strongly indoctrinated with appreciation of the maternal role in a child's upbringing. He was influenced by teachers of revolutionary temper and read Rousseau with single-minded enthusiasm. He intended to enter the ministry but gave up the idea when he failed in his first sermon. He became interested in law but soon realized that his political opinions would bar his advancement in that field. An ill-fated attempt at farming ended that possibility, but the experience led to the establishment of his first school for the orphaned and destitute children who then worked on farms. But even in the work that would eventually make Pestalozzi famous, failure loomed and bankruptcy overtook the great educator's initial efforts. For the next twenty years, Pestalozzi devoted himself to writing books and pamphlets on various topics.

His first volume, *Leonard and Gertrude*, appeared in 1781. It explained how Gertrude taught her children at home in an easy and natural way. When a school was established in her town, her methods showed that the instruction given in schools did not need to differ from those used in the home—only a wider range of interests was necessary in the school. The publication of this book finally brought Pestalozzi the notoriety necessary for him to advance his educational work. He became friendly with the philosopher Johann Gottlieb Fichte, who was important in the educational regeneration of Germany and who was able to introduce Pestalozzi's ideas to German educators.

At the age of fifty, he went to Stenz, Switzerland, to take charge of some orphan children. He taught eighty children of different ages single-handedly in the "manner of the home," which was nonsystematic. Experiments were tried, many with good results. Especially admired was his ability in developing character. He established a quasi-paternal relationship with the children and encouraged them to do physical work to accompany their learning. He believed in the value of work in itself, not just as a means for economic returns. He aimed to cultivate the fundamental powers of attention, observation, and memory—all of which he was able to accomplish with large numbers of children in his class.

He became head of the Training College for Teachers in the Castle of Burgdorf where he had help from a small band of teachers. There he ran an elementary day school, a boarding school, and a training college. In 1801 he published his famous volume, *How Gertrude Teaches Her Children*, followed by a series of books for parents and teachers written by Pestalozzi and his staff.

A change in government forced him to leave Burgdorf in 1805, and he settled in Yverdon where he again set up an educational institute in a large stone castle. The institute, which lasted for twenty years, included an infant department (mostly orphans), a secondary boarding school for boys, a normal school for young men, and a pedagogical seminary for trained and experienced teachers. Yverdon was visited by most of the noted educators in Europe and in America. Horace Mann reported while observing Pestalozzi's educational establishment that

music was everywhere in evidence. The teachers were masters of vocal music and they played upon one or more instruments as well. One was as certain to see a violin as a blackboard in every room. Singing was taught not only as an accomplishment, but as a means of recreation and socialization.[4]

Pestalozzi was successful here, but problems with helpers caused some troubled years and the school closed in 1825. He spent his last years writing and restating his educational doctrines.

He believed that the family furnished a model for the ideal school, where individuality and human qualities predominated. He had a deeper faith than Rousseau in the educational possibilities of ordinary life and had confidence in the ordinary peasant home as an instrument for education. As a result of this thinking, the teacher became much more important in Pestalozzi's thinking than in Rousseau's. Pestalozzi's greatest contributions were in the area of method, as his rather vague philosophy caused, both in Europe and in America, confusion as to which procedures were essentially Pestalozzian and which were older ideas and methods masquerading as new.

He was very concerned with the concept of "sense-impressions." The mind, believed Pestalozzi, begins with vague sense-impressions, which grow distinct, are followed by greater degrees of clarity, and evolve into description. A complete process of mental growth takes place when "clear images are transformed into definite ideas."[5] The objects are now seen in relation to other objects. The fundamental sense-impression was called *anschauung*. Sense-impression concerned the idea that knowledge enters the mind through the senses, and, thus, the *anschauung* forms the absolute foundation of all knowledge.[6] An *anschauung* lesson was a lesson in which the child sees, handles, or otherwise makes direct acquaintance with an object. The teacher's job was to make these sense-impressions separate from one another, hence to make them clear. These sense-impressions were to be introduced to children in units, their positions changed, and finally connected with the whole cycle of previous knowledge. Learning, then, must proceed in gradual steps from the near to the remote, from the simple to the complex.

Up to this point, Pestalozzi's ideas sound remarkably modern. But Pestalozzi was a faculty psychologist and as such believed that the mind possessed certain innate and latent faculties that could be developed in accordance with certain laws of nature. Education, believed Pestalozzi, should provide training for these faculties. The training was best accomplished through exercise. Each step along the way from the simple to the complex must be exercised until the learner has a clear and precise grasp of that material. Michael Traugott Pfeiffer and Hans Georg Nageli interpreted this concept in their *Gesangbildungslehre* to mean that each stage in the music learning process must be exercised until each student in the class, even the most dense, could repeat it perfectly. This interesting but strange concept Pestalozzi endorsed as being the embodiment of his educational theories as applied to music education!

Pestalozzi's psychology was based on instructional method, as he was less concerned with the mental processes and activities of the mind. Introduced to the teachings of Bodmer, Breitinger, and Steinbruchel at the *Collegium Carolinum*, Pestalozzi in turn influenced educational thought for years. Pestalozzi believed that instructional methods should be geared to human growth and proceed imperceptibly and thoroughly. Although Pestalozzi did not discuss curriculum in a precise way, he believed that the subject matter to which the learner was exposed had to be compatible with the growth and development of the child. When the subject matter was determined, attention had to be given as to the correct sequence in which the material was presented.

He believed in a similarity between the laws that control the mind and those that control physical nature. Although sense-impression was the absolute foundation of all knowledge, Pestalozzi recognized that a learner is subjected in nature to a sea of confused sense-impressions. The responsibility of the teacher was to isolate these sense-impressions one from another and then to place these separate impressions "in different changing positions before our eyes."[7] From this the child was impelled from confused and vague impressions to clear ideas.

Pestalozzi entertained ideas as to how a teacher was to question his students, or the means whereby instruction in school was to be accomplished. Here the lack of understanding of the followers of the Swiss educator easily manifests itself. Clearly Pestalozzi turns from a teacher-centered instructional situation to one where the child may freely express himself along certain loosely acceptable lines, as drawn by the teacher. Pestalozzi tells us not to talk too much to the child

but to enter into conversation with a child; not to address to him many words, however familiar or well chosen, but to bring him to express himself on the subject; not to exhaust the subject, but to question the child about it, and to let him find out, and correct the answers. . . . The attention of a child is deadened by long expositions, but roused by animated questions. Let these questions be short, clear and intelligible. Let them not merely lead the child to repeat, in the same, or in varied terms, what he has heard just before. Let them excite him to observe what is before him; to recollect that he has learned, and to muster his little stock of knowledge of materials for an answer.[8]

Pestalozzi believed this method to be built on laws of nature and requiring very little assistance from the teacher. The teacher "merely watches lest any external force might hinder or disturb the order of Nature in the development of the individual powers, he sees to it that the development of the individual power finds an unimpeded course according to its own laws."[9] Even the *Gesangbildungslehre* of Pfeiffer and Nageli is an inordinately teacher-centered text, and this volume was endorsed by the master himself and used as a music text in his school.

Pestalozzi himself asked Michael Traugott Pfeiffer and Hans Georg Nageli to present a textbook in singing which would represent Pestalozzian theory. Pfeiffer had opened a progressive school in Solothurn in 1804 but was enjoined from teaching Pestalozzian theory in the community by the authorities. Nageli was one of the most outstanding Swiss musicians. He was at one time or another a publisher, composer of vocal and instrumental music, teacher, writer, and choral director. Their completed work was entitled the *Gesangbildungslehre nach Pestalozzischen Grundsatzen*, or *Method of Teaching Singing According to Pestalozzian Principles*.[10]

The book was large and in its foreword it established its intent to demonstrate a new orientation to music instruction. Gone was the almost universal aim of the time to train children to participate in the musical portions of the church service. Rote learning was decried and the German chorales were considered inappropriate by these authors to be used as instructional materials for children. While some schools in Germany did teach music reading, most were content to teach the church melodies by rote. By removing material that the children could not understand, the authors succeeded in approaching at least one of the principles of Pestalozzianism, even though its result was political rather than pedagogical.

But the specific method sparkled with technical and detailed suggestions concerning the manner of instruction. The teacher was to sing all the exercises with a clear voice. It advocated strict discipline in order to prevent bad habits from forming. The division of the singing hour was specific, as too long an exercise would be tiring to the children. Students must not talk when the teacher turns to write on the "board." The singing ought not to be held before nine in the morning or after seven in the evening, admonished Pfeiffer and Nageli, and when and how often a review must be held was discussed by the authors. Suddenly from the generalities of Pestalozzi's philosophy came a set of mandated rules for the instruction of music. If the child used the wrong rhythm, the authors advised the teacher to use the terms *correct* and *incorrect*. If the child committed an error with regard to the melody, the correct expression for the teacher to use was *clear* and *unclear*. Each step was prescribed, and nowhere was there any mention of ideas the children might have had concerning the music they were to study. All direction came from the teacher in the *Gesangbildungslehre* and the children followed. The concepts of self-activity, sequence of instruction, or even sense-impression were lacking from this introduction. But in an age when music was taught to children by rote using only church chorales, and when music theory was taught by the memorization of rules, and when "learning" was the mere recitation of the correct rules and catechistic answers, then the principles as laid down by Pfeiffer and Nageli perhaps represented a considerable improvement.

The main body of the book consisted of detailed drills on various problems of rhythm, melody, and dynamics; combining rhythm, melody, and dynamics; and dictation. The elements were completely separated, and each element was to be studied apart from another. At the end of 208 pages of exercises, the child was then introduced to Nageli's one-voice songs. (The delay in the introduction of song material was recognized by Pfeiffer and Nageli and was remedied in later editions of the work.) The authors were sensitive to the problems that the *Gesangbildungslehre* created. They advised classes that had some background in music to jump to the singing of songs as soon as possible. With this admission, a degree of flexibility was suggested which creates a suspicion of the supposed rigidity alluded to in the text itself.

The politico pedagogical event that must be considered was the replacement of the chorale with pieces of music more in keeping with a child's nature and the needs of his age. This occurred later in America when the psalm and hymn tunes were gradually replaced with children's music which Lowell Mason and other so-called Pestalozzians considered better suited to children.

Pestalozzi himself had little to say regarding music teaching. He concerned himself with the effects of music on the moral education of children. In a *Letter on Early Education*, Pestalozzi gives us an illuminating perception of his views on music.

Now that I am on the topic, I will not let the opportunity pass by without speaking of one of the most effective aids of moral education. You are aware that I mean *music*, and not only are you acquainted with my sentiments on that subject, but you have also observed the very satisfactory results which we have obtained in our schools. The exertions of my excellent friend Nageli, who has with equal taste and judgement reduced the highest principles of his art to the simplest elements, have enabled us to bring our children to a proficiency which on any other plan must be the work of much time and labor.

But it is not this proficiency which I would describe as a desirable accomplishment of education. It is the marked and most beneficial influence of music on the feelings, which I have always observed to be the most efficient in preparing, or as it were attuning, the mind for the best impressions. The exquisite harmony of a superior performance, the studied elegance of the execution, may indeed give satisfaction to a connoisseur; but it is the simple and untaught grace of melody which speaks to the heart of every human being. Our own national melodies, which have since time immemorial been resounding in our native valleys are fraught with reminiscences of the brightest page of our history and of the most endearing scenes of domestic life.

But the effect of music in education is not only to keep alive a national feeling; it goes much deeper; if cultivated in the right spirit, it strikes at the root of every bad or narrow feeling, or every ungenerous or mean propensity, or every emotion unworthy of humanity.[11]

Pestalozzi expressed satisfaction with the work that Nageli was doing and with his text, but Pestalozzi had little idea of the technical aspects of music or music teaching. To Pestalozzi, the exquisite harmony of a superior performance was good for a connoisseur, but he preferred the simple untaught grace of melody which speaks to the heart of every human being. The paradox was that the changes that were to occur on both sides of the Atlantic in the instruction in music were to be associated more and more with Pestalozzi; the name of the master was all that was necessary to dignify any change in the teaching methods of the day. Changes in educational philosophy and methodology were long overdue, but it would take many more years before the children themselves would be free to respond in an original and creative manner in the field of music education.

PESTALOZZIANISM IN AMERICA

The beginnings of Pestalozzianism in this country can be traced to as early as 1806 in an article in the June 6 issue of the *National Intelligencer* describing Pestalozzian principles. Other articles followed, not only in the same periodical but in several 1819 issues of the *Academician*.

Joseph Nicholas Neef was probably the first Pestalozzian disciple to come to America. He had been acquainted with Pestalozzi and had taught music, gymnastics, and French at Burgdorf. He went to Paris through the invitation of the Philanthropic Society of Paris and there met William Maclure who had just come from Switzerland where he had observed and become enthusiastic about the Pestalozzian school. Maclure had amassed a fortune in Philadelphia and had decided to devote the rest of his life to geological study and to educational reform. While on a diplomatic mission to

France in 1804, he became interested in Pestalozzian ideas. He asked the great Swiss educator to come to the United States but Pestalozzi declined citing problems of age. Pestalozzi then suggested Joseph Neef. Maclure offered to pay Neef's expenses to America if he would open a school and teach according to the Pestalozzian method.

Neef accepted the invitation and arrived in this country in 1806 opening a school in Philadelphia three years later. In 1812 he moved the school to Village Green, Delaware County, Pennsylvania, but—except for the fact that he had the future Admiral David Farragut in his class—his school there failed. Neef was described as "a man of unusual abilities and eccentric character, a profound scholar, a deep and original thinker, a thorough philosopher and an honest man." He was "firm-knit, sinewy, compact of form with a bright, dark eye and close-cut coal black hair, the figure and gait of a well-drilled, graceful soldier, the face of a Roman Tribune, the mind of a sage, and the heart of a child." [12]

Maclure brought other Pestalozzian teachers, as well as texts, from Europe. The entrepreneur returned to Europe in 1819 where he studied in Scotland followed by a move to Spain where he lived for nearly five years and where he planned to establish an agricultural school similar to that of Pestalozzi. His newly purchased tract of 10,000 acres was repossessed by a new Spanish government, and Maclure found himself in the United States again in 1824. He then invested $150,000 in an educational experiment in New Harmony, Indiana, in 1826 and petitioned the Indiana legislature for the incorporation of the institution under the name of the New Harmony Educational Society. The state senate believed that the school was to teach atheism and the bill failed by a vote of fifteen to four. [13]

The experiment in communal living as well as in Pestalozzian principles lasted less than two years. Maclure was the superintendent of education while Neef served as headmaster. Unusual for its time, boys and girls were treated equally and given the same kind of education. In addition, there was an infant school for preschool children. When the community broke up in 1828, Neef moved to Cincinnati and later to Steubenville, Ohio. There he taught schools for the next six years after which he returned to New Harmony in 1834. There he lived until his death on April 8, 1864.

Neef was well indoctrinated into the Pestalozzian method. His

Sketch of a Plan and Method of Education gives us some insight into the methods he may have used in New Harmony.

We know that music was taught at this school but we do not know from direct evidence exactly what or how it was taught. But from Neef's writings it is possible to reconstruct some of his concepts and from that make certain judgments concerning his philosophy and practices in the teaching of music. His book was published in 1808 and was the first pedagogical book written in the New World and published in the English language.[14]

Neef concerned himself with the division of music into component parts. He started by fixing his attention upon the tones of the human voice and examining their nature. The student was asked to determine whether one tone was higher than another. Different intervals would be tried including semi-tones. The student had also to become aware of notes of longer and shorter duration, the author stating that "duration of tone is a measurable quantity."

He devised a new set of syllables for singing: ta, ra, ma, fa, and la. This innovation was thought by Neef to cause the children to distinguish the semi-tones with greater precision. An interest in harmony was demonstrated where the children were admonished to discriminate between intervals which produced an agreeable harmony and others which caused an "unpleasant and unpleasing dissonance." * Following the discrimination of the various musical concepts, the children were allowed to "speak the musical language, or to make use of the vulgar expression, to sing." Later, dictation was incorporated into the lessons. And to round out the music instruction, Neef gives us good advice for our music classes.

Our third and last operation, shall consist in reading our own musical writings; to which, in the sequel, we shall add foreign compositions. In this way, I think we shall not merely acquire a tolerable knowledge of vocal music, but also lay a good and solid foundation for instrumental music.[15]

If we can understand the variable nature of pedagogical procedures that were all identified with the Swiss master, then we must say that Neef was an excellent Pestalozzian.

While the country eventually needed a Lowell Mason to teach, publicize, and sell the tenets of Pestalozzianism, such men as Mac-

---

* Pfeiffer and Nageli intentionally ignored the treatment of harmony in their volume that was endorsed by Pestalozzi.

lure and Neef did their part. The Western Literary Institute and College of Professional Teachers held a meeting in Cincinnati in October of 1834 and there announced that Pestalozzi and his plans "are both so familiar to every well informed person, [and] that it is unnecessary here to dwell on them."[16] It is more than likely that Neef, who spent six years in Cincinnati and Steubenville, Ohio, helped to make Pestalozzianism and its principles familiar to these educators. The experiment in New Harmony was visited by many educators from both Europe and America, and all were unanimous in their praise. Even William C. Woodbridge, who was destined to play such an important role in the dissemination of Pestalozzianism in New England, visited New Harmony in 1825 and was undoubtedly impressed by what he saw. Unfortunately, the experiment in New Harmony was short-lived, but the role it played in the influence and spread of Pestalozzian principles was considerable. The time had not yet come to make Pestalozzi's name a household word, but the world of education was in the process of becoming sensitized not only through the work of Joseph Neef but also in articles and through school experiments such as the Infant School Society of the City of New York, whose *First Annual Report* came out in 1828 and the *American Journal of Education* of January/February 1829. The next decade would see a renaissance and a public beginning to focus on the long somnolent educational problems of this country.

WILLIAM C. WOODBRIDGE

An important conduit to the dissemination of Pestalozzianism in America was William C. Woodbridge. Not a musician himself— not even able to read or sing music by note—Woodbridge thrust himself in the center of educational reform with the specific aim of changing the system of teaching music and to see that vocal music was taught as a regular branch of school instruction. He was born in 1794 and graduated from Yale in 1811. He taught in an academy in Burlington, New Jersey, and later at a school for the deaf at Hartford, Connecticut. He went to Europe in 1820 with the idea of remaining there for one year to study and travel. He became impressed with Pestalozzi's work at Yverdon and became excited over the work of Philipp Emmanuel von Fellenberg regarding the

agricultural phases at the institution at Hofwyl. He returned to the
United States eager to pursue a crusade for the introduction of vocal music into the common schools. Returning to Europe in 1825
he spent three months with Pestalozzi and Fellenberg, followed by
visits to Pestalozzian schools in Germany. Woodbridge remained
in Europe for four years while he collected data on the status of
European education. Returning to the United States again in 1829,
he participated in the Society for the Improvement of the Common Schools, which had been organized in Connecticut. Its purpose was to improve the common schools, to organize institutions
for the training of teachers, and to achieve better facilities for the
education of women.

He recognized that the best means to propagate the improvement in education was to publish a journal devoted to that purpose, so in 1831 he purchased the *American Journal of Education*
from William Russell. He changed the name of that publication to
the *American Annals of Education and Instruction*. He remained
its head until 1837. The journal functioned as a high-grade educational review, octavo in form, and each month containing around
forty-eight pages. Dr. William A. Alcott acted as associate editor.
The publication eventually lost a great deal of money, but it did
succeed in presenting numerous articles concerning Pestalozzianism. Although the propagation of Pestalozzianism was not always
an unqualified success in the United States, it must be recognized
that William C. Woodbridge was important not only for his interpretation of the German reform movement but also for his ad-
vocation of music as a regular subject in the common schools.

ELAM IVES

The tenets of Pestalozzianism tended to be vague and ill-defined
particularly in music education. Nonetheless it is possible to discuss the various ramifications of what passed for Pestalozzianism
in music education and perhaps to look at the whole movement as
a manifestation of reform in education. In so doing the name of
Elam Ives stands out as one deserving attention in the movement
toward the acceptance of music as a regular branch of instruction
in the public schools of America.

Ives was born in Hamden, Connecticut, on January 7, 1802, the
sixth of thirteen children. His father was a successful farmer and

later a pioneer manufacturer of small carriage hardware in neighboring Mt. Carmel.[17] At twenty, Ives married Louisa Todd and began duties as church choir director and singing school master. It is not known where Ives received his musical training or when he moved from Hamden to Hartford. But at the age of twenty-eight he was already established at Hartford where some few years earlier he was introduced to the William C. Woodbridge version of Pestalozzian music instruction. Woodbridge was between trips to Europe and took that opportunity to acquaint the local music teacher with the Pestalozzian precepts as he understood them.

Ives may not have had a reading knowledge of German at this time, so the original works of Pfeiffer and Nageli must have presented a considerable challenge. Yet so quickly was Ives able to overcome the obstacle that within a few months after he began teaching in Hartford, the author was able to submit to his Hartford publisher the manuscript of his *American Elementary Singing Book, a Concise Manual on Pestalozzianism.*

By 1830 elements of Pestalozzian instruction appeared in Ives's publication of *American Psalmody* and presented the first division of music instruction into rhythm, melody, and dynamics. The same year Ives moved to Philadelphia, but not before he left the manuscript of his latest children's song book *The American Elementary Singing Book* with his Hartford publisher, F. J. Huntington. While in Philadelphia, he set himself up as principal of the Philadelphia Musical Seminary, a one-man school. On May 27, 1836, he and his Philadelphia pupils gave a concert in New York's Constitution Hall, and he announced at that time that he planned a move to New York City where he would establish a musical seminary. He accomplished his goal that summer, and by September 1, he was ready to present his New York pupils in a concert. He did the largest portion of his writing and teaching while in New York and Brooklyn returning to his home in Hamden probably in 1863, where he died one year later.

While Ives was not the first to put Pestalozzian principles to work in America, he was without question one of the first to embrace Pestalozzian concepts of music education, which, one can reasonably assume, were put into practice in his schools. The success of Ives's school can be substantiated from an article written by William C. Woodbridge, "On Vocal Music as a Branch of Common Education," in the *American Annals of Education and In-*

struction. Woodbridge commended Ives's work in the highest terms.

The attempt was made to teach the elements scientifically to a class in an infant school; and so complete was the success of Mr. Ives in this plan, that a professional musician, who heard them after a few weeks' instruction observed, in a letter on this subject: "I entered upon the examination of the system with some prejudices; but the more I examined it, the more I was convinced of its superiority over the common method, especially in the simple manner in which the principles of music are presented to the mind of a child."[18]

Woodbridge continued his endorsement of Ives's teaching method and skill, commenting upon the large classes in Philadelphia "whose performance has produced general delight." He remarked about the appearance of the *Elementary Singing Book* which employed, according to Woodbridge, the general principles of Pfeiffer.

In Ives's *Manual of Instruction in the Art of Singing*, the author tells us of the large numbers of pupils who have been instructed according to his method.

The following Manual embraces those principles of music education which have been established by actual experience in the instruction of about five thousand pupils. In its arrangement it is strictly inductive and practical.[19]

An interesting change in Ives's method can be traced to the second edition of *American Psalmody* (written in collaboration with Deodatus Dutton, Jr.), published in 1830. The author points out that the principal difference between the first and second editions is in the system of teaching. The second edition embraces the "inductive system" which he believed could be applied to "almost any science." Howard Ellis draws our attention to the introduction of notes and values which graphically shows the changes that occurred in Ives's method and philosophy after his introduction to the so-called Pestalozzian method. In the first edition Ives introduces notes and values this way:

Of the Time of Sounds

By time is meant the duration of a single sound, and the periodical succession of any number of sounds; or, the measure and movement of sounds.

A complete knowledge of musical time consists in understanding the following particulars, viz: the names of the notes, and their corresponding rests—the geometrical proportion of the notes—the division of notes into equal measure—and Accent and Rhythm.

Of the Names and Formation of Notes and Corresponding Rests

The semibreve is a white note resembling the letter O, when turned upon one side. Its rest is a hyphen adjoining the under side of the line.

In the second edition of *American Psalmody*, the material is presented with a significant difference.

PART I

Elements of Rhythm, or practical exercises
relating to the time of sounds

LECTURE I.

1. Your attention is now called to the Rhythmical differences, or the differences in the duration, or time of sounds. In all the following exercises the teacher will need a time-keeper. Maelzel's Metronome is by far the best. If he has not this, a pendulum that will vibrate seconds will answer. Let him place the time-keeper so regulated as to vibrate seconds, in the full view of the pupils. This instrument vibrates once in a second. Sing *Ah*, and prolong the sound while it vibrates four times.

2. Now sing *ah*, and make each sound just half as long, or while the time-keeper vibrates twice.

3. Sing *ah* again, and make each sound one quarter as long as at first, or while the time-keeper vibrates once. Repeat these exercises several times separately.

4. You have now learned three varieties in the duration of sounds. Now you are to learn the signs for denoting each of these varieties. (Write a semibreve on the blackboard.) o

This is the sign for the longest sound which you have made, or that which you continued four seconds. The signs for sounds are called Notes. This being the longest, is called a whole note. The difference in the time of sounds is designated by the different forms of the notes.[20]

The material to be taught is now categorized into sections, that is, rhythm, melody, dynamics, elements of articulation, and an explanation of musical terms. Every effort is made in the second edition to present the thing before the sign. If practiced in the classroom, Pestalozzi's theories of *anschauung*, or sense-impression, have been faithfully carried out.

William C. Woodbridge was a friend of both Lowell Mason's and Ives's. About the same time that Ives left Hartford for Philadelphia, Woodbridge left Hartford for Boston. Perhaps Woodbridge volunteered an account of Ives's teaching and perhaps Woodbridge may have shown Mason some of Ives's manuscripts. Ives was having difficulty finding a publisher for some of his works; by 1831 he had completed ten books but was successful in getting only four of them published. Ives needed Mason's stature and prestige, and so the *Juvenile Lyre* was launched as a joint venture in 1831. Mason claimed this to be the first school songbook published in this country. (This claim was made in Mason's *Normal Singer.*)[21] Ives was not mentioned as the co-author. Robert W. John believes that Ives may have written or compiled most of this book. The title page contains neither of the co-authors' names, while only the signed preface indicates the compilers. John believes that Mason wrote the preface and Ives was responsible for most of the remainder of the book. Ellis informs us that the *Juvenile Lyre* was a collaboration between Mason and Ives but with Mason mainly responsible for the work.[22] Songs in the book were taken from those of Nageli and G. F. Kübler with voices sometimes added by Mason. Both authors give credit to William C. Woodbridge by stating that "a large portion of [the songs] are translated from the works which were collected by the Rev. William C. Woodbridge."

It is interesting that the volume contains none of the usual "instructions" which sets it off from the typical publications of the time or even other publications of both Ives and Mason; although a volume by Augusta Peabody, *The Child's Book for the Use of Schools and Families*, published one year earlier by Richardson, Lord and Holbrook, also contained no theoretical introduction. (*The Child's Book* is thought to be by Peabody but it was published anonymously.)[23]

Ives's previous opus, the *American Elementary Singing Book* (published the same year as *Juvenile Lyre* in 1831), does not include three-part tunes until the pupils have been brought through a total of twenty-seven numbered lessons, each consisting of questions and answers, observations, and examples. Only after lesson twenty-seven does the author begin with three part songs. The *Juvenile Lyre* begins immediately with three-part songs all similar in form except the last, "Suffer Little Children to Come Unto Me," a piece written by Mason for his children's choir and one performed by them at the Park Street Church on July 4, 1830. The instrumental bass parts are interesting and unique, as nothing quite like this can be found in Mason's works. They seem closer to Ives's propensities than to Mason's. Ives was listed in the *American Musical Directory* for 1861 as a teacher of "pianoforte, violin, and singing." He may have considered himself more of an instrumentalist than a singer.

But Ives and Mason had a falling out for reasons that are not entirely clear at this time. Frank Metcalf tells us (in his *American Writers of Sacred Music*) that a Mr. Deodatus Dutton versified many of the hymns in the *Juvenile Lyre* (as well as the Ives-Dutton *American Psalmody* of 1830) but had received no credit for his work. And Ives received no credit either, a circumstance which could have caused a rupture of feelings between the two men.

CHAPTER VI

Lowell Mason and His Times

THE EARLY YEARS of the nineteenth century saw the gradual reawakening of interest in the idea of public education in New England. This unique region of the country urged the establishment of schools everywhere almost from its earliest days.

The schools of the country were in a state of neglect in the early nineteenth century. State aid to the schools of New York was discontinued in 1800, and the school law of 1812 followed the example of those in New England in turning to the misguided district school system. Under the system, communities as small as 150 people could divide their towns into as many as six districts, each with its own board of education and each with the power to hire and fire its own teachers.

The first school law in Massachusetts in 1789 legalized the district system, and eleven years later the district was empowered to tax the local communities for school support. In 1827 the legislature required the districts to appoint school trustees who could employ teachers and select textbooks. But, instead of encouraging local control in the best sense, the system deteriorated into local public feuds. Again in 1827, the Massachusetts legislature, through the efforts of James G. Carter, required the establishment of a tax-supported high school in all towns or districts of five hundred or more families.* In those towns or districts with a popula-

---

* In 1821 the Boston school committee opened the English Classical School which was renamed the English High School three years later. This school, which was probably the first public high school in the country, was for boys who wanted to become mechanics or merchants. Boston already had a Latin School.

tion of at least four thousand, courses in Latin and Greek were mandated.

Schools were still not free to all as the notorious rate bill allowed the school districts to levy a tax on all parents of school-age children who could afford to pay. Poor families were required to take a pauper's oath to be excused from the levy. When a charge was decreased or remitted, it served to stamp such beneficiaries as paupers.[1] So insulting was this prospect that poor people avoided schools, receiving no education at all. So insidious did this become that in the state of New York a move to abolish the rate bill was made as late as 1850 only to be defeated by a popular vote. These infamous bills kept hundreds of thousands of children out of the schools in Connecticut as late as 1868.

The Society for Establishing a Free School in the city of New York was chartered in 1805 by the legislature. By 1815 it received aid from the common school fund of the state. A little more than a decade later it changed its name to the Public School Society of New York. Its new charter permitted it to accept tuition from those who were able to pay. There was then an immediate decrease in attendance as there were many parents who were too proud to confess their poverty.

In Pennsylvania it was customary that every man should pay for his own education from private funds. An 1809 law in that state authorizing the payment of tuition fees for poor children prevented free schools from being established until 1818. Ten years later in Pennsylvania over half of the estimated 400,000 children in the five-to-fifteen-year age group were not enrolled in any school at all. Most were unwilling to take the pauper's oath.

GROWING SUPPORT FOR EDUCATION

By the 1830s, there was a movement for school reform in almost all states outside the South. With Andrew Jackson in the White House the nation entered a new era of the common man. Educational leaders in many states—James G. Carter and Horace Mann of Massachusetts, Henry Barnard of Connecticut, Thaddeus Stevens of Pennsylvania, John Swett of California, Caleb Mills of Indiana, and Calvin H. Wiley of North Carolina—led and responded to a great awakening of public responsibility for the common schools. Through their writing, traveling, and speaking, they demonstrated to the citizens of the nation that the common schools required reform and that large percentages of the school-age population were in truth not in attendance at any school.

In 1834 the Pennsylvania Free School Act provided for local taxation and some state aid for the schools. Each of the 987 school districts held elections to determine whether to accept the provisions of the law. Over one-half of the districts voted to accept, yet a bitter state senate repealed the bill. However, the indomitable Thad Stevens, leader of the House, refused to reconsider the act. Persuading the senate to accept an amended version of the law, he finally succeeded in making the law stronger.

The growing support for education reflected the belief of nineteenth-century intellectuals in the infinite perfectability of man. This idea of the Enlightenment—that mankind shares the spark of God and is divine—was given voice by Ralph Waldo Emerson in his speeches and writings. Emerson supplied the philosophical basis for the entire reform movement. One of the most sweeping humanitarian crusades in history embraced not only the institution of the common school but also antislavery, temperance, and women's rights. A recognition of the poverty and slums of the nation's cities led to the belief that improved opportunities would ameliorate these problems. Workingmen's organizations took up the call. A Philadelphia Working Men's Committee, in 1830, exclaimed that in some districts no schools whatsoever existed, while Robert Dale Owens, an early leader in the New York Workingmen's party, published an essay on public education in New York's *Daily Sentinel* in April 1830. He called for education at public expense, which would eliminate the "growing stratification" in American society.

High schools were founded in Portland, Maine, in 1821, and in New York City, in 1825. One year later, a high school for girls opened in Boston, but believing that its popularity would bankrupt the city, the mayor closed it two years later.

In the northern states the lyceum plan of Stewart Holbrook was received enthusiastically. Holbrook's plan in the 1820s called for an organization of local societies for mutual instruction in science and utilitarian subjects. The first lyceum was in Millbury, Massachusetts, in November of 1826. Within a year several nearby villages formed lyceums and joined at Leicester in a county association. Dues of one dollar were assessed for books and equipment and members collected plants and geological specimens. In 1831 state and local lyceums united into a national federation. The vision and purpose now expanded to embrace education on many levels, especially in the common schools, and to promote a general diffusion of knowledge.

In 1835 the Pennsylvania Free School Act was made stronger. It provided for local and county taxation and for state and local supervision of the schools. Districts that refused to carry out the provisions of the act were denied state funds. This act set the pattern for reform efforts in other states.

The reform during the 1830s was not easy. Reform in education went hand in hand with the abolitionist movement; the leaders of one were often the leaders of the other. Even in the North during this period, abolitionists faced angry mobs, and the democratic ideal of a truly universal education was treated with suspicion by many.

The 1830s was a period of materialism in America, the people idealizing a philosophy of expediency and utility. The frontier was the region least sympathetic to the problems of education. The rough life of the frontiersman "nourished an indifference and an amused disdain of the school. . . . [T]eaching was a job for him who had failed elsewhere, or had time on his hands."[2] The "three R's" were taken for granted, but anything further smacked of aristocracy. The ancient doctrine that education of the masses would be dangerous to society was held in high esteem by the "classes." The poor believed that public education would stamp them as paupers, and many believed that public education was an invasion of parental and family function. A truly democratic school system "could not be established in any American state while human slavery was lawful in any other."[3]

Massachusetts was the first state to make a viable effort to improve the system. James G. Carter, one of the early leaders, launched his campaign to improve the common schools immediately after his graduation from Harvard in 1830. He published newspaper articles deploring the current neglect of the common schools and criticizing the legislature for offering no legislative support for almost forty years. The then-prevalent system that condoned untrained teachers, irregular attendance, and short terms was denounced for what it was—an almost total disregard for the education of the children of the state. He criticized the Lancasterian school idea showing that quality schools cannot exist without an appropriate expenditure of money. Good schools must be graded, provided with uniform texts, and, most important, staffed by competent teachers. As a former district schoolteacher, Carter was most bitter about the prevailing district system of organization.

Carter worked vigorously for educational reform at the state legislature level. He was responsible for the law of 1827 by which the state vested in the town school committees the powers that had been held previously by the school districts and that had proved so unwieldly in practice.

In 1835 Carter was elected to the Massachusetts legislature, and two years later, as chairman of the House Committee on Education, he pressured a reluctant legislature to create the first effective State Board of Education in the United States. In 1837 Horace Mann was asked by Edmund Dwight to consider the secretaryship of the new state board. To the surprise of all, the young lawyer and senator, with a promising political career ahead of him, accepted the post.

Mann—a humanitarian and reformer, champion of the oppressed immigrant, supporter of humane treatment for the mentally ill, activist about the sale of lottery tickets and alcoholic beverages, worker for the preservation of the separation of church and state, defender of the freedom of the press, and an ardent abolitionist—attacked the problems of education in his state with characteristic energy. He served as secretary of the State Board of Education from 1837 to 1848. During these years he labored for the cause of public education on an average of fifteen hours a day. He spent no time for diversion and rarely visited friends. His salary of $1,500 a year did not include provisions for travel or clerical help. Mann did his own writing and correspondence until his strength was nearly exhausted.

Mann traveled throughout the state preaching the cause of school reform. He appealed to the self-interest of each group. The propertied class was told that adequate taxation for the support of schools was "the cheapest means of self-protection insurance." He founded and edited the *Common School Journal* to inform teachers and to influence public opinion, and he set up normal schools to improve the preparation and quality of teachers.

Mann's influence on education swept beyond the boundaries of his home state reaching into New York, other New England states, and the West. The careers of Horace Mann and Lowell Mason paralleled one another, although there was little interaction between the two men except for the remark of Mann that he would walk miles to attend a teaching lecture by Lowell Mason, so impressed was he with the teaching abilities of the Boston musician. Both men devoted their lives to the education of children, and Mann and those like him in other states helped to create a public climate for improved educational opportunities.

EXPANSION OF CULTURAL ACTIVITIES

In the urban areas of the United States during the nineteenth century there occurred a steady expansion of cultural activities. Opera was heard for the first time in New York; the important and later influential Boston Handel and Haydn Society was founded in 1815; German immigrants brought their musical talents and organizational zeal to America and formed numerous singing societies in those sections of the country in which they settled; the Philharmonic Society of New York was founded in 1842; and the Mendelssohn Quintet Club in Boston in 1849. Although no music conservatories were established as yet, a gradual but important increase in American instrument manufacturing began to supply an already-existing market of Americans who wanted to learn to play.

European artists visited the United States during these years. Their musical sophistication caused mixed reactions among the American public, although it did help to create a demand for the best in art music. European music teachers also came to America, setting up musical shop either in a school or in their home. Many who could perform did so either by playing solos or forming an ensemble and touring the countryside. The first German singing society appeared in Philadelphia in 1835 followed by a society in Baltimore one year later. The *Der Deutsche Gesangverein* was established in Cincinnati in the 1830s. In the 1840s other *sangerbunde* were organized in New York, Boston, Charlestown, Buffalo, Pittsburgh, Cleveland, Louisville, and Saint Louis. The surge of interest in musical societies at this time attests to the continuing rise of musicality of our young nation. Between 1785 and 1840 there were more than one hundred musical societies in Massachusetts alone.

The fountainhead of these societies was the Boston Handel and Haydn Society. This organization helped stimulate interest in amateur choral groups throughout New England. It was almost solely responsible for the elevation of musical tastes and technical accomplishments in New England during the early years of the century. The organizational structure, missionary zeal of its members, and important publications during the first half of the nineteenth century did much to spread the gospel of European art music among a population still somewhat isolated from the mainstream of European culture. In 1816 the Boston Handel and Haydn Society brought out Handel's *Messiah*; in 1818 it published Haydn's *Creation*; and from 1820 to 1832 it published a four-volume series of anthems, oratorios, and miscellaneous choral works called *The Boston Handel and Haydn Society Collection of Sacred Music*.

The Boston Handel and Haydn Society stimulated the founding of smaller societies in towns and rural areas of New England. Meetings of the various societies were usually all-day affairs. With the routine business done early in the day, the members could enjoy a "public exhibition of sacred music." They would organize themselves into a choir and perform the music they had previously rehearsed and learned. In addition to the attraction of the music, the day became a pleasurable social event as well. The music societies, touring concert performers, and growing interest in European art music helped set the stage for the most important figure in American music education.

LOWELL MASON

An indefatigable worker, a promoter par excellence, an outstanding music teacher, but also a product of the darker side of the nineteenth-century cultural ethic in this country, Lowell Mason was a complex giant of a personality. He promoted the musical education of children not only in Massachusetts but throughout the country. He often, however, borrowed musical material from others without attention to the niceties of scholarly convention. Lowell Mason promoted music education and his own publications to an eager public. He was an important figure in advancing the Pestalozzian method of instruction, even though his knowledge of Pestalozzianism was highly tenuous and his selling of its principles in relation to music instruction bordered on the fraudulent. But Mason's influence on behalf of the education of children was positive and far-reaching. In an era when American schools were only beginning to improve, when public sympathies were only beginning to be aroused, the city of Boston thought enough of the possibilities of music education to begin the teaching of vocal music in the Hawes School in 1837. It was to take the rest of the century for city after city to introduce the regular instruction of vocal music into the schools, first as an experiment, and then on a regular basis.

Lowell Mason was born in Medfield, Massachusetts, a village eighteen miles southwest of Boston, on January 8, 1792. He was the son of Johnson and Catherine Hartshorn Mason, the sixth generation of New Englanders. Johnson Mason was a prominent and influential man in the village, acting as the town clerk for nineteen years, town treasurer, and member of the legislature. In addition he was a merchant dealing in straw bonnets and a schoolmaster. There was no absence of musicality in the Mason home or in the small community in which they lived. Barachias Mason, Mason's grandfather, a 1742 graduate of Harvard and a Medfield schoolmaster and selectman, conducted singing schools while Johnson Mason played several musical instruments, particularly the cello. At the age of seventy he led the bass section of a chorus in his community.

Mason spent his first twenty years in Medfield, assisting his father in the sale of bonnets and learning as much music as his town could offer him. He attended a singing school, learned to play whatever instrument that came to his attention, and by the age of sixteen seemed qualified to conduct his first singing school.

He appeared to have no interest in becoming a professional musician, but at the same time Medfield appeared to Mason to lack opportunities for business and commerce. He joined friends and together on a trip by wagon, they made their way to Savannah, Georgia. Upon arriving, Mason took up the profession of bank clerk. Though his first year was not particularly happy, his insatiable energy and devotion to music prompted him to become a worker in the Independent Presbyterian Church as well as choirmaster and organist. In these posts he remained for seven years. He helped organize and superintend the only Sunday school in Savannah and perhaps the second one to be organized in America. Here he received his first experiences in the teaching of children. It was in Savannah also that he received his first "legitimate" instruction in harmony and composition when he became a student of F. L. Abel, a native of Germany who had arrived in Savannah about the same time as Mason. While teaching in Savannah, Mason felt the need for a suitable collection of psalm and hymn tunes harmonized in a correct European manner. He formed a manuscript collection for his own use with the help of Abel. The basis for this collection was the *Sacred Melodies* of William Gardiner. Gardiner's book had the correct figured bass. A large selection of tunes from the instrumental works of Haydn, Mozart, and Beethoven were adapted to English psalms and hymns.

In 1821 Mason visited Boston with the hope of finding a publisher for his collection. He soon discovered that there were too many collections already and that no publisher cared to take a chance on another tune-book collection. He only wanted, however, sufficient copies for his personal needs in Savannah. He opened negotiations with the Boston Handel and Haydn Society, then in its sixth year. The society was already famous but was in financial difficulties. The society, with its small membership and limited income, was unsure whether to take a chance on an additional publication. A compromise was reached. Dr. George K. Jackson, a sound musician and author of *Treatise on Practical Thorough Bass*, was to judge the merits of Lowell Mason's opus. An obese man with a fondness for drink, he nevertheless had a keen mind. Jackson listened to each tune in Mason's collection, mumbling either an approval or a suggestion or two while sipping from a bottle of gin. The young man might either accept or reject the suggestions according to his own judgment. At the following meeting of the two men, the older man's expostulations were all but forgotten.[4] Some pieces by the doctor himself were added to the collection and the whole was certified as follows: "It is much the best book of the kind I have seen published in this country, and

I do not hesitate to give it my most decided approbation." Abel, Mason's teacher, wrote a similar document which appears on a page of the first edition.

And so in 1821 (the book is dated 1822) the *Boston Handel and Haydn Society Collection of Church Music* appeared. The real story of its birth is lamentably concealed in the introduction to the first edition.

The society have for some time become engaged, with much labor and at considerable expense, in collecting materials for the present work; . . . These works are among the materials to which the Handel and Haydn Society have had access, and they have exercised their best judgements in making such selections from them as would most enrich the present work. They consider themselves as peculiarly fortunate in having had, for the accomplishment of their purpose, the assistance of Mr. Lowell Mason, one of their numbers now resident in Savannah, whose taste and science have well fitted him for the employment, and whose zeal for the improvement of church music has led him to undertake an important part in selecting, arranging, and harmonizing the several compositions.

Mason was not at that time named as editor. He was still unwilling to make music his profession. Mason was named as editor only in the ninth edition, by which time the collection had become highly profitable to the Boston Handel and Haydn Society and to its author. The book enjoyed an immediate success and a subsequent run of twenty-two editions. Fifty thousand copies were sold between 1822 and 1858 with the profits divided between Mason and the society. The Boston Handel and Haydn Society became financially secure, and in time this same success encouraged Mason to choose the profession of music.

Mason returned to Boston in 1827 and started to teach vocal music in classes as he had in Savannah. He organized the first singing schools for children in Boston that year. In his first classes only six or eight enrolled but soon the number increased rapidly. These classes were continued gratuitously for six or eight years, and it was not uncommon for Mason to have between five to six hundred children in these classes. Mason had few assistants at this time, yet the children invaded his church rooms in ever-increasing numbers.[5] We know little of what was taught in these classes, but instruction of children in music was new. Few thought that children could be taught to sing and most believed that talent was exceedingly rare. It should not have been difficult for Mason, whom we must recognize as a superior teacher, to get impressive results for that time even from very large classes. We also know that the alto part was usually not sung in the average church choirs of Boston during the time immediately before Mason's arrival.[6] It was difficult to find singers skillful enough to sing this part! To a citizenry unused to even a reasonable quality of choral singing in church, Mason's contributions to the singing must have appeared exceptional.

While teaching these children's classes, Mason published his *Juvenile Psalmist* in 1829, a book of thirty-two pages, half of which was taken up with a catechistic treatment of the rudiments of notation and some simple hymns in three and four voices. This may have been the first American song book written especially for children.

By the 1830s, Mason was introduced to what he considered to be the Pestalozzian system of music education.

Manual of the Boston Academy of Music

Mason's introduction to the works of Pfeiffer and Nageli and Kübler, through the good offices of William C. Woodbridge, kindled an interest in the pedagogical procedures of the great Swiss educator. He became the country's most important leader in the dissemination of his understandings of Pestalozzianism. The ninth or 1831 edition of *The Boston Handel and Haydn Society Collection of Church Music*[7] begins to show his conversion. The introductory rules were rewritten, demonstrating his newly acquired affinity for the form of question and answer.

Three years later Mason published his famous *Manual of the Boston Academy of Music, for Instruction in the Elements of Vocal Music on the System of Pestalozzi.*[8] So popular was this volume that a run of eight editions followed, the last appearing in 1861. Its aim was to place instruction in vocal music "on the same footing with instruction in the other branches of common elementary education."[9] The essence of this new system was that each thing would be taken up one at a time and thoroughly examined and practiced before another would be commenced. The knowledge was to be acquired by the pupils themselves and not from the dictation and direction of the teachers. The teacher must lead the students to the desired information, excite their curiosity, and "fix their attention." The system precluded the teacher from singing continuously with the scholars in the hope that the children would be "guided by their own ear and skill." Mason stated that his sources were "various; but always derived from personal experience, or the written experience of others, and never from mere theory." Mason continues in his introduction to the *Manual.*

The system must be traced to Pestalozzi, a Swiss Gentleman of wealth and learning, who devoted his life and fortune to the improvement of the young. . . . He obtained the services of Pfeiffer and Nageli, who, under his patronage, drew up a very extensive work on elementary instruction in vocal music. Other works on the same general principles, were afterwards published by Kübler, another distinguished German teacher, in which much improvement was made on the original treatise of Pfeiffer and Nageli. These German works have been introduced into this country by Wm. C. Woodbridge, the well known geographer and editor of the "Annals of Education"; and these have been made the basis of the following work.[10]

Mason suggests an organization of subject matter calculated according to the growth and development of the children. His infant classes were supposed to be taught only a few of the first lessons, and those by imitation. Mason suggested, and quite correctly, that these exercises should aim "chiefly at the formation of a musical ear and the management of the voice." They were to learn to sing a scale, slowly at first, then gradually faster and faster. Rote singing of measures and phrases in rhythm and melody could be tried followed by easy songs with words.

The regular classes were to begin with the formal instruction in vocal music "occupying two or three hours in the week." The areas of rhythm, melody, and dynamics were to be treated separately, although Mason informs us that in practice they could be pursued together. One-fourth of each meeting "should be occupied in lessons for tuning and giving flexibility to the voice; and the rest of the time divided between Rhythm, Melody, and Dynamics." Mason suggested that melodies with appropriate words be sung. They could be learned entirely by imitation "without books or notes." Mason had no aversion to rote singing at this time and his reasons demonstrate a sensitivity to a practical classroom environment.

There is no objection at all, to learning tunes by rote, under the direction of a judicious teacher. It is only objectionable when in consequence of

singing the syllables appropriate to solmization, the pupil is led to suppose that he is singing by note, while his voice is guided solely by others.[11]

Mason valued rote singing as a device to "enliven the mind, to
strengthen and improve the voice, and cultivate the ear."

In the *Manual*, the author suggests that a suitable room be used
where the scholars have the opportunity to sit as well as to stand, a
room outfitted with a large blackboard about six-feet long and
four-and-a-half wide, with several five-line staves drawn on it.
Also suggested were large cards with "rhythmical relations" and
those modulations which were felt to be most useful. Mason believed the piano to be the most suitable instrument for giving the
pitch but a violin would do. The scholars should also have "black
books" to note the substance of each lesson and from which they
might study between class periods. And, of course, Mason's own
Juvenile Lyre was recommended as a suitable text for the children
while for adult classes, *The Choir or Union Collection of Church
Music* was suggested. The body of the *Manual* itself consisted of
181 pages of hundreds of short exercises in the elements of music.

But Mason was not the author of this work for which he
claimed credit. The *Manual* was in reality merely a translation of
the *Anleitung* by G. F. Kübler, while Mason acted not as the author of this work but as editor.[12] Ellis tells us that Mason added
some editorial changes but the paragraphing of the original was
followed faithfully by Mason. The insertions and deletions which
appeared throughout the text were not of sufficient consequence
to demonstrate a substantive difference between the two works.[13]

Though Mason's "Introduction" was basically Pestalozzian, his
material, taken from Kübler, varies from the tenets of Pestalozzianism as given by Pfeiffer and Nageli in their *Gesangbildungslehre*, a work endorsed by Pestalozzi himself. Both an extended
discussion of harmony as well as the inclusion of the minor mode
are a part of the *Anleitung* that Mason used for his *Manual*, while
Pfeiffer and Nageli believed these elements to be too difficult for
inclusion in a text for children. But Mason suggested in his "Introduction" that his "method" would take several years for the children to complete.

It is impossible to go thoroughly through this course of instruction with
children, in a less time than two or three years, two lessons being given
in a week. An adult class may indeed go through the course in a much

shorter time; but even in adult classes, if sufficient time is taken for prac-
tise, two years' instruction will be found little enough.[14]

As Pestalozzi himself had comparatively little to say on the subject
of music education, it is now evident that the garden of Pestalozzianism in music education tended to grow somewhat out of
control.

The *Gesangbildungslehre* was more concerned with the techniques of teaching rather than with theories of learning. In this the
Gesangbildungslehre and the *Anleitung* are similar. The *Gesangbildungslehre* includes no ideas about human growth and development, no real confrontation of sense-impression, or *anschuung*, no
provision for self-activity on the part of the learner, and little syn-
chronization of material with the process of maturation. If such a
volume can be approved by Pestalozzi himself, then the *Anleitung*
may also be equated with Pestalozzianism and hence so must Mason's *Manual of the Boston Academy of Music*.

Knowing how much Mason understood about the nature of
Pestalozzianism at that time is less important than recognizing
Mason's role in the current school reform movement. Also important to know is that Mason's understanding of Pestalozzi's principles grew and matured over the years. It is significant that almost
any change in educational procedures during the first half of the
nineteenth century passed as Pestalozzianism.

What is surprising, however, was Mason's plagiarism. Did Mason realize that his borrowing without attributing his source was
unethical and dishonest? Perhaps he did not. (He could have admitted in the first edition of the *Manual* that his material came
from Kübler, which would have cost Mason nothing in sales.)
Seven years later he did admit in his *Carmina Sacra* that his *Manual* was indeed a translation of the work by Kübler. Mason need
not have admitted even this much, and perhaps no one would have
bothered to translate the *Anleitung* and check this work page by
page against the *Manual*. Also, conventional tune books of the
early 1800s, with their oblong format, were all but universal. It
was common knowledge that authors borrowed from each other's
volumes. Whole sections on the theory of music and how to teach
were lifted from one book to another with little concern either for
originality or legality. Such perhaps was the ethical background
that prompted Mason to have the *Anleitung* translated and its ex-

ercises used in his *Manual of the Boston Academy of Music*. The introduction to the *Manual* was Mason's, and what he delivered he believed to be Pestalozzian.

The Boston Academy of Music

With these problems in mind we can now observe that Mason taught his classes along Pestalozzian principles after his "conversion" by William C. Woodbridge, and that this new system of instruction worked significantly better than the system Mason had previously used. Mason was reported to have taught very large classes. It must be assumed that he did much to keep the children interested. What remains unclear is the degree of learning that took place in the Bowdoin Street Church each Wednesday and Saturday afternoon. The children were taught free providing they promised to attend for the entire year. We know that his instruction included the elementary rules for singing, the rudiments of music, and note reading using syllables. It is not known whether Mason's children attended both Wednesday and Saturday or just one of the two days. Perhaps Mason used assistants at this time, but who they were or how many there were is unclear. From our point of view it seems almost impossible to teach such large numbers of children all the singing and music reading that has been reported. All sources describing these classes are either secondary or are reports from people particularly friendly to Mason.[15]

But important public concerts were given in 1832 and in 1833 to show that children could be taught to sing and to spark interest in the teaching of vocal music in the schools. The choirs of children filled the galleries of the Bowdoin Street Church. The performances were reported to be "enormously successful."[16]

Out of these public concerts grew the Boston Academy of Music, an influential organization whose principal aim was to promote music education according to the principles of Pestalozzianism. A subsidiary aim was the promotion of publications which flowed prolifically from the pen of Lowell Mason. The academy was organized January 8, 1833. Samuel Eliot, a president of the academy, reported that the academy was "an association of gentlemen who were to promote musical education in the community in every way which was within the reach of their efforts."[17] Mason was hired as a professor whose responsibility was instruction. But Mason was the moving spirit behind the academy; it would not have existed without him. Although the official function of the academy was promotional, its professors were at first occupied principally with giving instruction in voice, piano, and thorough bass. The most important of Mason's lieutenants was George K. Webb, one of the founders of the academy who shared the direction of the choir in 1834.[18]*

Once the academy was formed it assumed responsibility for Mason's children's classes. Any child over the age of seven was admitted at no fee providing he or she agreed to continue in the school for at least a year. At first the directors of the academy thought of charging a tuition fee for the children, but such a practice was never effected. Adults, however, did pay. The children's classes were open to boys and girls of all denominations, took place two days per week, and were one hour in length.

Lowell Mason quickly recognized the inadequacy in the supply of qualified music teachers. In the 1830s Mason and the Boston Academy of Music began to fill this need. In August 1834, the academy advertised a course of lectures "by its professors" based on the Pestalozzian system. Teachers or those already acquainted with music could receive instruction "devised by Pfeiffer and Nageli" for ten to fifteen days, two lectures per day. That year twelve people were attracted by the advertisement and took the course. The following year the number enrolled jumped to eighteen. In succeeding summers the number increased to more than two hundred and attracted teachers from all over the country.

When the academy first opened in 1833, classes were held under the Bowdoin Street Church in rooms that could house about four hundred pupils. The following year the chapel of the Old South Church was used two afternoons each week for George K. Webb's class of one hundred pupils. In 1835 the Boston Theatre was changed to a music hall and its name changed to "Odeon." There the academy gave concerts including choruses, cantatas, madri-

---

* The choir was important in the musical life of Boston up to the year 1838 after which time its influence declined. By this time the academy was focusing its attention on instrumental music and on its juvenile choir. The choir concerts were curtailed in 1839 following a disagreement between Mason and Webb, which prompted Webb to leave the academy to assume the presidency of the Boston Handel and Haydn Society the following year.

Other instructors at the Academy in addition to Mason, were Jonathan C. Woodman, who organized a children's chorus in 1837–1838; A. N. Johnson, who succeeded Woodman; Henry Schmidt, who conducted the orchestra from time to time and who was somewhat later given faculty status at the academy; and Joseph A. Keller, hired in 1836, who was orchestra director and instrumental teacher.

gals, and glees. Eventually an orchestra was organized which also performed there. On August 5, 1835, the headquarters of the Boston Academy of Music was moved to the Odeon.*

The first president of the Boston Academy of Music was Jacob Abbott, the principal of Mount Vernon School. Mount Vernon was a private school committed to the teaching of music, as were so many other private schools during the nineteenth century. In 1835 the presidency of the academy was assumed by Samuel Eliot, who was prominent in city affairs when the groundwork was being laid for the introduction of music into the public schools of Boston. Eliot became chairman of the school committee in 1837 and mayor of Boston in 1838.

The first official reference demonstrating an interest in the inclusion of vocal music as a part of the school curriculum came from the Snelling Report issued in December 1831. George H. Snelling reported to the Primary School Board of the City of Boston that including music in the curriculum of the Boston schools was indeed desirable, and the report urged its adoption into the primary schools of that city. After strong opposition the committee adopted the following resolution on January 17, 1832:

Resolved: That one school from each district be selected for the introduction of systematic instruction in vocal music, under the direction of a committee to consist of one from each district and two from the standing committee.[19]

From a speech by William Woodbridge we learn that Snelling presented to the Primary School Board of Boston "an elaborate report strongly urging the adoption of music as a regular course of study in our primary schools."[20] A partial experiment was made, but the plan was not fully carried out. It was only much later, in 1864, under the direction of Luther Whiting Mason, that music was introduced into the primary schools of Boston.

Unfortunately, little additional information exists regarding this early attempt in 1832 at public school vocal instruction. Who attempted to do this teaching and why it failed is unknown. Mason, nevertheless, was most impressed by this report and by the experi-

---

* Its auditorium had a seating capacity of 1,500, and the building had several teaching rooms. The cost of an organ and extensive renovations were paid for by the members of the academy and by the rental of the auditorium to outside groups. The building was leased for two five-year periods, first in 1835 and then again in 1840.

ment, and it may have been that the resolution led to the establishment of the Boston Academy of Music in 1833. The evidence, however, is purely circumstantial. But the sequence of events is quite logical in the light of what we now know of Lowell Mason.

Introduction of Music into Boston Public Schools

Mason was an extraordinary promoter. What he may have lacked in intellectuality and originality, he made up for in resourcefulness and perseverance. It is highly conceivable that Mason perceived an underlying receptiveness in Boston to the idea of teaching music in the common schools. Mason had every confidence that success could be achieved, and his previous experience had proved this to himself if not yet to the general public in Boston. With the establishment of an academy of music, Mason could launch an offensive on several fronts. An organization with important people as officers could help promote the political efforts being made behind the scenes—so important in the implementation of a controversial and perhaps expensive change in the school curriculum. At the same time, Mason could continue teaching his children's classes which had become so successful. These classes could be publicized more and taught with the influential backing of a musical academy. And through the academy Mason could systematically work toward the inclusion of vocal music in the common school curriculum. Arguments favoring the introduction of music in the schools appeared in various publications. Samuel Eliot described the virtues of the study of music. By giving instruction in music, "the whole musical talent of the place will be discovered; and those who have the best powers for the study, and the strongest inclination for it, will have the means to cultivate the talents, which . . . would long have continued unknown to themselves."[21]

Finally, in 1837, Mason and the Boston Academy of Music achieved the results they had worked for. From the Kemper-Davis Report of that year, vocal music was described as "not a newly fashioned notion" but as an art and science that could go back for its defense to the time of Aristotle. The idea of music education was criticized. Many said that not all children could learn to sing and that the study of music would impair discipline. But the recommendations of the Kemper-Davis Report were accepted except for one final obstacle—no appropriations were forthcoming. The report recommended that vocal music was important in "every system of instruction which aspires, as should every system, to develop man's whole nature." The trouble with public education, said the report, was that "it aims to develop the intellectual part of man's nature solely, when for all the true purposes of life, it is of more importance to feel rightly, than to think profoundly." The report recommended that experiments be tried in four schools of the city, but on September 19, 1837, the city council failed to appropriate funds. At that point Lowell Mason volunteered his services in one of the schools gratuitously. In November 1837, the school committee passed the following resolutions:

Resolved, that in the opinion of the school committee it is expedient that the experiment be tried of introducing instruction in vocal music, by public authority, into the public schools of the city.

Resolved, that the experiment be tried in the Hawes school in South Boston under the direction of the subcommittee of that school and the Committee of Music already appointed by this board.[22]

Mason began teaching at the Hawes School either in November or December of 1837. The Groves Dictionary American Supplement states that Mason began teaching in October of that year.[23] If true, one would suspect that Mason clearly understood that the school committee was about to give its permission to him to do this and that Mason was only anxious to begin his teaching. If he did so, no official record of this teaching exists for this earlier date.

By August 1838, Mason's success was sufficiently obvious that the school committee gave its official endorsement to his endeavors. Mason was put in charge of music for all the schools and was authorized to hire several assistants (A. N. Johnson, G. F. Root, A. J. Drake, and J. C. Johnson). The subcommittee on music gave Mason full authority to hire his assistants directly. The assistants' contracts (if there were any) were with Mason, not with the school committee. The assistants were responsible to Mason for their work and received $80 per annum for each school in which they taught. Mason's budget of $130 per school included the assistants' salaries, $20 for the rental of the piano, and $30 for Mason to keep for his superintendence. Some of the schools, however, were taught by Mason himself, and for teaching in these schools he received the full teaching amount.

The school action of 1838 specified additional regulations which, to a certain extent, are revealing in themselves. Though the school committee believed that music should be taught, they stipulated that "not more than two hours in the week shall be devoted to this exercise" and that "the instruction shall be given at stated and fixed times throughout the city, and until otherwise ordered."[24] One suspects that Mason may have been a little casual about his schedule of instruction during his first year of teaching at the Hawes School or perhaps the classroom teachers believed that—then as now—the music program took too much time from their work. The school committee also affirmed that "during the time the school is under the instruction of the teacher of vocal music, the discipline of the school shall continue under the charge of the master or masters of the school, who shall be present while the instruction is given, and shall organize the scholars for that purpose, in such arrangement as the teacher in music may desire." The problem has an interestingly modern ring, and the school regulations legislated the rules carefully.

These regulations continued with little change until 1849. By 1851, however, there were some significant changes. Two lessons of thirty minutes duration each were given weekly. The teachers were paid $100 yearly and, interestingly enough, were admonished to "instruct personally." Could it have been that at an earlier time either Mason or his assistants did not teach personally but at times sent a substitute when the press of affairs arose? One could easily believe that Lowell Mason was busy. He promoted music education in several states and continuously worked at his publications. He demonstrated various teaching techniques in the field of vocal music instruction at workshops. Though Mason had by this time severed his connection with the Boston schools, it was not unlikely that the school committee had a clear idea of whatever problems ensued while Mason was teaching.

H. W. Day was the publisher of the *American Journal of Music and Musical Visitor*. Day was a singing school teacher in Boston, a compiler of tune books, and an enemy of Lowell Mason's. In November 1844 he charged Mason with running the music department of the Boston schools on a sectarian basis and other "obliquities."

Music continues in the public schools under the superintendence of Mr. Mason, and we rather fear that the matter of teaching is managed in a sectarian manner. Mr. Mason is a Congregationalist, and every school, or the teaching of music in every school, is in the hands of Congregationalist teachers, except one and he, a Unitarian—Mr. Baker, who was for some cause dismissed. But the hornets flew around and he was restored. The teachers are all employed by Mr. Mason and we do not think that there is much effort made to secure men the most experienced, but rather such as are pledged to one narrow system of teaching, and such as will sell one man's books—such as are under one man's thumb.

There are certainly Methodist and Baptist teachers, and those as make no particular religious professions, who are truly able and competent to teach, but they are not employed. The City Council will probably not long allow this monopoly. In this way, music must ultimately die or dwindle into insignificance. Let the teachers of music be employed as other masters are to take their own plan of instruction . . . music will soon approach a standard of perfection—but this is impossible under a monopoly.[25]

Day suggested improvements that could have saved the city of Boston money, such as buying rather than renting pianos and eliminating the office of music superintendent, which would save the city $50 for each school or a total of $800 for the year. Day also criticized Mason for his instructional inefficiency, claiming that "no progress was made, and that the children possessed little musical knowledge at the age of fourteen and after three years of music instruction given by Mason or his assistants."[26] Somewhere between the inimical writings of one person and the laudatory writings of a great number of others lies the truth about the man who was Lowell Mason.

Day discusses Mason's understanding of Pestalozzianism: "Many suppose that Pestalozzi was a distinguished music teacher, that he perfected and published a complete system of instruction and gave it to the world, and that we have had the good fortune to have it introduced with great success into this country—all of which is incorrect, having no foundation in truth. . . . The *Manual*, of the Boston Academy of Music we are told by a German, is principally a distorted and garbled translation of a little work by Keibler [*sic*] with some additions by Mr. Porter, who prepared it for the press, and has no more claim to Pestalozzian [*sic*] than Smith's Grammar, and indeed not half so much." Howard Ellis found Day's criticism of Mason's *Manual* to be basically accurate. Although Mason's translation of Kübler's *Anleitung* was not "distorted and garbled," as Day tells us, the *Manual* still represents only a translation of Kübler's work with some editorial additions and is not an original presentation of Pestalozzian principles for music education, as Mason claims.

In November 1845 Lowell Mason was removed from his position of superintendent of music in the Boston schools. Today the reasons are as veiled in innuendo as they were in 1845. Of the school committee's twenty-six members, only thirteen members (less than quorum) were present to vote on the resolution to dismiss Mason. Eight voted for it, three against, and two abstained. After his dismissal, the board affirmed the "integrity and competency" of Mason. An article in Boston's *Morning Post* of October 10, reported that

it seems to have been a last resort, when every vestige of hope had fled of reinstating Mr. Mason, by a friend of his, to render Mr. Mason's unpleasant situation as soothing as possible and take off the sharp edge of the effect on Mr. Mason's popularity. Special meetings of this kind are generally attended by those specially interested. The belief has been expressed that had all the committee been present, this resolution would have shared the same fate of Mr. Mason's petition [for reinstatement].[27]

Mason, of course, publicly expressed his surprise at the action of the board. In the Boston *Mercantile Journal*, September 13, 1845, he asked if there had been

any want of ability, faithfulness, fidelity, gentlemanly conduct toward committee or teachers or kindness to pupils and charges affecting my professional or moral character.

And the reply the same day by Charles Gordon, chairman of the subcommittee on music, gave the only reason for the committee's unfavorable action:

As you had held the office several years and had enjoyed its benefits so long it was proper to give to Mr. Baker, who was represented to be a distinguished and successful teacher of music the encouragement of the office. There were no charges.

The *Mercantile Journal* took Mason's side editorially and rapped the school committee for its inept decision. It could not understand the logic of dismissing a competent teacher because of his very competency and replacing him with another to enjoy "the encouragement of the office." But then Day reported that Mason had shown favoritism in his appointments of teachers and that he had used for his profit his own books in instructing the classes.

The Boston *Daily Atlas* replied on October 13, 1845, that the cause of Mason's dismissal could not have been the mere rotation in office. Two members of the music committee claimed that they acted for the good of the schools.

On October 14, the *Mercantile Journal* published the following letter by Lowell Mason requesting the opportunity to meet the challenge to his competency as superintendent of music:

To the School Committee of the City of Boston:

Gentlemen: Having been very unexpectedly, and as I think very unfairly, deprived of the office of master of music of the grammar schools, an office which I have held ever since the introduction of music into the schools, and so far as I know to the entire satisfaction of the Committee; and having had no charge made against me, or any satisfactory reason assigned as the cause of my removal, nor any opportunity of justifying myself, or of presenting my claims to the office; I take the liberty to address you, respectfully requesting you to take such measures as you think proper, to cause such an investigation of the circumstances as will place the matter in a proper light before the public, enable me to meet the charges, if there are any, and save my professional character from essential injury.

> With sentiments of great
> respect,
> Lowell Mason

A day earlier Mason had written to the Reverend Mr. Sargent of the school committee, requesting that a reason for replacing him be given. John T. Sargent replied the same day:

Lowell Mason, Esq. Dear Sir:

. . . the reasons which influenced Dr. Dale and myself, in the votes tending to displace you from your position as teacher of music in the schools, were of a nature not affecting or touching your general character. They were founded partly on some suspicion of favoritism on your part in the selection of your assistants; a question whether those assistants were the best, all things considered, and a conviction that other things being equal, some rotation, or exchange of their offices might be desirable.

> I am, sir, respectfully, etc., yours,
> John T. Sargent

James C. Johnson, one of Mason's assistants, believed that there was a plot by two young "outsiders" to have Mason removed and that such a plot was political in nature. He did not, unfortunately, divulge the names of those suspected or go into detail. Johnson wrote fifty years after the fact.

It reads singularly now 1895 but it really happened, that, after some years of tranquil and successful music teaching in the schools, it occurred to two young teachers, outsiders, that it was a great outrage that the important "offices" of school music teachers should be filled by others and not by themselves; and strange as it may appear, they actually succeeded, by shrewd political management, in ousting Mason and his helpers, and introducing themselves in their places. The writer asked one of them if successful and faithful teaching would not count for something, in the way of keeping one's school. But he was told, in substance, that "To the victors belong the spoils."[28]

The school committee never fully cleared Lowell Mason, and at this time we have no conclusive evidence whether Mason was unjustly accused and a victim of a political plot or whether there was at least some validity in the charges made delicately by Sargent and like a hammerstroke by his enemy H. W. Day.

Other factors possibly affecting the political climate could have easily made the move by the school committee more understandable. In 1845 Horace Mann was instrumental in securing the first school survey. Prior to this time oral examinations were given by members of the school committee. Now, in 1845, written tests were given to the pupils in grammar schools. The published summary of test results was a shock to the Bostonians. The average percentage of correct answers given by the children was minimal. There is no evidence, however, that music was included in these examinations. But the school committee was unusually sensitive to any sign of a defect in the organization of the schools. It would seem that the committee might have overreacted at such a time to criticisms, either real or imagined. Whatever Mason's faults, his detractors have been all but forgotten, and Mason's philosophy of teaching music to all children has become a tenet of the music education profession today.

In a similar manner music was introduced into the schools of certain larger urban centers in the North. Always a grass-roots effort preceded its introduction, and always, when it succeeded, the promotion was led by a well-trained musician especially interested in the education of children. It would be the end of the century before music could be described as being universal in the nation's schools. The study of the introduction of music into the schools of Cincinnati, Hartford, Buffalo, Chicago, and numerous other cities presents as interesting a story as that of Boston.

MUSICAL CONVENTIONS

Musical conventions developed early in the nineteenth century in response to the need for training those who conducted singing schools and were directed toward the singing teacher himself. The first musical convention may have been suggested by the New Hampshire Musical Society of Goffstown. The first meeting lasted for two days and was held at Concord, New Hampshire, in September 1829. Subsequent conventions were held in 1830 at Pembroke and in 1831 at Goffstown. These early meetings were held under the leadership of Henry Eaton Moore.[29]

Lowell Mason and his colleagues at the Boston Academy of Music introduced their own version of the convention in 1834, at which time the professors of the academy gave lectures on the method of teaching as set forth in the *Manual of the Boston Academy of Music*. The enthusiasm of those attending was such that the convention became an annual affair of the academy. The next year eighteen persons attended lectures again on the *Manual* and on taste and style in church music.

The following year several innovations expanded the convention concept. Discussion sessions were introduced allowing the teachers to express different points of view and to exchange ideas concerning their common problems. At the completion of the sessions the group as a whole endorsed the Pestalozzian system of music education as interpreted by Mason's *Manual* and registered their support for the inclusion of vocal music as a regular branch of study in the common schools. A detailed report of the 1838 convention of the Boston Academy of Music appeared in the *Boston Musical Gazette*. By this time and through the promotional zeal of Lowell Mason, the convention had become a significant force that was to affect musical taste and instructional techniques for many years. Sixty participants attended the 1838 convention to hear lectures on the elementary principles of music and on harmony and thorough bass and to receive exercises in singing. The sessions served as a model for similar meetings held elsewhere in the country.

8:00 A.M. to 10:00 A.M.	Meeting of the convention
10 A.M. to 12 noon	Lecture on the elementary principles and manner of teaching, by Lowell Mason
12 to 1:00 P.M.	Lecture on thorough base by George J. Webb
3:00 P.M. to 4:00 P.M.	Glees: George J. Webb at the piano, Lowell Mason conducting [30]

The convention passed a resolution against the use of the fixed Do method of teaching music reading.

By 1840 this group, sensing their significance, named their convocation the National Music Convention, and one year later the program began to reflect those necessary and pragmatic skills which have been the trappings and fittings of the music teacher's métier. That year George F. Root presided over a period of voice instruction. His autobiography gives us a vivid picture of his classes in vocal instruction.

There were perhaps twenty present at that first meeting. I took each one separately, all the rest looked on or occasionally joining, and sang a tone with him either an octave higher or an octave lower, and showed him and all how much more resonance and blending there was when the tone was produced with the throat more open, and when he could not readily change from the way to which he had been accustomed, I devised such means as I could think of to help him, much to the interest of the class and sometime to their great amusement. [31]

The 1841 convention saw a controversy between those who were concerned with the teaching of music and wanted only lectures and those who were more interested in the performance of the great masterworks and wanted no lecture. Always interested in the training of teachers, Mason and his supporters managed to dissolve the National Musical Convention only to become the American Musical Convention. Those preferring the emphasis on masterworks then formed a competing group and renamed their organization the National Musical Convention. Three years later even the American Musical Convention became disenchanted with Lowell Mason and the Boston Academy of Music and in 1844 voted to move their convention to New York City.

By 1845 the daily plan of instruction demonstrates the thrust of these early teaching-training exercises, which may represent the first instrumental clinic to be held in this country.

Tuesday, August 12

    10:00 A.M.   Meeting. Singing of a few tunes from *The Choral* (a collection prepared by Baker and Woodbury).

    3:00 P.M.   Glees. From *No. 1* or *Glees for the Million* (also by Baker and Woodbury).

Wednesday, August 13

    8:00 A.M.   Mr. Bond met with those interested in instruction on Brass Instruments. Ten or twelve were present.

    9:00 A.M.   Singing from *The Choral*.

    10:00 A.M.   Lectures on Thorough Base by Prof. Woodbury. Intervals of the scale were taken up and analyzed. Remarks on the common chord.

    3:00 P.M.   Glee Singing.

    8:00 P.M.   Chorus Rehearsal. Haydn's *Creation*.

Thursday, August 14

    9:00 A.M.   Principles of Elementary Instruction by Prof. Baker. Remarks on the difference between an art and a science. Division of the subject into four parts; recognition and explanation of characters dealing with length, then pitch, then tone and finally combinations of sounds. Rhythm defined as accentuation. Time beating advocated because of the advantage gained by exercising two faculties.[32]

Benjamin Baker was Lowell Mason's successor as supervisor of music in the Boston public schools and Isaac Woodbury was a prominent writer of hymn tunes and a teacher. The conductors of the convention lost no time in using and ostensibly promoting the music books which they had compiled.*

Directors of the conventions enjoyed ample opportunity to publicize the conventions as several were editors of musical papers and magazines. Isaac Woodbury was the editor of the *American Monthly Musical Review and Musical Pioneer*. Theodore Seward was the editor of the *New York Musical Review and Gazette*, along with William Bradbury. Bradbury's success was such that he was forced to advertise in his journal the locations of his next trip to the West for the purpose of giving "musical conventions."

---

* Although our own age distinguishes between the sale of merchandise and the profession of teaching, the nineteenth century made no such ethical distinction. *Caveat emptor* was the law of the marketplace.

I intend to spend the month of October and perhaps November at the West, in the vicinity of Chicago, Ill. Am already engaged at Beloit, Wis.; Janesville, Wis.; Burlington, Iowa; Peoria, Ill.; Princeton, Ill.; and in correspondence with several other places.

The object of this notice is to request other correspondents in the Western States especially, who, are expecting me to "hurry up" their applications before my time is completely engaged. I shall hold conventions of three days each (in some cases, 2 days), and arrange them so as to spend the least time possible in travelling from place to place.[33]

Lectures were developed on musical topics and especially on the art of teaching singing classes. Those attending were in constant practice during these sessions which ended with one or two concerts. So popular were these sessions that audiences attending the final concert could hear a thousand-voice chorus singing the oratorios of Handel or Haydn, occasionally with orchestra and organ accompaniment.

The curriculum included sight-singing, practicing new music, trying new books, and venturing into works of the great masters. The handbills that were often distributed, which seemed to be programs for a concert, were in fact catalogs of large auction sales of "larger and smaller musical works."[34] Conductors circulated their methods while dealers and publishers disposed of unsold materials. Those who organized and conducted the conventions held virtual monopolies over who could sell materials.

Numerous critics of the conventions expressed concern about the flagrant enthusiasm of the convention directors for the sale of their own musical materials. Others were disturbed at what they considered to be the low level of musicality. But such an arbiter of taste as John Sullivan Dwight defended the conventions because he believed they were a proper vehicle for improving the musical taste of the public.[35] Henry S. Perkins, a prominent teacher and conductor of musical conventions, believed the convention to be a democratic institution, a bastion of the people's music. As late as 1887 he wrote, "Critics of the convention were an ignorant element quick to criticize American composers, singers and methods."[36] It is perhaps ironic that conventions were defended, on one hand, for being a means for improving the public's taste and, on the other hand, for being a bastion of the people's music.

The festivals and conventions were popular. Trains and steamboat companies offered half fare to those attending the music festivals. The happy singers journeyed homeward carrying new books and oratorios, some new hints on the teaching of music reading, and a rekindled enthusiasm for the art of vocal music. Thus, a population was gradually changing and cultivating its musicality.

The Western Vermont Musical Association was perhaps typical of the many that were formed during the mid-nineteenth century. In a resolution in 1858 the association exercised the conviction that "the cultivation of vocal music with appropriate instruction and instrumental accompaniment is a powerful auxiliary to promote good manners, good morrals [sic], intellectual culture, social happiness and especially peace and permanent Christian emotions." [37] The meeting of this association, in December 1858, remained in session for three days. It opened on the first day with a singing of "Old Hundred" and closed on the third day with a public concert.

The first and second hour of each day were opened with "exercises and vocalization pertaining to the cultivation of the voice." Articulation, expression, enunciation, and style were presented under the direction of the president, Mr. W. W. Partridge. The remainder of the time was spent in the practice of glees, songs, church psalmody, anthems, and choruses. The whole was "accompanied with such remarks and criticisms as the occasion suggested, calculated to improve the style and taste in Music and musical performance in general." [38] At the October 29, 1859, convention of the Western Vermont Musical Association at Middlebury, Vermont, the festival was under the direction of Professor Benjamin F. Baker of Boston. The attendance was reported to have been larger than any previous meeting. The exercises were carried on principally with the practice of sacred vocal music. "Efforts of Prof. Baker were directed at correcting pronunciation faults in tone, manner and drill requisite to the accomplishment of this object." In these efforts he was reported to have had "no superior."

He cannot tolerate the careless, sing-song, heartless manner of performance so common with superficial musicians, but strives to impress upon his pupils the important truth that one can not sing well, when he does not thoroughly feel, and distinctly appreciate. —The heart must be warmed, animated and aroused; the soul must be atuned in harmony with the sentiments embodied in music and language, or singing will be vapid and lifeless. [39]

Another example of this type of activity can be observed in Virginia. The first musical convention in that state was organized by the Richmond Sacred Music Society in 1855. The society engaged W. C. Van Meter, a distinguished New York teacher, and George F. Root. The convention lasted from March 17 to 20, 1855, with tickets at fifty cents rather than the usual two dollars. The first meeting of the convention at the Second Baptist Church of Richmond included choral singing, solos, and musical criticism by George F. Root. The members of the convention appointed a committee of three to investigate the condition of musical activities in Richmond and make recommendations for their improvement. Of the five recommendations, the first was that another convention should be held in December 1855 to establish the Southern Musical Institute for imparting a more thorough musical education "especially for preparing teachers and choristers for their important work." The convention was to last four weeks, and the chorus and singing classes were to use the same book as far as practical; the *Hallelujah*, a Lowell Mason publication, was recommended.[40] The convention also invited Mason and Root to take charge of the gathering and advised those in attendance to familiarize themselves with Mason's works.

The Richmond Sacred Music Society had been organized in 1840 with John Williams as president. Meeting frequently in the evenings for choral practice, the organization was a direct result of the constant singing school activity in the Second Presbyterian Church. Their first concert one year later included teachers and professional musicians who served as singing masters and combined their efforts with those of their students and other interested amateurs. The program included works of Mozart, Handel, Haydn, Beethoven, and Rossini.[41] Between the years 1844 and 1851 there was no evidence of concerts or other activities by the society, but in 1852 Mr. S. S. Stevens, a gentleman who had conducted singing classes for adults and children in Richmond since 1845, became conductor of the society. For ten years Stevens had taught both vocal and instrumental music as well as the "elements" at the Ladies Collegiate Seminary. Although the society gained the support of many interested citizens, many of its members felt that little improvement had been realized in the musical taste of the public or in the performance of church music.

But the musical convention did seem to be working toward that ideal. The second convention, under Mason and Root, was held from December 14 through 20, 1855, at the Baptist Church. The Southern Musical Institute reached the crest of its success with the two conventions, but it ceased to function following the second. Perhaps the society believed that its goals had been achieved. It made the public conscious of good music in the city and imported the best teachers from the North for purposes of demonstration. It helped create the interest and the need for the establishment of music instruction. Perhaps as a result of these efforts, there followed after 1855 a significant increase in the number of music teachers in Richmond.

But there were some in Richmond who resisted the arts, believing that the arts could not thrive when a country was in a stage of vigorous development. In 1851 John Peyton Little, a prominent Richmond physician, wrote:

In fact, the fine arts have never flourished in Virginia. They require for their sustenance not only wealth and taste, but age, and a certain state of society that cannot precisely be called decayed or debilitated; yet it is, at the same time, one where the vigor of the State is on the wane; . . . These arts do not flourish in an agricultural country like Virginia; they belong not to men, or to a community immersed in the cares of State, or employed in building up new commonwealths.[42]

The arts did make slow but steady headway, however, although not always with the same degree of enthusiasm in all sections of the country. In Richmond, the development of the arts, if not its public school system, related to the German immigration into that city. Richmond established a free, tax-supported public school system in 1869, soon after the city began its recovery from the Civil War, but unfortunately it did not introduce music into the curriculum until 1899.

CHAPTER VII

American Educational Thought in the Mid-Nineteenth Century

EDUCATIONAL PATTERNS IN THE SOUTH

THE SLAVERY-based society prior to the Civil War and the post–Civil War policy of segregation did much to impede development and expansion of the public school system in the South. Southern resources were inadequate to maintain two public school systems. A social system that grew out of the disastrous Reconstruction and that had its roots deep in the antebellum South sharply restricted innovation, as all changes had to be compatible with a biracial society.

When General Lee surrendered at Appomattox, public education was as disorganized as the Army of Northern Virginia. The colleges and academies were closed, and the punitive northern policies of the Reconstruction destroyed any basis for educational reform for at least a generation. In the face of human desolation and racial conflict, the development of the public schools was postponed. The southern states were helplessly in debt from the fraudulent and extravagant spending of the reconstructionist governments and were overburdened with millions of uneducated ex-slaves. For decades, the southern states remained in economic chaos.

The South, at the start of the Civil War, had made only a weak start at establishing a public school system whereas the North had made significant progress toward strengthening its public schools. Inadequate taxation, a tolerance for casual attendance, and—for the poor—the stigma of charity hampered the common school. The illiteracy of the Negro was almost universal while most white children were without formal schooling. The white establishment in the antebellum days viewed the education of the slave as dangerous and forbade it. Schools for Negro children at the close of the war were nonexistent.

The carpetbag governments following the Civil War did little to improve the situation. Graft and looting of funds ran rampant, and a succession of exorbitant debts barred the way to an adequate tax system for public school support. But constitutional mandates did come out of these legislatures for the creation of common school systems and a mandate for the education of blacks. As late as 1876, when the radical governments of the Reconstruction were finally ousted from the seats of power, the implementation of these mandates was a long way from fruition. Traditional southern conservatism and social polarization impeded educational reform and contributed to the disillusionment of reformers. In Richmond, Virginia, where a tax-supported public school system was introduced at the relatively early date of 1869, the comments of John Peyton Little demonstrate the spirited debate even before the Civil War about the merits of a tax-supported school system.

It is better to place education under church influence, than under that of the State. . . . The government cannot, itself, educate the community; it can only act by a cloud of irresponsible and ignorant school-masters; nor would it be right for it to exercise the power, if it possessed the ability of imparting a good education. . . . Schools originated and sustained by private, or denomination enterprise, are best; of such kinds are the schools in Richmond.[1]

Following the restoration of democratic rule, an immediate retrenchment was promulgated as a result of the extravagance of the carpetbag governments, and public education bore the brunt of the economies during those years. A state official in Virginia announced that "it [would be] better for the State to burn the schools," while another believed that the idea of using taxation to support free schools was socialistic and "imported here by a gang of carpetbaggers."[2] Under radical rule the longest school term attained was one hundred days, while it took until 1900 for the Democratic administrations to restore this figure as the mandated school term. The funds expended per pupil reflected the differences between regions; in 1890 the national average was $17.22 per pupil, and state expenditures ranged from $3.38 in South Carolina to $43.43 in Colorado.[3] As a result of the short-sighted policies of the governments, illiteracy, even among the white population, was increasing.

In Tennessee in 1872, Colonel James B. Killebrew, assistant superintendent of schools, discovered "that while the white population had increased only 13 per cent during the preceeding ten years, white illiteracy had increased 50 per cent."[4] Some southern states as late as 1897 were spending less than fifty cents per capita annually for the support of schools, and school teachers received in some southern states less money than the law allowed for the hire of convicts. One-fifth to one-fourth of the schoolhouses were log and without outhouses. Only 168 of the more than 7,000 schoolhouses in Virginia had provisions for ventilation and these were considered as models when suggestions were made for improvement. School terms of sixty to ninety days were common, but less than 60 percent of the children were enrolled in school and less than 40 percent attended daily.

Similar conditions afflicted the New England schools in the 1830s and 1840s, but the southern states were facing these problems in the last decade of the nineteenth century. It is reasonable to suppose that an expanded list of course offerings was almost impossible when the school systems were in such a state and when the limited curriculum was taught by barely qualified, often inept teachers. State departments of education were undeveloped, and state superintendents were no more than clerks or, in the words of Edgar Knight, "pitiful political appendages—politicians, soldiers, patriots, or patrioteers."[5] No public high schools of standard grade were in existence in the South, and no southern states had enacted any compulsory school attendance laws. When such proposals were suggested, the argument was returned that the time was not yet ripe for such an advanced step.

The few colleges and universities of the South were not much better and did not rank with those in other sections of the country. Contributions, which were beginning to pour into the coffers of higher education of the North, failed to reach those of the South. The colleges and universities of the South had only one-tenth of the productive funds of their counterparts in the North, only one-seventeenth of the scientific apparatus, and only one-seventh of the volumes in their libraries. The annual income of one private university alone in the East exceeded the annual income available for higher education in eight of the southern states. In the South no important publishing houses existed and few libraries, while illiteracy was almost universal among blacks and prevalent among whites. A war and a social condition produced economic destitution and bitter racial conflict, which perpetuated an educational inertia.

The most effective agencies to work toward the improvement of education in the South were the Conference for Education, the Southern Education Board, and the General Education Board. Through these organizations, and others like them, improvement began to take place. The campaign for the improvement in southern education won the immediate approval of the southern press and the support of the leading people who were engaged in school work in the South. College and university professors, lawyers, and businessmen—all builders of public opinion—supported an improvement in what was by the 1890s an embarrassment to the region. The practical problems of the schools were discussed in the same manner and terms that were argued so effectively sixty years earlier in Massachusetts by Horace Mann and in Connecticut by Henry Barnard. Better buildings, increased school funds, and better trained and certified teachers were necessary. People discussed the ways and means for the improvement in education. Popular education in the South was a subject whose time had come. By 1903 the General Education Board was formed for the purpose of coordinating efforts with the Southern Education Board, which was responsible for the investigation and collection of data concerning the educational conditions in the South and the rendering of financial assistance within the limitations of the board's finances.

The South was beginning to extricate itself from the educational morass brought about by its political, cultural, and economic disasters. The North, in turn, was an industrial and economic giant, benefiting from the common school reform established in the years prior to the war and expanding the curriculum of the common school system not only in vocal music but in the arts and sciences as well.

IN SEARCH OF A PHILOSOPHY

The post–Civil War years saw the rapid transition from a predominantly rural and agricultural society to an urban and industrial way of life. Monopolistic corporations brought about new ways of producing and distributing goods. Social and cultural problems of both the North and the South would erupt and would, in time, be reflected in the educational aspirations and the changing culture of the people. New approaches to complex public issues would require governmental innovation as large numbers of immigrants poured from Europe into America's teeming tenements and as the end of the western frontier closed a time-honored escape route.

American educational thought was still influenced from abroad. Pestalozzian ideas flowed into this country after 1865 and affected the teaching methods used in the normal schools. But memoriter learning was still a conspicuous part of education though much lip service was paid to the influence of Pestalozzianism. It took the combined philosophical efforts of Johann Friedrich Herbart and Herbert Spencer, followed by John Dewey, before rote or memoriter learning retreated from the schools of the nation.

Herbart (1776–1841), one of the first educational psychologists and one largely responsible for discrediting the concept of faculty psychology, was the ideal scholar-pedagogue. Appointed to the chair in philosophy at the University of Konigsberg (a chair made famous by Immanuel Kant), he lectured for twenty-five years, wrote *Text-book in Psychology* (1816) and *Psychology as a Science* (1824), and conducted pedagogical seminars and a small practice school for students preparing to teach.

Herbart believed that the primary aim of education was moral development, the production of good men of moral stature. He separated psychology into a distinct branch apart from metaphysics. Education would develop into a science through his efforts. "Those . . . who have no true psychological insight," he wrote, "rarely understand anything of education."[6]

Herbart believed that interest was an essential component of learning, which, if not present spontaneously, should be introduced artificially by the teacher. Ideas would be self-activating and induced through association.* His translation from theory into practice involved four important "steps of instruction," namely, clearness, association, system, and method.[7] He emphasized the importance of teaching skill rather than mental discipline. Herbartian disciples formalized the great psychologist's methodology, but Herbart himself was more flexible. He never regarded his systematic method as rigid.

Herbartian concepts were popularized in the United States by several Americans, notably by Charles DeGarmo and Charles and Frank McMurry who traveled to Germany and studied the Herbartian practices at Jena. Upon returning to the United States, they published textbooks based upon Herbartian psychology, which were rather widely used in the normal schools of the country. DeGarmo's *Essentials of Method*, appearing in 1889, was widely read, and Charles McMurry published his *The Elements of General Method Based on the Principles of Herbart* in 1892. Educators were intrigued by the psychologizing of instruction and attached themselves to the trappings of Herbartian terminology. The result was a new interest in a methodology of secondary school teaching and a stimulation of studies delving into the nature of the learning process, all of which helped to discredit the concept of faculty psychology. Herbartianism "might well have marked the beginning of the scientific study of education in the United States."[8]

With the work of Herbert Spencer (1820–1903), the scientific emphasis on the problems of education arrived in earnest. There appears to be some controversy concerning the actual impact of the work of Herbert Spencer on education in the United States. A. Theodore Tellstrom quotes Harvard's Charles Eliot as crediting Spencer's thought with having had a distinct, but unconscious, influence upon American education.[9] Perhaps the philosophy of Spencer reflected the American ideals of dynamic pragmatism and the frontiersman's utilitarianism. His ideas were couched in the

---

* Herbart's concepts of *apperception*—that is, the understanding of a new idea from its context or the understanding of new words or experiences through their relationship to other ideas—are not accepted by modern psychologists, at least in the original terms of their author. Herbart's concept recognized no creative thoughts or no essentially new ideas. Intellectual creativity merely meant the synthesis of ideas on a higher level.

guise of the scientific. Reluctant to attribute ideas to a doctrinaire source, American educators would not easily credit Spencer.

Nineteenth-century man came under the influence of the Darwinian concept of man's infinite perfectability. The means toward this perfectability was through science or the "scientific," a concept pioneered by Bacon and carried on through the nineteenth century and passed down to the present day. Darwinian philosophy stressed evolutionary growth. The theory of biological growth encouraged child development and helped undermine the rigidity of the traditional classroom. The older theology was challenged, and the idea of an immutable social order was repudiated. Darwin's concepts led to the idea of infinite progress, both socially and biologically.

Spencer bitterly attacked the existing practices in education. He found the same catechistic and rote learning processes in England in the nineteenth century as Heinrich Pestalozzi found in the German and Swiss education of the eighteenth century. Little changed in methodology as one educational orthodoxy replaced another.

As a contrast to rote learning, Spencer would have the children demonstrate their own inferences from a set of circumstances. They should be *told* as little as possible and induced to *discover* as much as possible. He favored physical education, which coincided with Rousseau's naturalism, while his object teaching followed that of Pestalozzi. He was a great pioneer of progressivism in education and did much in anticipation of John Dewey. Spencer's general aim of education was moral training and included five important activities: one, those leading to self-preservation; two, those essential for self-support; three, those concerned with child-rearing and parenthood; four, those necessary for good citizenship; and, five, those relevant to leisure time. Spencer termed his philosophy synthetic because it attempted to establish a set of principles which could be "verified empirically by science."[10] Education, in short, was preparation for life.

Though sympathetic to the theories of Pestalozzi, Spencer was deeply disturbed over the abuses that passed in the name of the great Swiss educator.

In practice, the Pestalozzian system seems scarcely to have fulfilled the promise of its theory. We hear of children not at all interested in its lessons,—disgusted with them rather; and, so far as we can gather, the

Pestalozzian schools have not turned out any unusual proportion of distinguished men,—if even they have reached the average. We are not surprised at this. The success of any appliance depends mainly upon the intelligence with which it is used. It is a trite remark, that, having the choicest tools, an unskillful artisan will botch his work; and bad teachers will fail even with the best methods.[11]

Spencer's own theories were more than a little related to Pestalozzian ideals. In a criticism of what Spencer regarded as standard teaching practice he charged that

nearly every subject dealt with is arranged in abnormal order: definitions and rules, and principles being put first, instead of being disclosed, as they are in the order of nature, through the study of cases. And then, pervading the whole, is the vicious system of rote learning—a system of sacrificing the spirit to the letter.[12]

How could music education have thrived and prospered with the country eagerly reading, digesting, and experimenting with the educational concerns of Spencer? The answers seemed linked to the entire psychological and pedagogical amalgam that is American education. American educators have traditionally appeared enthusiastic about various educational messiahs who have materialized from time to time. But historically the choices have not been many. Subjects have been either organized by the teacher for the alleged good of the children, or much of the same curriculum has been left to be discovered by the child. The process could be either pleasant or unpleasant depending upon a variety of circumstances within the educational environment. Teachers may pay lip service to a philosophical point of view while changing little of their instructional routine. Lowell Mason's initial concept of Pestalozzianism followed this pattern. Rather than telling the students the basic theoretical information to be memorized, Mason, and of course many others, only altered the order of the subject matter and substituted questions and answers. The answers were not the children's responses to the musical stimuli but prearranged teacher-conceived answers that were to be memorized by the children. The philosophical change appears slight. But Lowell Mason was a successful teacher and, like so many others, succeeded irrespective of method.

As Pestalozzianism was defined for the convenience and interpretation of various educators, so Spencer's concept of "scientific"

education was defined so broadly by Spencer himself as to fit almost any method of education and included the arts which were
recommended by Spencer. He approached music education from
the point of view of a critic.

But perhaps it will suffice to instance the swarms of worthless ballads
that infest drawing-rooms, as compositions which science would forbid.
They sin against science by setting to music ideas that are not emotional
enough to prompt musical expression; and they also sin against science
by using musical phrases that have no natural relation to the ideas expressed; even where these are emotional. And to say they are untrue, is to
say they are unscientific.[13]

Spencer's idea of "science" no longer implies a method but is
here related to truth or philosophical realism. The philosopher is
troubled over the nature of popular taste, which is always fashionable to disparage. But to say what is true or untrue in regard to
art and to call the former science and the latter not becomes very
dangerous to education and to art. Its execution becomes censor-
ship. Spencer's understanding of Chinese art demonstrates these
dangers. Not at all a prophet he shows a Kiplingesque perversion
of an artistic "white man's burden."

In what consists the grotesqueness of Chinese pictures, unless in their
utter disregard of the laws of appearance—in their absurd linear perspective, and their want of aerial perspective?[14]

Spencer favored the inclusion of the arts in the curriculum of the
schools, but he was careful to give them a secondary role. He believed that the fine arts and belles lettres represented the efflores-
cence of civilization, and "should be wholly subordinate to that
knowledge and discipline in which civilization rests. *As they occupy the leisure part of life, so should they occupy the leisure part
of education.*"[15]

Of course Spencer was not entirely anti-art. He also said that
"without painting, sculpture, music, poetry, and the emotions produced by natural beauty of every kind, life would lose half its
beauty."[16] But that the arts should be elevated to the level of equality with more practical subjects and studied with a dignified academic posture seemed not to have been in Spencer's scheme of
things. As a divergence from the more important subjects, Spencer
advocated, "short breaks during the school hours, excursions into
the country, amusing lectures, [and] choral sings."[17]

It had become axiomatic during the nineteenth century that the study of music would make more efficient the study of the academic curriculum. Once established it only became necessary to prove that its pursuance was predicated on scientific principles. As these principles were vague and contradictory, and as music itself was universally considered an attraction in those schools in which it was taught, then the defense of the art, whether on aesthetic or ancillary grounds, was ordinarily successful. It was only necessary for educators—music or classroom, nineteenth century or now— to repeat the currently popular catchphrases to take part in what has become an almost continual process of reform in the schools. Music was growing in popularity as a school subject, and all gradations of methodology during the latter half of the nineteenth century were perceived by their authors as "scientific."

CHAPTER VIII

Music in the Private Academies and Select Schools

T HE FORMAL training of music teachers passed from the con ventions and institutes to the ever-growing normal schools and private academies. These arose not only to meet the needs of a population seeking an adequate secondary education but also to train teachers. In 1800 there were 102 academies in existence; fifty years later the number had increased to 6,083. Of these, 1,907 were in New England.[1] During the nineteenth century these schools were the backbone of secondary education in America.

Not all academies developed in the same way. The first such schools were for young men; not until later were separate schools for girls founded. In rural areas or in sections of the country where nonboarding schools were difficult to maintain, coeducational institutions were started. The institutions took on various names such as seminaries, female academies, college institutes, or public academies.

The academies differed from the Latin grammar schools and the small private schools of the day. These academies were often boarding schools which were supported variously, mostly by philanthropic endowment, partly through tuition fees, and occasionally through limited state funds. Ordinarily there was a board of trustees that hired a principal who, in general, supervised all aspects of the school. In many instances the principal had much discretionary authority in matters of curriculum and was often responsible for attracting students to the school. Advertisements appeared almost everywhere and each school claimed to provide "thorough" and "scientific" instruction. School catalogs were distributed generously describing the various offerings, listing the teachers, and discussing the objectives and facilities of the school.

The curricula of the academies varied widely. The classical elements of the Latin schools were combined with a more utilitarian content. They catered to a new middle class that required a wide and diversified curriculum. In New York between 1787 and 1900, over a hundred different subjects were offered at one time or another. The core of the curriculum was the study of English grammar and literature. Science became popular early in the century along with courses in "natural philosophy" (almost a general science course), astronomy, chemistry, and botany. The study of geography became popular later in the century as did American history.

Music was added to the curriculum under one or more special teachers. As the music teachers ordinarily received their fees directly from the students who enrolled in the courses, it became necessary only to find a willing teacher of music in the area. The music offerings were undoubtedly popular as schools often competed with one another in the number and scope of these courses. Some gradually increased their offerings until the school began to resemble a conservatory of music.

The extensive curriculum and the popularity of these privately supported educational ventures demonstrated a strong practical and democratic leaning. Such schools offered a terminal education for those who had no thought of attending college. It was a viable institution between the limited-function Latin school and a comprehensive high school. It prepared its students for a changing business and commercial world. A tuition fee was required, but in many schools it was low—no more than a few dollars per term—and many schools allowed children from the same family to attend at reduced charges. All but the poorest of families could afford these schools if they desired.

MUSIC IN THE PRIVATE SCHOOLS AND ACADEMIES OF NEW ENGLAND

Records of music instruction exist from some of the earliest academies. In 1778 Samuel Phillips, Jr., and his uncle John Phillips founded an academy at Andover, Massachusetts, and at Exeter, New Hampshire three years later. Both institutions offered music instruction from their inception. The official "Act of Incorporation" dated October 4, 1780, at Andover reveals the importance of music to the founders of the school.

That there be and hereby is established in the town of Andover, and County of Essex, an Academy, by the name of *Phillips Academy*, for the purpose of promoting true piety and virtue, and for the education of youth, in the English, Latin, and Greek languages, together with Writing, Arithmetic, Music and the art of Speaking; also practical Geometry, Logic, and Geography, and such other of the liberal Arts and Sciences, or Languages, as opportunity hereafter permits, and as the Trustees, hereinafter provided, shall direct.[2]

The Exeter Academy had the same purpose as its sister institution in Andover.

In 1820 the Westfield Academy in Massachusetts provided music for their students "if desired." The Morsom Academy in Massachusetts offered music at least from 1811 to 1816 as one of the trustees of the school was the Reverend Samuel Willard, compiler of the *Deerfield Collection of Sacred Music*. The American Literary, Scientific, and Military Academy, at Norwich, Vermont, made music available at a special fee. Other optional courses were Hebrew, French, and fencing. In 1825 Captain Alden Partridge, the school's superintendent, reported that both fencing and music were popular and that the students made good progress in these subjects.

Music was considered a particularly appropriate subject in private schools for young ladies. The Young Ladies Academy of Philadelphia was founded in 1786 by John Poor who later compiled a tune book especially for his students.[3] Benjamin Rush, one of the trustees of this institution, a professor of chemistry at the University of Pennsylvania, and a signer of the Declaration of Independence described the course of study of the young ladies. The girls studied English, writing, bookkeeping, geography, vocal music, dancing, history, travel accounts, poetry, essays, and the Christian religion. Rush said that "vocal music should never be neglected in the education of a young lady in this country. Besides preparing her to join in that part of public worship which consists of psalmody, it will enable her to soothe the cares of domestic life."[4]

Interestingly enough, Rush did not approve the study of instrumental music as he believed that its cultivation would take too much time and would cost too much. This point of view was challenged, however, by John Swanwick, another trustee of the academy, who delivered an address at the quarterly examinations October 31, 1787, and gave his approval of the study of both vocal and instrumental music in the education of the young ladies.

In 1803 the trustees of the Freyburg Academy, in Maine, recorded that "in addition to the sciences now taught in this Academy, that music, instrumental and vocal be attended to by those students who have talents and inclination to improve them, under such regulations as this Board with the advice of the Instructor shall see fit to establish."[5] The board of trustees of that institution approved the purchase of two flutes and two violins for the students.

The academies also became the training ground for common school teachers and often included a class in school-keeping. In those schools that not only offered courses in music but also courses in school management, it is reasonable to suppose that some of the music students became the music teachers of the next generation.

The Contributions of Samuel Read Hall

The first normal school was opened at Concord, Vermont, on March 11, 1823, by the Reverend Samuel Read Hall. Prior to this time, there had been a few abortive efforts. Jacob Eddy, a Quaker and town clerk of Danbury, Vermont, held a fall term for the training of teachers in the 1780s, but no information is now available on how long this school remained open.[6] Also, in an attempt to furnish New Hampshire with a regular supply of well-qualified teachers, Mr. Joseph Noyes of Franklin, New Hampshire, founded an institution named the Instructor's School. Its principal for many years was Captain Benjamin M. Tyler, a graduate of the Norwich, Vermont, military school. During the spring and autumn terms a teachers' class was formed. The school was successful for only a short time as it lacked a satisfactory endowment and was, perhaps, ahead of its time.[7] Perhaps in response to the influence of Lowell Mason, Hall became one of the early advocates of the teaching of vocal music in the common schools. Hall moved to Concord in 1822. The population of Concord was 806 people, most of whom were farmers. The professional men of the town consisted of an attorney, a doctor, and a minister. The town with its 806 citizens tried to support nine school districts, seven of which had schoolhouses. Very much affected by the impotent district school system, Hall immediately set about to effect an improvement in the education of the town.

Hall discovered that the time of the children was largely wasted because of the deficiencies of the teachers. He believed that in no way could he accomplish more for the children of his community than to teach the teachers. A course of study was arranged and teachers' classes formed during the first year; the next year a regular normal course was instituted. Lectures on school-keeping were given during the spring and autumn of each year and were intended to illustrate some better methods of teaching and classroom management. One year later, in exchange for an agreement that Hall would remain in Concord as pastor, the town agreed to allow Hall to conduct a school for the instruction of those who wished to become teachers.

On March 11, 1823, Samuel Read Hall opened his school for the training of teachers in his own home. Soon outgrowing its quarters, the Columbian School (as it was called) moved to a vacant room above the general store. In time these quarters also proved inadequate and Hall turned to the citizens of Concord for help. A building was erected on the low ground across the road from the Congregational Church—the place of the normal school. The two-story building, constructed of brick and heated by a sheet-iron stove, was incorporated as the Concord Academy with Hall and seven others acting as the board of trustees.

Hall admitted a class of very young people who served as models in demonstrations. He published a book, *Lectures on School-Keeping* in 1829, which was one of the earliest books published on that subject in the United States and by far the most influential book of its kind.[8]

Hall's book was immediately successful. Within two weeks every copy of the first edition was sold. A second edition was equally popular. In May 1832, James Wadsworth, commissioner of education in New York State, "placed an order for 10,000 copies of the *Lectures on School-Keeping* and authorized a copy to be placed in the hands of the trustees of every school district in the state."[9]

In 1829, about the time of the publication of the *Lectures on School-Keeping*, the trustees of the Phillips Academy at Andover, Massachusetts, were looking for a principal to head a new English department in their school. Hall's book aroused sufficient enthusiasm that the trustees of the school offered the position to Hall. Concerned about his continually poor health, Hall at first declined the offer but soon changed his mind and accepted the appointment in the fall of 1830.

At this time Phillips Academy was divided into three departments, the Normal or Teachers Department, the General Department designed to prepare young men for business, and the Boys Department or Model School. The teachers' department was only a nominal part of the academy and was administered as a separate institution. Its object was to "afford the means of a thorough scientific and practical education, preparatory to the profession of teaching." [10] Hall was obliged to run this institution according to his own judgment. He was responsible for both the length and content of the courses of instruction. In the third term of their senior year, students attended Hall's course on the art of teaching.

In 1832, six years before the great Hawes school experiment, Hall published his *Lectures to Female Teachers on School-Keeping* at Andover. No direct evidence exists to prove a connection between these lectures and Hall's daily contributions to his classes, but it might be guessed that Hall's students in the 1830s at Andover received some instruction in the values and methods of vocal music teaching in the common schools. Hall seemed fully conscious of the influence of the Boston Academy of Music and the influence of William Bradbury and his admonitions concerning the teaching of vocal music in the schools.

If these observations are correct, Hall's students might have heard the following during his lectures:

It is very important that the instructors of young children should be able to sing. All, who have ever seen the operations of a well conducted Infant School, will need no argument on this point. But it may be proper to refer others to the interest, which even infants universally manifest in hearing musick. The "lullaby" of the mother or nurse, is one of the most grateful sounds, that falls on the young child's ear. It calms his agitated feelings, and lulls him to repose, or causes him still to slumber after the demands of nature have been satisfied.

If the child is quieted and pleased, by merely *hearing* the notes of musick from others; will he not be much more delighted when he can tune his own voice to sound these strains? [11]

Hall discussed the values of teaching music by rote, a system that appeared to have had its roots in the Pestalozzian concept of *anschauung*.

Sounds, like colours, cannot be described in words. They must be taught by examples, patiently repeated and carefully attended to, until the ear is familiar with them; and gradually extended, as its powers of discrimination are increased. I have known cases in which persons who said they could not distinguish one note from another, have found no difficulty in doing it, as soon as a few notes had been sounded before them, and the use of the appropriate terms had been illustrated. . . .

. . . Whoever heard of an individual who spent whole days, for several years together, in singing, who did not find an ear for it? But we have few examples of men who pronounce a foreign language without obvious errors, even after years of study or residence in a country where they speak it incessantly. Until we are presented with individuals who were taught musick as they were taught language, from their childhood, and who still cannot distinguish or imitate musical sounds, there is no reason for admitting that any considerable number of persons are naturally destitute of an ear for musick. [12]

Hall quotes an unidentified writer in the *Education Reporter*, a periodical of his day, on the methods desirable in the instruction of vocal music:

The object is not to give fifty or sixty children a system of thorough instruction and knowledge in the theory and practice of sacred music;— that is the business of a life. And secondly, the object is to diffuse among them so much knowledge, taste, skill and love for the employment, *as shall make them wish to pursue it*. We are aware that in the arts of life, we want the *principles* of operation; and not a list of almost unmeaning technicalities; and they surely will be such to those who are not skilled in the practical part of any art or business, although they may be extremely useful to a skillful operative, as means of generalization and as they offer greater facilities for understanding the whole of his subject in every relation. [13]

Hall was astute in his observations on how children learn. His interests were sufficiently universal that there was hardly a school subject that escaped his interest. In 1836 Hall prepared *A School History of the United States*, jointly with A. R. Baker of Andover, the first book to emphasize the chronological method of teaching history and the first book to contain a chronological chart to accomplish this end. In the same period as *Lectures to Female Teachers*, Hall wrote *The School Arithmetic*, *The Child's Friend*, and *The Teacher's Gift*.

Hall worked hard for the improvement of schools in Massachusetts. In 1832 he founded the School Agent Society, an organization dedicated to the improvement of education in New England and New York. The society sent eight agents into these regions, and circulars were published in the hope of improving the status of the common schools in these areas. In 1834 the headquarters of the organization was shifted to Boston where the name of the group was changed to the American School Society. Unfortunately the society lacked funds and eventually ceased to exist. The work was sufficiently influential, however, to awaken the people of Massachusetts to the needs of the common schools. Three years later, Horace Mann was appointed secretary to the State Board of Education of that state. In 1836 Hall, with George B. Emerson and E. A. Andrews, wrote a "memorial on the superintendent of common schools." This paper was read before the state legislature of Massachusetts. The authors advocated the establishment of a state board of education and a superintendent of common schools. Through this letter and through the work of the American School Society and the American Institute of Instruction (another society of which Hall was a founder), the legislature of Massachusetts enacted the "Act of 1837," which set the stage for the reform of the common school. Only at a later date were other states to follow Massachusett's lead.

In Hall's last years, a life-long interest in geology culminated in the publication of the *Alphabet of Geology*, or *First Lessons in Geology and Mineralogy*, believed to be the first of its kind ever published. The text answered a need at a time when geology as a school subject was growing rapidly throughout New England.[14]

On June 24, 1877, Hall died and was buried at Croydon, New Hampshire, his native village. His work in the preparation of teachers will never be forgotten, but his contributions to the early history of music education deserve to be better understood and more fully appreciated.

It is significant that Hall's contributions to the teaching of vocal music were aimed at the instruction of young ladies. Hall's earlier book, *Lectures on School-Keeping,* did not mention the instruction of music at all. One wonders whether Hall had any thoughts on the teaching of vocal music at this time or whether instruction in music was considered to be so exclusively the province of female education that Hall would not deem it appropriate to mention it in relation to the instruction of both sexes. Another important consideration in this connection involves the dates of Hall's two volumes on teaching, which predate Lowell Mason's Boston school experiment. *Lectures on School-Keeping* bears an 1829 imprint and was written while Hall was still in Vermont, and *Lectures to Female Teachers* bears an 1832 imprint and was most likely written at Andover where Hall had the opportunity to become acquainted with the educational work of William Woodbridge and Lowell Mason.

Hall was not alone, of course, in his concern for the training of teachers and in his early recognition of the values of music in the common schools. The academies, particularly, were charged with the responsibility of training teachers not only for the common schools but for the academies as well. Almost everywhere in the country where academies and select schools operated, teachers' classes were organized. By modern standards such a single teachers' course would be inadequate, but at the time it was the only means available to supply the country with the needed teachers.

Hall himself reported that he received no benefits of instruction on how to teach:

Permit me to remark here, that for what I attempt to impart to you, I am myself indebted principally to experience. When I entered the same field of labor, in 1816, there was scarcely a paragraph in the weekly newspaper, or a single book or even a tract within my knowledge, intended to aid the teacher in knowing how to instruct and govern a school.[15]

New Hampshire had more than twenty-six-hundred schools in the 1820s, but no record of arrangements for the special training of teachers can be found. Those committees whose job it was to hire teachers for their schools staffed them as best they could—with college students needing to earn their tuition for a year or two; with young women of good general education; and with others who by "reason of fullness of information, special tact, zeal and earnest effort, became admirable teachers."

The private academies and select schools for young ladies became the early institutions for the training of teachers in the country. Beginning around the middle of the century, these private schools developed a spirited competition with one another in the variety and the thoroughness of their instruction. As courses in music proved to be popular with the students, and presumably their parents, such courses appeared with greater frequency in the catalogs of these institutions.

In the 1850s a teachers' course at the St. Johnsbury, Vermont, Academy was organized, and as this school also offered music courses, one can surmise that this institution along with so many others like it acted to produce the next generation of music teachers.

The course of study will include the higher English branches, a thorough training of classes in the elementary studies, with reference both to the acquisition of an accurate knowledge of the same, and the proper methods of teaching them to others.

An Experimental Class will be formed, which will recite under the supervision of the Principal, but in which each member of the class will, in turn, act as teacher, the design being to furnish the members with the opportunity to try their capacity to teach, and to perform successfully this chief duty incumbent on them in the School Room.

There will be frequent Lectures and Discussions, in connection with the Recitations, upon Modes of Teaching, Government of Schools, and other topics relating to the Teacher's calling.[16]

In the Bakersfield Academy, Vermont, catalog of 1854, a teachers' class was formed to meet twice per week during the fall and spring terms. "Special attention [was] paid to the *matter* and *manner* of teaching, and the best method of governing Common Schools."[17]

The Contributions of Others

Antedating the early efforts of Samuel Read Hall to train teachers at Concord, Vermont, Emma Willard opened a female school in Vermont. No branch of female education lacked interest to Willard. She engaged in teacher training, in a rather rudimentary sense, and from her later writings, it seems that music education played a role in her school. The school was opened in her own residence in 1814, the year her "Plan for Female Education" was written. The plan was later addressed to the New York state legislature and was conceived as a basis for reform in the education of women. Although her school was not organized primarily for the purpose of training teachers, this training did take place. Early in the nineteenth century Willard described how this was done. "I then betook myself to the training of teachers. In this way I continued to educate and send forth teachers, until 200 had gone from the Troy seminary before one was educated in any public normal school in the United States."[18]

Willard's early ideas of the purpose of music in her schools tended to be rudimentary: "I called all my girls onto the floor, and arranged them two and two, in a long row for a contradance; and while those who could sing would strike up some stirring tune, I, with one of the girls for a partner, would lead down the dance, and soon have them all in rapid motion. After which we went to our school exercises again."[19] The function of these exercises was to keep warm, a not unusual problem in the early schools of New England. But later when Willard addressed the legislature of New York with an articulate plea for equal educational rights for women, her presentation to the all-male assemblage mixed modesty with a defense of the arts.

I should not consider it an essential point, that the music of a lady's piano should rival that of her master's; or that her drawing room should be decorated with her own paintings, rather than those of others; but it is the intrinsic advantage, which she might derive from the refinement of herself, that would induce me to recommend to her, an attention to these elegant pursuits. The harmony of sound, has a tendency to produce a correspondent harmony of soul; and that art, which obliges us to study nature, in order to imitate her, often enkindles the latent spark of taste—of sensibility for her beauties, till it glows to adoration for their author, and a refined love of all his works.[20]

As female seminaries sprang up in all parts of the country and more academies opened their doors to young ladies (if only to relieve their ever-present financial stringencies), increasing numbers of young ladies from these institutions assumed teaching responsibilities in the nation's schools. As art and music played such an important role in the curricula of these academies and select schools, it can be surmised that instruction in the arts was implemented by these teachers. The subjects were taught without apology at these schools and seemingly with a clear understanding of their true place in the educational spectrum.

One such school where the so-called ornamental subjects were introduced without apology was the Burlington Female Seminary in Burlington, Vermont. This seminary, like so many others like it in the country, taught music with conviction. Providing inspiration and impetus to the seminary was the Reverend John K. Converse. The young minister felt the need for a female seminary in Burlington soon after his arrival in that town in 1832. The town enjoyed a university, but few local residents attended. No local schools for young ladies could be found, and parents of means had to send their daughters elsewhere for an education.

Converse called a meeting of several prominent citizens of Burlington one snowy February evening. He gave no indication of the purpose for the meeting but all who were invited attended, moved by curiosity and interest. Converse broached the subject of a female seminary with such eloquence and enthusiasm that subscriptions for aid were soon forthcoming.

The school experienced an initial success, but soon the patronage decreased and the school seemed on the verge of closing. Converse then took over the principalship himself, purchased additional buildings, and worked to reinvigorate the school. His daughter wrote that he "commenced with ten pupils, before the term was half out he had nearly doubled the number. Before three years had passed he had nearly one hundred pupils, and over fifty in the music-class alone."[21]

Converse remained principal of the seminary for some twenty-five years, and during that time he educated nearly three thousand young women. He was not only an able administrator but he loved and practiced music throughout his life. Such a talent enhanced his church services and established a vigorous music program at the seminary. He would procure lecturers at his own expense to deliver addresses in art, philosophy, and music. He would often sing in the evenings, accompanied at the piano by his wife, and he enjoyed playing his flute.

Every catalog of the seminary reflects the commitment of its principal to music. The 1838 catalog was typical.

CONDITIONS OF ADMITTANCE

Boarders per annum, $140, or $70 per term, half payable in advance. This sum entitles the pupil to board, lodging, room rent, fire, lights, etc., and tuition in any or all branches included in the extensive course of English studies pursued in the Seminary, and Latin. Extra charges are made for music, including practice, $12 Drawing, $5 French, $3 Singing, $1 for piano pupils, $2 for others. Pupils are not received for a shorter period than one quarter, unless specified on entrance. Deviation from this rule is made in case of sickness.[22]

Those pupils who selected music—and astonishing numbers did—were given careful instruction within the framework of a well-organized curriculum. In the 1850–1851 catalog of the seminary 107 young ladies were reported to have taken music.

In order that young Ladies may attain the true ends of musical instruction, they should be taught Thorough Bass, and also Vocal Music, that they may accompany the Piano with the voice. We have therefore added Thorough Bass and Vocal Music to the usual lessons on the Piano, and the charge for the whole is $10 per Quarter.

A small deduction is made from the above charges in the case of two pupils coming from the same family and rooming together for one Term or more.

No other charges, not here specified, are ever made in the term bills, except a trifle for carriages to and from church, in unpleasant weather, and for printing the annual catalogue.[23]

Only about fifteen miles from the Burlington Female Seminary was the Essex Academy. The school prided itself on its music program and made provisions for its study from the earliest days of the institution. The music instruction at all private academies was sufficiently popular that in the times of financial exigencies (which were fairly often), the schools would turn to music in the hope of attracting students to the schools. The Essex Academy was no exception. In the school catalog for 1870 is the following:

MUSIC

Special advantages are afforded for a thorough study of music. The best teachers to be procured are employed in this department, whose object it is not to teach the pupils to dash off a few trashy pieces to astonish the ears of admiring friends, but to have them well grounded in the rudiments, and to have each difficulty thoroughly mastered before they are allowed to proceed. Parents wishing to have their children obtain a thorough and complete musical education will do well to patronize this school.

That year the catalog of the school presents a structured program for voice and piano.

FIRST YEAR (*Piano*)

Five finger exercises—major scales—exercises from Richardson, Bertini—or Beyer—Czerney's First Studies; Four pieces thoroughly learned, two from memory.

VOCAL

Studies of the Registers, Variations of the scale, Book first Concone's Fifth Lessons or equivalent. Eight songs, three of which must be classical.

SECOND YEAR (*Piano*)

Major and Minor Scales, Arpeggio Chords, Chromatic Scales, Czerney's Exercises in velocity, Book First and Second Kohler's Special Studies, Six pieces, three from memory, Public playing.

VOCAL

Chromatic Scale, Arpeggio, Portamento, Book 2nd Concone's Fifty Lessons or equivalent, Eight pieces chiefly classical.

THIRD YEAR (*Piano*)

Scales in thirds and sixths, Arpeggio Chords, Double notes, Czerney's Finishing Exercises, Eight pieces, four from memory, including Symphonies by Mozart, Beethoven, etc., for four or eight hands, Public Playing.

VOCAL

Expression, Recitation, Exercises from Concone and Penseron. Twelve pieces, chiefly from Operas and Oratorios.[24]

East of the Essex Academy just a few miles from the state capital of Vermont was an institution priding itself on its fine educational product. One of the most respected academies in Vermont, the Barre Academy was incorporated by the legislature November 13, 1849. The academy building was completed in 1852, and that year the school opened. The principal of the academy, Jacob S. Spaulding, came to Barre with a reputation made by the successful management of the academy at Bakersfield, Vermont. Dr. Spaulding remained at Barre twenty-eight years. Without benefit of an endowment, he maintained a vigorous educational program. The list of faculty is of interest to our study.

INSTRUCTORS

J. S. Spaulding, A.M., L.L.D., Principal
Mr. C. H. Cook, assistant principal
Mr. D. G. Hill, assistant principal

Miss E. M. B. Felt, Preceptress and Teacher of Ornamentals
Mr. Irving Emerson, Teacher of Instrumental Music
Miss Alice L. Tenney, Teacher of Instrumental Music
Mr. J. M. Kent, Teacher of Penmanship
Mr. C. H. Cook, Teacher of Vocal Music
Miss A. L. Tenny, Teacher of Vocal Music
Mrs. B. M. Plimpton, Matron[25]

Three teachers out of eight were hired to teach only the arts, while two instructors did service both as music teachers and as teachers of academic subjects. It must be observed, however, that the special music teachers were expected to receive only the monies obtained from their pupils. The academies could not hope to underwrite the cost of such instruction. But the additional attraction of music and drawing to the school offerings, even if not always in the prescribed curriculum, helped the academy to prosper by drawing students.

Speaking in an article in the *Teacher's Voice* of March 1854, Z. K. Pangborn comments on the too low rate of tuition prevalent in the Vermont academies and obliquely refers to the cost of music instruction in these schools.*

In some schools, French, German, Italian, Penmanship, &c., are charged $1.00 extra. Besides these, Music, Vocal and Instrumental, and Painting, penciling and Embroidery are taught; but when it is remembered, that, in most cases, all the money received for instruction in these last named studies or accomplishments, as they are ordinarily called, is required to pay the salaries of the teachers who give the instruction in these branches, it will be seen that they offered no reliable income to the school, unless indeed an undue prominence is given to them, which is sometimes the case. It is usually the case that these accomplishments cost all they come to—sometimes more.[26]

Pangborn was as familiar with the various programs in the academies of that state as any person. He was a leader in the educational affairs of Vermont, and his publication *Teacher's Voice* appears to have been widely read during this period. His observations were most likely accurate. If it is true that instruction in music did not offer a reliable income for the school, it was also true that the music courses were a source of attraction to students and parents alike. If the academy that offered instruction in music

* Z. K. Pangborn was also the principal of the St. Albans Academy in Vermont.

became more desirable to pupils and their parents, then it must be supposed that there was a widespread desire and need to study music in the schools.

In the Vermont State School Report of 1858, instruction in music at the Barre Academy was commended.

In the Barre Academy, music is taught as regularly as any branch, and the session of the Institute was opened with music by the choir of the Academy, under the lead of Mr. I. N. Camp, the Assistant Teacher of the school and instructor in music, and such music as would go far to dissipate the doubts of the veriest sceptic as to the desirability of making vocal music an ordinary exercise in every public school where it can be done.[27]

It is difficult to know with precision just how the music instruction took place. The academies and select schools almost universally talked about the thoroughness of instruction. From contemporary accounts it must be believed that the more successful schools achieved that. A few of the schools published complete courses of instruction in music. These are sufficiently well thought-out that the modern reader cannot but be impressed at their scope. Those schools that did not publish such a curriculum can only allow us to guess or take the word of an alumnus who may have remembered, usually in glowing terms, the experiences of his youth.

MUSIC IN THE PRIVATE SCHOOLS OF RICHMOND, VIRGINIA

During the early nineteenth century, a thriving singing school movement in Richmond led directly to an increasing number of music courses in the private academies of the city. Successful singing masters and private music teachers were appointed to the faculties of these institutions. By 1830 almost every private school in Richmond included some phase of music instruction, with the singular exception being a classical school for boys.

While there were few Virginians concerned with music or musical development around 1800, the gradual expansion of music study paralleled the development and improvement of public performance. Churches assumed a major role, not only in the area of sacred music but in that of secular as well. As in New England, the church served as host for the singing schools and gradually included them in their Sabbath schools program.

Nevertheless there were many educated Virginians who ignored all possibilities for cultural development in their state. For them no place existed in their society for either public support of or instruction in the fine arts. They believed that only the private classical schools should be maintained. As a result, institutionalized music study emerged gradually in Richmond.

Instruction in music first appeared in the small private schools for girls. One of the earliest of these schools was the Fitzwhyllson's English School, operated by William Henry Fitzwhyllson from 1800 to 1824. A performer on the string bass, Fitzwhyllson was one of the founders of the Richmond Musical Soceity which presented popular concerts in Tanbark Hall.

In 1803 Mr. and Mrs. Cornillon's School offered the study of French and music. That same year a Mrs. Randolph's School advertised that music would be taught on demand. Music in the public sector of education was slow to develop during the first three decades of the century.

The Lancasterian schools, where older students were expected to teach younger, were introduced into Richmond in 1816. Although these schools did not teach music, they were generally well-received by the citizens of Richmond. Olson tells us that these schools produced good results and served to emphasize the value of free schools for the poor as well as for the financially secure. They seemed to awaken interest in popular education in Virginia and evolved into a tax-supported school system by 1869, an early date for such an achievement in the South.[28]

Between 1830 and 1845 a steady development in the instruction of music was paralleled by a corresponding improvement in the quality of public performance in Richmond. Increasing numbers of European performers augmented the city's concert life. A more cosmopolitan influence supplemented what was earlier an indigenous musical development. Foreign performers served to encourage rather than discourage resident musicians. Between 1812 and 1830 most compositions that were performed were by American composers. Between 1803 and 1845 musical taste had changed in favor of European composers. The later examples of the singing school in Richmond, beginning in the third decade of the century, have an aura of the Boston reform about it. By 1845 almost all singing activities were absorbed into the Sabbath school program, and references to Lowell Mason's *Manual of the Boston Academy* appear commonly in the newspapers of Richmond.

Perhaps the earliest published concern about music came in 1840 from the *Southern Literary Messenger* in an article written by its editor, T. W. White, entitled *Thoughts on Music*. White called music a necessity in the culture of any people. Referring to that music found in the churches and singing schools, he believed that music was good for the soul of any man.

About the middle of the century the German immigrants began to influence the musical life of Richmond. The Virginia Gesange-verein was organized in 1852, a singing society that was the first organization to make secular music a community enterprise in Richmond. By 1855 the Gesangeverein was presenting operas, choral works, and theatrical productions. Inspired by this orga-nization, other groups formed, such as the Mozart Society, the Wednesday Club, and the Sabbath Glee Club, all amateur groups. German performers and teachers took up residence in Rich-mond around in 1850. E. Loebman, William Grabau, Heinrich Schneider, C. W. Thilow, were some of the many. Loebman was a violinist associated with the armory band, and he played for balls and parties. Grabau, Schneider, and Thilow taught in "Lefebvre's School," a school reported to have had the best music instruc-tion.[29] Herbert P. Lefebvre was the proprietor of a private school in Richmond in 1852. The school offered music instruction of an unprecedented scope and quality for the city at this time. Of a fac-ulty of fourteen, six were teachers of music, a faculty which was considered the finest in the city.

By 1855, music instruction was still found most often in private schools for girls. Edward Valentine, a sculptor in Richmond, said that many of the city's residents believed that music was not a "logical study" for boys in the classical school. But boys did take private lessons from the many outstanding private teachers of the city.

Richmond of the 1850s had a population of forty thousand and could and did sponsor concerts by touring artists. At a Jenny Lind performance in 1850, ticket prices ran from $8 to $105 for a single ticket! By the latter half of the decade, music was accepted as both a serious and an ornamental study.

CHAPTER IX

Educational Growth and the Expansion of Music

THE EMERGENCE OF THE PUBLIC HIGH SCHOOL

HIGH SCHOOLS in the United States developed in a number of ways: some private academies on the brink of bankruptcy closed their doors one day and reopened them the next as public high schools; others were created specifically as high schools to fulfill a need; still others grew from common schools by virtue of expanded course offerings. For a period, some public high schools came under the control of colleges that sought to approve only those high schools they considered worthy. The high schools resisted this trend, however, and realigned with the common school and expanded their programs. Advanced subjects such as algebra, natural philosophy, and Latin were favored.

Public high schools appeared in Pennsylvania in the mid-1830s, perhaps as a result of the pioneering efforts in New England. While some early high schools were no more than private academies, there were genuine public high schools in Honesdale, Carlisle, and Norristown by 1836. Institutions with more extensive offerings were established just a few years later in Harrisburg, Lancaster, and York. The larger communities set up separate schools for boys and for girls, as was the custom in New England. Pennsylvania law required that any local high school that accepted the property of an academy must assume its educational obligations as well.

Many academies in Pennsylvania had received state funds upon the condition that all eligible children be provided with an education. By the end of the century there were one hundred schools in the state, most of which were in the larger towns. The school law of 1901 in Pennsylvania, authorized the creation of township and union high schools, giving impetus to the centralization of schools and paving the way toward the expansion of the high school concept in that state.

The high school in Middletown, Connecticut, came into being as a result of a special law of 1839 that gave the town permission to grade its schools. Although the town voted for the high school, only 252 children, half the number of children in the town between the ages of nine and sixteen, attended the school. It must be presumed that the remainder either attended a private school or did not attend any school. The new high school was conducted in a church basement, and, as was the custom, there was one department for boys and another for girls. The school became free in 1861, but in its early years it charged a fee of four dollars per year. Its early curriculum was not fixed, but it aimed to prepare some of its pupils for college and others for practical life. Within ten years, three curricula were established—an English, a classical, and a mathematical curriculum. Later a normal curriculum was added with courses in professional subjects, practice teaching, and a review of "the common school branches."

Like the high school of Middletown, Connecticut, most high schools developed slowly. Without strong antecedents, a new society struck out tentatively in new directions. Unwilling to copy the stratified high schools of Europe, which were committed to the perpetuation of a rigid class system, the high schools of America improvised pragmatic ways to meet the particular needs of Americans. Course offerings included business skills as well as Latin grammar. Later manual training and industrial arts were added. The schools were not wedded to an ideology but continued to be flexible, responding to the pressures of society.

As the public high school became more commonplace, it was only natural that instruction in vocal music be carried into these schools. Problems existed in the articulation of instruction between the grammar schools and the newly expanding public high schools. The issues of what to teach and on what level were addressed when the National Education Association established a forum from which to air these concerns. According to the minutes of the National Education Association in 1886, in the "Music Education Department," Mr. Aaron Gove, a superintendent from Denver, Colorado, requested information on the subject of managing a high school when "music plans have been often changed," and "when pupils come in from lower grades and when they come in from other schools."[1] N. Coe Stewart, an important music educator of this period, admonished the administrators and music teachers who treated high school students as beginners in music. He assured those in attendance that they were not.

Many of the problems of articulation between levels have now been bridged, but others remain intractable. The struggle to effect a suitable curriculum for high school students both in music and in general studies will be taken up in detail in a later chapter.

THE EXPANSION OF PUBLIC SCHOOL MUSIC

It is almost too easy for a historian to trace the emergence of public school music as it unfolded in Boston. Music did come early to Boston, and that city had the luck or foresight to employ some of the most gifted and influential music teachers of the nineteenth century. As we have seen, however, music education was not confined exclusively to the larger urban centers but spread throughout the country from the private academies and normal schools. But whether it be music, drawing, or geography, an enriched curriculum in the public schools had to await an adequate, tax-supported common school system. In general, music developed in the high school as the popularity of that institution grew.*

Two factors had to exist before music could become part of the common school curriculum. First, there had to be grass-roots support for an influential music teacher in the community. If this teacher, as, for instance, the case of Lowell Mason, was able to stimulate considerable public support for the "experiment" (as it was usually called), the introduction of music into the curriculum was successful. The second factor was a viable common school

---

* It is interesting that the city of Boston, which pioneered in the introduction of music in the grammar schools of that city, waited until 1864 before these opportunities were made available to the children at the primary level.

system. If a community insisted on as little an expenditure of tax dollars as possible, an expanded curriculum would have been impossible. The erstwhile promoter of an expanded music education would be driven into private teaching, a private academy, or a nonmusical occupation.

The introduction of vocal music into the school systems of the nation did not approach even deliberate speed until the last two decades of the century. In 1886 General John Eaton, the United States Commissioner of Education, reported that less than 250 school systems were teaching music regularly. During the next three years, however, a gain of 33 percent was recorded in the number of places employing special music teachers.

An important political institution, founded to advocate an expansion of the curriculum and to improve the general state of education, was the state teachers association. In Vermont, for example, a group of important educators met in Montpelier in 1850 to organize the Vermont Teachers Association. This association marked the beginning of a school reform movement in that state that was to have far-reaching results in both the improvement of common school education and in the vigorous promotion of an expanded curriculum in the common schools. The association advocated the inclusion of vocal music as a regular course of instruction almost twenty years before such programs began to emerge in the schools of the state. The *Vermont Chronicle* contained the following announcement:

TEACHERS' CONVENTION

The undersigned would invite The Teachers of Academies and other Schools in Vermont, and also all earnest friends of Education, to meet in Convention at Montpelier, on Wednesday, the 16th inst., at ten o' clock, A.M., for the purpose of organizing a State Association of Teachers; and also to discuss and adopt such Resolutions as expressed their views upon the subject of Education in Vermont.

J. K. Colby, *St. Johnsbury*	Rev. J. E. King, *Newbury*
C. G. Burnham, *Danville*	Ira O. Miller, *Peacham*
Rev. Asa Brainerd, *Danville*	L. O. Stevens, *Hardwick*
C. B. Smith, *Ludlow*	B. B. Newton, *St. Albans*[2]

The Vermont Teachers Association immediately proceeded to work toward the solution of the educational problems of the state. As there appeared to be an immediate need for a strong public relations arm of the organization, the first resolutions in 1851 aimed at establishing a state journal of education, using as its model the *Massachusetts Teacher*. As a committee deliberated about this matter, A. K. Pangborn, a well-known educator from St. Albans, Vermont, volunteered to undertake the publication of such a journal on his own responsibility. The journal was published for several years and encouraged the inclusion of vocal music in the expanded curriculum and the improvement of teacher training.

In 1854 the association girded itself for its most important work, that of promoting a state board of education and naming a state administrative officer. The association sought to emulate the good work of Horace Mann and the State Board of Education of Massachusetts and to create an executive to carry out educational reform. A resolution of August 23, 1854, showed their interest.

Resolved, That in the judgement of this Association, the interests of education in Vermont, would be greatly promoted by an efficient supervision of the same, and that it is expedient to establish a State Board of Education, with authority to employ a Secretary, or other agents to infuse life and energy into the system and thus to secure the elevation of our *common schools*.[3]

The work of the association made sufficient impression upon the governor and legislature in 1856 to warrant a detailed report by the Joint Committee on Education from the House and Senate as well as considerable space in Governor Ryland Fletcher's message to the legislature of that year. The joint committee was of the opinion that the problems of education required immediate legislative action. The committee made a strong plea for teachers' institutes, reasoning that the mere acquisition of knowledge was insufficient for teaching children; teachers needed to know how to impart this information. The committee noted the value of teachers' institutes where the teachers of the state might receive instruction in imparting learning.[4]

Perhaps in a more important declaration the committee recommended the appointment of a board of education, maintaining that such a board would be highly conversant with the problems of education in the state and could thereby make recommendations for proper school legislation.

Governor Fletcher, in his message to the legislature in October 1856, stressed the importance of an efficient and well-regulated common school system.[5] He confessed ignorance of the actual condition of the schools at the time and lamented the fact that no state superintendent of schools had been appointed and no statistical report had been made since 1851, although required by the law since 1845.*

By the strength of his action, an "Act to establish a Board of Education" was approved by the legislature on November 18, 1856. The act provided for a state board of education and the election of a secretary to the board who would act as the executive officer responsible to the board. Elected to that important post was John Sullivan Adams, a Burlington lawyer and one-time school teacher. Adams's interest in educational affairs was continuous, his capacity for work enormous, and his power over an audience hypnotic. The board charged him with the task of bringing new life to the common schools of the state. It expressed confidence in the fundamental structure of the system as it existed and admonished the new secretary that the system was capable by its own natural growth of meeting the growing wants of "our communities." The secretary was charged with the responsibilities of enlightening the public concerning the aims of the board of education regarding their common schools. He was to elicit the views of intelligent persons in the state regarding the problems of the schools and was to acquaint the public with the school laws so that the statutes already enacted could be enforced. He was advised to collect statistics for a clear and instructive report to the legislature at its next session. His report showed a widespread disregard for the school laws already enacted and anticipated some of the problems that were to face the subsequent secretary as he began his duties.

Adams observed that the success of the teacher-training institutes depended upon community interest and the general condition of the common schools. Before holding an institute Adams visited as many districts as possible. Though some institutes had taken place ten years earlier, they were still comparatively unusual in 1857.[6] They would not become a widespread and accepted part of education in the state until Adams succeeded in selling such a program to the people.

---

* Though the preceding superintendent requested statistical information during his term of office, little actual information was collected because of the neglect and oftentimes incompetence of the local district superintendents.

Adams collected school statistics. The dismal state of the common schools in Vermont could only be guessed at until the actual statistics were collected. When the facts and figures were finally available, they told a devastating tale of the squalor and impotence of the common school system. Adams believed that only through the dissemination of adequate statistical information—the number of school districts, the number of children, the average attendance, the thousands absent from school, the time and money lost by the employment of inferior teachers, the value of school houses, the expense of select schools, the average attendance at school meetings—would the people of the state feel the need for central control and a unified effort toward the improvement of the system. In such a Herculean task he succeeded nobly. In the course of the next ten years much was accomplished, and Vermont was able to join the educational mainstream led by Horace Mann, Henry Barnard, and so many others.

Among the most important agencies promoting school reform, the various local teachers associations were cited by Adams in the 1859 school report for their excellent work in arousing public sentiment for the improvement of the common schools. In a state preoccupied with costs, Adams reminded the citizens that the teachers association "costs comparatively nothing" and acts as an important agency for the improvement of the schools.

There were many in Vermont who were well aware of the expanding common school curriculum elsewhere in New England. The teachers associations in Vermont reflected this awareness in their reports and proceedings. The concern of a few regarding the widespread absence of music programs in the common schools slowly awakened general interest, which led to the gradual introduction of such programs into a few of the larger systems of the state in the nineteenth century.

But the common schools of Vermont were a long way from embellishing the curriculum with music and art. The school attendance figures were so shocking when they were finally known that many curriculum changes had to await an improvement in the law regarding the collection of statistical information. In the 1857 school report Adams said, as much with sarcasm as with accuracy, that a quarter of a million dollars was spent on education with no real knowledge of where the money went.[7]

Although there were rules and regulations regarding school attendance, there seemed to be a general parental lack of responsibility in this matter. In Burlington, the local superintendent of schools reported that a large number of parents were lax in their efforts to secure school attendance. "Children stay out for anything and nothing; to pick berries, to go fishing, to attend a fair or circus or music convention, to entertain company, to make visits out of town, to do small chores, or to run errands." [8]

Thus, it is not at all surprising that the enriched curricula at this time were left to the academies. The public schools were of such a marginal nature that the introduction of vocal music into the common schools had to await reorganization of these schools, the uplifting of these common schools in the estimation of the Vermonters, and the provision by the state legislature of the necessary legal controls. The school reports did succeed generously, and the people of Vermont and the legislature responded by bringing more and more children into the common school system of the state.

The buildings themselves were in incredible condition. The following describes a schoolhouse in Vermont around the middle of the century. Such schools were commonplace.

All the covering upon the frame was hemlock board, feather edged and nailed on. There were no clapboards on the outside, nor plastering nor sealing upon the inside. The chamber floor consisted of loose board laid down, being neither jointed nor nailed. The lower floor was the same, and there was not one window in the room. All the light, except what came through between the boards, was as follows: there were two or three holes cut through the boards of the side and end of the house. These were filled up with newspaper,—Spooner's Vermont Journal,—which was oiled to let the light through and fixed into thin strips of wood, and made fast. These were all the windows we had. Often when I first came into the room I could discern but little. In this cold, dark, inconvenient place, I spent three months instructing others according to the best of my ability. [9]

The Reverend John K. Converse, superintendent of schools in Burlington in 1863, describes a school in Vermont's largest town as "a miserable shanty—built just fifty years of age, and whose original identity has scarcely ever been disturbed by either carpenter, mason, pointer, glazier or the scrubbing brush; amply ventilated through broken windows, and no danger of suffocation to the children for the want of fresh air." [10]

With such facilities, it is not difficult to see why enrichment of the curriculum was so long in coming. The effective teaching of even the common branches of education was hampered by the condition of the school houses and the almost incredible lack of apparatus. One cannot but wonder how music programs could have ever developed in such an atmosphere. With some difficulty, however, they did appear. Perhaps they would have come sooner had not Adams resigned his position in 1867, ostensibly because of ill health but perhaps more because of political pressures on a man already overworked and greatly underpaid for his services. Adams did much to encourage the promotion of an enriched curriculum in the common schools, and the introduction of vocal music was a subject in several of the school reports of the 1860s.

The curriculum of the schools in Vermont in the first part of the nineteenth century showed almost no expansion. The reading and writing of the colonial schools, grammar, spelling, and arithmetic were introduced in 1789. Somewhat later, in 1826, geography was added. Almost no further change in the curriculum occurred until 1857 when the history of the United States became a required subject.

As the schools improved and the curriculum expanded, there was parallel pressure for the inclusion of art and music in the schools. This began tentatively in the 1850s and gradually gained momentum through the next decade. Although music was recommended as a subject, the teachers were under no obligation to teach it. Nevertheless it was considered of sufficient importance that prospective teachers were quizzed as to their qualifications in this area before a teaching certificate was granted.

The following questionnaire used in the 1860s is an example:

1. On the first line, write your full name, age, and residence.
2. On the second line state how long experience you have had in teaching.
3. Where do you expect to teach the coming term?
4. At what wages?
5. When is the term to commence, and how long is it to continue?
6. Have you ever taught in that school?
7. Do you sing? Do you intend to have singing in your school?
8. What works have you read on the subject of education?
9. What educational periodicals do you take and read?
10. Write a complete list of the branches required by law to be taught in common schools of Vermont.[11]

The appearance of questions on the examination for a teacher's certificate showed that the classroom teacher was expected to teach whatever music there might be in the curriculum. There was a state wide movement favoring instruction in vocal music in the schools, but the state's tradition of independence retarded its mandatory implementation. As the curriculum of the common schools finally expanded, it was only a matter of time before the arts came to be recognized as an important educational commodity. As early as 1855, articles promoting vocal music in the common schools began to appear.

At a meeting of the Vermont Teachers Association in 1855, L. S. Rust, of Burlington, read an essay on the importance of teaching vocal music in the common schools. Interest was such that in the *Proceedings* of the organization in 1857, a resolution was passed that "vocal music may be made a very effective instrument of moral training and good government; and we earnestly request the teachers of this State to secure its introduction into their respective schools."[12] One year later, in 1858, the Reverend Edward W. Hooker, of Fairhaven, Vermont, addressed the association on "Music: its Importance in Relation to the Common Schools."[13]

There were obstacles to be faced however. Antagonists put forth those time-honored arguments: music instruction would take time and would therefore interfere with other studies; only the favored few could learn to sing; children would be injured by singing; and, even, children would lose their voices by singing. These criticisms were forthrightly attacked by the proponents of music education.

In the annual school report of 1862 Adams vigorously promoted music in the common schools. Although he was not ready to suggest that music be taught as a regular course of instruction, he recommended that schools should open and close with vocal music. "If a knowledge of music and a capacity for its enjoyment, renders a man more happy, and generally makes him a better man at home, it must make him a better citizen: and if this is true, it is difficult to see any very valid reason why music should not be to a certain extent taught in the public schools."[14]

As in Boston in the 1830s, the prevailing ideas about education in Vermont in the 1850s and 1860s were concerned with material values. The education most prized was that which would give the young people the secrets of commercial success. Then as now, those who raised their voices for the arts represented a minority. In a society that sanctified the practical and the material, those who believed in aesthetic education were forced to defend the arts in terms that were understandable to the majority. Vocal music was praised as a means of discipline and a contribution to the "moral culture" of children in school. It helped children to adjust easily to the necessary concentration at the beginning of a school day. It "infused a habit of method and harmony into a whole school."[15] It allowed teachers to fill odd moments of the school day, moments when recitation time was limited, when it was not yet time for recess, or when some recreation was needed. Children could then be rested and occupied. Vocal music could also help as an aid to elocution. It would help children to learn to speak English well, to cultivate the voice, and to develop correct expression, pitch, and modulation. Verses committed to memory and repeated could influence a child's life and soul. The words would be made familiar by association with melody and would not be easily forgotten.

But not all defenses of vocal music in the schools were extrinsic in nature. The realization that music was indeed an art was not by any means lost. Some who defended music on ancillary grounds were quick to add that music was itself an influence in its own right.

Besides, there are influences for good derived from *music* alone. Its tendency is *refining*. A character touched by the sweet breath of music can not be rough and coarse. The sharp edges will be smoothed off. Music, more than any other human influence, awakes the tenderest sensibilities. It can touch chords that will vibrate to every emotion. The swelling tones of an organ, floating into the soul, carry with them a spirit of devotion. The strange harmonies of an orchestra paint for the ear every passion of the heart. In martial strains is a fire that keeps glowing a soldier's fortitude. If the heart throbs with gladness, or sighs with sorrow, music is its best expression. And this power to stir the emotions is such, that it often affects those who are impervious to other influences. We see this in religion. Hearts long shut fastened against feeling, may be unlocked by music. Men that will neither be frightened by warning, nor won by entreaty, nor forced by logic are often melted by the sweetness of a simple hymn.[16]

An unidentified writer in the *Vermont School Journal* in 1864 not only zealously promoted the inclusion of vocal music in the school curriculum but showed a remarkable understanding of many of the general problems of learning. In countering the argument that the inclusion of music in the curriculum will "take time and will interfere with other studies," the writer readily admitted that such a subject would "take time."

So does the study of reading, writing and arithmetic. Yet no one would say that either of these should be given up for geography. And then it does not depend all together upon the *time* that one is occupied, in order to succeed in obaining a complete mastery over a study. Some will accomplish more in an hour's time than others will with two or three. Nor is this owing entirely to different degrees of talent, but to the earnestness and zeal with which the one applies himelf and the other does not. Thus more progress will usually be made by three hours' daily practice upon the piano, than when six hours are devoted to it, for the reason that the mind and body become exhausted after a certain time, and further practice without rest is useless.[17]

Adams, as the first school officer of the state of Vermont, recommended the inclusion of vocal music as a common school subject in 1866.

There can be little doubt that if all the common and graded schools were required to give instruction in Book-keeping and Physical Geography and in Composition, much more of practical benefit would result from their efforts. And if by a change of law all the public schools, of every grade, were required, whenever the District so order by vote, to furnish adequate instruction in Vocal Music, Physiology and Drawing, the chief ground manifested for the preference of private and select schools would be taken away.

It may be remarked also, in regard to the topics last named, that properly used they may be made to exert a powerful influence upon our schools, in a direction where such influence is very greatly needed.

Why not then, in the common school, let Music and Drawing be allowed a fair chance to contend with roughness, coarseness and profanity in obtaining a permanent and formative power over the characters of the children of our State?[18]

Music did not appear in the common schools of Vermont with anything like a dramatic flourish. Its acceptance was gradual with many individual school systems not adopting music until very late in the century.

MUSIC EDUCATION IN CINCINNATI, OHIO

Cultural activities in Cincinnati developed in a different way. Early settlers in that city brought with them a predisposition for culture from the urban centers of New England. Following the pattern set by his brother Lowell, Timothy Mason helped found the Eclectic Academy of Music in that city in 1834 to promote music education in the West. Timothy Mason was responsible for the first music classes in the Cincinnati schools.

A second institution important in the promotion of music in the schools of Cincinnati was the Western Literary Institute and College of Professional Teachers. This organization, like the Vermont Teachers Association, met annually to discuss the problems of education and the need for the introduction of vocal music in the schools of the city.

An important figure in music education in Cincinnati was Calvin E. Stowe, a member of the faculty of the Lane Theological Seminary. In 1836, Stowe and his bride, the former Harriet Beecher, went to Europe where he studied the schools of Germany. Upon his return he reported his findings to a meeting of the College of Professional Teachers in a report called "The Course of Instruction in the Common Schools of Prussia and Württemberg." At that time Stowe stated his beliefs that all who could learn to read could learn to sing.

Stowe described a school for the reformation of youthful offenders in the United States. While he toured the halls, he heard some "beautiful voices" coming from an adjoining room. Upon entering he found twenty boys "sitting at a long table, making clothes for the establishment, and singing at their work."[19] Stowe was advised that the "rogues" were always kept at singing while they worked, and while they sang, "the devil could not come among them at all, he could only sit out doors there and growl, but if they stopped singing, in the devil comes."[20] Stowe informed the legislature that all children from six to ten years of age, "who [were] capable of learning to read, [were] capable of learning to sing, and that this branch of instruction [could] be introduced into all of our common schools with the greatest advantage, not only to the comfort and discipline of the pupils but also to their progress in their other studies."[21]

William F. Colburn was a student at this singing class and was later allowed to teach music in the schools providing that no cost should accrue to the board of education. Colburn did this for one year in 1844. The report of the board of trustees was singularly enthusiastic about the results.

The result has been in every way satisfactory and has been the means in some measure of inducing the Board as well as the public to come to the conclusion that music ought to be introduced into the schools as a regular branch of instruction. In whatever light we view it, whether as a means of social enjoyment, of moral influence, or intellectual improvement, it seems to have a happy effect upon the pupils. The Board has accordingly appointed a committee to report a plan by which hereafter, music may be regularly taught; this committee will probably report at an early session of the new Board, and we trust that our successors may enjoy the privilege of adopting a plan by which music may be regularly taught to all the youth in our schools whose parents desire it.[22]

Of the fourteen schools in Cincinnati in 1844, one was singled out on June 26, of that year and subjected to an examination. Before an audience of "Visitors and Inspectors," the children were summoned without warning to Wesley Chapel and examined on "Youth Choir's Companion," the song book then used by Colburn. That the results of this examination must have been successful was demonstrated when the board appointed Colburn the teacher of music with a munificent salary of forty-five dollars per month and hired a Mrs. E. K. Thatcher to assist Colburn at a rate of twelve dollars per month.

A second report by Timothy Mason and Charles Beecher at a meeting of the Western Literary Institute made a plea for the inclusion of vocal music into the city schools. They declared, in substance, that all men could learn to sing, that vocal music would be of physical, intellectual, and moral benefit to the children, that a public relations campaign be effected to acquaint the public with the benefits of such instruction, and that teachers be adequately prepared for this work. Communication must have been appropriately swift between Timothy Mason and his brother in Boston as the date of this report was 1837, contemporaneous with the Boston movement to incorporate music into the common schools of that city.

There must have been considerable sentiment favoring the inclusion of vocal music into the school day, as shortly after the report to the College of Professional Teachers, there were signs that individual classroom teachers took up the challenge and the music teaching process was started. The annual school report for 1838 stated that music was taught in some classrooms on a voluntary basis. When the College of Professional Teachers met again in October 1838, Timothy Mason conducted a group of Cincinnati school children who sang for the teachers.

In 1839, Charles Aiken arrived in Cincinnati from Pennsylvania. There he met Dr. Reuben D. Mussey, who became one of the greatest surgeons of his day. Like Aiken, Mussey was a graduate of Dartmouth College and had come to Cincinnati to participate in the development of a new and vital community. Walter Aiken, himself an important music teacher in Cincinnati, described Mussey as a cellist "of no mean ability," and it was through his influence that in 1842 a singing class was established in the basement of the Sixth Presbyterian Church.[23] Charles Aiken taught temperance songs there and the "new" movable Do system that was introduced a few years earlier in Boston. In this class were "musicians, laymen, and children" taught free of charge according to the methods used by Lowell Mason half a continent away.

It is unclear whether Charles Aiken was sent to Europe by the Ohio legislature, but he was requested by a resolution of that body to collect facts and information about the German schools and then report his findings to the next general assembly. When he returned, he submitted a report of about seventy pages, which was reprinted by the Massachusetts legislature. The music education of two states was affected by this report, and, as a consequence, so too were the schools of the nation.

The Universal success and very beneficial results, with which the arts of drawing and designing, vocal and instrumental music, moral instruction, and the Bible, have been introduced into these schools, was another fact peculiarly interesting to me. I asked all the teachers with whom I conversed, whether they did not sometimes find children who were actually incapable of learning to draw and sing. I had but one reply and that was that they found the same diversity of natural talent in regard to these as in regard to reading, writing and the other branches of education, but they had never seen a child that was capable of learning to read and write, who could not be taught to sing well and draw neatly, and that too without taking any time which would at all interfere with, indeed which would not actually promote, his progress in other subjects.[24]

When Charles Aiken began his duties in the Cincinnati schools, the exclusive teaching of music was not sufficient to occupy his hours. His instruction of music was confined to the more advanced classes supplemented with the teaching of Latin and Greek in Herron's Classical Seminary. He graduated from Cincinnati's Lane

Theological Seminary in 1847, and prior to his appointment as superintendent of music, he taught at the Woodward and Hughes high schools. Aiken became the first superintendent of music on September 25, 1871. In addition to his administrative duties and his unusual qualities of leadership, Aiken aided in the preparation of *The Young Singer* (1860) and *The Young Singer's Manual* (1866) and was solely responsible for editing *The High School Choralist* (1866).

During Aiken's eight years of superintendency, improvements were made in systematizing the music instruction. The first edition of *The Cincinnati Music Readers* was prepared under his leadership, and examinations were utilized to improve instruction. Charles Aiken was recognized at his retirement in a statement in the 1879 annual school report as having laid "the foundation of a high musical culture, not only with the pupils but with the public at large."[25]

In 1844 stress was placed on the "moral, intellectual, and recreational" values of music. Music was treated as a discipline first and as an art second. Walter Aiken looked back fondly from his position as director of music for the Cincinnati schools in 1924 and remembered with pride the hard work and discipline which were required of the children for the "First May Festival" in 1873. They sang "Lord God of Hosts, Author of our Being," by Mehal.[*]

Music was introduced into the primary schools of Cincinnati soon after its general introduction. A Mr. E. Pease taught music to children as an experiment in 1853. A resolution of December 18, 1854, required the primary teachers to teach music, and one year later Charles Aiken began giving instruction in some of the lower grades.[26]

Perhaps the most famous music teacher to have taught in Cincinnati was Luther Whiting Mason. He taught there from January 1856 until October 1864.[27] Mason enjoyed a singular success with his teaching of the children. He later went to Boston where he introduced music into the primary schools of that city, published his

---

[*] First came the choir of eight hundred voices of the intermediate schools singing in three parts, unaccompanied by instruments and with overpowering volume. Then the theme was passed over to four hundred basses and tenors of the high schools and then given forth by the combined forces of the different choirs. It was all over in two or three minutes but away down on the stage musicians were wiping their eyes, some had risen to their feet. A feeling of awe had come over them.

National Music Course, and achieved an international reputation as an educator.

Following the retirement of Charles Aiken, G. F. Junkermann became superintendent of music. Born and trained in Germany, Junkermann had worked as a laborer, clerk, and bookkeeper as well as a professional musician and teacher of drawing, arithmetic, and German before joining the faculty in Cincinnati in 1872. An ardent supporter of sight singing as a requisite musical skill, the new superintendent of music caused this element of instruction to be stressed in the Cincinnati schools, and there is some evidence to show that his students achieved some skill in this art. He built a staff that included instrumentalists as well as singers, and he formed a music teachers' orchestra.

Walter Aiken remembered Junkermann in colorful detail.

The children of the schools always looked forward to a treat when they saw Mr. Junkermann get out of his buggy with his old 'cello under his arm. . . . Mr. Junkermann was held in high regard by each member of his cabinet. Once every month upon a Saturday morning as regularly as the seasons would come and go he would insist upon an hour of orchestral practice with us, whether we wanted it or not. After the practice he would read us the riot act in good old fatherly style based upon his personal observations during the past month. It must have been a good thing for us. At any rate we regularly expected it, and I think would have been disappointed if we had not gotten it.[28]

Upon the retirement of Junkermann, the position was assumed by Walter Aiken.

MUSIC IN THE SCHOOLS OF COLUMBUS, OHIO

Music education seems to have been introduced formally into the schools of Columbus in 1854, as that date can be identified in the *Minutes of the Columbus Board of Education* when that body employed a special teacher of music. But Miriam B. Kapfer tells us that there is evidence to indicate that music was taught in the Columbus schools at least from 1847 and perhaps earlier.[29]

As in Vermont, the beginnings of school music in Columbus were closely related to the early development of free education. The first schools of Columbus were "subscription schools" and were not supported by public funds. The town was laid out in

1812, but it was not until 1826 that the first publicly supported
school opened its doors. For the next twenty years its support was
hardly adequate for the maintenance of a good school. As a result,
the private schools of the city prospered and received attention
from parents concerned about the education of their children.

On February 3, 1845, the General Assembly of Ohio granted a
special charter for the organization of the public schools of Columbus. At that time the management of the public schools of that
city consisted of a board of education with six directors. The city
was the first in Ohio to establish the position of superintendent,
and for this post Asa D. Lord was elected. Lord was a medical doctor but also a person deeply committed to the problems of common school education in his state. He held the office of superintendent from 1847 to 1854. Lord immediately set himself the task of
organizing a high school department which he and Mrs. Lord
taught, graduating their first high school class four years later.

With the beginning of Lord's superintendency, music became a
more important part of the curriculum. As detailed courses of instruction were published in the years following, the study of music
appeared as a regularly established branch of study from the elementary levels through the high schools. Grade school children
in Columbus learned to sing by rote, and singing was included
among the required "exercises for the ear and closing the school
day. All Columbus grade school teachers were required to conduct a fifteen- to thirty-minute period of "general exercises" of
which vocal music as well as most of the basic subjects were to be
included.

The high school studies were arranged into several departments
including reading, declamation, and music. Under this classification either "vocal music," or just "music" was listed in the courses
of instruction for the years 1848 and 1851.

Lord edited school journals during the 1840s and 1850s in the
hope of gaining support for public education in his city. As music
performances were good for public relations, concerts of school
children took place periodically. The children sang their class music in addition to various choruses. The singing of the classes was
interspersed with exercises in geography, reading, and "mental
arithmetic."

The holding of public examinations was a tradition during the period in most schools. They were held at the close of a term in order to give the public an opportunity to observe and evaluate the work done by the teachers. They also served to advertise the "success" of the school. As music performances lent themselves to these functions they were a conspicuous part of the exercises. Kapfer reports several titles of songs that were learned by the high school classes between the years 1847 and 1851 and that were sung at the annual exhibition in March of 1851, such as "Song of Freedom," "Fair is Our Native Land," "Be Kind to Each Other," "Land of Our Fathers," "But Near the Wood," and "The Rock of the Pilgrims."[30] There can be no doubt of the patriotic emphasis.

In Lord's "First Annual Report of the Superintendent," dated July 1848, the superintendent describes the values of the concerts.

For the purpose of awakening a deeper interest in the schools in the minds of parents and guardians, a series of Juvenile Concerts was commenced in September last and continued at intervals during the winter. These have generally been given in the largest churches in the City which have often been filled to overflowing, and through the addresses made in connection with them and the school exercises introduced, have furnished to many, who might never have visited the schools, an opportunity to become acquainted with the system and to feel a deep interest for its success.[31]

Then, as now, newspapers often carried reviews of these public performances, which, in the majority of instances, were most complimentary. It is impossible, therefore, to ascertain the true merits of any performance of children by reading contemporary reviews. But we can know that performances took place and were well-received by the audiences, which (then as now) consisted primarily of the parents of the young musicians. An 1851 account in the *Ohio State Journal* draws attention to a performance at a high school exhibition.[32] "The music by the choir, led by Mr. Dryer, the teacher, and composed entirely of school children, added much to the interest. This branch of education, we are glad to say, is made a prominent one in our system." And in another school recitation in December 1852, Dryer was complimented again on his work and indicated that his students were "making efficient progress in the science of music. There are several fine voices, and the general effect of the whole choir, when singing together, is very pleasing."[33] Elam Dryer was described as "long, and somewhat lank, in body, and his bass voice was as rough as a cross-cut saw; but he was good-natured and kind-hearted, and the old men and women in Columbus today [1905] could testify that he made the boys and girls sing." [34]

This program was typical for its time.

Programme

PART I

1. Sound our voices long and sweet, ... Chorus
2. In the valley I would dwell, ... Chorus
3. Mountain Song .... Chorus
4. When night comes o'er the plain, ... Chorus
5. Thy will be done .... Chorus
6. Farmer's Song .... Chorus
7. Gentle thoughts, O, give me them, ... Quartette
8. Tis well to have a merry heart, ... Chorus

PART II

1. We roam through forest shades .. Solo and Chorus
2. See our Bark .... Trio
3. The Alpine Echo .... Chorus
4. Hark! a low and soulful Anthem .... Anthem
5. Dream on .... Chorus
6. I've wandered in dreams .... Duett
7. Lutzow's wild Hunt .... Chorus [35]

An admission charge of twenty-five cents for adults and fifteen cents for children went toward the purchase of equipment for the school.

MUSIC EDUCATION IN BALTIMORE

Baltimore developed a common school system without the compulsion of state law. Although the city gave ample patronage to its private schools, its common schools never developed the stigma of "charity schools" which became so devastating to schools in many other areas.

Around the turn of the nineteenth century, Baltimore began to emerge as the cultural hub of a young country. It possessed a fine natural harbor, and, as a port town, it engaged in extensive trade in tobacco and grain. As its trade expanded, increasing numbers of

immigrants settled there. By 1800 the population of Baltimore had
reached thirteen thousand. A vigorous theatre life, the availability
of concerts, and a considerable number of music teachers combined to make that city the fountainhead of artistic life in the state.

In contrast to the Anglo–Saxon populations in eastern and
southern Maryland, the ethnic makeup of Baltimore was more diverse, which tended to generate a varied culture. Aristocratic
French, escaping from the French Revolution, arrived in Baltimore
bringing with them the music they had grown to love in the old
country. One group of French musicians participated in a concert
of vocal and instrumental music on May 25, 1790. Their programs included "Grand Symphonies" by full orchestra, overtures,
opera songs, and instrumental solos.[36] Before 1800 the French influence was dominant in Baltimore. Following the War of 1812,
an expanding trade with Germany brought immigrants of that
nationality to the city, and the Germans came with their well-
developed predilection for the best in European art music, both
vocal and instrumental. In 1828 an assistant theatre manager went
to Germany to obtain a *corps de ballet*. He returned instead with
five instrumentalists, among whom was a young man of seventeen
named Henry Dielman. Dielman became one of the founders of
the New Musical Association, which sponsored performances and
stimulated interest in the works of Haydn, Mozart, and Beethoven. Dielman became the recipient of the first doctor of music
degree conferred in the United States. It was bestowed by George-
town University and presented by the president of the United
States, Zachary Taylor.[37]

Providing a vigorous musical environment were a number of
self-employed music teachers. They offered a wide range of instruction from vocal and instrumental to private or group lessons.
Thirty such teachers appear in the *Baltimore Directory* for the
year 1855, and the number doubles for each decade thereafter. In
the years immediately preceding the Civil War, a revival of serious
opera occurred and minstrel shows became popular. Even during
the war citizens of Baltimore could hear performances of the *Barber of Seville, Don Giovanni, Faust*, and *Tannhauser*. Thus during
the last half of the nineteenth century, there were improved opportunities for professional and amateur musicians. Orchestras were
employed for the theatres on a regular basis. Choral societies, organized and made popular by the German immigrants, grew away

from a religious orientation and developed ethnic and secular functions. Musical associations composed mostly of amateur musicians such as the Rossini Musical Association, the Haydn Musical Association, and the Baltimore Amateur Orchestra, were popular.

Coming into existence early in the nineteenth century, the societies, or "musical associations" as they were often called, aimed to perform the larger vocal works of some length and technical difficulty. These societies were not an outgrowth of the American singing school but were instead direct offshoots of the European singing societies whose aims and ambitions were reflected by the Baltimore prototypes.

Early choral societies studied and performed sacred music. The Cecilian Society enjoyed the patronage of John Cole, who published several tune books which were dedicated to this group. The society was associated with the St. Paul's Episcopal Church of Baltimore. As early as 1803, concerts of the *Messiah* and *The Creation* were performed by societies with the talent and ambition to undertake the challenge.[38] As early as 1821, oratorios were performed by groups with as many as two hundred singers and accompanied by orchestra. At such times works such as Pergolese's *Stabat Mater*, Mozart's *Requiem*, and Masses of Haydn and Beethoven were performed.

Though the early choral societies tended to identify with the various Baltimore churches, the immigrant populations of Germany and central Europe gave the societies a more secular emphasis. German choral societies were active by 1837. Soon after the first concert of the Liederkranz Society in 1837, at least six other societies emerged, all conducted by musicians of German extraction. Orchestras were also commonly associated with these groups. Fisher reports that newspapers were brimming with notices of choral activities between 1838 and 1848.[39]

These activities gave Baltimore a luxuriant atmosphere for the cultivation of the arts. Music education as a subject in the public schools was a logical next step. There is some evidence to show that these vigorous choral societies were a strong stimulus for the teaching of public school music, which was initiated officially in 1843. When music was taught in the public schools, interest in the choral societies did not diminish as it did in the singing schools. Singing schools were designed solely for the instruction of music, while the choral societies were organized primarily for the performance of music. As the instructional portions of the societies' work were gradually taken over by the public schools, more time became available for practice and performance, and presumably with a more literate group of singers.

In 1812 the state legislature of Maryland provided the first funds for primary education in that state. The idea of formal schooling grew slowly, but eventually the concept of general education for all became widely accepted. In 1825 the Maryland legislature made provision for a unified public school system under the direction of a state superintendent. Each county was divided into school districts under the control of a board of county school commissioners. Individual counties could choose not to participate in the plan which, in effect, made the plan optional. Local populations still had to persevere in their work to establish individual schools and school systems. Baltimore passed a city ordinance creating a board of school commissioners in 1828, and one year later there were public schools in that city.

The first schools taught only reading, writing, and arithmetic, but soon the curriculum began to grow in response to the interests and pressures of the people. By 1843, when music was first introduced, the schools were teaching "natural philosophy," physiology, history, composition, and elocution, in addition to the three basic subjects.[40] In 1839 the city's first high school was established. The school was only for boys, but five years later two other institutions for girls were authorized. Their curricula were similar to those of the private academies of the day with two distinct areas of study: the Classical curriculum, designed for college preparation, which featured the study of Latin and Greek along with courses in higher mathematics; and the English curriculum, which included the study of modern languages, general mathematics, English composition, bookkeeping, and often related business courses.

A much-needed state normal school opened in 1843, a rather early date considering that the high schools of that city had only been in existence for four years. Music was the first of the arts to be admitted, and its inclusion undoubtedly grew from the zeal of the city of Baltimore.

At the earnest request of many citizens and patrons of the schools vocal music was introduced. The experiment was first made by teaching on Saturdays in such schools as formed classes, leaving it with the teacher, Mr. Wilder, to make his own arrangements with the scholars. At the opening of schools in September the board having discovered that the experiment had become highly popular and was calculated to benefit the schools materially, determined to appoint a teacher of vocal music.[41]

Levy Wilder was a musician who came to Baltimore sometime before 1841. He organized singing school classes and led one of the German choral societies. He attended a national music convention at Boston organized by Lowell Mason in 1836, which demonstrates an early pedagogical interest.[42]

Reports of the *Baltimore Sun*, of July 29, 1843, warmly commended Wilder and his students and strongly encouraged the continuation of the music instruction. The concern for public relations was not lost upon the school administrators of the day. Large audiences of pleased parents could only help the cause of popular education in every community.

A rather substantial increase in the school population prompted the school commissioners to appoint a second music teacher in 1845 in the person of William Tarbutton. Tarbutton enjoyed a long tenure as music teacher in the Baltimore schools and was described in the 1863 *School Report* as an "accomplished instructor." He compiled and arranged the first public school music book to be used in the Baltimore schools.[43]

The music program gradually expanded during the years following the Civil War until there was a maximum of five teachers. While, in general, it can be said that music as a school subject was indeed popular, there were critical voices heard, and such was their nature that then, as now, the music teachers and the friends of music involved themselves in a continuous campaign to rationalize the existence of this instruction in the schools. Most of the defense of music was extrinsic with much emphasis placed on the moral values of the instruction. Perhaps because its acceptance was poor, music instruction was discontinued in the high school for boys in 1865.

Ruel Shaw who had joined the music staff in 1868, campaigned to reinstate this music instruction. Shaw noted the "refining effects" of such instruction upon the boys, and, significantly, he deplored the attitude of the boys in certain elementary schools. He suggested that a more serious exposure to music would improve their manners, but his protestations were of no avail, and music was not to be taught in the Central High School for boys until the next century.

The musical experiences of the students in Baltimore can be divided into two general categories, the theoretical, and the practical. The theoretical studies included the learning of the names of the notes and the musical terms and acquiring some knowledge of keys, chords, and chord progressions. The practical skills included vocal exercises, scale drills, note reading, sightsinging, and rote singing.[44] The two categories obviously interacted, but an effort was made to keep the practices separate. Fisher observes that this practice was probably a carryover from the singing school, and in general we can say that such artificial divisions were characteristic of educational practices prior to the popularization of the child-study ideas later in the century.

The music specialists were constantly concerned with the progress of the children in learning the theoretical aspects of music. No child seemed too young to be exposed to the mysteries of note names, keys, and chords. The music specialist believed that such intellectual exercise stimulated the faculties and placed the study of music on par with the so-called academic subjects. In 1860 it was expected that two-thirds of the instruction time given by a music teacher be devoted to the learning of theoretical principles, while the remainder could be spent in singing.[45]

Examinations were carried out at regular intervals. The examinations were noted in the 1857 "Rules of Order," as described in the Thirty-First Annual School Report which emphasized individual recitation. Ten years later public quarterly examinations were given with the questions being written on the blackboard. After a time the examinations came to include both theoretical knowledge and performance skills.

By 1872 those students who wished to enter the female high schools were required to answer the following questions concerning a musical example that was placed on the blackboard:

1. Write the names of the notes in the first four measures.
2. What notes are taken flat in this example?
3. What kind of notes does the second measure contain?
4. Explain on which notes the beats occur in the second measure.
5. In which measures do the rests occur?

6. Write the names of the notes in the last four measures.
7. In what key is this example written?
8. Explain the beats in the fourth measure.
9. How many sixteenth notes are there in this example?
10. What are the names of the dotted eighth notes in this example? [46]

The theoretical aspects of music were taught by the music specialist almost exclusively. The classroom teacher presided over the rote singing of songs, much to the consternation of the music specialists who considered exercises in music reading in syllables to be the preferred manner of instruction. In 1857 teachers were instructed "not to consume the time allotted for music lessons in teaching of singing by rote merely." [47] In 1871, J. Harry Deems, a music teacher appointed to the music staff three years earlier, complained that primary classes were singing by rote when he started to teach in the city schools, while there was some evidence to show that some of the classroom teachers did nothing at all regarding music. *

It is significant that it took the popularity and prestige of Luther Whiting Mason's *National Music Course* (after 1883) and its emphasis on rote songs in the primary grades before the music teachers of Baltimore began to realize and accept the efficacy of the rote song experience. By 1890 one of the objectives for the primary grades was the singing of "easy" and "pleasing" rote songs.

Fisher effectively points out that by 1885 the music staff of the Baltimore schools had diminished to the extent that the classroom teachers became primarily responsible for the teaching of music. As the classroom teachers believed themselves incapable of teaching the more theoretical aspects of the art, rote singing may have appeared to them to have been the natural solution to the requirement of music teaching. And with the appearance of the Luther Whiting Mason series, the rote song method achieved a dignity and legitimacy of its own.

During the nineteenth century classroom teachers received little

---

*J. Harry Deems was the son of James Monroe Deems, a Baltimore musician and teacher. J. Harry Deems studied piano and violin under his father's instruction and played in some local orchestras as a boy. At the age of twenty he was chosen over fifteen competitors for the position of music teacher in the Baltimore schools. He was the first local musician to take such a post and was a young man who had no previous experience in the teaching of singing schools. He was considerably younger than the two other music teachers who joined him that year.

training in music. In an effort to help this situation, occasional training classes in music were held for the classroom teachers in the Baltimore schools. But these were not maintained in a consistent way, and many of the classroom teachers remained unable to teach the theoretical aspects of music. It was therefore likely that what music was taught was recreational and by rote. The music specialists visited the classes about once a week where they gave instruction in the theoretical branches of the art, while the remaining music lessons under the direction of the classroom teacher were given to rote singing.

From 1843 to 1845 one music instructor was responsible for teaching nearly three thousand students. There was, undoubtedly, little time for classroom visitation and instruction. With the number of public performances that were required, it is reasonable to suppose that the music specialist spent the great bulk of his time rehearsing the children for the exhibitions. From an early time, sensitive decisions were required between the instruction of children in the classrooms and the public relations values of exhibitions and performances. Such problems still concern the music educators of today.

In 1845 a second music teacher was hired, but the public performance versus classroom teaching problem was, of course, not solved. The presence of a second teacher merely gave a sense of competition to the two instructors and the separate districts. The competition manifested itself in the public performances and made that aspect of the music program even more important. In 1851, William Tarbutton, the teacher of music for the western district presented a concert involving about four hundred students. The concert, presented at the "New Assembly Rooms," a public meeting hall, consisted of selections by the elementary school pupils with the assistance of a group of girls from the Western Female High School. In attendance at the performance was the mayor of the city and at least fifteen hundred persons.[48] At a concert the following year, attended by about twelve hundred persons, the mayor again was there and used that forum for some impromptu remarks in defense of the public school system which, at the time, had come under fire by certain conservative factions who expressed opposition to the continuation of public education. Again the music program was used only in part for the cultural edification of the

students. Its principal role in the minds of public and school officials was political.

Methodology in the Baltimore Schools

Music reading skills were sought by the music teachers, and various devices and procedures were used to accomplish these ends.
There was also a logical concern for vocal quality. In 1859 syllables were used in the hope of accomplishing both objectives. The
exercises were to be sung carefully with attention being given to
the quality of voice. The solfeggio exercises were of progressive
quality.

One of the early books published in Baltimore and used in the
schools was *Vocal Music Simplified*, by James Deems, father of J.
Harry Deems. Deems, Sr., came to Baltimore in 1839 and published his book ten years later, one of the early music books
adopted by the school commissioners for use in the schools. The
solfeggio was to be sung with fixed syllables at first, then sung with
the neutral syllable "ah." *

In the 1870s the debate between movable and fixed Do raged.
The movable Do was used in many school systems of that day,
while the fixed Do came from European practice and was in use in
American conservatories. In 1871 the debate in Baltimore centered
around J. Harry Deems who favored the fixed Do system and Ruel
Shaw who liked the movable Do. Both J. Harry Deems and his father favored the European practice, believing that the method was
simpler and would facilitate reading. The Peabody Conservatory,
in Baltimore, taught the fixed Do method, and both father and son
were affiliated with that institution. Shaw believed that the movable Do system required less time to teach and was easier for the
purposes of intonation and for singing in all keys. He proclaimed
that the system of movable Do was fast gaining ground and would
supersede the fixed Do system. And in Baltimore as finally in most
other schools, the movable Do system emerged victorious.

The universal use of music books came slowly to the city. In
1846 books were used in both the male and female high schools,
the first book used being the William A. Tarbutton, *Music for the*

---

* About 1865 an experiment used what was then called an "elocutionary" system, which
was merely a type of speech song using the notes of a major scale and apparently applied
to various kinds of learning in the school. But the method was short-lived and only a few
teachers in the city used it.

Public Schools, Selected and Arranged. This sixty-four page book contained graded exercises and songs, three-part pieces for two treble voices and bass. Unlike the earlier books written for singing schools, Tarbutton's volume omitted the theoretical introduction but emphasized original graded music reading exercises without words. It was arranged methodically "in sets," introducing each key including scales and chords. Following the exercises were several songs that were suitable for the techniques learned. As the book progressed, the rhythms used became more difficult. The book was one of the first of its kind to be written expressly for use in the public schools.

In 1857 when A. J. Cleaveland replaced Tarbutton as music teacher, Cleaveland's book *The High School Vocalist* probably replaced that of Tarbutton. While this book was similar in nature to the Tarbutton opus, Cleaveland succeeded in having his book published commercially.* In addition to Cleaveland's experience as music teacher in the Baltimore public schools, he also taught music at a singing school as well as the local academies.

In the 1840s only the high schools had books. Few books were provided at that time for the elementary schools. Apparently a need was sensed as in 1848 the school commission provided a collection of songs for elementary grades, but paradoxically, in a system that prided itself on the teaching of music reading skills, no music whatsoever was included in this book. Only the words were available.

By 1864 books were used in the elementary grades, and, in 1869, Ruel Shaw complained in a school report that Lowell Mason's *Young Singer*, part I, which was successfully used in the grammar school grades, was particularly unsuited for use in the high school.

In the 1880s the universally popular *National Music Course* was introduced into the schools of Baltimore and its rote-note system of music instruction became a staple there for ten years. In the 1890s the three-volume *New American Music Reader* was used and became the first series used by the Baltimore schools and compiled by Baltimore musicians. The series was written by J. Harry

---

* Books especially written for the public schools were not the only books used in music classes in Baltimore or in other towns and cities. Often these schools used singing school material as well. These latter books were readily available, and publishers, sensing an expanding market for their books, included on the title pages of these volumes the many places the books could be used. See chapter X, "The Great Publishing Carnival."

Deems and John Wehage, who were the "music superintendents" in the city schools. The series called for a systematic approach to music reading using charts and calling for the students to chant the letter names of the notes. It is interesting that no syllables were used.

The use of charts was first introduced into four primary classes in the eastern district school of Baltimore. Soon two-thirds of the two hundred classes in the district were using the charts for music reading exercises.[49] The primary grade teachers were expected (ordered) to use the charts after each regular visit of the music specialist.

The use of instruments as a teaching tool cannot be taken for granted by modern students. Pianos were in use in the high school classes, but the less expensive cabinet organs were used in the lower grades. Levi Wilder was reported to have used his violin to accompany the children as they sang for one of the first public exhibitions in 1843. We know also that A. J. Cleaveland played the flute and violin, while J. Harry Deems was a violinist. As late as 1870, J. Harry Deems initiated a series of four concerts for the purpose of raising money to purchase organs for the school rooms.[50] Voluntary funds had already provided several organs for the schools. Two years later about half of the schools had such instruments, but it would be 1887 before all primary and grammar schools would be so endowed.

The "Remarks" from the Annual Report by the Committee on Music in 1876 are most revealing about the state of music education in Baltimore at this time and, in a general way, are typical of the nature of music programs during the last part of the nineteenth century. That year the school commission concerned itself with the teaching of music reading, but this concern only mirrored the philosophy of the music specialist. Later in the 1880s when Luther Whiting Mason's *National Music Course* was accepted, the rote-note approach became suddenly viable. The final aims of music education had still not changed much, as the rote aspects of the curriculum were limited to the primary grades, and the students were still required to read at sight as the *ne plus ultra* of their musical experiences.

One cannot help but wonder whether the music specialists met their classes with the regularity implied by their schedules. The

Music Committee showed concern lest the music supervisors shirk their responsibilities. It has already been shown that the regular quarterly examinations had to include the theoretical branches as well as the practical. It seems clear from the warning of the Music Committee that the theoretical aspects *were* often shortchanged in favor of the more popular practical aspects of the music study, that is, singing.

The committee concerned itself with the schedule of music teaching, certainly implying that the daily instruction in music was not always adhered to, and the three lessons per week grammar school schedule, at least occasionally violated. The only way in which the Music Committee could enforce its standards was by way of the quarterly exhibitions or public examinations.

The concern over the classroom teachers who could not teach music was apparent at the end of the "Remarks." The idea of the availability of a Saturday normal school to give the classroom teacher this instruction must be considered, even today, with respect. We do not know at this time the number of classroom teachers who availed themselves of this opportunity, but, from one point of view, it must be observed that there were sufficient numbers of nonmusical teachers to exercise the concern of the Music Committee.

Remarks

1. The Music Teachers are requested to conform strictly to the Schedule, as no deviation will be permitted without special permission from the Committee on Music.

2. The questions for the semi-annual examination of the classes in the Primary, Grammar, and Female High Schools will be prepared by the Committee on Music, and will be based on *the Theoretical Part, as well as the Exercises and Songs named in the Schedule.*

3. In imparting vocal instruction in classes, reading at sight must be regarded as a first consideration.

4. The attention of the teachers is directed to Art. XIV, Sec. 1, of Rules of Order which requires daily instruction of Music in the Primary, and three lessons per week in the Grammar Schools. Violations of this rule must be reported by the music teachers in their Quarterly Reports.

5. Musical Exhibitions of the Primary, Grammar and Female High Schools, showing the proficiency of class-singing and reading at sight,

will take place at such time as the Committee on Music may direct.

Singing prima vista, or at sight, constituted one of the principal features of the exhibitions in question. Whilst the Grammar Schools showed the same proficiency as on former occasions—reading at sight one, two and three part exercises, prepared by musicians not connected with the Public Schools, and in the presence of the audience assembled—the Primarians and pupils of the English-German Schools gave unmistakable evidence of the strict adherence to the schedule, since they acquitted themselves with equal precision and correct intonation in the foreign musical examples placed before them.

In the Female High Schools the before named subject—sight-singing— has received more attention during the past year. As the Grammar School pupils, entering those schools, are better prepared in this subject, we confidently assert that a successful result will hereafter necessarily follow.

In accordance with the prevailing munificence, three graduated from each of the Female High Schools—the usual number—were sent to the Peabody Conservatory of Music for examination, prior to admission.

Your Committee, in conclusion, desire this Board to direct the attention of those school teachers who are incompetent to impart musical instruction to the Saturday Normal School. The music class is instructed by a graded system, and all availing themselves of this advantage must be greatly benefited.

H. B. Roemer,	J. H. Henderson
C. B. Bayly	Jos. K. Milner
J. L. Lawton	*Committee on Music*[51]

Lowell Mason

Charles Aiken,
from Charles Gary's *Vignettes*

Luther Whiting Mason

Will Earhart, from a portrait by Malcolm Parcell

Frances Elliott Clark, from the cover of *Musical Monitor*, November 1920

John W. Wainright

F. Melius Christiansen

Shinichi Suzuki

CHAPTER X

The Great Publishing Carnival

TUNE BOOKS from the 1840s to the 1880s were aimed at various groups of singers in the hope that the authors' might sell their books as widely as possible. Hundreds of titles appeared during the period, and millions of copies of these music books were sold. The *Golden Wreath*, by Luther O. Emerson, was published in 1856 by the Oliver Ditson Company and sold 300,000 copies before 1872; Robert Loury's *Bright Jewels* was issued in 1869 and sold 500,000 copies in four years.[1] Horatio Palmer's *Song Queen* in 1867 sold 200,000 copies, while Lowell Mason's famous *Carmina Sacra*, brought out in 1841, sold over 400,000 copies in ten years. Between 1850 and 1860 more than sixty-five school music books were published, and new editions of older books were being printed. Robert W. John tells us that in the nineteenth century tens of millions of music books of all kinds were sold. Not all of them, of course, were used in the public schools. But because of the versatility of the collections and the adroitness and entrepreneurial skill of the collectors, each volume was used in a diversified manner.

Between 1840 and 1880 the Oliver Ditson Company gradually bought the publishing rights to more and more music books so that, by the latter part of the century, it became the largest single publisher of tune books. The John Church Company of Cincinnati became the largest of the Midwest publishing companies. Ralph Baldwin tells us that at least the *Carmina Sacra* and the *Jubilee* were commonly used in the public schools toward the end of the century.[2]

The oblong format was still standard, and a theoretical introduction, often thirteen or fourteen pages, was almost universal. While these theoretical introductions were rather complete, little attempt was made to give the students practical exercises from which to learn. In the *Collection of Secular and Sacred Music*, by Palmer, assisted by Emerson, a fairly complete theoretical introduction appears but the drill exercises seem rather elementary. In a period of controversy regarding methods of instruction, particularly music reading, the authors seem to throw up their hands helplessly in regard to the confusing philosophies of the day.

No attempt is here made to introduce a system either new or old. Every teacher must explain each new part in his own way. We have only endeavored to suggest the order in which the new ideas should be introduced. We continually refer back to the THEORETICAL STUDIES, where a full explanation of each new idea will be found. The scale, staff, short notes, Double Bar etc., should all be explained and illustrated upon the blackboard, before commencing these exercises. The successful teacher never tells *what he is going to do*, but *does* it; in other words, he makes his explanation *short* and *sharp*, and turns at once to the exercises which involve it.[3]

ROTE VERSUS NOTE

Controversies surrounded the teaching of music reading throughout the nineteenth century—rivalries which have not been reconciled to this day. Lowell Mason, in his understanding of Pestalozzianism, believed in the thing before the sign, or rote before note. But it must be stressed that Mason was much concerned about reading and, as we have discovered, wedded to the appropriateness of drill. Those who later advocated rote singing placed the emphasis on song rather than on mechanical drill. The song itself was the basic material by which the children would learn to read. Only after a wealth of material was sung by rote would the teacher begin a regimen of syllable identification and syllable drill. The note-reading advocates believed that the child must learn the tools and the means of using them before songs should be sung. Those tools were the mastery of the use of syllables. The greatest battles came during the last thirty years of the nineteenth century, and, like so many great philosophical issues, a resolution has not been found.

Charles Farnsworth alluded to a final reconciliation, if not an agreement, in a September 1914 article in the *Music Supervisor's Journal*:

Another very interesting feature of the Minneapolis meeting was the opportunity given for so thorough an inspection of two well developed systems of teaching, headed by such strong personalities. This opportunity alone would have been worth the expense of the meeting. There is perhaps among some a rather amateurish emphasis on the value of method. Every strong teacher will have his or her way of doing things, but it does not follow that such a way is best for different persons under different conditions.

Joseph Bird published a pamphlet in 1850 entitled "To Teachers of Music" in which he objected to Lowell Mason's rote approach as advocated in the *Manual of the Boston Academy of Music*:

Teach a class by rote and the "Elements" and a few will read, but the greater number give up in dispair. . . . We believe that the only way by which reading music will become as universal as the reading of our language is by changing the system, and making books and teaching from them in the same way we do from our reading books.[4]

In 1861, the Oliver Ditson Company published Bird's *Vocal Music Reader*. It was not a "series" in the strict sense, but it was a significant step in the direction of a multiple book idea whose time had now come. A distinct need for a graded music series became evident when music was introduced into the primary schools of Boston in 1864.

Lowell Mason receives the credit for the first graded series books with his *Song Garden* (Mason Brothers), the first two volumes of which were published in 1864 and the third appeared in 1866. Mason's series was not regularly adopted as a set, perhaps because the third book was too difficult. John tells us that the schools of Washington, D.C., used the second book alone in 1866.[5] The first and second books were used in 1871 in the Saint Louis schools. With the later series books, partial adoption was uncommon. Although books were progressively arranged, each book was complete in itself.

George B. Loomis published the second series in his *First Steps in Music* in 1868. Loomis's series served more as a prototype to later examples than did that of Mason. Loomis's second book was published at his own expense in 1869, while his third was published in 1871 by Iveson, Blake, Taylor, and Company of Chicago and New York.

Loomis began teaching in the Indianapolis schools in 1866, having been recommended by Lowell Mason. Eleven years later he helped found the Indiana Music Teachers Association, one of the first state music teachers associations. Starting with little or no materials of instruction, Loomis was forced to improvise. Out of this need was born the *First Steps in Music*.[6]

The first book begins with a one line staff around which are several pages of exercises. There follows a two line staff plus additional pages of exercises. The author's aim was to teach the children to read notes throughout the thirty-seven pages of the first volume.

The second book comprises a group of short songs using various numbers of staff lines.*

FIRST STEPS

Numbers appear on various lines or spaces which tell the singer which scale step is represented. In the above example we find the number four on the third line. Counting down from four the learner discovers that "one" or "do" is in the first space. But before we deduce that the numeral is merely a substitute for the usual key signature, we find that Loomis did not necessarily have that in mind. The numeral "3" might appear on the second space still implying or giving a cue to F major. The book presupposed no musical knowledge on the part of the teacher, a consideration that was to become increasingly commonplace in music series book production.

The third book of Loomis's series is 142 pages in length. Time

---

* John tabulated the number of songs using various numbers of staff lines: three songs with one staff line; eleven songs with two staff lines; twelve songs with three staff lines; three songs with four staff lines; and three songs with five staff lines. No clefs or time signatures are in evidence.

signatures are introduced on page 54 and easy two-part songs introduced on page 74. The remaining pages of the volume contain two-part songs (with one exception) usually in parallel thirds or sixths. No accidentals appear in these songs. The songs themselves were composed mostly by the author and are described by John as "short pedantic tunes." No excellent song literature was presented here, only short didactic tunes whose principal purpose was obviously to teach children to read.

Loomis sets the stage for his third book with the following introduction:

We now enter upon the third book of the series, and if the first and second books have been mastered by teachers and pupils, we have reached the stage in our progress when with the more advanced age and intelligence of pupils, and additional experience of the teachers, we may move forward with quickened pace, and with less fear of meeting with serious obstacles.[7]

The publication of the three-book series was taken over by Iveson, Blake, Taylor and Company, and the name of the series was changed to *Progressive Music Lessons*, and two more books were added. In 1898 the American Book Company bought the publishing rights to the series. The books were widely used in the Midwest in the 1870s and 1880s.

THE NATIONAL MUSIC COURSE AND LUTHER WHITING MASON

Luther Whiting Mason was the father of the American graded series. His *National Music Course* was accepted throughout the country and was translated into German to be used in the schools of that country. (In Germany the *National Music Course* was translated as *Die neue Gesangsschule*.) The books which he wrote from 1870 to 1875 set the pattern for most series books for the next fifty years.

Mason was born in Turner, Maine, in 1828. He taught in the Louisville, Kentucky, schools in 1852, where from contemporary evidence he must have distinguished himself as a teacher of vocal music. In 1857 Mason left Louisville to begin teaching in the schools of Cincinnati. He became acquainted with the school music books of Christian Heinrich Hohmann, one of the great German pedagogues of that period. Hohmann's small graded books in four parts were based on Nageli and his Pestalozzian interpretations. Each book included between thirty-one and forty-one pages. Oliver Ditson had published a translation of Hohmann's method in 1856 under the title of *Hohmann's Practical Course*.

In 1864 Luther Whiting Mason went to Boston to organize that city's primary music instruction. Music instruction in the primary schools was new in this country and Mason immediately sensed the need for instructional materials that would fit the requirements of children of many ages. In 1870, using *Hohmann's Practical Course* as his model, he compiled the *National Music Course* which was published by Edwin Ginn. The course was the first completely planned method, and its popularity was such that it was adopted by the Japanese government following the author's three-year visit there as governmental music supervisor. (School music in Japan was referred to as "Mason-song.")

The *National Music Course* was a group of seven graded books—five readers and two supplementary books, an intermediate book containing books two and three, and an abridged fourth reader. Mason included a set of charts to assist in the instruction.

The song material in the *National Music Course* was taken largely from German sources and included numerous German folk songs. Mason became the first advocate in this country of the use of the "song method" when teaching children to read music, and the series represented the first major break with the dominating influence of the singing school books. John tells us that "it sounded the death knell for the tune-books in the public schools and was the beginning of the end of the tune-book in America."[8]

Mason presents his philosophy:

The proper view to take of a child learning to read is, that he is learning to recognize in printed or written forms, the words with which he is already familiar in speech. We only surround him with difficulties if we regard his reading at this period as the means of extending his vocabulary.[9]

He used the Tonic Sol Fa system of music reading, a system which was used in England and started by Eliza Glover and "perfected" by John Curwen. It became the accepted method of music education in the primary schools of England. It was based on the system of movable Do and taught tone relationships initially by means of a tone ladder which was followed by syllable notation or just the first letter of the sol-fa syllables. No staff was used. The time was indicated by the distances between the syllables and an unusual system of commas, dots, and dashes. The system precipitated much controversy in this country, but it seems reasonable to assume that those who believed in the system and used it well accomplished the desired educational results. The adherents of the system believed that by eliminating the staff in the early stages of music reading, the teaching and learning of the art would be simplified.

The system never really caught on in this country as teachers were reluctant to learn a new system of notation when it was realized that the real music was written on the staff. Classroom teachers, when they taught music at all, were wedded to the didactic idea that the primary function of their music teaching was to teach the staff.

Ever since it became apparent in the nineteenth century that for music to become a regular branch of school instruction classroom teachers would have to teach it, their fitness to do so has been continuously debated. Many taught rote singing but on such a primitive level that Luther Whiting Mason, the premier advocate of this system of instruction, was disturbed:

This kind of singing (singing as it happens) is not altogether useless, as in many cases there is a freshness and energy about it that serves to awaken a love for singing, and to furnish a basis on which to build a subsequent course of musical instruction. But there is a wide distinction between this haphazard singing and genuine 'rote singing.' The latter is the most important part of instruction, in vocal music. Genuine rote singing implants at the beginning true musical impressions. It leads to a discrimination between a musical and unmusical style. A child will learn more easily, and enjoy better singing in a good rather than a bad style, if he has the right examples at the start.[10]

The second book of the *National Music Course* was for intermediate grades and sought to teach music reading through the introduction of the C major scale. Other keys followed. But Mason believed that if sufficient efforts were placed on the C major scale, the children would have no difficulty moving to other keys. The analogy between language learning and music reading was not then considered as natural as we now believe. But the remarkable popularity of Mason's series stands as proof that his system was used, if often inexpertly, by many school systems and large numbers of teachers in the country.[11] Mason expressed confidence in the ability of the classroom teacher to teach the essence of the art in his *Second Music Reader*, published by Ginn, Heath and Company in Boston:

Many teachers may not feel confidence in their own musical powers sufficient to enable them to carry out the work as they feel it ought to be done. But if we wait till all are competent to give the best instruction, it will be a long day before good music becomes as common as all desire it to be.[12]

Mason himself must have been an outstanding music teacher. In an exceedingly complimentary letter written by five members of the Germania Band who were on tour in Louisville and who visited Mason's classes, a picture emerges of Mason's skill and efficiency in the teaching of his children's classes.

We have been astonished at the success you have met with in regard to instructing pupils thoroughly and in so short a period, and do with pleasure acknowledge that we consider your mode the most practicable ever experienced. You have succeeded in a few months to make the pupils sing the scale in all intervals, and as thirds, fourths, fifths, etc. without their hesitating one moment, and have succeeded in making them thoroughly acquainted with the rudiments of music, without stuffing their heads with far-sought, and to the children, incomprehensible expressions.

We are also pleased with their remarkable ability to write down any sound or note of the scale, such as you sing them, and their bold outpourings of their little voices, not showing any fear or uncertainty in soloing their exercises.

Closing our remarks on other matters, we would add, that if vocal music was to be taught like this all over the states, we should hear less faulty singing and piano playing, such as amateurs, without any good basis of the art, are usually tormenting our ears with.[13]

Not all teachers were as successful as Mason, and often the rote aspects of the instruction degenerated into mere entertainment. In a demonstration class given by Mason and reported by J. Baxter Upham in *Dwight's Journal of Music* in 1873, we find that Mason gained the attention of his pupils by singing to them an easy melodic phrase within the range of their voices.[14] The children were then asked to repeat after him. The students' attention was aroused by appealing "to the imitative faculties which young children possess in so great a degree of perfection." Attention was given to the proper voice quality and to "smooth and pleasant intonation." The children were to be trained in the following: a proper position of the body; the right management of the breath; a good quality of utterance; the correct sound of the voice; a good articulation; and an intelligent expression of the sense. The children were allowed to sing only in the middle register of the voice. In rote singing only the first six notes of the G major scale would be attempted. After the voices had been well practiced they were extended upwards and downwards "to a judicious extent, taking care *not to strain* the voice in the least degree." It was pointed out that many of the best songs for juveniles used only the first six notes of the scale. Easy musical phrases and rhythmical structures were next taught in double and triple time and by rote. After this experience the children were taught the simplest forms of musical notation.[15]

The second year of primary instruction emphasized the different kinds of notation and rests, and the nature "of quadruple and sextuple time." They were introduced to the chromatic scale and to the key of G and F majors. The third year emphasized the understanding of intervals of the major diatonic scale.

The grammar school instruction of music covered about six years. "The lowest class carried the pupil over a rapid review of the primary material." Rote singing was for the most part abandoned, and the children were then expected to begin to read the notation of simple musical phrases at sight. "Children were taught to recognize any sound of the scale by its scale name, and produce the same at the dictation of the teacher. This still further to educate the ear. This is followed by a representation of the sound upon the musical scale, which trains the eye together with the ear."[16]

Drill exercises and practice with charts were followed by triad practice and two-part songs together with the beating of time. Upham suggested that by the second or third year the children would have had sufficient knowledge that any chorale in any one of nine different keys could have been sung by the pupils at sight.

The third year began with the study of triads on different degrees of the scale and the study of intervals and seventh chords. Upham points out that the fundamental principles of this instruction were given by the classroom teacher with the aid and general direction of the professional music supervisor.

And we take it for granted that all the regular teachers can do their part in such instruction. It requires, in the system we have been considering, no special musical ability, or previous training, for the acceptable performance of this work. An *aptness to teach* only is necessary, and any person who is fitted in other respects to hold the responsible position of teacher in a public school has the ability, we contend, to learn in a very short time (under the direction of a competent professional head), how to teach the elements of music, as well as the other studies required in our common schools. Nor is it necessary that the teachers should be able to sing in order to be successful in this branch of study, though of course it is an aid.[17]

The *National Music Course* was by far the most popular music series in the 1870s and the early 1880s. Almost all teachers were familiar with the material contained in these volumes. But by the second decade in the life of the series, a reaction began against the very familiarity of the rote song approach. School people were growing concerned lest music instruction decline to the level of mere entertainment. Schools were rapidly accepting music as a regular course of instruction, and the singing of rote songs was not recognized as contributing to a student's aesthetic understanding and musical literacy. The rote song was only looked upon as idle entertainment by many, and if the carefully prepared lessons of Mason's were not followed, the music lessons could have easily become just that. The reaction emerged in the person of Hosea Edson Holt.

THE *NORMAL MUSIC COURSE* AND HOSEA EDSON HOLT

Hosea Edson Holt was a colleague of Luther Whiting Mason. He came to the Boston public schools in 1869 to take charge of the grammar school instruction in music. He was an expert in school music pedagogy with a strong musical background. As a young man he had been a woodturner but had found time to teach a singing school. He served as a bandsman in the Civil War, and at that time decided to devote himself to the profession of music. After studying with Benjamin Baker and John Wheeler Tufts he taught music at the Wheaton Seminary and the Bridgewater Normal School. He worked with his teacher John W. Tufts on the *Normal Music Course*, which was first published in 1883 by D. Appleton and Company. The publishing rights were secured two years later by the Silver Burdett Company whose entry into the field of publishing began with this series and continued with many of the best school music books. The following vignette comes from a person who knew Holt:

Mr. Holt was to a very marked degree a magnetic personality. He was distinctly a genius but not of the forbidding, self-centered type; on the contrary, always gentle, encouraging, optimistic. With an inexhaustible fund of new ideas, he was impatient with conservatives, and created many antagonisms among the believers in the *status quo*. This led him to conflict (sometimes in the courts) with his reactionary opponents, and,— he always won his case.

Mr. Holt was a born teacher, but, as a genius, he was never contented with imparting merely established ideas. He felt keenly the inanity of the musical material culled from German sources, and chose one of his former instructors, John W. Tufts, as the maker of teaching materials which should embody the highest musical training for pupils in our public schools.

Hosea Holt was a most vociferous critic of the rote approach, and in an address before the music division of the National Education Association, Holt expressed his potent sentiments. Forty-five thousand dollars worth of pianos were purchased for the schools of Boston in order to accommodate the rote-note approach to music reading. Twelve hundred dollars alone were spent yearly on tuning. "This great outlay is not only unnecessary, but . . . these pianos have been a *positive hindrance* to real intelligent progress in vocal music on the part of both teachers and pupils. One piano in each Assembly Hall is sufficient for all purposes."[18] Holt quotes the following musical example that was used as an examination piece by the Boston Board of Supervisors who were investigating the effectiveness of the music instruction. The report of this board indicated that only "from one-half to two-thirds" of the whole sang the piece well, and the children had had eight years of music instruction.

Holt recognized that the future of music teaching lay in the hands of the classroom teacher if only she or he could be trained properly. "*Thousands* of teachers in our public schools would teach music *most successfully* could they only be shown that they can teach music just as they teach other studies, and it is not necessary for them to sing either *for* or *with* the children in order to do the most successful work." To Holt's credit he believed that an underlying musicality must pervade the music instruction. "It is very important that children should sing from the beginning none but well-written exercises and songs. Everything should be *musical*. We can never establish a true musical taste so long as we give children unmusical exercises and songs for practice." Holt was not clear about how the correct pitch was determined. He implied that the children should develop an acute sense of relative pitch in three years of practice in the primary schools. He believed that children should be given systematic practice in the "study of tone or the pitch of sounds. They should not only know and be able to give instantly the sounds of the scale in their relation to each other, but should be perfectly familiar with each sound in its relation to every other key." This knowledge was to be gained in three years of primary school. Holt believed that this instruction in pitch and scale relationships must precede the instruction in instrumental music. "We must withhold the use of *musical instruments* as a means of instruction or as aids in singing." [19]

The *Normal Music Course* was a carefully graduated series of five books or "readers" with three accompanying books, the *High School Collection*, the *Euterpean*, and the *Aoedean*. Each had a selection of works by "well-known" composers. Tufts warns us that the readers must be pursued in a regular order as "any departures from this rule would prove of serious detriment to the student." Twenty-four exercises were included in the first reader using just the first two notes of the scale. As the exercises progressed, other notes were added until the whole scale appeared. Later, the study of intervals was introduced.

Sight-singing exercises were the foundation of the series. The song material attempted to include techniques which were previously learned in the singing exercises. Chromaticism was common.

The third volume of the series contained some sight-reading exercises that were quite difficult for the children. Some parts tended toward the contrapuntal that each child could be singing a melodic part.

The *Normal Music Course* became enormously popular; its disciplined emphasis on music reading appealed to educators and to a public interested in scientific learning and in an approach that demanded rigor and formidable exertion by the child. Music teachers could evaluate the musical progress of the child by monitoring his sight-singing ability, which became the *sine qua non* of musical progress. By the end of the century the note-reading method had won a victory, and the *Normal Music Course* enjoyed the flattery of numerous imitators. But public philosophy as well as taste is ephemeral, and the pendulum of expert and public opinion swings back and forth. The problems of teaching music reading were not solved by Hosea Edson Holt and John Wheeler Tufts, any more than they were solved in the 1870s by Luther Whiting Mason. New philosophers were on the horizon and the teachers of music soon forgot their antecedents. Tradition is reinvented by each new generation wedded to progress and to the Darwinian obsession with the infinite perfectability of man.

The average song content varied little in the school music books prior to 1900. It showed almost no influence from outside the school with the exception of the Civil War years when patriotic songs increased. Walter Jones classified the song material into the following areas: seasonal, home, school, occupation, baby and childhood, sports, patriotic, with nature and religion comprising half the songs.[20] The songs themselves were usually in only a few sharps or flats with about twice as many songs in sharp keys as flat. Jones discovered no minor keys in his analysis and speculates that the difficulty of singing them in syllables may have been an important contributing factor of their neglect.[21]

OTHER PUBLICATIONS AND AUTHORS

Although the *National Music Course* and the *Normal Music Course* were the most popular of the school series books during the last half of the nineteenth century, other important additions to the school music library must be mentioned. Charles Aiken of Cincinnati, an early advocate of the movable Do as a system of instruction to be used in the public schools, wrote the *Cincinnati*

Music Readers, which was published by John Church in 1875. His *High School Choralist* and *The Choralist's Companion* were welcome contributions to the song literature for older students. Aiken borrowed from the great masters and other European composers whom he believed to be meritorious. He believed that children should be exposed to as fine a musical quality as possible given the child's level of maturity. Not all writers of school music books concerned themselves with the quality of the selection. Most books of this type written before 1900 contained songs the majority of which were composed by the author. Songs composed by other composers were rarely credited. Only a few books included material from composers we now regard as great masters, and only rarely did the author tell his pupils that such an exposure would result in an improvement of musical taste. It was expected that a knowledge of the fundamentals would thereby result in appreciation.

The works of Phillipp Friedrich Silcher of Germany, John Ryke Hullah of England, and Guillaume-Louis Bocquillon-Wilhelm of France were favored by Aiken. In 1892 the *Cincinnnati Music Readers* was expanded to five volumes by Aiken's colleague in Cincinnati, G. F. Junkermann.

In 1895 the American Book Company entered the lucrative field of music series publishing with its *Natural Course in Music,* prepared by Frederic H. Ripley and Thomas Tapper. Both men believed that instruction in music should be simple and divorced from artificial encumbrances such as charts, hand signals, or any artificial, nonmusical devices which would serve to separate the actual music from the learner. As children learn a language by natural aural means, so music should be taught the same way. The theory, or technicalities of music were to be learned late. The developmentalism of the child-study movement was making itself felt in the school music pedagogy of that day.

The American Book Company began sponsoring its "New School of Methods in Public School Music" in Cataumet, Massachusetts, at the home of Ripley, in 1895. Classes were reported as being held on Ripley's front porch and in his living room. Not to be outdone by their competitors, the American Book Company held a second institute the same year in Chicago. W. S. B. Mathews appeared as guest lecturer and observed on the pages of *Music* (a periodical of which he was editor) that other instructors at the institute included both Ripley and Tapper and C. C. Birchard.[22] The 1902 class of the New School of Music Methods was divided into five departments; the theory and art of teaching music in the schools; voice culture; form, melody, and harmony; sight singing and the practice of teaching; and music history.[23]

The normal institutes were all successful, and that each attempted to indoctrinate its students with the exclusive merits of one teaching philosophy did not seem to confuse the students. Students were usually drawn to a particular institute because they sympathized with its approach. The institutes filled a needed pedagogical gap while the state normal schools were in the process of development. It is to the credit of the music teachers themselves that they experienced the need to upgrade their skills. The instructors at the institute were all knowledgeable and experienced educators, many with national reputations. The educational results could only have been of a positive nature. W. S. B. Mathews summarized the importance of the institutes with a plea in his magazine in November of 1901.

In order to be prepared to teach singing in the public schools, you need the following subjects well mastered: First you ought to be a singer and a good reader of notes. You must have a complete musical terminology and be able to define correctly any musical term at sight. (This quality is very rare.) You must have a comprehensive oversight of the system of textbooks you are to administer. It would be better if you knew all the systems thoroughly, as to their material, their ideas and the methods in which their authorized exponents desired them to be administered. As this is rather a large problem, the best thing will be at first to select one of the latest systems (because when an adoption is close the new system has the advantage with school boards who are nothing if not progressive) and attend the summer class of that system—if it has one.[24]

CHAPTER XI

Music Teacher Education
1823-1914

T HE REFORMERS in Massachusetts were well organized and
their influence with the political powers of the state showed
the way toward permanent, statewide improvement in education.
This improvement was to be given the force of law.

James G. Carter and Horace Mann had their doubts about a
teacher-training program that consisted of one course in school-
keeping at a local academy. The need for normal schools was recognized, and by 1865 there were fifteen such institutions in ten
states: Massachusetts, New York, Connecticut, Michigan, Rhode
Island, Illinois, Minnesota, California, Maine, and Kansas.

MUSIC IN THE NORMAL SCHOOLS

The curriculum of the normal school generally consisted of a review of those subjects usually taught in the common schools and
courses in school-keeping (school management). Often a model
school was available where the students could observe and practice teaching techniques. Some advanced work was offered but
usually it was not too different from that offered by the academy.
Admission requirements were low. Music instruction was offered
both at many private academies and at the normal schools from
their beginnings. The normal schools tended to prepare teachers
for classrooms in the rural areas. Most normal schools themselves

were isolated from the larger population centers. The few normal schools that were in operation by 1865 prepared only a small fraction of the teachers needed for a population of thirty-five million people. The rate of increase in the number of normal schools was about twenty-five new schools each decade through to the end of the century. By 1900 there was a threefold increase in the number of normal schools in 1871, but the population had doubled and new compulsory attendance laws greatly expanded the need for teachers. The normal schools could barely meet the demand. By the end of the century most rural teachers "still obtained their licenses upon examination after attending a school for teachers for a short time or even without professional training."[1]

The curriculum of the normal schools expanded from one to two, three, and finally four years and maintained a close connection with rural education. In the nation's cities the high schools maintained normal classes for the training of elementary teachers but seemed reluctant to establish normal schools of any standard. Horace Mann attempted to discourage high school normal classes and the comparable classes in the private academies and select schools. He believed correctly that the normal school graduates were better teachers than the graduates of the academies or of the high schools.

An 1847 advertising circular of the state normal school at Lexington, Massachusetts, boasts that "all the school attends to vocal music, drawing and composition during the entire year." And during the last half of the nineteenth century, as normal schools increased in number, the music offerings expanded to include courses such as harmony, music history, and instrumental music lessons.

The adequacy of facilities and books varied widely. Professor Albert Miller, instructor of vocal music at the Michigan State Normal School at Ypsilanti from 1854 to 1858, commented that "the school had no books, no instruments, no facilities for teaching music. Classes were organized in vocal music and required of all students without exception. Many pupils took additional work in harmony and composition. There was also solo and quartet singing."[2] No doubt Professor Miller was successful improvising the required materials as the substance of the quotation implies.

The early normal schools provided teachers for the elementary and grammar schools of the country, and the courses were designed to provide the requisite skills. Only in the last two decades of the century was specific instruction given for music teachers. Previously, the music subjects were offered as electives and for general cultural purposes.

Because music courses were universally popular, the normal schools competed with each other to provide students with course offerings as wide and as interesting as possible.

In a statement from the 1873–1874 catalog of the Missouri State Normal School at Warrensburg, the omnipresent description of its musical offerings appears.

Vocal Music—the importance of music as one of the branches of education is fully recognized. Vocal music is taught throughout the entire course, both theoretically and practically and teachers are advised to make it a part of the course of instruction in every school with which they may be connected. Lessons are also given in instrumental music by the instructors of the school.[3]

A complete description of the music offerings at the Michigan State Normal School for the 1868–1869 school year gives an interesting insight into the music curriculum of that school and demonstrates how the eternal problem of music reading was to be approached.

MODEL SCHOOL

Primary Grade—Pupils are taught to sing easy songs by rote, beating time, and to sing the major scale by applying the syllables Do, Re, Mi, etc., and the numerals. The proper use of the voice is taught by imitation.

Grammar Grade—Exercises on the blackboard and from the school song books must be sung by note. Pupils are also required to sing the major, minor and chromatic scales by applying syllables and numerals. Songs sung by rote and the cultivation of the voice by imitation.

HIGH SCHOOL

In this class, pupils are required to sing entirely by note. Solfeggios, scales, solos and two and three-part songs. Boys being subject at this age to a change of voice, are not allowed to sing.

NORMAL SCHOOL

Class in vocal music, musical notation, singing and writing of the major, minor and chromatic scales in all of the keys. Explanation and writing of the intervals, cultivation of the voice and the physiology thereof and methods of instruction.

CHOIR OR ADVANCED CLASS

Practice of church music, selections from the works of the great masters, glees, solo and quartette singing.[4]

Obviously, the rote-singing method was then in vogue in order to introduce the beginning elements of tone and time. The grammar-grade children received not a little drill in the use of syllables. It appears that high school girls did most, if not all, of the singing at that level. But the interesting question still remains: what happened to the boys' musical development while their voices were in the process of changing? Perhaps they sat and listened, perhaps they were excused from the singing class, or perhaps they became alienated from singing. It must be remembered, also, that this course of instruction occurred at a normal school, and the young children were there for purposes of observation as well as of learning. What the potential teachers learned there, they were likely to take with them to other schools. If high school boys were not allowed to sing, the musical repercussions were undoubtedly substantial.

The curriculum was not designed specifically for teachers of music but for classroom teachers. Yet it must be recognized that early teachers of music did pass through these programs. Those who possessed a more natural ability and played the piano or sang before they entered the normal school could have easily found themselves teachers of music. These teachers, who later may have attended the normal institutes for music instruction, began to study methodology more intensely, to attend lectures on music history, and to study harmony, the latter two disciplines being conspicuously absent from the normal schools. Just as the institutes sponsored by the publishing companies geared their instruction to their own series books, so the state normal schools tended to gravitate to one or another point of view in regard to the instruction in music reading.

Instruction in vocal music at a normal school was ordinarily inadequate for the preparation of a music supervisor. Most courses of study were aimed toward the needs of the classroom teacher, most of whom were expected to teach their own vocal music. During the last three decades of the century the normal school curriculum became increasingly stable with most schools requiring two years of training and some schools offering two additional years. The potential classroom teacher was expected to receive an exposure to music varying from one-half to two-thirds of an academic year on music. The Kansas State Normal School Catalog of 1869–1870 required two terms of music instruction.[5] The first term consisted of vocal exercises, "daily recitation and study of the rules of notation," practice in music reading, and some pedagogy. The second term included the "singing of glees, quartettes, and choruses."[6]

Then, as now, periodic criticisms emerged as to the quality and extent of the courses in music for classroom teachers. George B. Loomis addressed the 1870 convention of the American Normal School and National Teachers Association about the qualities he thought essential for teaching. He was concerned that the teachers have a "practical and general knowledge of the science" and that the study be systematic and thorough. The prospective teachers should study the culture and training of the voice so as to set a good example for the children. They should have knowledge of the vocal organism so as not to undermine the voices of children. They should acquire a "knowledge of the more intellectual or mechanical part of the subject. This will enable pupils to interpret what is written in song language with independence." The teacher should "understand the power of music as an educational force," and she or he "should, after having gained a knowledge of the subject, become conversant with the best methods of imparting a knowledge of it."[7]

But the average classroom teacher would never approach the aspirations of our educational leaders in the field of music, and conversely there would never be a sufficient supply of music specialists to give daily instruction in music to children. Frank A. Beach, of the Kansas State Normal School at Emporia, suggested that music be a regular subject to be included for the certification of grade school teachers. He stressed the need for appropriate supervision of those grade school teachers who were having difficulties with music instruction.[8] While the musical education of the classroom teacher fluctuated widely from one institution to another, the special education of the music teacher improved during the last three decades of the century.

The training of music teachers began as an adjunct to the regular teacher preparatory programs. The normal schools were already teaching music not only because it was a required skill but also because of the almost universal popularity of the instruction. Soon a number of normal schools expanded their offerings in music to include special courses for the training of music supervisors in the public schools or for those whose ambitions included musical pursuits outside the schools.

The Pennsylvania State Normal School at Mansfield was one of the first to organize a separate department for those students who wished to specialize in music. Its catalog of 1871–1872 describes the music courses of the State Normal Academy, which were divided into four departments:

The Vocal Department. Embraces everything pertaining to voice culture or vocal music, both sacred and secular as applied to solo or chorus practice, from the usual popular styles to the classical works of our greatest masters.

The Theoretical Department. Includes notation, thorobase, harmony and musical composition.

The Aesthetical Department. The one to which all others become subservient and without which no one is able to acquire a proper taste and style, as it quickens the musical perceptions and develops the facilities in such a manner that they become susceptible to the beautiful effects that may be produced by the resources obtained from instrument, voice or composition.[9]

The Instrumental Department. Includes every instrument in general use, in church, parlor, orchestra or brass band.

Students could take the full program or elect only those that interested them. Those students who wished to graduate "in music" were required to complete at least three branches: "1) the theoretical course, 2) some instrument (usually piano or organ), and 3) voice culture."[10] One course in the teachers' class was also required.

The Michigan State Normal School at Ypsilanti also provided a special music curriculum for the prospective music supervisor. Its normal conservatory opened in 1881 with a curriculum offering piano, organ, violin, "violin-cello," and voice culture.[11] The four-year curriculum for music for the Michigan State Normal School in 1882–1883 showed an increased specialization in the last three years.

FIRST YEAR

Any one of the other courses which the student may select with the approval of the principal.

SECOND YEAR

First Term	*Second Term*
1. Elements of vocal music with methods of instruction	1. Advanced vocal music and voice culture
2. Algebra	2. Elementary Physics
3. Rhetoric	3. English Literature
4. German, French or Latin, Essays	4. German, French or Latin, Essays.
Instrumental music may be substituted for either 2, 3, or 4.	Instrumental music may be substituted for 4.

THIRD YEAR

1. Harmony	1. Harmony
2. Voice Culture	2. Voice Culture
3. Principles of Teaching	3. Principles of Teaching
4. German, French or Latin. Essays	4. German, French or Latin. Essays.
Instrumental Music may be substituted for 4.	Instrumental music may be substituted for 4.

FOURTH YEAR

1. Musical Composition and Literature of Music	1. Solo Singing
2. Solo Singing	2. Literature
3. Language or Literature	3. Professional training in Arithmetic, 10 wks. in Grammar, 10 wks.
4. Practice teaching. Essays. Instrumental Music may be substituted for 3.	4. Practice teaching. Essays Instrumental music may be substituted for 2.[12]

The increased course offerings in instrumental music are of interest. Until the last third of the century, instrumental music in a catalog almost universally referred to the study of the piano. Only occasionally would the violin be offered as an elective. But toward the end of the century increased offerings in instrumental music became more available, and some years in advance of the instruction in instrumental music in the public schools.

The curricula at the Michigan State Normal School, and others like it throughout the country, began to look more impressive. Of course we cannot know which courses were well taught or what the performance standards were either in the instrumental instruction or the theoretical courses. Nonetheless, we can make two general observations. One, opportunities for music instruction of various kinds were on the increase. Public school systems were adopting music as a regular course of instruction, and the academies and normal schools were competing in an effort to achieve a reputation (or, in the case of the private academies, to keep their doors open for yet another year). Two, educational leaders in the field of music were imbued with an artistic determination to raise standards on all levels.

EARLY MUSICAL INSTITUTES

The nation's schools of higher education did not flock to the cause of preparing teachers of music. In 1916, in a survey of 117 schools, only 23 percent were found to be engaged in programs for training music supervisors.[13] The establishment of textbook institutes fulfilled a vital function in the education of a music teacher.

Normal institutes evolved from the convention and date from the middle of the century. Rather than a few days, the normal institutes remained in session for three or more weeks. The institutes were held once a year, usually during the summer months. Again, those who attended were often the singing masters, but by this time they were joined by public school teachers, private music teachers, and church officials. According to George F. Root, the idea of the normal institute was suggested by Root to Lowell Mason about 1850 or 1852. Root believed that the usual three-day sessions of a singing convention were insufficient to give music teachers the requisite skills and information. He suggested that a three-month period would be preferable. In April 1853 the New York Normal Musical Institute met with Lowell Mason as conductor.* The institute was in session from April 25 through July 20 with fifty-one people in attendance. The enthusiasm was such that plans were made for another meeting the following year.

In 1857 a normal institute was held at North Reading, Massachusetts, Root's summer home. Its daily schedule of activities, supplied for us by John Sullivan Dwight, begins to show a modern pedagogical concern for the musicianship and skills necessary to teach vocal music successfully in the schools.

---

* The faculty included William Bradbury, Thomas Hastings, and R. Storrs Willis. Assisting with the private vocal and instrumental lessons were Clare W. Beames, John Zundel, E. Howe, Allen Dodworth, U. C. Hill, and Osborn Oxnard.

NORTH READING NORMAL MUSICAL INSTITUTE FOR 1857

Daily Routine

8:30–9:15. Elementary Class in Vocal Training with particular attention to all that is essential to correct vocal performance.

9:15–11:15. Familiar lecture on elementary music, and methods of teaching, including an example of the true mission of song, its relation to man's creative nature; and the furnishing of teachers with a knowledge of those principles which, having their foundation in nature, shall serve as a sure guide for their future work.

11:15–12:00. Advanced class in Vocal Training. Practice of Solfeggi, style and facility in execution.

2:30–3:15. Teaching exercise, during which time some member of the class assumes the position of teacher, subject to the criticism of the other members. Time is occasionally taken for musical performances by individuals, also subject to the criticism of the class and teachers.

3:45–4:15. Advanced class in Harmony, Composition and four-part writing.

On particular days certain of the above exercises are laid aside for practice of glees and chorus singing under Mr. Webb, whose long experience and excellent qualifications in this department are too well known to need comment.[14]

Reactions from those in attendance were positive if we are to believe the published comments and letters presently available to us. One such observation was published in the *New York Musical Review and Gazette*,[15] and although one would not expect an extensive criticism of the institutes from this source, the reactions are nevertheless of interest.

All the classes come together for the opening exercises; and here the plain song of the people, the impressive chant, and the appropriate anthem are producing deep and lasting impressions on our minds. We are forgetting gradually musical performances and vocal display, and making this exercise more and more an act of graceful worship.

After this, Dr. Mason's work of demolishing our noble systems of teaching commences. But we have one comfort, which is, that we really see that we are learning a "more excellent way."[16]

Problems in learning the techniques of harmony were presented by George F. Root according to the Pestalozzian principle of the "thing before the sign."

In the afternoon our harmony lessons came, and here all our previous notions are knocked into Pi. Instead of being told that certain chords and progressions are wrong because they look so, we are compelled to sing and listen, sing and listen until we ascertain for ourselves whether they are so or not.

Mr. Root, seating himself at the piano-forte played successions of chords, modulating into keys both closely and remotely related to the original and the class was called upon to decide by ear the character of each successive chord; in what key, whether direct or inverted; what particular inversion, etc. Another year and this class will be ready to pass to a higher region of the art and attack canon and fugue.[17]

Pedagogical experience and training was achieved in the time-honored manner of selecting members of the class to act as teachers followed by a critique by both teachers and students.

And how we quake in our shoes when we are called to give a lesson to a singing class, to be criticized by the other scholars and the teachers. In this thing especially we are treated shamefully; for we have been told a thousand times that we are something quite remarkable in the way of teaching singing schools, and after we get through, to hear one, and another, and a dozen or more get up and pick us all to pieces.[18]

In an institute held in South Bend, Indiana, in 1870, the curriculum was expanded to include music literature and history. Special instructors for this branch were William Mason, Lowell's son and a renowned pianist, and W. S. B. Mathews, a well-known publisher and musical scholar. George B. Loomis was one of the general assistants. Much attention was devoted to the study and discussion of public school music and its problems. Illustrated lectures were given by William Mason and W. S. B. Mathews on an analysis of the piano music of various composers.[19]

Institutes were held almost everywhere during the 1870s. At an institute at Florida, New York, both Lowell and William Mason served as faculty; the grand old man of music education was now seventy-eight years old. Theodore Seward who led the institute was a former student of Mason's and collaborated with him in a book called *The Pestalozzian Music Teacher*.

The idea of a convention or a musical institute for the purpose of giving music instruction to teachers prospered. Toward the end of the nineteenth century several music publishing companies were engaged in a spirited competition in what was becoming a lucrative market in school music instruction books. It soon became apparent that the sales of series books could be enhanced if music institutes could be organized by the publishing companies themselves to teach the usual curriculum of pedagogy, but emphasizing the special philosophies and methods of their own publications.

On October 1, 1886, the Ginn Company organized classes for classroom teachers in the use of Luther Whiting Mason's *National Music Course*. Organized under Mason's leadership, the classes adopted, in general, the teaching programs of the normal institutes and were called the National Normal Music School.[20]

During the first year of operation the school met daily from October 1, 1886, until September 2, 1887. Its first faculty was headed by Luther Whiting Mason and assisted by eight prominent music supervisors and teachers from the Boston area. The instructional organization was divided into the primary, grammar, and high school departments. It must have become apparent that an institute in session for the whole year became cumbersome and obviously limited its students to those who either worked in the Boston area or who did not work at all. Thus, the next year the institute was held during the summer months only. The curriculum was organized so that a supervisor's diploma could be achieved by the students after three summers of instruction. The institute was a resounding success. Soon the Ginn Company began holding two institutes simultaneously, one in the East and the other in the West, with the instruction based on Mason's *National Music Course*. In addition to pedagogy, the institute taught harmony, history of music, and sight-singing.

The success of this institute and the several others which followed lasted until the second decade of the twentieth century. The curriculum expanded as did the numbers of students who poured through the summer programs in search of information and improved techniques for teaching music to children. The 1914 session of this institute took place at Lake Forest College in Illinois where 357 persons attended from thirty states. The course included fifteen subjects related to school music, and credit had to be achieved in all before a diploma would be awarded.[21] In 1920 the Ginn Company announced that their institutes would be discontinued. The nation's colleges, universities, normal schools, and conservatories had taken over pedagogical instruction; the Ginn Company and other publishing companies like it returned exclusively to publishing.

In 1884 Hosea Holt, the inveterate competitor of Luther Whiting Mason, organized a Normal Institute of Vocal Harmony at Lexington, Massachusetts. Holt's emphasis on music reading became the prominent aspect of those institutes following the philosophy presented in the *Normal Music Course*.

Though a strong critic of the rote approach, Holt still believed in the "thing before the sign," a Pestalozzian precept that was universally accepted during this period. But he disagreed on what constituted the "thing." Holt criticized the rote approach saying that the "thing" was not the song as advocated by Mason and others. Learning by imitation was anathema to Holt who could only accept the rote learning of a scale. Knowledge was gained, believed Holt, by thinking not by memorizing. Proper training could be achieved only by "careful systematic cultivation of the mind through practice in thinking and producing the sounds in the scale."[22] Holt wanted to train teachers in the use of his system, and his Normal Institute of Vocal Harmony was the result.

When the Silver Burdette Company took over Holt's institute program and formed the American Institute of Normal Methods, Holt's philosophy and teaching methods were given a platform comparable to that of the *National Music Course*. The American Institute of Normal Methods met for the first time in 1889. Holt was the director and was assisted by other prominent music educators.[*] The 1901 meeting of this institute, held at Northwestern University, attracted more than one hundred persons.[23]

An advertisement appearing in the July 1894 issue of *Music* again reinforced the philosophy based upon the sanctity of note reading. Its somewhat defensive nature is not surprising for a pe-

* Leonard B. Marchall of Boston, Samuel W. Cole of Brookline, Massachusetts, and Fred A. Lyman of Syracuse, New York.

riod that witnessed a challenge to these concepts in the form of the child-study movement.

This institute stands for a principle in teaching vocal Music which has given it a National reputation. Wonderful results are now being obtained by Mr. Holt's New System of Vocal Harmony. This system of teaching is based upon the great truth that Musical Tones are established in nature in a certain fixed and absolute relation to each other, as much as the planets. To this fact Mr. Holt has applied a pedagogical principle, and has worked out a system of teaching vocal music that is based upon the laws of the human mind. This system of teaching is wonderful in its simplicity.[24]

The beginning of what might be called the modern concept developed from the child-study movement which had its roots in G. Stanley Hall's *The Contents of Children's Minds Upon Entering School*, which was published in 1883. Opposed to the traditional pattern of the child conforming to the school, the child-study idea reasoned that the school might better study and adapt to the child. To reflect this liberalization of thought, the *Modern Music Series*, compiled by Robert Foresman and Eleanor Smith, was published in 1898 by Scott, Foresman and Company. In 1901 the publishing rights were secured by the Silver Burdette Company which was corporately happy to be able to publish music series encompassing conflicting and competing viewpoints. Robert Foresman outlined the philosophy behind his *Modern Music Series*:

The child's first impression of music should be gained from good music, learned by ear and sung intuitively, his first conception of elements should be deduced from song and re-sung in the spirit of the song. These elements with their own characteristics should then be recognized and studied, and should be recognized as mere forms to be noted, remembered, classified and applied exactly as other scientific knowledge should be noted, remembered classified and applied, in order to be considered practical and useful.[25]

CRANE NORMAL INSTITUTE

One of the normal schools to achieve national recognition was the Crane Normal Institute, which was affiliated with the state normal school at Potsdam, New York. Julia Ettie Crane, its founder, came to the Potsdam faculty in 1884. She had been a student at the school and came burdened with the inadequacies of her own school experiences. Julia Crane accepted the position at Potsdam with the understanding that she would be allowed to implement her plans for expanding the music curriculum of the school. One year later the Special Music Course was instituted, a curriculum for the education of music teachers that was to remain virtually unchanged for decades. Crane wanted to emphasize a commonality between the preparation of a music teacher and the preparation of a musician.

The course in theory at the institute included instruction in all major, minor, and chromatic scales. It emphasized all signs and terms used in music. The student studied intervals, triads, and seventh-chords in addition to part singing and finally harmony. Her large classes of voice students were indoctrinated with the precepts of subduing harsh tones and of avoiding a forcing of the voice.[26] Her potential teachers were instructed in the art and science of arranging subject matter into a logical course of study. Model lessons were given for purpose of illustration. Simple melodies were analyzed so the students could determine the proper accent and phrasing, and elementary writing exercises were given so that young children would have a proper introduction to rhythm and pitch. The principles of good teaching were observed and their application to the teaching of music investigated. And last, the then-current music books were examined and compared.

The model school was the backbone of the music student's association with teaching. Each pupil was assigned a model school class. After a period of observation, he taught for a period of twenty minutes per day for ten weeks. Directed by the normal school faculty, the students met weekly for a discussion of their common problems.

Crane published a *Teachers' Manual* in 1887, a book which was to influence the training of music teachers at other institutions. She was able to reconcile the differences between the rote and note methods of music teaching, borrowing one idea and then the other when they could be justified philosophically and empirically. Rote singing should be stressed in the primary grades, according to Crane, the children receiving value from an imitative experience. The teacher should emphasize the training of the voices at this time and allow the natural awakening of the emotions to take place. Note reading was to be taught in the grammar grades and approached through the scale. Her three steps in learning the scale followed the almost universally recognized principle of "the thing before the sign."

1. The pupil must hear the scale before he can sing it.
2. After hearing the scale, pupils can learn to sing it accurately.
3. When children can sing the scale, the symbols can be learned.[27]

The last three decades of the nineteenth century were tentative years for the education of music teachers at normal schools. The direction was correct but the aims and standards were divergent. Changes in society's expectations often acted as a catalyst to changes in curricular offerings and institutional standards. Students could attend normal schools in the 1880s and 1890s without the benefit of a high school diploma. As a high school education became more universal, it soon became mandatory for students to have achieved this distinction before entering a normal school. General academic course offerings were increased and their contents strengthened, a manifestation that resulted from the improved educational skills of prospective students. By the early years of the twentieth century, it became necessary for students to have already had a modicum of musical experience before entering a normal school. Slowly, the course offerings themselves were strengthened and deepened. That which took one semester to complete eventually took two or more semesters. Requirements in applied music were more clearly defined.

The child-study movement influenced at least the course descriptions and the various statements of philosophy as they appeared in school catalogs. Julia Crane substantially rewrote her principles for the education of children in music in her *Teachers' Manual* of 1915.

Period of Infancy. Not under the direct control of the teacher. Stress given to the importance of providing the right kind of music education so that pupils as future parents can provide a wholesome musical atmosphere for their children. If the pupil enters kindergarten, the teacher can furnish some of the means through song and rhythm by which play is enriched by elements peculiarly enjoyable to the child.

Transition Period. Sixth to eighth year (first and second grades). Music should be presented to the child almost entirely by ear. Through songs and games, through marching and dancing, experience with music fundamentals is gained.

Eighth to Twelfth Year. Period of acquiring formal learning. This is the time for drill, discipline, technique. It should pave the way for enjoyment of the higher realms of music in the seventh and eighth grades and in high school where attempts to teach fundamentals are likely to fail.[28]

In 1914, the results of a national survey of 164 institutions for the training of teachers showed that only 43 offered curricula for the training of music specialists. While the length of time for the completion of the requirements varied from one to five years, the usual time was two years. The courses, with the number of schools teaching them, were as follows: [29]

- Elementary Theory and Sight Singing (41)
- Harmony (37)
- Counterpoint and Composition (18)
- Instrumentation (16)
- History, aesthetics, appreciation (37)
- Voice (private and class) (37)
- Piano (26)
- Conducting (32)
- Methods (39)
- History of Education, Pedagogy, Psychology (32)
- Practice Teaching (32)

Elementary theory and sight singing were universally accepted by these institutions, which is not surprising considering the popularity of sight singing as a vehicle for music education or the sole avenue toward musicality (depending upon one's point of view). That the study of counterpoint and composition occur infrequently should also not surprise us as these skills were considered rather advanced with little or no thought that they should be useful in the instruction of children. The acceptance of instrumental music as a branch of public school instruction was still a few years away, so a course in instrumentation is far from popular. Still, it is surprising that the study of the piano was not reported with greater frequency. Perhaps that instrument was so universally studied that many schools merely expected its students to have a reasonable acquaintance with it. It is also possible that some schools may have worked out an informal agreement with a local piano teacher to give lessons to those students who were in need.

But many schools offered an impressive array of courses. The Iowa State Teachers College for the school year 1910–1911 offered a comprehensive two-year program. Though light in academic general course requirements, the school attempted to give its students at least an exposure to a rather complete spectrum of music offerings:

FIRST YEAR

First Term:	*Second Term*:	*Third Term*:
Psychology	English Literature	Nature Study
Rhetoric	Psychology	Voice
3rd Term Music	4th Term Music	6th Term Music
Sight Singing	Sight Singing and	Methods
Elementary Harmony	Methods	Harmony
Voice	History of Music	History of Music
	5th Term Music	5th Term Music
	Harmony	Ear Training
	Voice	Advanced Sight
	Physical Training	Singing
	Literary Society Work	Piano

SECOND YEAR

First Term:	*Second Term*:	*Third Term*:
Sound	History	History of
Elocution	School Management	Education
7th Term Music	8th Term Music	Voice
History of Music	Appreciation	9th Term Music
Harmony	Harmony	Supervision
Conducting	Child Voice	Harmony
Observation	Practice Teaching	Theory
	Physical Training	Practice Teaching
	Literary Society Work	

Piano and voice taught privately.
Term—12 weeks of daily recitation (1 hour).
Not all classes met five days per week.[30]

The curricula at the various normal schools, colleges, and universities were, for the most part, slow in offering courses for the preparation of music teachers. If the music teaching profession was to achieve a degree of dignity, lack of standardization could not be allowed to persist. In 1907 the Music Supervisors National Conference was organized, and it served as a forum for the discussion of a more standard curriculum. In 1921 the Educational Council of that body made an extended report and included a four-year projected curriculum for training music specialists. The council's formula, which included three-fourths music and professional courses to one-fourth general studies, set a precedent for decades.

The council recommended that the time required for the course of study be four years, after which the "Mus. B. or the Mus. B. in

Education would be awarded." Entrance requirements specified that the student be graduated from high school and have "the ability to perform at the piano at the grade two level." The student was to be able to sing a hymn at sight, to be in possession of an agreeable singing voice, and to have "a quick sense of tone and rhythm." Of the ninety hours of courses, sixty were to be devoted to music study and thirty to the study of pedagogy. The academic area included such courses as English, history, dramatic expression (speech), modern languages and science, while the pedagogical requirements included educational psychology, principles of teaching, conducting, methods for grades, high school, and orchestra; and practice teaching. The following music courses were suggested: [31]

a. Piano
    (covering at least the third grade)   8 hours
b. Voice   4 hours
c. Theory   16 hours
    (harmony, form and analysis)
d. Ear Training   8 hours
    (Melodic and harmonic)
e. Music history and appreciation   8 hours
f. Orchestration and practical work instruments   8 hours
g. Electives   4 hours

This movement toward standardization was an important beginning. As the musical interests expanded during the course of the twentieth century, the requisite offerings grew to fulfill the needs. Those needs, which included instrumental music classes, ensembles—large and small—music appreciation, and various creative activities, are all part of an interesting and exciting expansion of music in the public schools.

CHAPTER XII

The Child-Study
Movement and the Psychologizing
of Education

P SYCHOLOGICAL research during the latter part of the nineteenth century and continuing into the twentieth laid the
groundwork for the progressive movement in education. Its effect
on the acceptance of the arts, in addition to many other subjects,
was significant.

During the nineteenth century, the most popular conception
of learning was based on faculty psychology. Its theory was first
formulated by Christian von Wolff in 1734 and somewhat later
in 1785 by Thomas Reid, a Scottish philosopher. The doctrine
viewed the mind as a spiritual entity apart from the body and
unique to man. The mind could be studied by introspection, believed these philosophers, and evidence of the way one felt in-
wardly was sufficient evidence of the way the mind worked.

In the United States the most generally accepted theory was that
the mind was divided into three separate faculties: the will, or voli-
tion, which enables man to act; the emotions; and the intellect.
The proponents of this theory were largely concerned with the faculty of intellect, of which scholarly knowledge was viewed as the
most important. The acceptance of faculty psychology provided
the intellectual rationale for the idea of mental discipline. This
concept has been defined variously as the ability to remember or

the sharpening of the wits. The concept of mental discipline assumed that the mind required training for its fullest development. Only abstract subjects such as the classics, philosophy, and mathematics would provide the sharpening of intellect. Intensive drill and practice along with the cultivation of the memory were standard procedures in the nineteenth-century schoolroom. A mind so trained could transfer its powers to whatever application was required. By the turn of the nineteenth century, faculty psychology was still the prevalent guide to methodology and curriculum. Modern psychologists today cannot agree on the manner in which the mind works, or even on a definition of *mind*, but they are in unanimous agreement in their condemnation of the concept that the mind is composed of trainable faculties.

Darwin did much to break down the older concepts of an independent mind and body and suggested that the mind was a product of evolutionary growth. William James set the problem to rest in his *Principles of Psychology* when he wrote that no longer should one refer to the mind as divided into separate powers or "faculties."[1] He believed that the transition between the thought of one object and the thought of another was no more a break in the thought "than a joint in a bamboo is a break in the wood." James described mental activity as a continuous flow, and any subdivision of the mind as unwarranted. The psychological concept was to influence profoundly the development of American education. The human mind could now be thought of as a behavioral instrument which allowed man to change his nature and modify his environment.

G. Stanley Hall became the first to formulate a psychological system based upon these ideas to be used in the instruction of children. He studied experimental psychology under Wilhelm Wundt in Leipzig, and at Harvard he received the first doctorate in psychology. He later founded the first psychological laboratory in America at Johns Hopkins University in 1883. Four years later he founded the *American Journal of Psychology*, the first journal of its kind to be published in the United States. When Hall assumed the presidency of Clark University in 1889, he succeeded in making that institution a famous center for research in the study of child development.

Hall believed that the mind and body evolved in a parallel fashion through a series of stages from the earliest history of man through to modern civilization. He conceptualized that the individual "recapitulates" this evolution as growth and development takes place.

Hall was strongly attracted to the questionnaire as a psychological device. His first monograph, *The Contents of Children's Minds Upon Entering School*, was developed from its use. Though it was not the scientific instrument that psychologists today endorse, the study attracted wide attention. His study concluded that the concepts of children vary greatly with each change in environment. Hall suggested that parents and teachers acquaint children with "natural objects" which would increase the conceptual range of children's minds.[2]

Hall was a tenacious advocate of Darwinian concepts and the latter's "recapitulation theory," and attempted to explain the psychology of adolescence and early childhood as manifestations or "consummations" resulting from organic changes within the body.[3]

A prolific writer and an author of more than a hundred questionnaire studies during his years at Clark University, Hall became immensely popular and his ideas made him a national leader of the child-study movement. Hall, like John Dewey and Francis Wayland Parker of Quincy, Massachusetts, placed the child at the center of the educational process. He believed that the school should adapt itself to the various natural stages of a child's growth. While the antecedents of Hall's psychology go back to Pestalozzi and Rousseau, and even to Comenius, his theories, as well as those of others, brought about a change in the thinking of the public and of the educational establishment in relation to the school curriculum.

Hall was not insensitive to the values of music in the education of children. A paper delivered to the music department of the National Education Association in 1908 waxed eloquent concerning the psychological aspects of music and its relationship to children. While much of his discourse was strangely unscientific and rhapsodic, a final series of observations demonstrate a sensitivity to the functions and philosophy of public school music, problems which have not been completely solved to this day.

Much school music is now chosen merely with reference to some scheme of pedagogic, systematic progression. Much method here is a sin against the holy ghost of music itself. Every tune introduced should have a moral and aesthetic justification and should be admitted to the school canon only after careful deliberation and for good and sufficient reasons. And then and only then music will be rescued from its present abject subordination and given its rightful, commended place in the curriculum as the trainer of the feelings which are three-fourths of life.[4]

Hall wanted "to break away from all current practices, traditions, methods, and philosophies" and to establish a curriculum "based solely upon a fresh and comprehensive view of the nature and needs of childhood."[5]

The work of John Dewey probably had a wider effect on educational theory than that of any other. Dewey showed the necessity of connecting the work of the school with life outside the school. Like G. Stanley Hall, Dewey believed that real education must be based upon the nature of the child. The mind is a growing affair, demanding continual stimuli from social agencies for its development. One learns by doing, to swim by swimming, to talk by talking to people, and to think by attempting to solve real problems and not by memorizing mere formal exercises. In Dewey's *School and Society* (1899) among other writings, the philosopher insists that school "is not a preparation for life except as it reproduces the typical conditions of social life." It is not a preparation for life, but is life.

In *How We Think* (1909) Dewey gives life to the idea that all learning takes place in attempts to remedy inadequacies of past experiences, and past experiences become the material out of which the future is shaped.

John Dewey was born in Burlington, Vermont, in 1859, the year that Darwin's *Origin of Species* was published. He graduated from the University of Vermont in 1879 and taught for short intervals in South Oil City, Pennsylvania, and in Charlotte, Vermont. He reentered the University of Vermont for a year of graduate study in philosophy where he studied under Professor H. A. P. Torrey from whom Dewey's ideas of child growth and development may have germinated.

It seems reasonable to suppose that Dewey's early influences in philosophy were not lost. Later, at the new Johns Hopkins University where he earned his doctorate, Dewey was introduced to the Hegelian idealism of George S. Morris and the experimental psychology of G. Stanley Hall. His interest in psychology continued at the University of Michigan where he taught for several years and where he worked with Morris who was also a member of the faculty. Darwin's experimental approach must be considered strongly influential, but William James's *Principles of Psychology* may have had the greatest single influence on Dewey in the formation of his mature philosophical thinking. Dewey's intellectual growth coincided with the rise of progressivism and militant social protest. In Dewey, the philosopher merged with the social activist. Dewey's own aims gradually shifted from the study of philosophy as a strict discipline to a broader view of social aims and the values of education that could contribute toward their solution. Philosophy for Dewey became an instrument for action in human affairs. He wrote in 1916, "Unless a philosophy is to remain symbolic—or verbal—or a sentimental indulgence for a few, or else mere arbitrary dogma, its auditing of past experience and its program of values must take effect in conduct."[6]

In 1894 Dewey accepted an appointment as head of the departments of philosophy, psychology, and pedagogy at the University of Chicago. He remained there for ten years. From 1904 until he retired, he was professor of philosophy at Columbia University. For fifty years he was regarded as the most important educational philosopher, and his practical influence on the schools of the nation cannot be exaggerated.

Dewey's famous Laboratory School was opened in 1896 with two instructors and sixteen children. By 1902 the school had expanded to a maximum enrollment of 140 pupils and twenty-three teachers who were assisted by ten university graduate students. With small classes and a unique innovative educational philosophy, the school became the most interesting experimental venture in American education. The Laboratory School was linked to the University of Chicago from 1896 to 1904. During this period Dewey and his staff attempted to develop a unified system from the kindergarten through to the college level. The Laboratory School was "child centered." The interests of the children determined the curriculum, and these interests were followed in whatever direction they would lead. Dewey believed in the importance of emphasizing the present. The teacher was obliged to recognize the immediate use of the child's interests while also moving the child in the desired direction. "This utilizing of interest and habit to make of it something fuller, wider, something more refined and under better control, might be defined as the teacher's whole duty."[7] Dewey's teaching and curriculum started with question marks rather than fixed rules.

Perhaps the key to Dewey's plan was flexibility. This plasticity extended from curricular design to methodology in the classroom. With a growing acceptance of curricular flexibility, the burden of defending music programs in the nation's schools became less strained. With the gradual demise of faculty psychology, it became less necessary to defend music education behind a phalanx of mental discipline. No longer was it necessary to suggest, as did Lowell Mason and William Woodbridge, that music instruction would produce a changed condition in the intellectual, social, emotional, and moral faculties. No more should any spiritual descendants of Horace Mann have to suggest, as did that great Massachusetts educator, that "vocal music furnishes the means of intellectual exercises," and that "all musical tones have mathematical relations." No more would a Dr. Rush have to defend vocal music in our schools by suggesting that singing was a means of "protection from the pulmonary diseases so common in our climate; and that "singing was employed with success as a means of arresting the progress of pulmonary complaints."[8]

The educational philosophy of John Dewey, aided by the psychological studies of G. Stanley Hall and so many others who helped to give childhood a dignity and existence different from that of adulthood, would set the stage for a phenomenal period of growth in twentieth-century music education. The century would see more functions taken over by the public schools with curricula of a widening and expanding nature. It would see a period of rapid technological changes affecting the methodology of school music instruction. It would see the rise of instrumental instruction in the public schools with the amazing phenomenon of the school band which was to replace the ubiquitous town band which had been so much a part of life in rural, nineteenth-century America. And it would see its progress threatened by a reaction to Dewey's progressivism as an insecure citizenry turned upon its educational establishment in the late 1950s at the real or imagined threat of the Soviet Union and as the educational mentality of the nation again turned from a child-centered approach back to concepts resembling the mental-discipline theories of the nineteenth century.

Our educators were irresolute, first adapting one point of view and then another, with the true nature of learning as elusive as ever.

CHAPTER XIII

The Music Educator and Music Appreciation

T HE TERM "appreciation" was and is used by musicians with
some apology. It never seemed to define precisely the understanding of music that the musician would like to imply, but it sur-
vived as a term because none other appeared to work as well. Will
Earhart, the philosopher and music educator par excellence of the
early part of this century was particularly troubled, not as much
with the philosophical implications of "appreciation" as with the
term itself.

I am sick of the word "appreciation" by which is often meant a desire to
find beauties that we really have not found at all. I am so tired of gush
from people who have not found anything to gush about, only wished
they had, and I do want to try not to foist any enthusiasm of my own on
young people.[1]

But Will Earhart continued to use the word "appreciation," undoubtedly for want of a better choice.

Richard Lee Dunham describes early efforts in the nineteenth
century to acquaint the concert-going public with the essence of
music in the hope of fostering a better understanding of both the
composer's art and the performer's. In 1824 Hans Georg Nageli
gave a series of lectures in various German cities on the nature of
music, lectures which were published in book form two years later.
Charles Burney, the eighteenth-century music historian, lamented
that so many treatises on the subject of music composition and

performance were written yet "none had appeared to help ignorant lovers of music learn to listen and evaluate music."

Francois-Joseph Fétis wrote the first widely circulated book on
the appreciation of music which was published in 1830.* A book
"for the edification of the listener," went through nineteen editions
in seven different languages. The author's purpose was an attempt
"to give general and sufficient information, on all that contributed
to the effect of the art of music, with as little use of technical language as possible."[2]

Later, in 1862, in the United States, John Knowles Paine was appointed to the newly created chair of music at Harvard University,
where he began a series of evening conversations on music for un-
dergraduates. His purpose was to provide historical and aesthetic
instruction in music for the general student of the university.

In the 1880s Thomas Whitney Surette, a staff lecturer for the
American Society for the Extension of University Teaching, in
Philadelphia, presented between one to two thousand lectures on
music in the United States and England. In the next decade and up
to the year 1906, he "lectured on music to people of all sorts and
conditions in villages, towns, and cities, at universities, at workingmen's centres, at schools, at convents, and at other institutions."[3] He reported that people were generally susceptible to music of the best kind and observed growth in the number of people
who were seeking music. He believed that he was able to observe a
trend whereby more men were accompanying their wives to musical performances as a result of his efforts in the area of appreciation. Surette illustrated his lectures on the piano. He wanted to
help members of his audience cultivate their own "powers of aural
observation" through his illustration of the music at the piano. He
believed that a single hearing was not necessarily beneficial, and
played a piece bit by bit until the listener could connect one part
with another and become thoroughly familiar with it. His lectures
were organized into a series of six or twelve weekly meetings, with
questions and discussion part of each session. Surette sometimes
used the pianola as a substitute for his personal playing. To his
credit, the lectures dealt with the music itself rather than with the
lives of the composers. Surette believed that the appreciation of

* La Musique mise a la portee de tout le monde

music consisted of two points: the emotional and the formal. The two elements coexist in every great piece of music. Real appreciation, believed Surette, took place when the listener was able to perceive each of the elements in its proper relation. He was very concerned about the diminished level of appreciation when insufficient organization meant too few lectures at a given location. "Peripatetic lectures," he said, "do not work well."[4]

In 1885, W. S. B. Mathews published one of the most important two-volume books of its kind on the appreciation of music. *How to Understand Music* was designed for use in the piano studio. Its preface stated its purpose:

As a text, the present work covers new ground. Its prime object is to lead the student to a consciousness of music as MUSIC, and not merely as playing, singing, or theory. It begins at the foundation of the matter; namely with the observation of musical phraseology, the art of hearing and following coherent musical discourse.[5]

A guide for teachers, the book gave pedagogical cues as to what compositions to play, what questions to ask the students, and what to expect in the way of answers. One to three page lessons were presented with much emphasis on musical form. Phrases, periods, themes, cadences, imitation, variation, and rhythms were indicated with the complex examples following from the more elementary. A list of compositions that might be performed followed each lesson. Mathews's analysis of the Fugue No. 2 in C Minor from the *Well-Tempered Clavier* gives us an example of the author's concept of his role:

In all these a leading subject is taken as a text not to come back to and repeat entire as in the Rondo and other binary and ternary forms, but to *work with*, to transpose and transform, to elaborate by means of harmonic treatment until an entire movement is built up out of it. This is the type of musical composition as it existed in Bach's time. Some pieces are more emotional than others, but all of them are built up on this plan. They contain *Musical Thought*. (These transformations of motive are equivalent to reasoning in language.) To appreciate them properly one needs to follow the idea through all its modifications and modulations.[6]

While the author addressed this book to the serious piano student, its nontechnical approach recommended itself to the general musical public. The book had a wide circulation and went through a number of editions. It became a widely mentioned reference by other authors of music appreciation texts well into the next century.

Henry Krehbiel, who served as American editor for the second edition of *Groves Dictionary* and as editor of the English language edition of Thayer's *Life of Beethoven*, was music critic of the New York *Herald Tribune*. In 1897 he wrote a book entitled *How to Listen to Music*.[7] As a music critic, Krehbiel had ample opportunity to observe the need for an appreciation text for those attracted to concerts, recitals, and the opera. His book was directed toward the "untaught lovers of the art."

This book has a purpose, which is simple as it is plain; and an unpretentious scope. It does not aim to edify either the musical professor or the musical scholar. It comes into the presence of the musical student with all becoming modesty. Its business is with those who love music and present themselves for its gracious ministrations in Concert-Room and Opera House, but have not studied it as professors and scholars are supposed to study.[8]

Krehbiel, like Mathews, believed that the perception of musical form was paramount to the understanding of music. To perceive form, the auditor must exercise memory and note the function of melodies and their repetition in the form of motives, phrases, and periods. An awareness of harmony and key relationships is desirable as well as that of rhythmic variations. Such sensitivities would allow the listener to observe unity in a composition. He held an autonomous aesthetic point of view, but as a musician of the nineteenth century, he could not ignore the programmatic aspects of the art.* But he warned his readers of excesses in the hands of lesser composers.

It cannot be too forcibly urged, however, as an aid to the listener that efforts at musical cartooning have never been made by true composers,

---

* The two principal aesthetic points of view during the nineteenth century were the autonomous point of view enunciated by Hanslick and the heteronomous point of view articulated by Wagner. By 1910 the majority of teachers and writers leaned toward the autonomous believing that the sole expression of music was through musical values arrived at through an analysis of melodic contours, formal principles, and rhythm. A few, however, did look beyond the formal principles to express the beauty of music in poetic and rhapsodic prose. Trained music teachers could translate the sounds into a purely musical point of view, but to the less trained, greater comfort was felt in a heteronomous treatment of the music. When a technical vocabulary is not readily available, a person turns to those things which he can more easily talk about, that is, how music makes him feel.

and that in the degree that music attempts simply to copy external things it falls in the scale of artistic truthfulness and value. Vocal music tolerates more of the descriptive element than instrumental because it is a mixed art; in it the purpose of music is to illustrate the poetry and, by intensifying the appeal to the fancy, to warm the emotions.[9]

The book includes information on opera, choral music, symphony orchestra, and piano with references to kinds of music and performance conventions of typical concerts. That portion devoted to piano music incorporates a section on historical style, while the final chapter discusses the author's role as music critic.

MARY REGAL

In the Central High School of Springfield, Massachusetts, during the last years of the nineteenth century, an amazing combination of music supervisor, superintendent of schools, and an outstanding music teacher organized what was perhaps the first music appreciation course in the U.S. public schools. She described her methods, procedures, and philosophy both to the music section of the National Education Association and to the Music Teachers National Association in 1910. The course was designed for those "who have not and never expect to have any technical proficiency."[10] She believed that its purpose was to "cultivate such a love and knowledge of music as would enrich the mental and emotional nature just as a love and knowledge of literature or painting or any other of the fine arts does."[11] Miss Regal herself performed on the piano and emphasized those works considered masterpieces, including the Beethoven Fifth Symphony, the Schubert Unfinished Symphony, the Tschaikovsky Fourth Symphony, the Overture to a *Midsummer Night's Dream* by Mendelssohn, Wagner's Overture to *Tannhauser*, the Schubert Variations from the Quartet in D Minor. Regal emphasized the training of the ear in order to enjoy the emotional effects of the works, not the accumulation of facts.

All other things are regarded as subordinate to the study of the masterpieces of music, which constitutes the main part of the course. An unremitting effort is made to teach the pupil to listen, which is not as simple a matter as may be supposed. There is perhaps no better training in concentration of mind than following a complex musical work in all its details from beginning to end. An instant's flagging of attention and the thread is lost. There is no recovering it as one may recover a lost paragraph by rereading it. The stream of tone flows steadily on.[12]

Like Mathews in *How to Understand Music*, Regal was concerned about her pupil's sensitivity to musical form. She started her classes with simple themes, such as the Haydn *Austrian Hymn* or the Schubert *B-Flat Impromptu*. The class was urged to observe and discuss the similarities and differences between the various phrases. She believed that a foundation could be laid for the future understanding of music through student perceptions of "repetition and contrast, rhythm and modulation." Most of the recitation was spent in listening to the musical compositions performed by the teacher. The student's attention was called to essential features, such as structure, key and mode, repetitions, and contrasts.

Regal's aesthetic orientation was aggressively autonomous. It must be supposed that her students received instruction in the pure tonal art unencumbered by vague flights of fancy and verbal pyrogenics.

While form is taken as the thread upon which our examples are strung, it is by no means the only quality of music to which attention is called. The "content" of music is, however, so inextricably bound up in its form that there is no considering it apart from its expression. Music can be expressed only by musical means. Sometimes words can suggest its meaning more or less, but the elaborate verbal interpretations by which the unmusical expect the inner meaning of music to be revealed to them have little value. The object of the course is to help pupils appreciate music *directly*.[13]

Regal's course covered a two-year sequence. The central point of the first year course was an interview of the various kinds of music with an emphasis on the formal principles governing the music. The individual musical examples were flexible depending upon the instructor's preferences. The second year course was devoted to specific piano works and songs, with the instructor emphasizing the beauty, structure, and harmony of each, although the content varied somewhat to enable the students to repeat the course. Comparisons were made between the various compositions and the styles of the respective composers. Performances were repeated so that the students had the opportunity to become truly familiar with the music. Regal's students concerned themselves with the history and development of music, with three or four standard symphonies, and with song and piano literature.

A recital series was also available as an adjunct to Mary Regal's piano, and artists of the first magnitude could be heard by the students as well as a few of the citizens of Springfield. Regal reported that such artists as Edward MacDowell, Marguerite Hall, Evan Williams, Leopold Godowsky, Harold Bauer, Leo Schultz, Gertrude Mae Stein, Corrine Moore Lawson, the Bannreuther Quartet, and the Adamowski Trio appeared in Springfield. Because Regal realized that the nature of appreciation was elusive and mere parroting of facts mocked the true aims, the course was offered without credit.

WILL EARHART

Another important music educator was Will Earhart of Richmond, Indiana. His important work began almost immediately after the turn of the century. An action by the Indiana legislature mandated that all high schools in that state offer an educational course in music that shall be more than "mere" chorus singing. Earhart concerned himself with the broad aesthetic ideas and strove to minimize the minutiae of historical development. He did not want his students to be only "subconsciously affected on the ethical side" but for them to know the composer of a piece, "when and where he lived and under what conditions, what manner of man he was, what he tried to do, how well he succeeded, [and] what the world thinks of him now." Earhart, too, was concerned that his students understand the form of a composition.

I wanted them to know what romantic and classical, polyphonic and monophonic meant; what "absolute" music meant; what descriptive music meant and how far it could go—and I foresaw here how, without my saying a word about it, they might get several glimpses into the larger reaches of life and art.[14]

Earhart's course was called the "Critical Study" class.

Earhart made a list of sixteen great composers which he arranged from Bach to Wagner. He did not have the benefit of a phonograph and did not obtain a mechanical piano until 1904. The only performance possible, then, was for his classes to sing as a chorus. He identified the available choruses of those composers whom he wanted his classes to study. Original editions were sought for the musical honesty of the individual compositions rather than for the convenience of musical performance with groups. In addition to the choruses, the mainstay of the course, lists of piano, solo voice, vocal duet, and orchestra pieces were made with the latter performed on the piano.

Although the musicality of his mechanical piano was not always satisfactory, he found that the new device gave him flexibility in teaching his classes. He had to depend upon fewer guest musicians to play the works and could exercise greater control over the literature.

Unlike Regal, Earhart was concerned about evaluation in his appreciation course and worked out a rather traditional system. In addition to a library of musical works which were paid for by concert receipts, each student was required to keep a notebook and an outline of the course. Students compiled the facts of history and biography as homework, wrote themes for grades, and took written examinations. Grades were given as high school credit and applied toward graduation. Both the course in harmony and "Critical Study" were electives and received one-half credit per semester. The courses were open to all students who were not having difficulty with the required academic courses. Two hours per week were devoted to recitation, and both courses required two years each for completion. He reported an average of eighty to ninety students per semester.[15]

Sixteen composers were studied over two years, or four composers each semester. Facts about the music and the composers were taught at appropriate, though flexible, places. Dunham provides us with a list of subject matter included in a typical sequence of study in Will Earhart's classes:[16]

FIRST SEMESTER:

Handel	Choruses: "Surely He Hath Borne Our Griefs" and "Lift Up Your Heads" from *The Messiah*.
	Instrumental Music: "Pastoral Symphony" from *The Messiah* and "The Harmonious Blacksmith."
Bach	Choruses: "Have Lightning's and Thunder" and "Final Chorus" from *St. Matthew Passion*.
	Instrumental Music: "Louré" from Third Suite for Cello, *Italian Concerto*, *St. Anne's Fugue*, and *Fugue in G Minor*.

Rossini	Choruses: "Swift As a Bird" and "Hark, How the Horn," from *William Tell*, "Inflammatur," from *Stabat Mater*.
	Instrumental Music: *Overture to William Tell, Overture to The Barber of Seville.*
Donizetti	Choruses: "Hail to the Happy Bridal Day," and "Let Us Roam Through These Ruins," from *Lucia di Lammermoor*. "Would You Know," and "Hark to That Joyous Strain," from *Lucretia Borgia*.
	Instrumental Music: "potpourri," from *Lucia di Lammermoor*.

SECOND SEMESTER:

Haydn:	Choruses: "The Marv'lous Work," and "The Heavens Are Telling," from *The Creation*. "Hark the Deep Tremendous Voice," and "Hark, the Mountains Resound," from *The Seasons*.
	Instrumental Music: *Symphony No. 94 in G Major, "Surprise."*
Mozart:	Choruses: "Gloria," and "Sanctus," from *The Twelfth Mass*. "Each Voice Now Rejoices," from *The Marriage of Figaro*.
	Instrumental Music: *Symphony No. 40 in G Minor.*
Bellini:	Choruses: "A Chaplet of Roses," and "Fatal Day," from *I Puritani*.
	Instrumental Music: *Overture to Norma.*
Verdi:	Choruses: "Anvil Chorus," and "Miserere Scene," from *Il Trovatore*.
	Instrumental Music: *Il Trovatore Fantasia.*
Incidental subjects:	Symphony, string quartette, sonata, chamber music.

Earhart was called upon to report his activities in the area of music appreciation almost everywhere. He served as the chairman of a committee of the Music Supervisors National Conference to develop a course of study for advanced work in music in the high schools. Many accepted Earhart's appreciation course as a model.

ADVANCED STUDY IN MUSIC AT CHELSEA,
MASSACHUSETTS

In 1904 several educational organizations, led by the Educational Music Conference and the New England Education League, ap-

pointed a committee to prepare a statement on entrance requirements in various aspects of music education for submission to
the College Entrance Examination Board. The areas to be examined were: music appreciation, harmony, counterpoint, piano-
forte, voice, and violin.[17] The committee, comprising Walter R.
Spalding of Harvard, Lee Rich Lewis of Tufts, Henry D. Sleeper of
Smith, and Leonard B. McWhood of Columbia, worked nearly
two years after which recommendations were presented and accepted by the College Entrance Examination Board. The following
represent the recommendations of the committee in regard to the
study of music appreciation in the high schools:

1) A general knowledge of the principal musical forms—song, classic
dance, fugue, sonata (all movements), symphony—and of their historical
development; 2) A general knowledge of the lives and environments of
at least ten composers, including Bach, Mozart, Beethoven, Schubert,
Chopin, and five of the following: Purcell, Handel, Gluck, Haydn, Cher-
ubini, Weber, Rossini, Glinka, Mendelssohn, Schumann, Wagner, Verdi;
3) Familiarity with certain designated works. The works set for 1907 and
1908 are:

Bach:	Prelude I and Fugue I from The Well-Tempered Clavichord (sic). Gavotte from Sixth Violoncello Suite.
Handel:	Air with Variations ("The Harmonious Blacksmith")
Haydn:	Largo from String Quartet (Op. 74, No. 3).
Mozart:	Overture to "The Magic Flute." Symphony in G Minor (entire).
Beethoven:	Sonata Pathetique (op. 13) (entire). Larghetto from Second Symphony, Allegro con brio from Fifth Symphony.
Weber:	Overture to "Der Freischutz."
Schubert:	Moment Musical in F Minor (Op. 94, No. 3). Song, "The Erl King." Song, "Hark, Hark, the Lark."
Mendelssohn:	Scherzo from Midsummer Night's Dream. "Spinning Song" (Op. 67, No. 4).
Chopin:	Polonaise (Op. 40, No. 1). Nocturne (Op. 37, No. 2).
Schumann:	"Aufschwung" (Op. 12, No. 2). Song, "Im wunderschonen Monat Mai."
Wagner:	Overture to Tannhauser. Siegfried's Funeral March, from Gotterdammerung.

The test of familiarity will be conducted by the college or university
concerned. In this test the candidate will be expected to identify characteristic portions of the works set, when played by the examiner; and to

give intelligent information concerning the form and character of the works themselves. The test will not require ability to perform, nor to read from printed music.[18]

In 1907 the high school at Chelsea, Massachusetts, under the leadership of Osbourne McConathy, inaugurated a course of study designed to implement the recommendations of the committee. Its curriculum was divided into two parts. The first was a one-hour singing course required of all students. In addition, freshman students received one hour a week of sight singing. A weekly "choral period" included training in listening to music. The second part consisted of special elective courses including music appreciation, theory, orchestral ensemble, and applied music "with a plan for credited outside study."[19]

McConathy hoped that his course would help students to cultivate an intelligent appreciation of music, would "improve the quality and number of discriminating concert goers," and would help those who were planning a future career in music. Beginning in the student's sophomore year, one period a week was given to the listening to music with a corresponding emphasis on the study of musical forms, musical history, biography, and other "musical topics." The instructor was "an accomplished pianist" and equipment provided by the school included a pianola, rolls, and "music for laboratory work." In the first year, the students were exposed to a variety of compositions while the instructor pointed out various aspects of the forms. Examinations were given at the close of the year and included questions such as "What is meant by the words contrapuntal, folksong and symphony."

The instructor plays several characteristic selections which are unknown to the students, who are required to name the form of each minuet, gavotte, waltz. The teacher plays portions of the compositions which have been studied during the year, and the students are required to name them, and to describe some of their distinguishing characteristics.[20]

During the second year of the course, the junior students listen to various compositions that illustrate the historical development of music. The biographical information regarding the composers was carefully postponed until the next year. The students' senior year was devoted to musical biography, a short course in physics of music "under the instructor of sciences, a course in listening to the various orchestra instruments, and a course in contemporaneous musical matters." [21] The students were encouraged to read articles in magazines from the public library, and books on musical subjects were recommended and sometimes reviewed in the classroom. The students were encouraged to attend local concerts and the works to be performed were discussed at appropriate times.*

In the 1909–1910 school year enrollments of high school students of Chelsea averaged 27 percent of the total school enrollment for all four high school grades, while the freshman and sophomore classes alone attracted 30 and 31 percent of the class enrollments respectively. The figures showed a significant interest for an elective course.

GEORGE OSCAR BOWEN

George Oscar Bowen reported in 1908 on a music appreciation course in the high school at Northampton, Massachusetts, a course that most likely was initiated sometime between 1906 and 1908. The school was one of the first to establish, and one of the few to maintain, advanced courses in music for which credit was granted. Bowen, the music director of the Northampton High School, termed his work "more or less experimental and not perfected." The two-year appreciation class began in the junior year. Two prepared lessons were required each week, and two credits were allowed. There were eight pupils in the class. The students studied the formal growth of music, listened to the subject matter of a composition, and recognized the principal ideas and their treatment. They were given some history and biography, and papers were read in class on such subjects as the development of the suite and how the perfection of the violin and piano influenced its character. The influence of various composers toward the development of the suite was also noted. The students were given music to analyze from a structural and harmonic standpoint. [22]

OTHER CONTRIBUTORS

Considering the nature and number of discussions concerning music appreciation in the schools during the early years of the cen-

---

* The Chelsea High School also offered a theoretical course given two periods a week for four years. The elements of musical notation were reviewed, and chord construction and the harmonization of melodies were taught.

tury, it is reasonable to suppose that a renaissance of interest was occurring. But there were differing opinions concerning the approaches to this study.

Nelson B. Yardley, of Newark, Ohio, prepared a series of chorus concerts featuring the music of selected individual composers. Complete recitals were given featuring only the music of Mendelssohn, Haydn, or Gounod. Alice C. Clement, of Rochester, New York, was one of the earliest supervisors to use the gramophone in her appreciation classes. She pointed out that the gramophone had been less popular than the player pianos but had been helpful to the music supervisors in Saint Louis, Missouri, and Bay City, Michigan.[23] William H. Critzer, a supervisor of music in Ohio, decided to give his students the best in music to perform, and organized four years of choral singing around *The Creation*, the *Messiah*, *Judas Maccabaeus*, and *Elijah*.[24]

In 1908 Ada Fleming, supervisor of music in the Chicago schools, outlined an idealistic schedule for teaching music to all the students and defined the concepts of appreciation as a necessary constant in life. She believed in "exploring the realm of musical literature; interpreting, quoting repetition, contrasting rhythm; modulation; feeling musical content; discovering form." She wanted her students to study the dance form, rondo, sonata, and fugue.[25] Edward Bailey Birge, the master teacher from Indianapolis and historian of music education, noted the use of mechanical pianos in nine elementary schools of that city and plans for others. Twice per week a twenty-minute recital was given using those instruments. "The doors of the school rooms [were] opened and the children [sat] in order while the music [was] in progress." The titles of the compositions and their composers were written on the board. A memory test was given once a month when short excerpts were replayed and the children asked to remember the title and composer. Birge admitted that the work was still experimental but he believed that "the interest, pleasure and delight of the children in the music justify us in expecting very large returns for the time given."[26]

SOME MUSIC APPRECIATION TEXTS

In any study of music education it soon becomes readily apparent that a change or innovation in the teaching of music translates into the need for sufficient publications that reflect the change. Probably the most influential publication on the teaching of music appreciation was *The Appreciation of Music*, by Thomas Whitney Surette and Daniel Gregory Mason.[27] The volume passed through fifteen editions between 1907 and 1924. The authors were critical of many other books on this subject believing that they were either too technical or "too rhapsodic and impressionistic." *

Collateral readings were suggested at the end of each chapter, and short musical examples appeared throughout the text. A supplementary volume was published which included complete compositions and which were treated to a measure analysis. The authors believed that the use of this latter volume was vital. Surette and Mason considered the music itself to be the most important aspect of their instruction; the literature about the music was of secondary importance. The book was organized around the elements of musical form: motives and repetition, antecedent and consequent phrases; the suite, rondo, variation, minuet, and the sonata. The final four chapters were concerned with the music of Beethoven and were rendered in much detail. The book was mainly concerned with musical analysis and kept the flowery, heteronomous descriptions to a minimum. The authors emphasized larger instrumental forms rather than the larger vocal forms—the opera and oratorio. Dunham speculates that this volume was perhaps the first book on appreciation designed especially for classroom use. It was universally cited as a reference "by teachers, authors, and musicians more than any other book." [28]

Before the introduction of the gramophone for educational purposes, the Aeolian Company, an American manufacturer of mechanical pianos and piano rolls, published *The New Musical Education Courses*. A rather larger number of courses were published which included lesson pamphlets, piano rolls with special commentary printed on them, and sheet music or miniature scores. Single lessons or complete courses could be purchased, while some could be rented. Prices varied from eight dollars for a four roll course to one hundred dollars for a sixty-two roll course. A typical

---

*Dunham tells us that D. G. Mason's philosophy was in evidence when a historical point of view was required. Mason, in turn, was influenced by Sir Charles H. H. Parry who transferred Darwin's theories of evolution and natural selection to music. Parry's book *The Evolution of the Art of Music* (London and New York: D. Appleton-Century Co., 1893), attempted to make a case for the proposition that the art of music was steadily improving.

course consisted of twenty rolls for thirty-five dollars.[29] By 1908, nine such courses were available. A five-lesson series on Chopin was built around eighteen compositions representing most of the smaller forms. The course in opera contained one selection of twenty well-known operas, usually the overture. Twelve lessons were devoted to Beethoven, each lesson covering one complete work. Lesson IV of the twelve dealt with the Third Symphony; Lesson V, the Quartet in G Major, op. 59; Lesson VI, the Violin Concerto; Lesson X, the Trio in B Flat, op. 97; and Lesson XII completed the cycle with the Ninth Symphony.[30] Dunham compared the offerings of the Aeolian Company with the selection of compositions used by Will Earhart and deduced that Earhart must have used some of the piano rolls in his appreciation classes in Richmond, Indiana.

Earhart, too, found it necessary to publish a music appreciation text—a series of booklets devoted to various composers and their works. The first four books presented music by Haydn, Mozart, and Beethoven. Volumes on Verdi and Mendelssohn appeared in 1912. In the preface Earhart explains the format and his point of view. Each booklet consists of the following:

1. About thirty pages of choral selections representing the composer at his best in that particular branch of the musical art.

2. A biographical sketch of the composer.

3. A study of the composer's personality and genius.

4. A brief disquisition upon his place and authority in musical art, with an analytical study of the characteristic points in which he may be compared and contrasted with his immediate predecessors and followers.

5. A helpful glossary of musical terms, with abundant matter relating to the various musical forms and to the ideals of the composer and his times.

The end of the contrasted study of several great masters, each represented by a program showing his art at its most individual moments, must result in an appreciation of the works of these masters as well as in a deep and genuine musical culture which cannot possibly be secured in any other way.[31]

Daniel Gregory Mason's *A Guide to Music* was one of the several books on the subject of appreciation by that author and was intended expressly for children. Its language was simple but its many musical examples presupposed an ability to read notes. In terms understandable to young people, Mason described the aesthetic and spiritual qualities of music that can become accessible through study:

This book is intended to help you to listen in this thoughtful active way, by showing you some of the thousand little differences in pieces of music that, left to yourselves, you might miss. The differences taken one by one may seem very slight; but taken altogether they make up what separates the noble and everlasting works of genius from the trivial and meaningless jingles of the vaudeville theatre, the hurdy-gurdy, and the phonograph.[32]

THE INFLUENCE OF THE MECHANICAL PIANO

The mechanical piano held an important place in the teaching of music appreciation during the early years of the century, but by 1910 the rival phonograph began to assume a greater importance in the schools. The pioneer music teachers of appreciation—Will Earhart, Osbourne McConathy, Alice Clement, and Edward Bailey Birge—had all used the mechanical piano. For a very few years, the mechanical piano fulfilled an important role. In 1905 Charles I. Rice, of Worcester, Massachusetts, tells us that the mechanical player piano was destined to do more toward the popularization of good music than the combined efforts of the Boston, Chicago, and New York orchestras. Three years later Ada M. Fleming of Chicago echoed the sentiments of Rice, considering that the player piano was indispensable to the teaching of music appreciation. "The mechanical player doesn't mean mechanical interpretation; it means the presentation of otherwise impossible selections; it means perfect technique—and nothing less worthy; it means unlimited repetition if desired."[33] George Coleman Gow of Vassar College, however, suggested to the 1910 meeting of the Music Teachers National Association that the player piano lacked both the "sensitive adaptations of loud and soft to the requirements of each movement" and the ability to provide nuance and variety of color.[34] The Music Section of the National Education Association held at Boston in 1910 also debated the issues of the mechanical piano versus the phonograph.

John G. Thompson argued the importance of cultivating the aesthetic nature of public school students by exposing them to masterpieces of literature, painting, sculpture, architecture, and music. He endorsed the use of the mechanical piano, believing that the instrument made the consistent hearing of music literature possible for all schools.[35] Edward Bailey Birge believed that the player piano should be used first in the primary grades as that was the seemingly successful procedure in Indianapolis. Edith C. Westcott, principal of Western High School in Washington, D.C., used the mechanical piano rather freely in her school but was highly protective of the school phonograph, permitting only an "expert" to manipulate it. She used the phonograph with gymnasium classes to supply the proper musical rhythms and on patriotic occasions to lead "The Star Spangled Banner." Professor Lee Rich Lewis of Tufts College recommended both the mechanical piano and the phonograph believing that the music that the child hears should not be limited to that music which the child himself can perform. The mechanical aids "make it possible for the technically unskilled but well informed teacher to present to a class the representative works of all periods of art, and with the aid of copious existing literature concerning music, to lay a firm foundation of musical taste."[36]

But Frank A. Beach discovered the Achilles' heel of so many educational programs which start with such promise. While on leave from his position at the State Teachers College in Emporia, Kansas, he observed the music programs in a number of schools in cities of various size. He immediately noticed the poor use that so many schools made of the mechanical piano. Many were used as a "source of entertainment or revenue; only in rare cases was a definitely organized course in the appreciation of music in operation, or regular lessons in the lower grades conducted with a specific aim of developing intelligent listeners."[37]

CHAPTER XIV

Frances Elliott Clark
and Music Appreciation

FRANCES ELLIOTT CLARK was born Frances Mary Elliott, in
Scott Township near Angola, in Steuben County, Indiana, on
May 27, 1860. Her early education was at a rural school. She
could sing hymns at the age of four. A neighbor had a cabinet
organ on which the young girl took lessons and practiced for a
two-hour period following each lesson. She attended a singing
school at Swan, Michigan, where she acquired a solo soprano
voice and soon excelled her classmates. Not long afterwards, she
began her own singing school.

At the age of fourteen, she married John Clark, a woodsman
and surveyor. In 1880, yellow fever took her husband, leaving her
a widow at the age of twenty with a child on the way.

She summoned courage to plan a career for herself, and, as she
loved books and learning, she decided to become a teacher. She
had had only an eighth-grade education and so much studying was
needed. In 1884 she passed her county teaching examination and
began her career. She taught for four years in four different areas.

During the summer months she continued her education at the
Tri-State Normal College, being the second student to enroll in
that college when it first opened in 1884. There she studied voice,
participated in college choral groups, sang in the church choir, and
was in demand as a soprano soloist. In 1888 she graduated with
honors in a class of twenty-two. She studied with a Mrs. Linders

and Hattie Creel, the latter a product of the Cincinnati Conservatory of Music who believed in the coming profession of a music supervisor and encouraged Clark to pursue such a career. Both suggested that she attend the Ginn Institute in Detroit, which was the first fully organized school in the Midwest for training music supervisors. The school was established by Mrs. Emma Thomas, the supervisor of music in Detroit, and boasted Luther Whiting Mason as dean and Clarence Birchard as business manager. Other members of the faculty included a Mrs. Cox of Chicago, who taught children's songs, Professor Lott of Columbus, Ohio, who taught voice, and Professor Veazie.[1] Clark learned the Luther Whiting Mason philosophy of the rote-song approach to music learning, which she would use successfully and on which she would build. Clark attended two summer sessions and graduated in 1891.

While attending classes at Tri-State Normal School, she accepted her first position as a music supervisor at the Pleasant Lake School where she taught both elementary and high school levels from 1888 to 1890. In 1891, she accepted the position of music supervisor at Monmouth, Illinois, where she found that older methods of music teaching had been used. It was in Monmouth that Frances Elliott Clark demonstrated an organizing ability that was eventually to lead her to the top of her profession.

She became a member of the Women's Tuesday Music Club. In 1893 she represented that group at an organizational meeting of the National Federation of Music Clubs in Chicago, which had been called by Mrs. Theodore Thomas. The formal organization of the federation took place in 1897 when Frances Elliott Clark was elected to the board and served in that capacity for many years. In addition she served as chairman of school music, director of the Education Department, member of the executive committee, Second Vice President, and Chairman of Legislation. She also wrote an entire course of study for the junior clubs.

In 1896 she assumed the position of music teacher at Ottumwa, Iowa. Ottumwa, with a population of 20,000 when Mrs. Clark arrived, had enjoyed the services of a well-qualified music teacher who had achieved good results in all the grades. Clark immediately organized three choruses at the high school level, a freshman and a junior chorus that sang good quality training materials and a senior chorus with the skill to sing oratorios. Her senior chorus was reported to have sight read the "Hallelujah Chorus" at a sufficient level of skill that it did not have to stop, and it later presented the entire *Elijah* accompanied by two pianos and a reed organ. Two soloists were employed for the performance. Mrs. Genevieve Wheat sang soprano and Dean Frederick Howard of Drake University presented the title role.[2]

Recognizing the need to relate the performance of music to music history, she began a series of ten-minute talks in this latter branch before rehearsals of her senior chorus. The pupils had no books at this time, but the facts were placed on the blackboard. Subjects embraced in her ten-minute talks included the Rise of Opera; Bach, his life and work; Schubert; Schumann; Chopin; and "living" composers. These represented some of the first efforts concerning music appreciation along with Peter Dykema's study of Wagnerian operas at the Fletcher School in Indianapolis and Will Earhart's critical study courses, at Richmond, Indiana.

Frances Elliott Clark was an advocate of the rote-note approach to the learning of music. Her conviction of the efficacy of this approach sharpened in 1893 when she heard a concert by fifteen-hundred children at the Columbian Exposition in Chicago directed and trained by William L. Tomlins, originally from England. He was director of the Apollo Club in Chicago and created a sensation at the exposition with a demonstration of the artistic possibilities of the children's voices. The success of his groups made him famous throughout the Midwest. Mrs. Clark described Tomlins as the first to "present the spiritual power of pure tone production and the need of safeguarding the miniature voices of children."[3] This manifestation of the child-study movement gradually impinged on the votaries of note-reading with their exclusive preoccupation with reading by syllable.

Clark left Iowa for Milwaukee in 1903 to become Supervisor of Music in the schools of that city. Milwaukee, then a city of 450,000 people with a varied ethnic population, enjoyed many community choruses, male, female and mixed. Its citizens attended operas, oratorios, and chamber music concerts. Even restaurants and beer gardens employed large orchestras that played classical as well as the better popular music.

But little music had been taught in the public schools. Grade school children had sung German folk tunes from a book published by a Mr. Siefert "to the accompanying melody of Mr. P. M. Bach's violin."[4] No attempt had been made at sight singing or methodical progression. Clark used William L. Tomlins's *Laurel Music Reader* for the eighth grades, and *Progressive Music Lessons* built on the song idea for the lower grades. The superintendent of schools was himself a trained musician, which helped to create a sympathetic atmosphere in which the supervisor of music could work. He agreed that the new program should begin with grade school organization and supported Mrs. Clark's request for the many teachers' meetings that were necessary to organize the program. Confident leaders were found for the eighth grade choruses, and efforts were made to improve the quality of the children's voices through exercise. Part singing was introduced in the grammar grades; the fifth and sixth grade children were required to sing in two parts which were treated interchangeably to encourage flexibility. Songs of the "masters" were sung in the higher grades.

Clark believed that ear training should begin in kindergarten, and she pioneered a plan to encourage the children to respond vocally to the musical roll call of the teacher. Often the names of flowers or fruits were substituted for the children's own names. At a meeting of the International Kindergarten Union which met in Milwaukee, Clark's method of ear training was favorably received as the first to work out tonal problems in that manner.

In 1907, Frances Elliott Clark was vice-president of the Music Section of the National Education Association. Along with others she felt a concern that this organization and the Music Teachers National Association were not entirely meeting the needs of the music supervisors. In the January 1907 issue of the *School Music Monthly*, a call to a meeting at Keokuk, Iowa, was signed by twenty-six music supervisors including Hamlin E. Cogswell, president of the Music Section of the National Education Association; Frances Elliott Clark, vice-president; Philip C. Hayden, secretary; and Thaddeus P. Giddings and other leading supervisors. Responding to the invitation were 104 supervisors, who met in the Sunday school room of the Westminster Presbyterian Church in Keokuk, Iowa, April 10, 1907.

As Cogswell was ill, Clark was to preside over the meeting. Hayden presented his ideas on teaching the tonal side of music through progressive rhythmic forms, which were idiosyncratic and which precipitated a hostile demonstration by those in attendance. At length Hayden's sincerity was recognized and a degree of order prevailed as the delegates began to ask questions of the leaders of the conference concerning the best methods of teaching this and that branch of the music curriculum.* Frances Elliott Clark reported that "it became a veritable town meeting. . . . everyone giving and getting." The music supervisors had "never had such an opportunity, such a rich experience of close family without outsiders."[5]

After calling a recess, Clark conferred with other leaders at the conference and a consensus was reached that a program should be improvised and that the group remain in sessions for three days. By the second day it became evident to Clark and to others that more meetings of that kind would be desirable, and to do that required a special organization. She called Charles Fullerton to the chair while she proposed the suggestion to the group. C. C. Birchard spoke in favor of the idea of an independent organization and T. P. Giddings was ready with a motion to that end, which passed with only two dissenting votes. A committee on organization was formed with Herman E. Owen of Madison, Wisconsin, as chairman and Charlotte Field, of Findley, Ohio, as a member. The report making the conference permanent was brought to the final session and adopted by the group.

The first officers elected were Philip C. Hayden, of Keokuk, president; Charles H. Miller, of Omaha, vice-president; Stella R. Root, of Springfield, Illinois, secretary; Edward Bailey Birge, of Indianapolis, treasurer. The executive committee comprised Mrs. Frances Elliott Clark, of Milwaukee; T. P. Giddings, of Oak Park, Kansas; and Birdie Alexander, of Dallas, Texas. The conference included sixty-nine charter members. The next meeting was scheduled to take place in Peoria, Illinois, the following year. But Clark used her influence to have the meeting place changed to Cleveland where the conference would meet coincidentally with that of the National Education Association as Mrs. Clark was president of the Music Section of that organization. Hayden did not preside as president of the conference until the 1909 meeting in Indianapolis.

---

* Arthur Mason, Edward Birge, Charles Fullerton, Alys Bentley, Stella Root, Robert Foresman, Charles Congdon, Anna Allen, Elizabeth Pratt, E. L. Coburn, Alice Rogers, A. J. Gautvoort, Frances Elliott Clark.

At the 1910 meeting at Cincinnati, the first constitution of the conference was adopted as well as the official name—the Music Supervisors National Conference.

Certain patterns of the conference established at the first meeting in 1907 are preserved to this day:

- the meeting would be in the spring of the year
- visits to schools and places of interest would take place in the host city
- papers would be presented by important people
- demonstrations and discussions would take place
- informal discussions in groups would be encouraged
- songs would be sung in the lobbies and at mealtimes
- there would be business sessions
- a formal conference banquet would take place
- publishers would be encouraged to display their wares.

Perhaps Frances Elliott Clark's most significant contribution was in the area of music appreciation and, more particularly, in her immediate recognition of the educational values of the Victor Talking Machine. By 1903 some of the great artists had been recorded, and by 1906 Victor Red Seal Records began to be pressed. Still, a general feeling prevailed that the invention was merely a plaything.

Frances Elliott Clark reported her experience on first looking into purchasing a machine and some records: "When I heard the glorious tenor of Evan Williams singing "All Through the Night," truly my heart almost stood still, for nearly every fourth grade in the Milwaukee schools was singing that song." She thought of what it might mean to the children if they could hear the "beautiful tone quality, the sensitive phrasing, and the diction of this great artist."

I walked out of that room dazed as with an almost supernatural vision calling for action. Very soon thereafter I met on the street two of our most musical principals, Thomas Boyce of the First District, and Robert L. Cooley of the Twenty-Second District. I asked them what they thought of the idea of using records in the classroom, explaining that I saw great possibilities in it. Mr. Boyce said, "Try it out in my school." Mr. Cooley echoed the same wish. So they arranged with Mr. Parker of the Gimbol Brothers to send an instrument on a given day the following week when I should be in the First District, to see whether the children would listen attentively or only be amused.

I selected the records to be given, and almost wholly those songs which we were using in some of the grades. To the delight of all, the children listened, wonderingly at first, then seemingly enchanted with the beauty of the music which they had never before heard, and the giggles which had been anticipated were a revelation. In a day or two, another similar program was given in Mr. Cooley's school.[6]

In January 1910, Mrs. Clark met with the eighth grade teachers of Milwaukee, ten of whom were to bring fifty children each to participate in a demonstration. At the time the children enjoyed a repertoire of some fifty songs from the *Laurel Music Reader*. A Victrola and records were on hand. Neither the children nor their teachers had been told beforehand of the nature of the demonstration. When all were assembled, a concert took place. First the children would sing two or three songs, then recorded selections would be played on the Victrola. When possible, Clark followed the children's performance with a recorded example of the same piece. Following the playing of each recorded selection, she called the children's attention to the tone quality, phrasing, and diction of the concert artists. The principals in attendance were immediately impressed with the new teaching tool, and several immediately arranged for the purchase of a machine. Before the next such meeting, which was scheduled for the following June, there were over forty requests for concerts.

Frances Elliott Clark enjoyed a reputation for having created one of the best organized, best balanced, and highest quality music programs in the country. Her ideas spread nationally. In 1910, Miss Katherine Stone, supervisor of music in Los Angeles, California, visited the Milwaukee schools. Upon arriving home in California, she recounted her impressions of the music program in Milwaukee:

(1) the awareness of the teachers to the excellence of their music; (2) the matching of tones and the rhythmic activities in the kindergarten for the development of the child's ear and voice; (3) the extended tone matching and placement, as well as scale recognition, in the first grade; (4) the learning of many simple little "stunts" with the staff in the second grade—the placing of scales, creating of little melodies, and sight reading of melodies created by the teacher; (5) the clear sweet tones of the third

grade students as they sight read many songs and exercises from their primers; (6) the splendid two part singing (both parts) and excellent sight reading of the fourth grade; (7) the participation of all the boys as well as the girls in the many part songs sung by the fifth grade; (8) the rather queer but colorful whistling division for boys with changing voices as used in certain patriotic and boating songs sung in three parts in the sixth grade; (9) the three part singing of beautiful folk songs by the seventh grade chorus; (10) the well-formed resonant and flutelike tones and well nigh perfect enunciation of the eighth grade chorus singing "'quite classic songs,'" some having the melody in the bass to encourage new voices in that section; (11) the remarkably well-kept rhythm in sight singing, even in the lower grades; (12) the talking machines used as an integral part of the work, for cultural purposes, school marches, calisthenics, and school dances; [and finally,] (13) the work here is perhaps the best rounded and complete to be found anywhere, and may well refute all slander as to school music in this country.[7]

Mrs. Stone also began using Victrolas in her classrooms in Los Angeles, and T. P. Giddings, of Minneapolis, began to order Victrolas after a correspondence with Frances Elliott Clark. Mrs. Clark's demonstration of the use of the phonograph at the November 1910 meeting of the Wisconsin State Teachers Association introduced the machine and its educational possibilities to the teachers of that state. Soon all of the larger cities of Wisconsin were using Victrolas to help in the instruction of music.

F. E. Clark, Introduction of the Victor Talking Machine to the Milwaukee Schools

PROGRAM OF TEACHERS' MEETING

January 3, 1910

1. Chorus—7th grade, 10th D. No. 1 (Teacher, Miss Luebke)
   (a) "Now the Day is Over"   Bamby
   (b) "May Morning"   Denza

2. Victor
   (a) "Home, Sweet Home" (Sung by Patti)
   (b) "Last Rose of Summer" (Sung by Sembrich)

3. Chorus—8th grade, 6th D. No. 3 (Teacher, Miss Skelding)
   (a) "Annie Laurie"   Anon.
   (b) "Hark, Hark the Lark"   Schubert

4. Victor
   (a) "Lo, Hear the Gentle Lark" (Sung by
       Melba)
5. Chorus—7th & 8th grades, 1st D (Teacher, Mr. Boyce)
   (a) "All Through the Night"   Welsh Air
   (b) "Sextette from Lucia"   Donizetti
6. Victor
   (a) "All Through the Night" (Sung by Evan
       Williams)
   (b) "Sextette from Lucia" (Sung by Caruso,
       Sembrich, Scotti, Servarina, Joumet, and
       Daddi)
7. Victor
   (a) "Mad Scene from Lucia" (Sung by Tetrazzini)
8. Chorus—8th grade, 15D. No. 1 (Teacher, Mr. Simmons)
   (a) "Massa Dear"   Dvorak
   (b) "Merry Life"   Denza
9. Victor
   (a) "My Rosary" (Sung by Schumann-Heinck)
10. Chorus—7th grade, 9th D. No. 2 (Teacher, Miss Costello)
    (a) "Believe Me, if all Those Endearing Young
        Charms"
    (b) "Quail Song"
11. Victor
    (a) "Believe Me, if all Those Endearing Young
        Charms" (Sung by Melba)
12. Chorus—7th & 8th grades, 17th D. No. 1 (Teacher, Miss
    Redfern)
    (a) "He Shall Feed His Flock" (The Messiah)   Handel
    (b) "Estudiantina"
13. Victor
    (a) "He Shall Feed His Flock" (The Messiah)   Handel
    (b) "Estudiantina" (Played by Pryor's Band)
    (c) "Ave Maria" (Sung by Eames; Cello ac-   Schubert
        companiment Hollman)
14. Chorus—8th grade, 10th No. 1 (Teacher, Miss Oldewelt)
    (a) "The Merry Makers"

15. Victor
     (a) "Duet from Madame Butterfly" (Sung by   Puccini
         Farrar and Homer)
16. Chorus—8th grades, 6th D. No. 1 (Teacher, Miss Niesser)
     (a) "Serenade"   Schubert
     (b) "Blue Danube Waltz"   Strauss
17. Victor
     (a) "Blue Danube Waltz" (Played by
         Sousa's Band)
     (b) "Quartet" from *Rigoletto*   Verdi
     (c) "Anvil Chorus"   Verdi
                     (The Victrola operated by Mr. Parker)

Royden J. Keith, the representative of the Chicago distributors of the Victor Talking Machine Company, attended Clark's second demonstration in Milwaukee in June 1910. His report to the parent company was exceedingly complimentary to Clark. A. D. Geissler, the Chicago distributor for the company and the son of Louis F. Geissler, general manager of the Victor Talking Machine Company of Camden, New Jersey, sent four school principals to hear Clark's November demonstration. He then corresponded with Clark promising an opportunity for her to meet his father when the latter came through Chicago in December. Clark said that she wanted to meet Geissler in order to convince him that more and better records for children would be desirable. There were few instrumental records suitable for the older children, and none available for the primary grades. When she met Louis F. Geissler, he addressed her as follows:

The idea of using for children the beautiful records we are now able to make has long been an idea of mine. I remember as a boy in school using the little Chinese frame of colored balls for number combinations and have not forgotten them to this day. What children learn they keep. Therefore, it has been a thought of mine that if little children might hear this beautiful music while young, they will soon be grown and out into homes of their own. . . . I have interviewed sixteen musicians on the subject. . . . Not one of the sixteen seemed to have any idea of how to go about using records for actual teaching of music. You seem to have gotten it done. As you have made a success of it in one city, I think you can do it in all. We wish to open an educational department and want you to become its director.[8]

It required two months for Frances Elliott Clark to make a decision to join the Victor organization. She already had a fine professional position and would have taken over the supervision of the high school music programs in Milwaukee the following year. She also expressed a fear of losing status as an educator by working in a commercial venture. But in December of 1910, she accepted the position.[9]

Mrs. Clark arrived at Camden in 1911 to organize and plan an educational department. She made arrangements for making children's recordings. She attended all large gatherings of music educators and arranged proper exhibits. She coordinated printed literature with the recordings, and she kept up on teaching techniques in the schools, both in music and nonmusic areas. Within a year of her appointment, special children's recordings were released. Evan Williams recorded children's songs by Schubert and Schumann. Patriotic songs were recorded in high voice to be closer to that of the child's, and stories of operas were prepared in simple form.

In 1911 the Victor Company published its first educational catalog, and by 1924 the catalog was classified into subjects by grade, music appreciation, and correlation with other courses. At that time it contained almost three thousand selections.

In 1913 Clark announced a prospectus of a book written by Anne Shaw Faulkner of the Victor staff.[10] Faulkner's book, *What We Hear in Music*, was a four-year course in music history and appreciation to be used at the high school level. The book was re-edited and reissued by the Victor staff periodically and was one of the first books for music appreciation to be used in the public schools. Its major divisions included "The Principles of Music"; "The History of Music"; "The Orchestra and the Development of Instrumental Music"; and "The Opera and Oratorio." Each section had thirty lessons to be equivalent to a year's course. At the end of each chapter appeared a list of Victor records which could be used in the lessons. The book was an important pioneering effort.

In 1913 the second publications of the Victor Educational Department appeared. *A New Graded List of Records for Home, Kindergarten, and School* was an annotated catalog of Victor records. Though "merely" a catalog, its influence was immeasurable as it prescribed the nature of a child's preschool listening experiences and expressed the philosophy that a child should be exposed to music before he studies it, a concept pointedly similar to the study of language.

In 1914, Charles A. Fullerton, head of the music department at Iowa State Teachers College, became concerned over the dilemma of the nonsinging classroom teachers. He wrote Clark at Camden and asked whether a recording of children's songs could be made "by a fine artist" for use as a model in the schools. Mrs. Clark became excited by the idea and auditioned singers, choosing Olive Kline, a student of Herbert Witherspoon. Her record of children's songs was chosen from the elementary songbook *New Song Book and Music Reader*, published in 1910 by Fullerton and Gray. The ten-inch, black-label record (#17719) included eleven songs: "Jack in the Pulpit"; "In the Belfrey"; "Corn Soldiers"; "Naming the Trees"; "The Squirrel"; "The Windmill"; "Riggety Jig"; "The Singing School"; "Dancing Song"; "Dancing in May"; and "Mother Goose Lullaby." Fullerton experimented with the record in the college classes, in his laboratory school, and in county teachers' meetings. He noticed immediately that the elementary teachers became more confident in their teaching. The idea spread rapidly over the state. As other records of this type were added to the Victor educational catalog, Clark added explanations and commentary for each grade level as to the best way of using the records in the classrooms. The demand for these records always exceeded the supply. About five hundred recordings were made strictly for educational purposes under Mrs. Clark.

At a meeting of the Victor Educational Department at Atlantic City in 1915, Harold D. Smith presented a lecture to the assembly on the subject of correlating music with other subjects. The group recommended that Smith prepare a pamphlet. A result of his efforts was the publication of *A New Correlation*, a book that attempted to explore all avenues where the listening to records could be used with the study of other subjects. Record references and Victor numbers were included in the margins. Unfortunately, in many instances the relationships were artificial. A particularly interesting example of this appears on page 10 of this publication where it states that "no study of *The Last of the Mohicans* is complete until the class hears some of the old New England psalms."

In 1918 a questionnaire was prepared in an attempt to determine the extent of music education in the high schools of the country. The questionnaire was prepared by a joint committee of the

National Education Association, the Music Teachers National Association and the Music Supervisors National Conference. Osbourne McConathy acted as chairman. The results of the survey concluded that chorus singing in the high schools was almost universal. Orchestras were gradually becoming increasingly important, and courses in harmony and appreciation were becoming more common. Credit toward graduation for these subjects was being granted in a large proportion of these schools, and credit for private study outside the high school was given by 116 out of 359 schools in thirty-six states.

In 1920 the Victor Company published *Music Appreciation for Little Children*, the largest part of which was done by Edith M. Rhetts. It stated the fundamental principles of music appreciation which became generally accepted for all music educators, namely, that they should, one, help all children to experience and love music; two, provide opportunities for quiet listening; three, not confuse knowledge about music history and biography with music appreciation; and, four, evaluate the music appreciation program by observing the children.

In 1923, Frances Elliott Clark was to have brought out a publication that was to have been the culmination of her work in music appreciation. To be called "Learning to Listen, Listening to Learn," it was to emphasize appreciation from the first through the sixth grades in both urban and rural environments. But the book came out under a different title, *Music Appreciation with the Victrola for Children*, with a preface by Calvin B. Cady, a foreword by Frances Elliott Clark, and the authorship attributed to the Victor Educational Department staff. The 1930 edition received a shorter title, *Music Appreciation for Children*, and both editions included the motto on the title page: "Learning to Listen, Listening to Learn."

The book was designed to meet the needs of a child during the early sensory and associative period from the first to the sixth grades and was an expanded version of its predecessor, *Appreciation for Little Children*. The following principles for organization were given:

(1) A music appreciation course should be so carefully planned and purposefully given that it will command the same respect as that given to courses in literature and other subjects.

(2) The mere playing of music, be it ever so entertaining and delightful, is not necessarily educational.

(3) Children should hear music long before they are asked to master the symbols of the printed form, the rules of grammar of its language, or the techniques of its performance.[11]

The book discussed possible reasons why some people build up elaborate imagery while listening to music. It emphasized nationalism as expressed in folk songs, dances, customs, and instruments. It also concerned itself with rhythmic response through bodily motions. Clark stated that it was her belief that "no other work on the market touches the field served by this book. It is small and complete; its value is all meat from cover to cover."[12]

At the 1917 meeting of the Music Supervisors National Conference, increasing use of the Victrola in rural schools was reported. In Arizona, a group of grade school teachers used one in a "concert" in a nearby mining town. In Kentucky, a choral club sent a machine and some records to a rural school. In a rural district of North Dakota, a woman's club purchased a Victrola which was carried from school to school in the county. In Iowa, Friday Night Socials were held in one location followed by a ten-minute program of Victor records.

One of the earliest advocates of the use of the Victrola in rural schools was Charles A. Fullerton who inaugurated the "choir" plan in 1917. Fullerton employed recordings produced especially for him by the Victor Company. The records were played once for the class after which "obscure words were cleared up." The children then were invited to sing with the "lady" on the refrain. Later the process was reversed followed by the class singing alone. Fullerton demonstrated this technique with combined groups of community or county choirs. Fullerton used as many as five thousand students from all over Iowa in a state festival, and ten thousand at the Texas Centennial.

Through this means was music brought to the rural schools of the nation. County supervisors were employed to help standardize the work, and cultural advantages were brought to the children who would not otherwise have an opportunity to hear such music.

Frank Beach, the Director of Music at the Kansas State Normal College at Emporia, Kansas, sponsored lecture-concerts in that state in rural areas. Two Victrolas were constantly on the move and were booked eight months in advance. The lecturers began their program with folk music, then gradually increased the depth of their offerings culminating with the Beethoven Fifth Symphony. People came from miles around to attend these performances. Beach also related that the local telephone companies cooperated by connecting one hundred phones to the homes of shut-ins.[13] Beach's enthusiasm for the new machines mirrored the great values of listening to music in the classroom and in the home, values which remain significant to the present day.

From the early years of the century the mechanical piano served many schools and was the principal device used whenever appreciation was taught. As late as 1929, Alice Keith stated her belief that there was a certain kind of music appreciation which could best be taught through the use of player piano rolls and that all well-equipped music departments should be so supplied. Keith was a member of the Music Appreciation Committee of the Music Supervisors National Conference and was the educational director of the Radio Corporation of America, in New York City. Previous to her New York position, she supervised music in the Cleveland schools for three years beginning in 1926.

It is clear that a well-equipped school of the second two decades of the century had both the Victrola and the piano roll. Alice Keith described the equipment available at the Thomas Jefferson Junior High School in Cleveland, Ohio, but maintained that this was the only school in Cleveland like this. The school enjoyed the use of "twelve orthophonics and electrolas; a duo art, several pianos; dynamic super-heterodyne radiola; a complete supply of records not only for use in music classes but for use in geography, history, English and other classes wishing to vitalize their teaching by correlation." [14]

About the year 1910, the talking machine began to challenge the remarkable but not too versatile mechanical piano. By the time the United States entered the First World War the phonograph began to replace the earlier instrument as the chief means for the teaching of music appreciation.

Frances Elliott Clark observed that wherever the Victrola was introduced into the schools, there was an immediate realization of the potential of the instrument as an aid to public school music education. It became one of the greatest teaching aids ever for instruction in music and did more than any other one thing to bring good music within the reach of every child.[15]

Perhaps the most dramatic mechanical marvel of the century was the radio, first as a means of communication and later as an educational and cultural tool. The first radio programs were initiated in 1925 but received mixed reviews. By 1927, however, five great educational foundations came forward to finance research and experiments with radio programming and to foster organizations given over fully to education by radio. Educators were faced with the problem of introducing educational radio into the curriculum of the schools. The question was how the classroom teacher might make the best use of radio lessons, lectures, current events, dramatizations, and concerts of great music. Early experiments in educational broadcasting were made by Columbia University, the University of California, the University of Wisconsin, and the University of Alabama. Courses of study were given on public radio stations as well as on college-owned stations. The National Broadcasting Company gave courses in music appreciation and piano playing and engaged in other educational endeavors.

By the 1930s radios were considered a viable instructional tool. In the interest of education, schools competed for an adequate allotment of radio time to complement instructional purposes. Broadcasts throughout the nation for 4-H clubs by the United States Marine Band in Washington, D.C., was such an example. The programs were under the management of Roy Turner who organized a twelve-year sequence of programs covering folk music of many lands, "American music every child should know," and a study of opera. Notations and running comments were made by Turner. The plan was adopted from the work of the Victor Educational Department, and almost all selections used were from Victor records.

Alice Keith of Cleveland conducted what was probably the first course over the radio in 1925. In the 1930s, Donzella Cross Boyle was in charge of music appreciation programs on the Ohio School of the Air over station WLW in Cincinnati.

The director of the children's concerts in Cleveland was Arthur

Shepherd who, with Alice Keith, prepared a book entitled *Listening in on the Masters*. The volume may have been the first textbook written in this country for use by schools to prepare children for concerts given over the radio. Percy Scholes wrote two such books on the subject of music appreciation on the radio.[16]

When the depression hit the nation, the Victor Company was not exempt from difficulties. The enthusiastic and energetic traveling members of the Victor Educational Department staff were fired to trim the payroll. Only three people remained. The sudden rise in the use of the radio, however, made possible the extension of the Victor educational effort on a drastically reduced payroll. Frances Elliott Clark's department was the first to organize radio music for children.

In the 1920s the radio industry expanded considerably, from a few isolated stations in 1920 to 612 in 1931. By 1931 there were thirteen million radio receivers in use, representing 34 percent of the homes in the United States.

The book, *Listening in on the Masters*, by Alice Keith and Arthur Shepherd, was published in 1926. It served as the text for a year's course of study built around the youth concerts broadcast by the Cleveland Orchestra. The course objectives were listed in the introduction of the book.

1. Recognize particular themes and note their recurrence or change in the development of the composition.

2. Follow certain melodies in polyphonic compositions like the Bach Fugue, or in the first part of Bizet's *Farandole* from *L'Arlesienne Suite*.

3. Analyze the form of a composition (as minuet, song form, or sonata form).

4. Note the composer's use of dynamics, tempo, and tone color or in producing certain emotional or dramatic effects.

5. Study the history and mechanics of instruments used.

6. Note the musical characteristics that are the result of historical, geographic, or social conditions.

7. Consider the composer or school of the compositions presented.

8. In the case of vocal music, consider the vocal range and interpretation.

9. In vocal music, classify the composition as to form, specify-

ing whether it be folk song, near folk song, opera or oratorio. Obviously it would not be advisable to consider each composition from every angle.

The course was designed for children in the intermediate elementary school grades. The nationalities of the composers were discussed. Lists of materials to be used with the text were the sixth-grade book of *The Hollis Dann Music Series*, the *Intermediate Book* of *The Music Education Series*, Book Three of *The Progressive Music Series*, and Book Three of *The Universal School Music Series*. In 1929, however, special concerts were being broadcast for the first and second grades as well as for the junior and senior high schools.

In 1928 Walter Damrosch was approached concerning his willingness to present orchestra concerts on the radio for the benefit of children. He discussed the idea of a regular series of broadcasts with various educators who encouraged the venture. The Radio Corporation of America agreed to underwrite the project on an experimental basis, and in 1928 Damrosch began with two morning concerts, one for grade school children and the other for high schools and colleges. His was the first attempt to broadcast children's concerts nationally. He prepared a manual of questions and answers to be used in conjunction with his radio concerts for the classroom teacher and which were distributed free of charge during the current year by the Radio Corporation of America to those teachers whose pupils listened regularly to the Damrosch concerts. Damrosch received over ten thousand letters from schools. The American people tuned in, they "disarranged their schedules, and teachers had their children march to the assembly room to listen to the concerts."[17] The experiment was successful and the course was scheduled to be given again the next winter. In 1928 four separate concerts were presented. One was planned for the third and fourth grades; one for the fifth and sixth grades; another for the seventh, eighth, and ninth grades; and the last for high schools and colleges. Each concert was thirty minutes. They were scheduled on alternate Fridays at 11:00 and 11:30 A.M., eastern standard time. Over a two-week interval, one concert could be presented for each age group.

Dunham gives us a good example of this course in his quote from the *Teachers Manual* regarding a program featuring the

Mendelssohn Overture to *A Midsummer Night's Dream*, and *Dance of the Mosquito*, by Liadow, and selections from the *Pastoral Symphony* of Beethoven.

    1. Q. What happens to Bottom, the weaver, in *A Midsummer Night's Dream*?

    A. Puck, the fairy, changes his head into a donkey's head.

    2. Q. How does Mendelssohn introduce Bottom in the Overture to *A Midsummer Night's Dream*?

    A. By imitating the braying of a donkey.

    3. Q. What other characters does Mendelssohn portray in the Overture to *A Midsummer Night's Dream*?

    A. King Oberon, Queen Titania and their fairy subjects.[18]

There appears to be little interest in strictly musical matters with the major effort in the direction of programmatic suggestions.

    Questions from an April 26, 1929, concert aimed at high-school-age and adult listeners moved more in the direction of autonomous listening. "In what form is the first movement of a symphony usually written? Give a brief description of sonata form. In what form is the second movement of Beethoven's Fifth Symphony composed?" But other questions refer to programmatic conceptions and extra-musical reactions by the listener. "What dramatic concept is the first movement of Beethoven's Fifth Symphony generally supposed to express? What did Beethoven say of the principal theme of the first movement of his Fifth Symphony? What picture did Mr. Damrosch evoke as a possible interpretation of the second movement of the Fifth Symphony?"[19] The answer to the last question is suggested in the *Teachers Manual* as "a walk in a lovely garden, in which one finds a statue erected to the memory of some national hero."

    It must be recognized that the strengths of the programs outweighed their few weaknesses. In the New York City schools alone between three hundred fifty to four hundred schools had been equipped with "radio receiving sets," with more than two hundred thousand pupils in that city listening to the broadcasts on Friday mornings in 1930. The schools of Columbus, Kansas, were entirely equipped with radios as were Joliet, Illinois; Omaha, Nebraska; and Superior, Wisconsin. In Nashville, Tennessee, forty-two of the city's schools had radios, and in Beaumont, Texas, twelve schools were so equipped. Many schools had one central set in the school auditorium. The National Broadcasting Company estimated in 1930 that there were 5,176,960 children listening to these broadcasts of classical music as presented by Walter Damrosch.[20]

It was difficult for those west of the Rocky Mountains to receive these broadcasts because of the time differences. Not to be outdone by the Damrosch concerts, however, the Standard Oil Company of California sponsored broadcast concerts of the San Francisco Symphony and the Los Angeles Philharmonic Orchestra. The company presented the Standard Symphony Hour and beginning in October 1928 carried this symphony hour in conjunction with an educational half-hour broadcast.[21] The broadcasts were scheduled for the morning and were devoted principally to an explanation of the concerts which were to take place that evening. Arthur S. Garbett, educational director of the National Broadcasting Company, served as lecturer and coordinator for the series.

It soon became apparent that individual teachers could do much to enhance the scope and efficiency of the broadcasts. A teacher could conduct discussion sessions at the close of each concert. Visual aids like pictures of instruments and composers were used to reinforce the learning. It was also recommended that program notes be used in preparing the children for each concert.[22]

MUSIC MEMORY CONTESTS

Contests designed to test the student's memory of certain selected compositions became enormously popular after the First World War to about 1930. Edward Bailey Birge tried such a contest in an informal way as early as 1909 in Indianapolis. Once a month certain parts of pieces were played and the children attempted to recall the title of the composition and the composer. In 1916 C. M. Tremaine, director of the National Bureau for the Advancement of Music, tried a similar technique in his home in order to interest his own children in music. After suggesting a game in which the children would familiarize themselves with an assortment of classical selections available to them on piano rolls, he would award a prize to the one who could correctly identify the most compositions. After a disappointing early effort, one of the children was able to identify eighteen out of twenty compositions three weeks later. The child began to evince a greater interest in music, started to play the player piano regularly, joined a mandolin club, and indicated a desire to attend concerts. Pleased that his idea had worked, Tremaine talked to Mabel E. Bray, the supervisor of music in his hometown of Westfield, New Jersey. Apparently enthusiastic about the idea and with the cooperation of the superintendent of schools, the local paper, and local musicians, she carried out the first school memory contest in October 1916.[23]

Evidently the experiment became exceedingly popular. Tremaine reported to the Music Supervisors National Conference not only the success of the contest in his hometown of Westfield but also described similar contests in New Orleans in 1917 and in Utica, New York, in 1918. This latter event was reported to have had a thousand entrants. Tremaine described how impressed the Westfield community was with the ability of the students to learn the required information. By 1920 the music memory contest had become a popular musical feature in many cities, tending to foster the cooperation of the music clubs, the press, and the music dealers. Some orchestras of the moving picture theatres played certain selections that appeared on the approved lists for "music memory." Usually six to eight weeks were set aside for special training in memorizing the pieces. In the larger cities, preliminary contests were held in the schools with the winners competing on a district level.

In 1920 an impressive music memory contest was held in Dallas, Texas. The school children were exposed to the contest music in an intensive way. Fifty compositions were chosen for the contest, and the children were reported to have absorbed every note.[24] Some of the records were heard every school day during the student's thirty-minute music period. School concerts featured the selections in hour-and-a-half performances. The pieces would be heard "at school parties given at the homes of pupils for their classmates, on Saturdays, and in some instances on Sunday afternoons at the home of the departmental teacher of music. Children tested each other out by humming on the way to and from school and at intermissions."[25] The music dealers cooperated by giving two concerts every Saturday night during the eight weeks of preparation and kept an open house for the children every day during this time where the pupils, singly or in groups, could listen in booths to a phonograph or player piano. Studio teachers gave their students extra help on lesson days, and records and sheet music were sold.

By the time of the contest, 177 of the 270 contestants made perfect scores.

The music memory contest spread rapidly during the 1920s. In 1922 state contests were held in Indiana, Pennsylvania, Wisconsin, Michigan, and Ohio. The Interscholastic League of the State of Texas, which administered activities such as football, baseball, and debate, announced that it would supervise the music memory contests as a part of its annual program. In 1922 there were 405 music memory contests; two years later there were as many as 1,193 such contests.[26]

There was some degree of uniformity in the lists of compositions selected by various educators even in different parts of the country. This uniformity was encouraged by a list of recommended selections drawn up and published by the National Bureau for the Advancement of Music. By 1924 a supplementary list of 100 selections was recommended by Osbourne McConathy, Hollis Dann, Will Earhart, Peter Dykema, C. H. Miller, and Frances Elliott Clark, all former presidents of the Music Supervisors National Conference. There was a remarkable agreement by music teachers as to what selections seemed appropriate for the music memory contests.

Richard Lee Dunham describes the selections on the list as "short, in general, and possessed of one or more striking melodic, rhythmic, or harmonic characteristic which made them relatively easy to recall."[27] The melodies were generally singable and had few subtle characteristics. Most of the selections were taken from the romantic literature.

But there were certain problems inherent in contests of this kind for school children, problems that have concerned music teachers to this day. Although there were benefits deriving from the excitement felt by participants and from the broad-based public relations, there were also disadvantages. Some music educators deplored the interruption of the regular music class work in order that drill might take place for the contests.[28]

Thomas H. Briggs posed a number of philosophical questions relating to the contests in 1925.

How much knowledge and appreciation goes with recognition?

How long can interest be retained or increased in preparation for a contest?

Are there better means of testing than naming a composition?

What is the contribution of related information to the desired ends of recognition and appreciation?

What is the relation of success in recognition to further understanding and appreciation?

How may the accomplishment in a contest be utilized for continued enjoyment and education? [29]

In 1928, the National Bureau for the Advancement of Music expressed concern that the contests' overemphasis on competition led to excessive rivalry. Contests tended to magnify the importance of "those points which merely aid in recognition, at the expense of the true teaching of appreciation." The bureau criticized the emphasis placed on spelling and the time consumed at the expense of other music work, and it also observed a lessening of interest in the contests after the first two or three years of participation. [30]

Attempts were made to modify the contests to fit a more broadly based concept of appreciation. The Chicago Symphony supported the movement by playing for the contests as well as playing contest selections at the children's concerts. These contests were sponsored by the In-and-About Chicago Music Supervisors' Club which made an effort to turn away from the practice of learning the names and nationalities of the composers and toward encouraging a development of an understanding of five different areas of music that were graded according to the level of the student. Dance forms, musical nationalism, and the instruments of the orchestra were studied. High school students were responsible for the study of the composers, their styles, and their idioms. In Chicago weekly lectures at which the contest material would be discussed and played were given by Anne Shaw Faulkner on the radio. Outlines of the lecture were printed regularly in the Chicago Daily News. On three Friday evening broadcasts a month, Mr. and Mrs. Oberndorfer presented twenty selections for a memory contest.

On the fourth Friday short segments were played while contestants at home jotted down the name of each piece, its composer, period and nationality. These papers were in turn submitted for evaluation and the Daily News awarded prizes for the best set of answers. [31]

Prizes in the Chicago area were awarded not only to individuals but also to schools, making the contests a team effort.

Mabelle Glenn put her imprint on the memory contests in Kansas City where she placed special emphasis on the musical characteristics of the compositions under study. Miss Glenn asked her students to remember the number of times they heard the tune and to determine whether the tune was "dignified, changeable, sparkling, or stately." She also made three suggestions concerning the preparation for the contests.

1) Do not play too many compositions on the same day, 2) do not introduce the music for the purpose of the contest, but let the contest come as the result of a year's classroom work in music appreciation, [and] 3) do not slight the teaching of the musical qualities in the haste to present identifiable themes.[32]

It was inevitable that changes in the memory contest would occur. In Saint Louis, Agnes Moore Fryberger asked the students to write original poems and stories and provide drawings for their conceptions of the music being performed. The "Dallas Plan" asked the contestants for a recognition of form as well as the composer and title. In 1924 Sigmund Spaeth asked his students in his supervisor's course, given at New York University, sophisticated questions relating to the history of music. The compositions were heard for the first time by his students.

1. Do you consider this "program" or "absolute" music?

2. What is the outstanding element, rhythm, melody, or harmony, or does it achieve a balance among these factors?

3. What is its general rhythmic pattern, two beat or three beat?

4. Is it in major or minor mode or a combination of the two?

5. Is it composed of a distinct melody and accompaniment or are all the parts independent, homophonic or polyphonic?

6. If program music, is it descriptive, narrative, or merely suggestive?

7. If absolute, is it rhapsodic, contemplative, sentimental or purely incidental?

8. Has it any definite form or logical division into parts?

9. To what period do you think it belongs, classic, romantic, or modern?

10. What kind of piece do you think it is? Waltz, march, nocturne, ballade, sonata movement, overture, rhapsody, song, fantasie, mazurka, polonaise, intermezzo, caprice, operatic selection, etc.

11. Whom would you pick as a probable composer?

12. What would be a probable title?

13. Do you know the actual composer and title of the piece? If so, name them.

14. What is your opinion of the piece? [33]

The ultimate consummation of the music memory contest took place in Cleveland in connection with the third biennial meeting of the Music Supervisors National Conference in 1932. The contest was national in scope with study hints published in the *Music Supervisors Journal.* Those eligible to compete were the members of the 1932 National High School Orchestra and Chorus and the All-Ohio Band who were present at the meeting and scheduled to perform. Any other junior or senior high school student who had the approval of his or her music supervisor or teacher and could be present in Cleveland on April 6, 1932, could compete. The test was broadcast nationally from New York by the National Broadcasting Company with Walter Damrosch conducting. All students in the United States were invited to participate, but, of course, only those who were properly registered in Cleveland were eligible for prizes. The judges were members of the Music Appreciation Committee of the Music Supervisors National Conference. The prizes, three scholarships to any established summer music camp, were awarded by the National Broadcasting Company.

Following this contest, interest seemed to wane and fewer and fewer references can be found to memory contests. Several reasons can be cited for the decline. Instrumental music was growing enormously during this period. The various performing groups absorbed the better and more interested musicians of the school. Those students would normally be more interested in active participation rather than in listening, and the philosophy was reinforced by the educational establishment through the glorification of the "learning by doing" idea. In general, the music memory contest had somewhat over a ten-year vitality. It was not sufficiently a part of the culture of the United States to survive a longer period. Its weaknesses, which were apparent to many from the early days of the contests, eventually eroded its basic support. Those who had always been against contests pointed to the excessive nervous strain on the young participants. The emphasis on the teaching of a certain subject to the exclusion of others disturbed many. Many believed that the contests fostered the idea of winning at any cost. Some argued that the trips to contest sites created financial difficulties and anxieties regarding chaperoning.

But as the band contests started to flourish and the ideas of competition continued unabated, one must look to other, more subtle, forces that brought an end to the music memory contests and that, in another sense, signaled important changes. These changes resulted from the increasing importance of instrumental music in the nation's schools, an increasing perception of the child-study movement, and a more widely based curriculum that did not encourage all children to take general music on the high school level. Each of the old courses now had more competition, and instrumental music had a rare unmatched glamour. Not strongly encouraged by the music supervisors, the music memory contests became lost in the new wave of interest in performance. The special concept known as "appreciation" would merge with the performing experience on one hand and a multifaceted general music experience on the other.

CHAPTER XV

The Rise of Instrumental Music

IT HAS BECOME traditional that a discussion of instrumental music in the schools would begin with the turn of the twentieth century. While the year 1900 is still a good indicator of the time when instrumental music developed a foothold in the public schools, it must be equally obvious that all those people who played their cornets and trumpets in the town bands, purchased stringed instruments during the nineteenth century, and learned to play the piano as a "polite branch" had to receive their instruction from some source. An American citizen of the nineteenth century would have seen many schools and teachers of instrumental music right beside those omnipresent teachers of vocal music. These instrumental teachers opened schools and academies of music, giving not only private lessons but sometimes class lessons as well—a good fifty years ahead of the usual estimates of when the first class instruction started.

Residents of the larger urban areas of the United States had ample opportunities to hear the best of the European masters performed by symphony orchestras, which were fast becoming the bulwark of culture in our major cities. The New York Philharmonic was founded in 1842, and the Symphony Society of New York was founded in 1878. Two years later the Saint Louis Symphony was founded, and in 1881 the Boston Symphony began, destined to become one of the world's finest symphonic organizations. The European touring artists did much to stimulate interest in the study of instrumental music, and the European musicians sailing from their homeland to the New World brought with them their instruments and their art and, perhaps what is equally important, the desire to teach this art in their adopted country.

Almost all towns had a town band which provided entertainment. Patrick S. Gilmore's band toured and created a sensation with their Peace Festival of 1869 and World Peace Festival in 1872. Perhaps for the first time the country was exposed to the massed band concert, with chorus, orchestra, organ, cannon, and anvils! John Philip Sousa's band followed and, showing better taste, played both transcriptions and the great marches of its director.

Instruments were taught in the public schools of the nineteenth century but only in isolated instances; no momentum developed until after the turn of the century. In 1879 an instrumental teacher was hired in Lancaster, Pennsylvania, in the high school. As early as 1857 the first school band (or was it an orchestra?) appeared in Boston at the Farm and Trades School on Thompson Island. It was called a band but its instrumentation was reported as "tissue covered combs, three violins, and bass viol."[1] Two years later regular instruments were acquired and the organization paraded through Boston. The following public schools taught instrumental music before 1900: Wichita, Kansas, with Jessie Clark; Chelsea, Massachusetts, with Osbourne McConathy; Edinburg, Pennsylvania, with Hamlin E. Cogswell; Hartford, Connecticut, with James D. Price; New Albany, Indiana, with Anton Embs; and Sullivan, Indiana, with Ralph Sloan.[2] And as early as 1869, Walter Aiken was reported to have played in a school orchestra.

The prevalence of instrumental performance during the last century requires us to consider these teachers and their methods. The greater part of this instrumental teaching took place in academies, conservatories, music schools, and homes. Advertising, especially for successful teachers, was not necessary.[3]

EARLY INSTRUMENTAL TEACHERS: THE HOWELLS AND
THE BENJAMINS

We have already observed the rise and decline of the singing school and the sociology that surrounded the teaching and performance of vocal music. Its serious study had religious overtones, and the later practice and performance of oratorios was a most serious undertaking. From the church schools of the Middle Ages to the singing schools of eighteenth-century America, voice instruction had traditionally been taught in classes. Instrumental performance and study had quite another history. In Puritan New England the use of instruments in church was forbidden, and, as we have seen, the use of the bass-viol (cello) became accepted in the churches of New England around 1800 only with considerable controversy. Unlike voice instruction, instrumental instruction was ordinarily given privately. Most teachers of instruments believed that only one student could be taught at a time.

A few singing masters of colonial America also taught instruments, and by the mid-nineteenth century there were those teachers who combined singing class techniques with instrumental instruction in a class setting. They taught dance music: quadrilles, reels, and cotillions. Some even taught religious music. D. L. Elder taught music theory and instrumental music both privately and in classes in Knoxville, Tennessee, in 1839. Later in the century the University of Tennessee advertised in its *Register* that "vocal and instrumental music is given individuals or classes at the University."[4]

Charles Edmond Sollinger tells of the Howell brothers of Cotton Plant, Arkansas, in the decade before the Civil War. Cotton Plant was not far from Little Rock, a city which had between seven and ten private schools in 1838. A number of these institutions taught both instrumental and vocal music. James L. Howell and his brother Joseph taught music and sold instruments in Cotton Plant from 1849 to 1861. (After the Civil War, Joseph Howell returned to Arkansas, but it seems likely that James died in the conflict.)

The Howells taught violin in classes, using a pentatonic scale approach that employed the first and third fingers in addition to open strings for the beginning stages. The brothers had attended southern singing schools, and their musical selections followed the fasola traditions of southern hymnody.

Joseph Howell wrote his *New Class Book* around 1859. Sollinger reports that the text was intelligently and carefully written and neatly printed. It was the usual oblong shape and included a theoretical introduction. Its contents included a collection of songs in one, two, and three parts designed for students to play and sing at the same time. The book used round notes. Seventeen of the tunes were popular southern hymns. Howell's book also urged parents not to spend too much on a violin "without knowing what was being purchased," and he warned against buying a poor instrument as the student's progress would be hindered. "I have for years had daily experience in teaching and have seen, and constantly do see, not without concern and admonition, many a talented youth make an unsuccessful effort, who had promised fair in the beginning, and might have proceeded happily, had he in his hands a good violin." A "snakewood Amati" had been advertised as the most perfect violin. "It is not to be found in any music or fancy store in the South. I have therefore ordered, and do receive, directly from Europe once a month, a large number of these and others, the best that are made, for the express benefit of my schools, knowing it to be my duty to place in the hands of my students such an instrument as they can use successfully and satisfactorily, especially when they come before me daily and say: 'We are not judges of good violins, and must therefore depend on you to select for us.'"[5]

Across the continent in New York a family named Benjamin taught instrumental music, principally the violin. Lewis A. Benjamin, Sr., taught violin in classes around the middle of the nineteenth century, and Sollinger reports that he was the first to teach orchestral instruments in classes in the United States. He was a performer and teacher in New York City and Brooklyn between 1847 and 1891. He was associated with Isaac Woodbury in the New York Normal School in 1851 when they jointly published *The New York Normal School Song Book*. Benjamin formed beginner's instrumental classes according to age groups.

Benjamin organized a musical academy, which served both musical and social purposes. The classes were organized in the form of "societies." Each member paid dues of twenty-five cents per week each time they attended. In the advanced evening classes, dance music was the usual fare. The social contacts helped ensure the success of the school. But the students gave regular public concerts, and the "members were expected to take the part assigned to them as their duty to the academy."[6] The more qualified students were invited into classes free of charge if they committed themselves to remaining with the academy for a minimum of two years.

At the end of the first year, scholarships were awarded for the second year. In this way a nucleus of good players could be retained for the featured concerts. The scholarship students were required to participate in the academy for a full year, otherwise the normal fee of three dollars per quarter would be charged. Private lessons were available on the "pianoforte, seraphine, violin, guitar, and accordion &c." Ten dollars was charged for twenty-four lessons at a rate of five dollars per quarter. As is so often the case today with private entrepreneurial ventures in the field of music, instruments were rented and sold at the academy.

Lewis A. Benjamin, Sr., wrote *The Musical Academy* for his instrumental classes.[7] The book was twenty-five pages long and contained eighteen popular tunes of the day, mostly dance tunes, arranged in three parts, two treble and one bass.* The title of the 1851 volume reads "for Violin, bass-viol, clarionette, flute and other light instruments." But instruction was given chiefly for the violin with some technical aid given for the cello. Benjamin taught his instrumental students in classes. The three-part harmonizations of the tunes implied or suggested ensemble playing, and the cover and title page of *The Musical Academy* read, "designed for instrumental classes." The directions included in Lesson IV said "learning the letters of the bass staff may be omitted in class when the bass part is not performed."[8]

Lewis A. Benjamin, Jr., followed in his father's footsteps, becoming a music teacher in New York City and Brooklyn during the last third of the nineteenth century. He was a performer, a teacher, and an organizer of "free violin schools." In addition, he sold instruments and published music. He and his brother Frank operated the Benjamin Brothers Musical Academy in Brooklyn during the 1880s. Lewis Benjamin, Jr., organized and produced annual Children's Carnivals at the academy involving thousands of children—with the help of his wife Lillie, his brother Frank, his secretary Ernest Weiss, and perhaps his father.

The Benjamin Brothers Musical Academy offered free violin class instruction in the hope of enrolling as many students as possible, thus creating more opportunity to sell instruments, music,

---

* The title page implies that there were six other volumes published prior to *The Musical Academy*, and there were to be two additional volumes to be printed subsequently, but Sollinger reports that these additional volumes remain to be found.

and perhaps enroll some students for private instruction. In 1889 the academy's annual Children's Carnival featured an orchestra of three hundred students, all taught in the free schools by class instruction. Rules were instituted to maintain order. The student's membership was forfeited "if a member came earlier than the hour set for class, loitering in the hallways or around the door, engaged in loud talking, or made noise coming in or out of class."[9] Missed lessons required a written excuse, while four consecutive absences required a parent to present him or herself personally to the school to explain the reasons.

Instruments were sold aggressively by the Benjamins and probably represented a good share of their livelihood. The students and parents were advised to purchase instruments from the Benjamins where they would be assured of obtaining an instrument of "good tone, proper size and satisfactory in every respect." They claimed to sell guaranteed Italian, French, and German violins at wholesale prices of $4.50 to $75.00. The price included bow and rosin. Installment purchases could be arranged with two dollars down and fifty cents a week plus fifty cents carrying charge on violins under ten dollars. The ten dollar violins included a case ("violin box") but the less expensive instruments did not. A certain "new style" violin case sold for $1.50. Folding music stands sold for $1.50 while violin tuners were seventy-five cents. Sollinger tells us that chin rests were not supplied with the instrument but were sold separately to the students for one dollar! The ten dollar instruments were those recommended to the students while those in the thirty-five dollar to seventy-five dollar range were classified as "artist's" or advanced pupil's violins.

Frank T. Benjamin published his *Free Violin School* in 1889 from the same plates as Ryan's *True Violinist*. Apparently there was no ethical dilemma either for Benjamin or for his publisher, the John Church Company, that supplied the plates for the earlier volume. "Instructions for the violin" were included on pages 18 through 29 with the following subjects discussed: "Position of the violin; Holding the bow; Scale or Gamut; Plan of the fingerboard; The Scales; Scale of Flats, Sharps, and Naturals; On Bowing." An exercise for the open strings was followed by a group of scales in various keys. One or two tunes followed each scale in the appropriate key just introduced. Pages 30 to 79 contained mostly dance tunes: schottisches, quadrilles, reels, waltzes, polkas, marches, quicksteps, country dances, and some sentimental songs and operatic airs.

Benjamin's Children's Carnivals, which were presented to large and enthusiastic audiences between the years 1883 and 1891, represented good examples of massed performances that seemed so popular during that period. Most concerts featuring large groups of performers were usually choral, but the Benjamins successfully included large numbers of instrumentalists. The sixth such carnival presented by Benjamin took place on May 17 and 18, 1889. A full house of 3,500 people on each of the two nights crowned his efforts. The performance took place at the Brooklyn Academy of Music in the form of a musical variety show. It included a large orchestra, large chorus, solos by violinists and vocalists, a fiddling contest, and a guest soloist. Two thousand children took part. An orchestra of three hundred students of the Benjamin Brothers Musical Academy plus fifteen hundred singers from the schools of Brooklyn participated. The orchestra was seated in front of the green curtain on the stage, the boys to the right, and the girls on the left. The private class of Benjamin played the overture to "Nadjy" before the curtain was raised. As the curtain rose, the audience saw the remainder of the children from one side of the stage to the other and up on risers to the back "until the top row reached the flies in the rear." The girls wore white dresses with richly colored ribbons while the boys wore dark clothes. As the curtain rose, Lillie Benjamin directed the children in a chorus of "Our Nation's Song," as everyone waved banners in the air. The scene was reported in detail by the *Brooklyn Eagle* of May 17, 1889, with the writer declaring that the scene was "inspiring" and the singing was "good."

The Benjamins undoubtedly had much cooperation from the public schools of Brooklyn, and the school officials must have looked with favor on the efforts of the Benjamins to promote instrumental music. Letters from school principals were printed in Benjamin's book, *Free Violin Schools*, commending Benjamin's work. The brothers themselves taught in public school No. 34 for five years. The principal, F. R. Moore, praised their work highly and observed that the study of the violin had not interfered with the regular school work. Those who learned to play the violin in class participated in the exercises of the school. That the Benjamins could borrow fifteen hundred school children in order to create a chorus, itself demonstrates that Benjamin's relations with the schools were indeed cordial.

Frank T. Benjamin, Lewis's brother, and his wife, Ida, organized and taught free violin schools in Philadelphia and in Camden beginning in 1888. Following a similar pattern of promotion and teaching as his brother, Frank organized free violin schools at six locations in Philadelphia. He taught weekdays after school from 4:30 and all day on Saturday. Each evening Frank Benjamin also taught violin at the "violin college" at 2110 North Fifteenth Street. The total number of students at the six locations of his free school was more than five hundred, and all except beginners were proficient enough to play in the orchestra at the Children's Carnival of 1891 in that city. Sollinger estimates that between ten and twenty students were in each of the violin classes taught by Benjamin, and perhaps also by his wife. The purchase of Frank T. Benjamin's book, *Free Violin School* entitled the buyer to a year's free lessons.[10]

Benjamin was enthusiastic about class teaching of the violin. He invited parents to the school to discuss instructional problems and believed that class teaching provided added stimulus to the boys and girls who participated. All classes were graded with the highest called "first class" and the lowest "preparatory." Students remained in the preparatory class for as little time as possible and moved into the next class, usually within two weeks. As soon as a particular lesson was learned, the pupil was promoted, receiving a higher "class ticket," or having his book stamped appropriately. The method stimulated interest and enthusiasm in the early lessons.

Frank T. Benjamin also wrote a *Comprehensive Violin Method* in which he discussed his instructional techniques. Piano accompaniments were incorporated in all exercises and pieces. He believed that the pianist should play along with the violin student who should be counting aloud. Should the violinist play out of tune "the pianist will strike the note with the right hand and is not to proceed until the pupil has made his or her note to correspond."[11]

Frank T. Benjamin's 1891 carnival was most successful. Like the carnivals of his brother Lewis, the 1891 Carnival was a three-day affair with all performances crowded. The concert was attended by Governor Pattison and his family (the governor's son played in the Free Violin School Orchestra), by the superintendent of the Board of Education (whose son also played in the orchestra), and by "nearly every public school principal in Philadelphia and Camden." Twenty-five hundred school students participated. There was an orchestra of five hundred; a chorus of two thousand; solos; a violin playing contest; and a grand drill for the finale.

The inspiring mass performances of the children may have been important in creating enthusiasm for the reintroduction of vocal music in the schools of Philadelphia after an absence of twenty years. Vocal music was first introduced in 1869, but in 1877 city officials failed to appropriate money for the salaries of music teachers. For twenty years vocal instruction was not officially supported. During that time the principals of the various schools encouraged vocal instruction, which was paid for by the students. The teachers were called "penny-a-lesson" singing teachers. Sollinger speculates that the choir preparation for the carnivals was most likely accomplished during school hours by either Frank Benjamin or his wife, Ida, making them one of the "penny-a-lesson" teachers.[12] To reinforce the effects of Benjamin's promotional activities, the superintendent of schools recommended the reintroduction of vocal music into the public schools of Philadelphia in 1895.

THE CONSERVATORY SYSTEM

The conservatory system of teaching was borrowed from Europe. In many instances the European conservatories were sponsored by governments for the purpose of preserving a country's musical culture. Ordinarily, they were free for all, their directors realizing that musical talent was no respecter of social class. In general the curriculum consisted of applied music, solfeggio, harmony, and other theoretical branches. The aim of the conservatories was to produce excellent performers with broad musical backgrounds.

The European conservatory most imitated in America was the Leipzig Conservatory, an institution started by Mendelssohn in 1843. Many German musicians who trained there immigrated to the United States and became music teachers, and many American students who looked toward the Continent for the completion of their musical studies went to the conservatory at Leipzig. The school adopted class teaching as its principal system of instruction, believing that a situation wherein students could play for each other and for the criticism of the teacher was most desirable. In general the students in each class were at the same level of advancement. At Leipzig there were five distinct classes, but more were organized if necessary.

American conservatories had a somewhat different philosophy, which is not very surprising considering the cultural level of the United States during the nineteenth century. The American conservatory was aimed at people at all levels and abilities in the hope of generating a cultural renaissance among the masses.

The Leipzig Conservatory was particularly conservative. In 1857 its director would consider no music after Mendelssohn to be worthy of study or performance. Performances of Chopin and Schumann were rare, and the music of Wagner was not only un played but the composer was not mentioned as a musician. In general this conservative attitude was transmitted to the American conservatories.

While there have been several claims as to who first introduced the conservatory system to America, Eben Tourjée must be recognized as the first person whose results were significant and permanent. He was born in Warwick, Rhode Island, in 1834. In 1851 he began a business as a music dealer and taught music in the public schools and formed classes in piano, voice, and organ. He began publishing *The Key Note*, which later became *The Massachusetts Music Journal*. In these publications Tourjée first expressed his desire for an American conservatory of music.

In 1853 Tourjée tried to interest some Boston educators and musical persons in his plans, but they considered him an impractical dreamer. He then began a school of his own at Fall River, Massachusetts. At the Fall River Conservatory classes were offered in piano, voice, violin, and flute at a cost of one dollar for twenty lessons. Although a total of 560 pupils were enrolled, his expenses exceeded his income from the beginning and he abandoned the venture after two years. He moved to Newport in 1855 where he taught music in the public schools and where, undaunted, he began the Newport Musical Institute. After a three-year stint as director of the seminary in East Greenwich, Rhode Island, he went to Europe to study the textbooks and methods of the conservatories there. Although he remained only a year, he found time to make the acquaintance of and perhaps to study with Schumann, Cramer, von Bulow, Richter, and August Haupt. Upon returning to America he moved to Providence where he founded the Providence Conservatory of Music. His efforts now met with success, and only six years later, in 1867, Tourjée established the New England Conservatory of Music.

He became one of the principal spokesmen for the class system of instruction, which worked well when it was introduced in Boston. An indefatigable promoter, he organized and trained choruses of ten and twenty thousand for Gilmore's peace jubilees of 1869 and 1872. He received a doctor of music degree from Wesleyan University in 1872 and the next year was made dean of the College of Music of Boston University. His call to the nation's music teachers to form the National Music Conference for the purpose of developing a uniformity of approach to music education represented the first organized meeting of music teachers on a national scale. The organization became the Music Teachers National Association (MTNA) which was organized in 1876 with Eben Tourjée as its first president.

Americans believed that there were too many large classes in the European conservatories and so modified the European practice. Instrumental classes in this country varied between two and six students. The Boston Conservatory advertised four students to a class; New England advertised six; Peabody, four to six; Oberlin, two or three; Chicago, three; and Cincinnati, three.

Many music professors, however, rebelled against the conservatory system of class instruction, and the advent of the degree programs in music signaled its decline. The class method was continued for the study of secondary instruments in conservatories and colleges, but for the study of a student's primary instrument, private instruction was resumed. The conservatory system also declined with the growing popularity of class instruction in instrumental music in the public schools.

INSTRUMENTAL MUSIC IN THE PUBLIC SCHOOLS

There were considerable differences in approach concerning the teaching of instruments in classes. The conservatory system had small classes where the students played individually. The public school instrumental classes were larger, perhaps sixteen or even as high as thirty, and the students played together. The conservatories used method books most often from their European counterparts, while the public school classes used books especially prepared for the public schools in addition to some conservatory methods. Public school class instruction became a mainstay of instrumental teaching while the conservatory professors were, for the most part, happy to return to the concept of individual lessons.

The conservatory concept of class lessons was foreign to the public school music teacher, and when instrumental music began to appear in the public school music curriculum, teachers felt the need for an efficient and economical way to teach orchestral instruments. We have already seen that individual teachers had discovered instrumental class teaching and had put the system to use with an obvious degree of success. But in the nineteenth century the introduction of vocal music was problem enough with a citizenry barely able to accept the concept of public education and, by the standards of the next century, with a tight curriculum based upon the tenets of faculty psychology. The isolated practices of class teaching did not find a fertile soil on the national landscape.

But in England in 1898 there was an event that was destined to help change the course of school music teaching. The Murdock Company, dealers in musical instruments, began violin classes in the All Saints School at Maidstone, England, as an experiment in developing a love for orchestra music. Instruments, music, equipment, the organization, and the teachers were supplied by the Murdock Company of London. The classes were held under the supervision of the school, and payments were arranged in small weekly amounts, so the poorer children could afford lessons. During the first few years of its existence, almost a half million violins were sold by the Murdock Company in some five thousand schools. Charles Farnsworth heard a concert at Alexander's Palace that involved 1,450 instrumentalists from school orchestras in and about London. Massed performances were presented periodically to provide an outlet for the students, to promote the program, and presumably to stimulate additional business for the Murdock Company.

The First Annual Festival of the National Union of School Orchestras in 1905 featured 700 students. The number increased each year until there were 6,800 participants at the Tenth Annual Festival in 1914. That year the event was divided into two sections; 3,500 played in the afternoon, and 3,300 in the evening. The masses of violinists played to the accompaniment of a brass band! The First World War brought these activities to a sudden stop in England, but the idea was carried to the United States by Albert Mitchell, Paul Stoeving, and Charles Farnsworth.

The three wrote, taught, and lectured on the techniques they observed in England and were responsible for the promotion of this kind of class instrumental instruction in the United States. Albert Mitchell, a music supervisor in the Boston schools, was given leave in 1910 to go to England to study the class teaching methods used in England. When he arrived back in the country, he immediately organized violin classes in Boston. Mitchell held these classes after school with sixteen children per class. Three years later the results of his efforts were sufficiently impressive that his classes were admitted into the school day. He claimed Boston as being the first city in the United States to introduce systematic violin class teaching into the public schools. In 1918 he published a method for use with his classes.[13]

In addition to Mitchell who taught the classes, and Farnsworth who wrote the publicity, Paul Stoeving had much to do with the promotion of string class teaching in this country. Stoeving was a concert violinist, wrote books, and taught classes. He was educated at the Leipzig Conservatory and toured as a concert violinist until 1896. At that time he accepted an appointment as professor of violin at the Guildhall School of Music in London. He observed the Maidstone Movement, as it was called, and was duly impressed. He came to the United States to live in 1914 and that year reported his ideas and opinions to the MTNA convention at Pittsburgh. He described the tenth annual national festival to those assembled. His writings concerning the efficacy and procedures to be used for teaching stringed instruments in class are still as pertinent today as when they were written.

CHAPTER XVI

Early Bands in the United States

B AND S BECAME organized on a permanent basis in this country around 1800. In 1823 New York City had five prominent
bands, and bands were also organized in Allentown, Pennsylvania,
in 1828, in Barrington, New Hampshire, in 1832; and in Rohrs-
ville, Maryland, in 1837. Most of the early bands, however, were
associated with military posts or with local militia. In 1821 West
Point had a military band consisting of fourteen men: five clar
inets, two flutes, two horns, one bassoon, one trumpet, one trombone, one keyed bugle, and one drum.[1]

About 1834 the reed band, or those bands that had both reed
and brass instruments, became less important because of the increasing popularity of the brass band. This change in taste may
have been influenced by Allen Dodworth, the director of the Dod
worth Band of New York City.*

In the years preceding 1850, the minstrel band became popular. Traveling widely with minstrel troupes, these organizations
brought band music to communities that might not have been
so introduced in any other way. The minstrel band introduced
the "cakewalk," the first distinctly American contribution to the
march.

Patrick Sarsfield Gilmore's influence on the development of

* Dodworth also introduced the "over the shoulder" type of bass instruments common
in American bands until the later introduction of the sax horns.

bands and their music cannot be overrated. Gilmore directed brass bands in Boston and Salem, Massachusetts, before the Civil War and served as a bandmaster during the war. His ideas and conceptions always tended toward the spectacular. In 1864 he assembled a band of five hundred players and a chorus of five thousand school children for a Grand National Concert in New Orleans honoring Michael Hahn, the newly elected governor of Louisiana. He was responsible for bringing to this country the Grenadier Guards Band of England, the *Garde Republicaine* Band of France, the Kaiser Franz Grenadier Band of Germany, and the Johann Strauss Orchestra from Vienna. Gilmore was influenced by European bands, and in 1873 when he became director of the Twenty-Second Regiment Band of New York, he set out promptly to organize it using as a model the European bands he had heard in Boston. Within five years he had developed the prototypal concert band which became so familiar in this country. Sixty-six men played in Gilmore's band in 1878, thirty-six playing woodwind instruments including saxophones.

Gilmore's band toured the United States between 1876 and 1891. His concerts encouraged the ubiquitous town bands to reintroduce woodwind instruments, and the repertoire and standard of performance of his band inspired the town bands. Gilmore's band played, among others, Wagner, Liszt, Mendelssohn, Berlioz, Rossini, and Verdi. He played arrangements, of course, but it is important to remember that many in his audiences heard these composers for the first time.

What Gilmore started, John Philip Sousa improved upon. Touring the United States, Canada, and the world between 1892 and 1932, the great Sousa bands established new standards of perfection for both amateur and professional bands. But between 1910 and 1920 the colossus gradually lost its strength in a period of changing cultural values. As job opportunities decreased, the inferior bands exploited a shoddy type of showmanship. They charged less money for these efforts and were hired over the better concert bands. The steady employment of 1910 vanished by 1920. In addition those bands that played polkas, waltzes, and schottisches could not compete with the growing popularity of the jazz bands which were breaking out of their Storyvilles and saloons and becoming a musical force to be reckoned with.

The golden age of the town band—1870 to 1930—paralleled

that of the professional band. In 1889 there were ten thousand adult and juvenile bands in the United States. It has been calculated that Sousa's famous marches had been sold to eighteen thousand bands by 1897. Austin A. Harding wrote in a 1915 article in the journal of the Music Teachers National Association, *Proceedings*, that "there were more bands in the state of Illinois than there were towns." The Bureau of Music connected to the Louisiana Purchase Exposition of 1804 (the Saint Louis World's Fair) planned a series of band contests and sent circulars to nearly 8,000 bands. It is unknown how many of these bands were juvenile.[2]

Although a new and increasingly vital interest in public school bands began to emerge in the 1920s, there were many isolated examples of school bands prior to that time which were not yet part of a national movement. From *Trumpet Notes* and *Musical Truth*, advertising magazines for Conn and Dupont (later, C. G. Conn Company), boys' bands were mentioned at least as early as 1877, girls' bands from 1900, and mixed juvenile groups known as "kid" bands from about 1894.

From about 1900 industrial bands were promoted as a means of maintaining industrial peace. The bands were established in factories and large department stores. A 1901 article in *Music* magazine "extolled the virtues of bands as a panacea for labor unrest." The enterprise would cost only about $200 for twenty instruments with a fee for an instructor at just three dollars an evening once per week. The members could learn to play quickly and be able to perform at picnics within a month. These industrial bands flourished until the Great Depression.

College bands began to appear during the last years of the nineteenth century. In 1896 Purdue University had a band of thirteen members. One year later, the University of Wisconsin offered credit for band participation. The St. Olaf college band in Northfield, Minnesota, had a forty-piece band in 1902, and Baylor established a permanent band in 1906.

Isolated examples of secondary school bands can be found during the latter part of the nineteenth century. In 1884 Brother Maurelian, president of the Christian Brothers High School in Memphis, Tennessee, wanted his school to be of service to his community. He hired Professor Paul Schneider to organize a school band. The school itself taught students from the elementary grades to the college level, and the school band had representatives from every level. The band was maintained until the First World War when the college-level students enlisted as a group and the band was dissolved. Following the war the band was reorganized, and it remains in existence to the present.

Junius K. Abráms, of Live Oak, Florida, reported that he was teaching three bands in 1896, two for young boys and one for young men under twenty years of age. He identified himself in *Musical Truth* as "a teacher of high school bands." The same publication mentions a Greenville, South Carolina, public school band in 1897. The band was organized in 1893–1894 by E. L. Hughes, the superintendent of schools.

In 1907 W. Otto Miessner organized a band in Connersville, Indiana, with the idea of keeping boys "with changing voices interested in music." The following year the band played at a meeting of the Indiana State Teachers Association. Miessner wrote of his 1907 band:

It is one thing to *assemble* a group of youngsters who can *play* instruments and *read* music and train them how to play together. It is quite another thing to start from scratch and arouse the interest and teach kids to play and read music, develop facility and acceptable ensemble performance. The Connersville pupils were taught in groups (classes) of instruments employing similar notation and playing techniques, *viz.*; trumpets and cornets, horns, trombones, basses, flutes (piccolos), clarinets. All this was done before, between and after regular school hours.[3]

The Connersville band comprised about twenty boys in the 1908–1909 school year, with another twenty on the waiting list.

In November 1913, John W. Wainwright was a student at the Oberlin Academy in Oberlin, Ohio, and a part-time printer. That year he organized a boys' band. They played a first performance the following May at a Decoration Day parade, doing two funeral marches Wainwright had written especially for the band. Their young director told his boys that if they would work hard and prepare a whole program, he would take them to Washington to play for the president. The group rehearsed through the summer, and that fall the band was selected to take part in the "1914 Buckeye Corn Special Tour" to Washington, Philadelphia, and New York, a tour promoted by the State of Ohio Agricultural Commission. The Oberlin band played that year on the White House lawn for Woodrow Wilson.

The repertoire of the band included overtures, marches, waltzes, and novelties published by the Fillmore Music House, in Cincinnati. Arthur L. Williams, the cornet soloist with the band, recollecting his early years, related that among the favorite numbers were selections from *Martha*. Williams soloed on "When You and I were Young, Maggie," and "Calm as the Night."

Wainwright and his band toured northern Ohio, and there can be no doubt that his work inspired other groups to organize school bands. Similar bands were established in Wellington, Lodi, and Elyria, Ohio, as well as in other towns. Back in Oberlin, Wainwright organized a Negro boys' band, became the director of the college band, and continued his work with an adult community band. These organizations were all concert bands and marched only in community parades. Wainwright was one of the first in the country to discover the possibility of teaching boys and girls to play as a band from the very first. This concept represented a new idea in instrumental music teaching. Earlier, the students had to study and practice individually tending (according to Arthur L. Williams) to take up melody instruments for the most part. When instruction was given as a complete unit, it became possible to enjoy a balanced instrumentation from the start. Wainwright later became band director at the Fostoria High School in Fostoria, Ohio. There he employed profitably the same teaching techniques that he had used so successfully at Oberlin.

While the early years of the century saw the gradual awakening of the instrumental music giant, the principal concerns of the music educators in the country were in the area of vocal music. Concerns were expressed in these early days of the Music Supervisors National Conference for the appreciation of music in the secondary schools, the music appreciation movement in general, and the proper qualifications of music supervisors. Additional attention was given to the emergence of the school orchestra as a growing phenomenon, but the band movement was as yet unnoticed. In a report of the High School Music Committee in 1912, with Will Earhart acting as committee chairman, it was recommended that "efforts be made to secure accreditation for the following activities listed in the order of rank: chorus, music appreciation, orchestra, girls chorus, band, boys chorus, and glee club."[4] The group later recommended that credit be given for applied music study taken

outside school. After 1912, music educators devoted more attention to instrumental music but their concerns were mostly for the
school orchestra.

As bands entered the school program, they were publicized and
discussed. In 1914 Glenn H. Woods reported that the Oakland,
California, schools supported three bands and three orchestras in
its high schools. The system boasted twenty-two bands and nine
orchestras in its grammar schools. The Oakland Board of Education had generously provided $5,000 for the purchase of instru-
ments and employed a teacher to give free ensemble instruction in
the high schools. Woods spoke of the Oakland Club Band which
was sponsored by the city of Oakland and by various businessmen
who donated money. On Saturday nights the band would march
the streets and stand by the stores of those who had donated
money. As the band played, a crowd of appreciative onlookers
would gather to enjoy the music. Soon the crowd would drift into
the store to buy, and the investment in the band would be returned
with a profit.

In 1916 the defense quickens for the inclusion of a popular art
form in the schools of America. The school orchestra always had
as its model the best professional symphonic organizations and required no artistic rationale for its introduction, even though the
full symphonic realization would be rare. The school chorus also
could look back upon a long tradition of choir singing dating from
the nation's earliest days, and the singing organizations of the
nineteenth century sought to perform the world's best literature.
But the band arrived in the schools with a far different background. Always closer to show business than to rarified artistic
pursuits, the band, which was quickly attracting a student following, had to prove itself intellectually to the teaching profession.
The answer for the band lay in democratic and egalitarian principles, and F. M. Hunter, superintendent of schools in Lincoln,
Nebraska, expressed these sentiments at the 1916 meeting of the
Music Supervisors National Conference. His speech focused on
the development of "community thinking," and a "community
consciousness, which [enabled] communities to get together and
put the welfare of the whole people first." Hunter pointed to a
twenty piece band made up of "German-Russians" whose leader
was a young boy who "never had a day's professional life. . . . But

they filled the school twice to overflowing; there were seven hundred people there at the last concert."[5] In general, however, the music educators of 1916 were not interested in bands.

Three years later W. Otto Miessner spoke for the growing interest in instrumental music. The 1919 meeting of the Music Supervisors Conference in Saint Louis evinced a stronger interest in instrumental music than could be noticed at previous meetings. Miessner was then director of the music department at the State Normal School in Milwaukee. He believed in "democratizing" music by teaching all its branches.[6] As a product of the child-study movement and progressive education, Miessner stated that the music educator overlooked the individual child. He expressed the sentiment that a child who could not sing might be able to play an instrument. Instrumental music was now entering the public schools of our land expeditiously, and all that remained was to defend philosophically that which was already taking place. Instrumental music was, as it still is, an extremely popular branch of public education. Such a branch is easiest to defend when democratic principles are invoked.

Many changes took place in education and social services during the first decade of the century. Child health centers mushroomed from 20 before 1900 to 193 in 1910. The first child guidance clinic opened in Chicago in 1909. Hot lunches were offered to school children for the first time during this period, and school nurses joined the school staff for the first time in 1903. School playgrounds staffed by school personnel and financed by boards of education began to appear in 1905, and the boy and girl scout movements reflected this sudden rise in concern for the children of our nation. The establishment of the National Recreation Association in 1906 demonstrated a new concern with the problems of a productive use of leisure time. The period of political and social reform that was ushered in during this decade permeated all facets of people's lives; the changes in curriculum in the schools represented only a branch of the social upheaval taking place in the country.

In 1917, as Europe was ravaged by a war that was to accelerate the rate of social change, the Grand Rapids meeting of the Music Supervisors National Conference felt the first tremors of the explosion of instrumental music programs that was to occur following the Great War. The event was merely a demonstration of Albert Mitchell's *Public School Class Method for Violin*. A cello class demonstration followed using traditional private study materials. This represented the first public display of the efficacy of class teaching techniques at the national conference. Its timing was excellent. Instrumental ensembles could function to some extent depending upon private instruction outside the school, but a careful concern for instrumentation and a continuation of a sizable body of young musicians compelled the teaching of instruments as a part of the school day. That this could be done efficiently in classes was the information needed by the music supervisor. Another hurdle was passed on the way toward effective and vigorous instrumental music programs.

Two years later Edward Bailey Birge prepared a questionnaire to determine the status of instrumental music in the schools. Three hundred and fifty-two replies were received. Out of that number 79 percent reported school orchestras but only 24 percent reported school bands. Before 1920 the instrumentation and repertoire of the school band was primitive. The typical literature of that period consisted of marches, waltzes, two-steps, "smears," and ragtime. But as the concept of instrumental music grew, the band movement began to flourish. The 1921 meeting of the Music Supervisors National Conference demonstrated for the first time that those procedures that were readily accepted for school orchestra were also applicable to school bands. The next year a Committee on Instrumental Affairs was established * and promptly set itself the tasks of drafting a statement demonstrating the values of instrumental music, conducting a census of instrumental teachers in the public schools, suggesting the minimum requirements for instrumental music supervisors, listing suitable materials, and investigating the possibility of creating a journal of instrumental music.[7]

---

* While this committee was to take a strong hand in the development of the contest movement and at the same time contribute to the growth of the school band, its membership was not taken from the ranks of band directors. Jay W. Fay, the chairman of the committee, had recently moved to Louisville, Kentucky (1923), after several years in Rochester, New York, where he worked with instrumental groups. Eugene M. Hahnel, of Saint Louis, Missouri, was primarily interested in grade school orchestras. B. F. Stuber, from Akron, Ohio, was an orchestra director and had been a violin teacher all his professional life. Victor L. F. Rebmann was supervisor of music at Yonkers, New York, and was an orchestra director, although in 1920 he encouraged the inclusion of the high school band in the program. Only Russel V. Morgan, of Cleveland, Ohio, was active in establishing and conducting high school bands.

By 1923 the band became an important force in school music. It was no longer "an incidental school enterprise," it no longer acquired the services of a volunteer high school teacher who had had some band experience. It had a definite place in the school schedule with regular rehearsals under a trained instructor.[8] Most directors of school bands came from the ranks of professional musicians who had lost jobs with circuses and carnivals, vaudeville houses, or moving picture theatres. Many supervisors gave up time with their orchestras and choirs to start bands. Initially only a small percentage had previous school experience. The bands were often taught by those lacking certification and working on a part-time or substitute basis. Thousands of instrumental directors were completely unprepared. Many enrolled in correspondence schools to upgrade their skills at the same time that colleges and universities began to establish courses for instrumental teachers as high school graduates sought to become band directors.

The First World War gave a strong impetus to the public school band movement. The patriotic feelings induced at times of war were stimulated by band music. Emotional farewells and tearful homecomings were accompanied by the martial strains of the omnipresent regimental bands. These military bands required directors, and the supply of well-trained band directors was considerably below the demand.

The problem became apparent to Walter Damrosch in 1918 when he was in France under the auspices of the YMCA to tour the army camps. While in France, General Charles Dawes of the American army called upon Damrosch at his hotel and asked whether he would come to the general headquarters of the American Expeditionary Force at Chaumont on July 17 to confer with General Pershing regarding possible improvement in army bands. Pershing told Damrosch he had heard the crack military bands of France and England and was conscious of the inferiority of the American counterparts. Pershing wondered whether it might be possible to take the best players from among the bands then in France and to form a headquarters band of excellence, led by the best bandmaster among them "and in this way form a model which the others could endeavor to copy."[9] Damrosch responded positively to these suggestions and asked the general how many American bandmasters there were in France. Pershing said that there were two hundred such bandmasters, and it was determined that they would all be sent to Paris in groups of fifty every week together with a military band. Damrosch would test their efficiency in conducting, harmony, and orchestration.

Damrosch carried out his testing scheme allowing each bandmaster to conduct either the *Oberon* Overture of Weber or a movement from a classical symphony followed by a composition of their choice. He found most to be musically talented and ambitious, but they had "little opportunity for acquiring what we may call the technique of the baton." Many did not know how to beat time accurately. Damrosch believed that some opportunity had to be given them to learn the rudiments. He believed that a quick formation of a bandmaster's school was the only solution to the problem. He would use French musicians who had graduated from the Paris Conservatory and had won first-place prizes. He noticed that important instruments, such as oboes, bassoons, French horns, and flugelhorns, were lacking in the American band. Damrosch knew that some of the best players of these instruments were in the French army and obtained their names and whereabouts from the Ministere des Beaux Arts. A proposal was made to General Pershing that a music school be formed so that fifty bandmasters could receive intensive musical training and discipline for eight weeks. This class would be followed by a new batch of fifty. At the same time forty pupils each on oboe, bassoon, French horn, and flugelhorn would get similar training for twelve weeks. Damrosch devoted five weeks of intensive work to this project. The bandmasters were carefully examined, and during the evenings he "[worked] out the entire tuition plan of the school, down to the minutest details." [10] Two professors each for oboe, bassoon, French horn, and flugelhorn were engaged, and classes in conducting, harmony, and orchestration were initiated for the bandmasters. Damrosch also recommended that a performance be given once a week by members of the faculty in order that the students have an opportunity to hear the finest in art music. Damrosch reported a positive acceptance of these concerts.

With the end of the war many of these bandmasters and bandsmen may have looked for a place where they could put their special music education to work. For some the public schools provided just such an outlet. It is doubtful that General Pershing understood the effect of his suggestion on music education in

America when his musical concern in those war-filled days was the presence of a second-rate American military band at his headquarters! Spurred by what was an obvious feeling of patriotism in the summer of 1918, Walter Damrosch recognized the value of the military band upon the morale of the soldiers and worked hard at the age of fifty making his contributions to the war effort. It is doubtful that he considered the effects of this band school at Chaumont on the instrumental music programs of American schools.

Before the First World War those schools that had high school orchestras employed them for various functions: graduations, school assemblies, professional education meetings, and performing concerts. Following the war these functions were gradually taken over by the bands. The American band easily reflected this affinity or identification that the orchestra could not duplicate. The band was a mobile unit that could perform either outdoors or indoors. Its volume and sonority have been traditionally linked with a patriotic and martial spirit. Uniformed bands provided visual reinforcement of this patriotic feeling; and repertoire, both loud and rhythmic, was and is more accessible to the average public more enchanted with the popular art forms than with the masterworks of geniuses.

CONTESTS AND FESTIVALS

An important factor leading to the promotion and expansion of instrumental music instruction in this country was the music contest. A spiritual descendant of the Welsh *eisteddfod* which was so popular with the immigrants from that nation who came to this country just prior to the American Civil War to work in the coal fields, the music contest had an immediate appeal to an energetic and competitive American population. The first *eisteddfod* was held in Carbondale, Pennsylvania, in 1850 by the Welsh miners of that area, and an international *eisteddfod* took place in Chicago in connection with the World's Columbian Exposition in 1893. There were evening concerts with four afternoons devoted to contests in poetry, solo and choral singing, and harp playing. Fifteen choral societies including four from Great Britain competed for $30,000 in prizes. At that time the Choral Union of Scranton,

Pennsylvania, defeated the Salt Lake City Tabernacle Choir in the event for choirs of over 250 voices.[11]

There are only scattered references to music contests in the nineteenth century, but we do know that they existed and stimulated interest in the various musical activities. An article in the May 15, 1877, issue of *Trumpet Notes* stated that a band may profit more from one "well-regulated band contest than [from] months [of] the ordinary routine of band practice." A convention of cornet bands took place in Portage, Wisconsin, on June 7 and 8, 1877. Fifteen bands took part parading and giving concerts.[12]

That same year a "Grand Tournament and Musical Jubilee" took place at Port Huron, Michigan. Eight brass bands which were classified as to size and instrumentation, took part. The divisions separated reed bands and brass bands; reed bands numbering eighteen and over and brass bands of sixteen and over.* A large audience gathered in the Port Huron armory to hear the bands perform. A parade through the business section of the town was followed by an opening chorus at the armory. After a welcoming address there was a concert by the massed bands. Each band was required to pass in review before judges who classified each organization and evaluated their marching. On the second day the bands were rated on their concert performances according to instrumentation, harmony, tempo, appearance, attack, solos, and selection of pieces. Eight bands attended though only five competed—all brass bands. The selections performed by these organizations included the *Poet and Peasant Overture* by von Suppe; "Fantasia" from *Rose d'Amour*, by Bleger; "Fantasia" from *Martha*, by Flotow; and Selection from *Bohemian Girl*, by Balfe.

In 1896 several bands competed in Arapahoe, Nebraska, for a "Wonder Solo Trumpet." At Ruggles Grove, Ohio, on Lake Erie, bands came from all over that area in 1899 to be judged and to receive criticism. In Ottawa, Kansas, in 1897, $400 was offered to the winner of a first prize in a choral competition held in connection with a Chautauqua in June of that year. The required number was appropriately "Be Not Afraid," from Mendelssohn's *Elijah*. The first school contest was held May 22, 1897, presumably in or near Boston on the occasion of the New England Conference of

---

* The first prize for the reed band consisted of "one epergne, 28 inches high, with cut glass vase, large benton and two side dishes, gold-lined valued at sixty dollars." The second prize was one fruit stand valued at thirty dollars.

Educational Workers. Students from the third, fifth, and seventh grades competed in matters of interpretation and ability to sight-read. Original music was prepared for the occasion. The program also included competitive singing by the high school choral groups.[13]

The music competitions in Kansas were a direct result of the Welsh influence and their *eisteddfods*. The Welsh brought with them their love of music and established *eisteddfods* in several areas of the state, one of which was Emporia. The national festivals ceased about 1890, but their influence persisted. Some of the sponsors of the Kansas *eisteddfods* became music supervisors in the public schools. As the Welsh children went into the schools, music became a part of the annual county contest which included athletics and declamation. The discontinuance of the *eisteddfod* in the state occasioned the organization in 1912 of the first contest devoted to music in the public schools and was designated as the All-Kansas Music Competition Festival.[14] By 1919 contests increased in popularity and were expanded to other communities in the state. At least five such contests for high school students were held in the following locations: Kansas State Normal School, at Emporia; the State Manual Training Normal, at Pittsburg; the Fort Hays Normal School, at Hays; Bethany College, at Lindsborg; and the State Agricultural College, at Manhattan. The music contest at Bethany College was initiated that year and included events for organ, piano, voice, violin, violoncello, brass and woodwind instruments. Group competition that year was limited to girls' glee clubs. Small cash prizes were awarded for first and second place in all the events. Entrants were welcome from any state, the contestants not being limited to young musicians from Kansas.[15] In Emporia, Kansas, bands may have been included in the contests as early as 1916.[16]

The contest idea seemed to catch on in many other states. In Missouri, C. P. Kinsey, of Southwestern Missouri State Normal College at Springfield, organized a contest for choral groups in 1917. The first North Dakota music contest was organized two years later in 1919 on the campus of the University of North Dakota. Band events were included in 1921, and the contest had grown so large that year that elimination contests in seven districts had become necessary. In 1922 over six hundred high school students from forty-four schools participated in the finals.

The Oklahoma music contests grew out of the annual track and field events that were held on the campus of the University of Oklahoma. School administrators could not understand why the university should have tried to interest only half the students. As a result, the music contests were more or less forced upon the music supervisors. Some county music contests had been held as early as 1919, but by 1922 the events became sufficiently popular that elimination contests were required on the district level. These regional contests were held on the campuses of the six normal schools of that state. A band event was added to the state contest in 1920.

Band contests were initiated in Michigan in 1920 by J. Harold Powers, head of the music department at Central Michigan College of Education at Mount Pleasant. Four years later in 1924 the number of contestants increased dramatically when three teachers' colleges were included from the lower peninsula. From 1922 or 1923 the contests were held on the campus of the Michigan State College of Agriculture, now Michigan State University.

In Connecticut a music contest was held in conjunction with the State Agricultural Fair. Both bands and orchestras competed for prizes of fifty dollars, thirty-five dollars, and fifteen dollars. The first prize in 1922 was won by the Hartford High School Orchestra, while the second prize was won by the Warren, Massachusetts, Boys' Band. The third prize was awarded to the Waterbury Junior High School Orchestra, and the fourth prize went to the New Haven High School Orchestra. Each organization provided music for one evening of the week with the awards announced at the conclusion of the fair. W. D. Monnier reported that the musical work of the children stimulated more attention than the professional orchestras in the previous years.[17]

The first national school band contest was held in Chicago, June 4, 5, and 6, 1923. The contest was to give a national forum to the school band and served as a powerful stimulus to the school contest and festival concept that dominated secondary school music until the outbreak of the Second World War. The contest was responsible, in part, for the position of prominence that the school band assumed during that period. The letterhead and official correspondence called the contest "The Schools Band Contest of America," but the newspaper accounts called it a tournament.

The contest was the brainchild of the Chicago Piano Club, a music dealers' association of that city. This group was responsible for providing entertainment for the annual convention of Music Industries Chamber of Commerce, which was scheduled for June 3 through 7, 1923. Victor J. Grabel, the band director at the Cicero plant of the Westinghouse Corporation, told the entertainment committee about the popularity of the band contests in Wisconsin several years earlier when he had taught in that state. The officers of the Piano Club were enthusiastic and suggested to Carl D. Greenleaf, the president of the C. D. Conn, Ltd., as well as of the Band Instrument Manufacturing Association, that this industry seemed the logical choice to organize and finance such a venture. A fund of $10,000 was raised for expenses. The planning committee consisted of Carl D. Greenleaf, Bohumir Kryl, E. H. Kleffman, and Frank L. Beals. Kryl was the director of a popular touring band and was associated with the Conn Company in a promotional capacity. Kleffman had assisted H. H. VanderCook in the teaching of music by correspondence and had written articles on violin technique, orchestral violin playing, and interpretation. He had directed a band at Harrison Technical High School in Chicago since 1919. Beals was a retired army officer who had reorganized the high school cadet corps in Chicago in 1917 and 1918 and had continued to supervise military training after the creation of a junior ROTC in 1919. As all public school bands in Chicago were connected to ROTC, Beals was, in effect, supervisor of bands. A part of his responsibilities lay in the supervision of contests for the ROTC units and their bands.

The group met early in April to plan the project. The Conn Company had a list of all bands in America as well as practically all bandmasters. Notices of the contest would go out with dispatch. "The main difficulty was that there was not much time in which to raise the money in each community for a new undertaking—sending a band to a national contest. This was never heard of before."[18]

The preliminary announcement was mailed not earlier than April 3, offering $6,000 in cash prizes plus instruments, medals, and ribbons, to the best high school, grammar school, and military school bands. A first prize of $1,000 was offered in each division. When the first applications were received, Patrick Henry, an advertising agent who had been hired to organize the tournament and promote the interests of the band instrument manufacturers, "opened a barrage of newspaper stories about the tournament, announcing that 6000 students would participate, 200 bands from all over the nation."[19] One week before the tournament, Henry announced that 200 bands had been eliminated, implying that preliminary contests were responsible for the selectivity, and that thirty-five "carefully selected bands would appear in Chicago for the final contest." But the only eliminations were the results of insufficient funds by the individual bands and the reluctance of school officials to encourage their bands to enter a commercial contest. Thirty bands did appear for the tournament though fifteen were from Chicago and its immediate area.

The size and instrumentation of the competing bands varied considerably. The smallest group was from Paw Paw, Michigan, and numbered twenty-five. Its woodwind section consisted of three clarinets and a saxophone. There were bands of seventy and eighty pieces from Gary, Indiana, and Fostoria, Ohio. But only a few bands had oboes, bassoons, or French horns.

The marching contest was cancelled, and half the prize money for this classification was set aside and distributed among the ten bands ranked immediately below fourth place in the high school division. The contest judge was Lt. William H. Santelmann, director of the United States Marine Band. He was expected to rate each band on tone quality, expression, intonation, and precision. An award of ten points represented perfection in each category. A rating was also given for deportment.

The competition itself was conducted in Grant Park near the Congress Hotel and Art Institute. A temporary wooden bandstand was erected between Michigan Avenue and the tracks of the Illinois Central Railroad. A short distance away was a smaller platform for the judge and his secretary. The bands were to march from the pier to the bandstand. There they competed with the city noises as well as with each other.

There were shortcomings, of course, to this initial effort of a national contest. The employment of a single judge was criticized, while others complained that the adjudication standards differed from those previously announced by Henry's letters to the participants. There were no required selections, and each band was free to prepare whatever it could in the six or seven weeks between the receipt of the first notice and the tournament date. Of course some bands played selections that they had prepared for other contests. And there was no requirement as to size or instrumentation for the competing groups.

At the massed band concert on Thursday, June 6, C. M. Tremaine presented awards to the winning bands. The contest was won by the Fostoria, Ohio, high school band directed by John W. Wainwright.

Wainwright had come to Fostoria from Oberlin, Ohio, in 1919. When Wainwright began teaching in Fostoria, all instruction was given in classes. As progress warranted, the boys were promoted to private study. The early class work consisted of scales and rhythmic patterns. Ten to twelve boys were assembled in heterogeneous groupings of instruments. Within a month the boys presented their first recital. By 1922 Wainwright had organized a "ladies band," a junior band, and an orchestra. The groups had at their disposal $30,000 worth of instruments including two concert grand pianos, though many of the students purchased their own instruments.

Motivation was supplied by a generous quantity of performances. During spring vacations the boys would be taken by bus or "interurban" to play concerts and to visit the local attractions. The high school band played regular Sunday afternoon concerts, often with only one or two rehearsals. Different programs were presented each week with the exception of 1923 when the special contest selection was repeated. The performance stimulated sufficient public enthusiasm in Fostoria that $200 was raised by the town to send the band to the national contest.

Wainwright's own description of the event captures the flavor of the moment.

We were one of the last bands to be called to the platform during the contest, and by this time the strain which we had been under during the last few weeks and especially since arriving at Chicago had begun to tell upon the boys, to say nothing of their director. We started to play our number and everything went smoothly until we were about two thirds of the way through. Just as we were about to begin the cornet solo "Then You'll Remember Me," through some conflict of arrangements another high school band came directly toward us playing a lively march. Of course I had been holding our band down as much as possible as we were almost drowned out. What should we do, go on or stop? If we stopped probably we would be counted out. If we went on we would not be heard to advantage and one of the most effective spots in the number would be lost. Just before the cornet picks up the solo there is a hold followed by a pause. During ths pause I turned questioningly to the judges, [sic] then turned quickly back and went on. It seemed but an instant until they sent word out for us to stop. I did so by calling out to the boys "OUT on the end of the next measure." And not one of them but heard and followed the instructions perfectly. As soon as the other band was notified of its error, we started in again just where we left off and finished.[20]

Wainwright's band had the following instrumentation: three flutes, one oboe, twelve clarinets, four saxophones, thirteen trumpets, seven horns, three baritones, seven trombones, five basses, six drums. The Fostoria band had won with thirty-four out of a possible forty points. When the band returned home it was greeted with the shouts and whistles of a victorious army. The ladies' band struck up a march and Wainwright was presented with a floral baton. A parade formed. The band passed under the balcony of the Hayes Hotel where a group of girls "in the costumes of vestals showered the boys with flowers."[21] The returning conquering heros were treated to banquets and parties. The band had returned with a check for $1,000, a blue ribbon, a new set of timpani, a flute, and some other instruments given by individual band manufacturers.

It is not surprising that John W. Wainwright was elected president of the Ohio High School Band Association at its first meeting in 1924. Wainwright's energies seemed limitless. In 1925 he established the Ohio State Fair Boys Band. Two years later he built a music camp for the Fostoria Band on the shores of Oliver Lake near La Grange, Indiana. Initially called the Wainwright Band Camp, its name was later changed to the Limberlost Camp. The camp was to attract young musicians from all over the country. Wainwright left Fostoria in 1930 to accept a position at Shortridge High School in Indianapolis, Indiana. From 1933 to 1944 he assumed the duties of the head of the music department of the South Side High School in Fort Wayne. Increasing deafness forced him to give up his teaching in 1944. Wainwright then entered politics and won three full terms in the state legislature. Not wishing to give up music completely, he organized bands at the Indiana State Prison and in juvenile reform schools. He died January 4, 1960.

During the 1923 contest the secretary of the National Bureau for the Advancement of Music, Tremaine, listened to Carl Greenleaf describe plans for the future of the tournament. But Tremaine was disturbed about a contest whose organization was left in the hands of commercial interests. Tremaine believed that the best chance of success for ventures involving school students lay in control by organizations of educators. Greenleaf suggested that the National Bureau undertake the management of the 1924 contest. Tremaine agreed providing that the industry would underwrite the project and not interfere with the regulations for entrance, the repertoire, or the adjudication and performance procedures that were to be set up by the educators. This Greenleaf readily agreed to. Tremaine also agreed to request assistance from the Music Supervisors National Conference.

Before the advent of the First World War, the manufacturers of band instruments in this country were indifferent to the school market. The band tournament of 1923 convinced the manufacturers otherwise. After the war a weak effort was made by the Frank Holton Company of Wisconsin, and the J. W. Pepper and Sons Company to import European instruments. John W. Wainwright attempted to persuade the manufacturers that the production of moderately priced instruments for school use would be mutually beneficial for the music teacher and manufacturers, but to no avail. Carl Greenleaf rejected any suggestion indicating in 1920 that school bands represented less than 5 percent of total sales of band instruments.[22] While working in the sales department of the Frank Holton Company, L. G. McQueston, the director of a band at Lake Geneva, reported that efforts to encourage school bands using company funds were conducted without the knowledge of Frank Holton "who considered the projects wasteful."[23] Joseph E. Maddy believed that the 1923 tournament represented the turning point demonstrating to the manufacturers the potential strength of the school market.

Once the economic values were recognized, the industries proceeded vigorously. Greenleaf, speaking at a meeting of the Music Teachers National Association in 1930, defended the activities of the manufacturers in promoting instrument sales. He observed that the market in professional and adult amateur bands diminished greatly at the end of the First World War. In the eyes of the manufacturers, the sales were "dangerously reduced." The success of the industry "depended on the creation and maintenance of a market large enough to justify mass production." Musical instruments were harder to sell than most products as the sale depended upon the willingness of the buyer to work hard enough to learn how to play.

[These factors] made it necessary for the manufacturers to stimulate interest in the organization of new bands, and in many cases . . . to furnish elementary instruction, either free or at low cost. This has usually been done by the employment of local teachers or professional musicians. In other words, it became necessary for the manufacturers and dealers to organize and teach bands.[24]

Tremaine approached the Committee on Instrumental Affairs of the conference and convinced them that the National Bureau would support such projects without undue commercialization. The committee reluctantly agreed to plan a contest for 1924. The committee felt, however, that a national contest must indeed have a national scope. Every section of the country should be represented. The committee suggested a series of elimination contests, first in several states, then in each of five regions. No regional contest was to be held until five state winners had been declared and no national contest was to occur until at least three of the five regions had held competitions. To help guarantee the educational sanctity of the contests, a repertoire list was developed from which a required number was selected and from which a second number was required. The list included symphonic movements, suites, overtures, and symphonic poems—a considerable improvement over the typical literature played by most school bands. The required number for the competing high school bands was Safranek's *Atlantis*, and the junior high schools' required selection was the *Larghetto* from Beethoven's Second Symphony. But the new regulations created problems. Contests were held in thirteen states in 1924, but only five were in accordance with the new rules. As a consequence, the 1924 national contest failed to materialize. The required lists brought many complaints from the band directors, school administrators, music publishers, and instrument manufacturers. The band directors were accustomed to marches and novelty numbers, and the intricate parts of the selections on the approved list made a full score imperative. Not only would the reading of such a score have been exceedingly difficult for most of the band directors of that time, but no full scores were published for band until 1927. Many of the authorized compositions required oboe, bassoon, and French horns, instruments in short supply in most high school bands of the period. Many of the young high school bandsmen had learned their instrument by rote and required fingerings beneath certain of the notes. They were no match for much of the difficult music arranged by professionals.

The next year ten states adopted the new rules allowing for regional contests in Gary, Indiana, and Boston, Massachusetts. In 1926 five more states joined the activity making three regional contests possible and leading to the first national contest under the new rules at Fostoria, Ohio. Thirteen bands participated representing ten states. The Joliet Township High School Band, directed by A. R. McAllister, placed first; Fostoria placed second; Ogden, Utah, was third; and the Male High School of Louisville, placed fourth.

Perhaps as a result of the contest the National School Band Association was founded which later was to replace the National Bureau and the Committee on Instrumental Affairs of the Music Supervisors National Conference as the regulatory agency for band contests. Membership in the association was open to band directors as well as students. Reminiscent of the older nineteenth-century choral festivals, railroad fares were reduced for those participating, a practice which continued for a number of years.

Interest in the contests mushroomed during the next several years. As the state and national associations became stronger and accepted more responsibility for the contests, the National Bureau and the Music Supervisors National Conference could reduce their involvement. The Great Depression forced the cancellation of only one national contest, that of 1931. The rapid expansion in the number of contestants made it necessary to hold band and orchestra national contests in alternate years. It was soon necessary to equate each regional competition with a national contest.

The contest movement played a large role in the stimulation of instrumental music in the public schools. It seemed a logical extension of the music memory contest and a natural outgrowth of the American competitive nature. It was an easy and natural vehicle for a public relations tour de force. The contests spurred the formation of state and national associations for instrumental teachers which enabled discussion of problems and acted to raise performance standards.

In an effort to improve band instrumentation the Committee on Instrumental Music of the Conference suggested that one-half of the instruments in a band of sixty-eight members be woodwind. The existing school bands were rapidly in the process of becoming almost entirely brass. The saxophone and the trumpet were enjoying a great popularity. It was the wish of the committee that the clarinet choir be accepted as a substitute for the string section of an orchestra as was the case in the great bands of Gilmore and Sousa. The committee believed that no more than five saxophones should be used. Brass instruments should be used in pairs with the exception of four horns and three trombones. A storm of controversy arose. School administrators charged that such a scheme would only benefit the manufacturers of instruments. The manufacturers complained that their most profitable products had been discriminated against and that their European competition would benefit from a project that was financed by American businessmen. Music publishers lamented that their entire catalog would be immediately obsolete. The Committee on Instrumental Music rose to the challenge. A blue-ribbon commission consisting of John Philip Sousa, Frederick A. Stock, Edward Franko Goldman, Taylor Branson, and Herbert L. Clark was asked to develop a standard band instrumentation for a symphonic organization of seventy-two pieces. The special commission did not always agree, but the instrumentation they suggested became the standard for American bands to this day.[25]

The work of the Committee on Instrumental Affairs and its advisory committee resulted in radical changes in the manufacture of musical instruments, in completely new band publications by all publishers, and in improved performance standards—all of which might have taken a hundred years or more to accomplish had it not been for the high school band contest movement and the strength of the sponsoring organizations."[26]

The contest movement expanded to such Olympian proportions that by 1940 the district and state competitions which served as preliminaries for the national finals serviced a total of 10,000 bands, orchestras, and choruses; 7,500 instrumental and vocal ensembles; and 15,000 instrumental solos. Over half a million school students participated.

CHAPTER XVII

The Renaissance of the Choir

T HE METEORIC rise of instrumental music in the public
schools of the United States temporarily eclipsed high school
choral singing. The better choirs still attempted the major oratorios as had those of their fathers and grandfathers, and others
sang part-songs of a more trivial nature. High school singing did
not disappear, of course, but was merely taken for granted in the
flurry of curricular activity during the first two decades of the century. But gradually a new influence began to develop. It started
with the Musical Art Society of New York.

Frank Damrosch was the first supervisor of music in Denver between the years 1881 and 1885. He left this position to become
chorus-master at the Metropolitan Opera and assistant to his
brother Walter Damrosch. He was drawn again into music education when in 1892 he formed the Peoples' Singing Classes at
Cooper Union. The classes later developed into the Choral Union,
a performing organization of over twelve hundred members.

In the summer of 1893 Damrosch felt the need for a more satis-
fying musical experience and organized the Musical Art Society of
New York. The society was the first American professional chorus
to specialize in unaccompanied singing. Believing that there was
more to choral singing than oratorio and light part-songs, Damrosch sought to educate New York audiences to the beauties of unaccompanied choral singing.

A *cappella* singing was sufficiently rare that Damrosch was obli-
gated to use professional singers for his group. It became necessary

to raise at least $4,000 for this undertaking. With the help of Laura Post, Damrosch presented his plan for the Musical Art Society to a group of wealthy Newport women, who worked enthusiastically, and the society was oversubscribed by $500.[1]

The first concert of the society took place March 3, 1894, and the following program was presented:

"Sing Ye to the Lord"	J. S. Bach
"Stabat Mater"	Palestrina
	(Arr. Richard Wagner)
"Up, Up Ye Dames"	Henry Leslie
"Flora Now Calleth Forth Each Flower"	J. Stafford Smith
"Nachtwache" op. 104, no. 1	Johannes Brahms
"Thine Eyes So Bright"	Henry Leslie[2]

The event was of sufficient importance that the New York *Daily Tribune* gave two reviews of the society's efforts. "The society was ushered in with becoming modesty and many signs of honest devotion to art." The reviewer did not like some of the vocal solos and the English part-songs. He mentioned "some lack of blend, a smallness of tone, and intemperate tempos in the Bach motet." But the review was quite laudatory in describing the performances of the Brahms and the Palestrina selections.

The second concert was more of a critical success, and the reviews tended to reflect more accurately some of the problems inherent in the initial performance. In April the *Tribune* commented on the gains in "technical finish and spirit."

The singing of the choir was of a beauty and homogeneity of tone, a precision of attack and an elasticity that are seldom heard hereabouts; while it was plain that Mr. Damrosch's intentions were in large manner realized. The improvements made in these things since the Musical Art Society's debut showed that much may be expected of the organization if its plans are permitted to be carried out in future seasons of work.[3]

The aims of the society were carried out, indeed, as the organization lasted twenty-five seasons. It presented sixty-one concerts, and the number of singers increased from fifty-five to seventy. Solo selections became a subordinate part of the program. It set an example in style and in literature for college and professional musical societies that were founded at a later time. Damrosch's selection of literature included many works by Palestrina; numerous compositions by sixteenth-century Italian, English, and German compos-

ers; Bach motets, cantatas, and chorales; almost the complete catalog of German part-songs; Brahms's works in large choral forms;
selections from the Russian liturgy; modern English and American
compositions; and folk song arrangements. Many of these came
from Charles Bordes's *Anthologie des maitres religieux primitifs*.
Damrosch edited much music for the society, music which filtered
out to similar performing groups. The high schools were not far
behind and copied the musical work of the colleges. The unaccompanied singing that the society introduced had become accepted as
the ultimate manifestation of choral art. Damrosch wanted students and teachers to hear this polyphonic art at a nominal price.
Dress circle tickets were made available to them at half price, or
fifty cents. The one dollar balcony seats were given free to members of the Peoples' Singing Classes. The members could purchase
the remaining balcony tickets at twenty-five cents each. In time the
regular ticket prices doubled, but the cost to members of the Peoples' Singing Classes remained the same.

The society discontinued its activities while Damrosch was in
service in 1918 and 1919. One year later in 1920 financial difficulties forced the disbandment of the society. The $60,000 endow-
ment fund was $40,000 short of the amount necessary for con-
tinued operation. The existing endowment was turned over to the
Institute of Musical Art, a professional music school that Damrosch founded in 1905 and which later joined with the Juilliard
School of Music in 1928.[4]

Contributing to the public acceptance of the *a cappella* ideal
were various Russian singing groups that toured during the second
decade of the century. Among these were the Russian Orthodox
Cathedral Choir of New York City, The Ukrainian Choir, The
Russian Symphonic Choir, and the most popular group, the Don
Cossack Choir, directed by Serge Jaroff.

The Russian Orthodox Cathedral Choir was supported by
Charles R. Crane, who had lived for a time in Russia and had become impressed by Russian church music. He invited Ivan Gorokoff to New York City in order to build Russian choirs. Gorokoff
brought with him three tenors, two basses, and one "deep Russian
octave bass." Crane organized tours throughout the United States
around 1913. Their influence was such that choir directors made
special visits to the cathedral in order to hear this ensemble.

The most famous and successful of the Russian *a cappella* groups was the Don Cossack Choir which made its American debut November 4, 1930. Highly dramatic devices such as the use of the falsetto voice, sforzando openings, and vanishing pianissimo endings enhanced the showmanship of the group and made their concert appearances enormously popular. On the evening of their third concert in 1930 the police were obliged to clear the lobby after Carnegie Hall was filled.[5] The group was formed by officers in the Russian Imperial Army in a prison camp near Constantinople. For a time it functioned as a church choir for exiled Russians in Sofia, Bulgaria. Its thirty-six members wore the uniform of the Imperial Army and preserved the military bearing on stage. After each number its conductor, Serge Jaroff, would bow quickly and step immediately behind the chorus, thereby eliminating himself from the applause and simultaneously giving the pitch for the next number.

Other *a cappella* choirs toured the United States during the 1920s, groups which reinforced the solemnity of the *a cappella* ideal. The Sistine Chapel Choir made a ten-week tour of the United States in 1923. Perhaps a more important influence was the English Singers, a vocal sextet that toured this country between 1925 and 1928. Its programs consisted entirely of English madrigals, motets, ballads, and folk songs. The American public was initiated to the beauties of the English madrigal school through the skillful artistic performance of these works. The authentic practice of one voice to a part was generally unknown to America. The singers sat informally around a table giving an improvisatory quality to their performance without detracting from their musicianship.[6] Their tour in 1928 covered almost the length and breadth of the United States, and their tours continued over the next ten years.

THE ST. OLAF CHOIR

The most influential college choir of the period was from a small Lutheran school in Minnesota. Its choir set an artistic example for hundreds of high school and college choir directors, which has persisted to the present day.

The college was founded in 1874 in Northfield, Minnesota, by the Reverend Bernt J. Muus. In 1886 the school was renamed St.

Olaf College. Instruction in piano and voice was offered from the inception of the college while other music courses periodically found their way in and out of the curriculum. There were sporadic attempts to form student choruses.

The man destined to change the casual musical offerings of the school and to make the name "St. Olaf as famous in choir circles as Mount Rushmore and Yosemite" was F. Melius Christiansen, a Norwegian immigrant, who came to America in 1888. He had hoped to make his fortune as a violinist, but after two unsuccessful years he assumed the position of director of the Scandinavian Band in Marinette, Wisconsin, as well as that of choir director and organist at Our Savior Lutheran Church. Two years later he became a student at the Augsburg Seminary in Minneapolis, later transferring to the Northwestern Conservatory of Music in that city, from where he graduated in 1894. He returned to Europe in 1897 to attend the Royal Conservatory in Leipzig where he studied the violin with Hans Sitt and composition with Gustav Schrek. While he did not study choral music at this time, he listened to the *Thomanerchor* at the conservatory, a choir under the direction of his composition teacher, Gustav Schrek. The experience was to influence directly many of the vocal concepts he would later put into practice. He returned to Minneapolis in 1899 where he taught violin at the Northwestern Conservatory and played violin in the orchestra that was later to become the Minneapolis Symphony. Meanwhile at St. Olaf College, two of Christiansen's friends convinced President Kildahl that the Minneapolis violinist would be the ideal person to direct the college band, the Choral Union, and the St. John's Church Choir and to build a department of music at St. Olaf.[7]

Christiansen's first success was with the band. In 1904 he gave concerts in nine nearby cities. He arranged an exchange concert with the Norwegian Students' Chorus from Christiana (Oslo) University when the chorus was singing at St. Olaf in 1905. The band then toured Norway the next year in 1906.

Christiansen again spent a year of concentrated study of composition and orchestration at Leipzig. There he made arrangements of Norwegian Lutheran Chorales, which would later appear on his programs but with no credit given to himself as arranger. In 1907 he formed a choir for the specific purpose of a performance for a Conference of the United Norwegian Lutheran Church. The choir of forty voices comprising students and faculty from St. Olaf presented a service of hymns that was particularly well received. Almost in an exploratory effort to find the most suitable means of musical expression to fit his temperament, Christiansen organized a Male Octet the following year. As good public relations and touring were equated in the mind of its director, the ensemble toured Minnesota, South Dakota, and Iowa in 1908. Sixty-two concerts in forty-nine cities were presented. For these efforts a sum of $400 was earned for the school organ fund, and their audiences were treated to a goodly number of Lutheran Chorales.

The Choral Union under Christiansen's direction gave oratorio performances at the May Festivals. In 1909 the organization was divided into a male and female chorus and presented separate concerts. The groups were combined only for the commencement program.* In the spring of 1912 the choir adapted the name of the St. Olaf Lutheran Choir and began short tours.

The school officials never lost an opportunity to advertise. On their second tour in 1912, the choir sang at the annual meeting of the United Lutheran Church in Fargo, North Dakota. The choir manager approached two visiting delegates from Norway and discussed the possibility of a tour. With the approval of the delegates and the necessary preparations undertaken, the St. Olaf Choir toured the principal cities and villages of Norway, two cities in Sweden, and Copenhagen, Denmark. While some critics complained that the programs were of an overly religious nature and that the singing was cold, the Norwegian press was unanimous in its praise. They believed that there were no student groups in Norway to compare with the carefully trained St. Olaf students.

An important factor in the success and dedication of the choir was its sense of religious mission. Christiansen believed that his students would sing well only if they lived a noble Christian life. The constitution of the choir stated that the purpose of the choir was to serve God and the church. They believed their work to be a religious duty, their concerts religious ceremonies, and their tours religious campaigns.[8]

The most important tour was in 1920 when, under the manage-

---

* The two choruses remained essentially separate but combined in 1910 for a concert under the name of the St. John's Church Choir.

ment of the *Musical Courier* and impresario Martin Hanson, the choir toured the East and New York City. The tour was a financial success, and with the exception of some interesting criticisms in New York City, the tour was a critical success as well. From that year it became apparent that the St. Olaf Choir would enjoy a national reputation.

Richard Aldrich complained in the *New York Times* (April 28, 1920) about the rapid tempos "in the wrong places." He criticized the "trivial arrangement" of Luther's "A Mighty Fortress is Our God," with "meaningless scale passages in the inner voices." The critic of the *Musical America* had this to say: "There were moments, indeed, when it equalled in point of sheer virtuosity the best that either of the older organizations have ever done here and seemed virtually to establish a new local record for flawless finish and beauty of unaccompanied songs." But he criticized Christiansen's choice of music. He also noted the conductor's "mania for speed."[9] But at the same time the reviewer described the singing as "perfect beyond cavil in balance," [and] . . . trained to a precision of attack and release of almost uncanny perfection." He noted the choir's "practically flawless intonation. It yields instantly whatever nuance, whatever subtlety or vivid perfection of rhythm, whatever plasticity of phrasing its conductor may summon." The "freshness of voices" was commented on as well as "the complete technical ease with which they manage even the most complicated arrangements of voice parts, rhythmic accents, and dynamic graduations." Such acclaim was typical of the various reviews that crowned the choir's efforts.

The college made money as a result of the tour and attracted students with the growing reputation of the choir. In 1927 a new music building, known as the building "built by a song," was erected at the college. It was financed by funds earned by the choir. The students received no money but the tours produced an income of between $12,000 to $30,000 each year.[10] By 1963 St. Olaf had become the largest of all Lutheran colleges with a full-time enrollment of 1,993 students.

More and more of Christiansen's compositions appeared on his programs, and those directors attracted to Christiansen's careful *a cappella* style naturally tended to adopt his published works as well. In 1938 in a survey of seventy-five high school choral directors, preferences for *a cappella* compositions were given in the following order: compositions by Christiansen; Noble Cain; arrangements of spirituals; modern Russian compositions; early German (Bach); early Italian (Palestrina); modern English; early English; early Spanish; early Netherlandish.[11] Though Christiansen's compositions were criticized because of their "excessive elaboration," a lack of inspiration, and "overblown Romanticism," his works sold. His arrangement of "Beautiful Savior," sold 117,900 copies during a twenty-nine year period.

He enjoyed at least ten hours of rehearsal per week but worked most carefully on a relatively few compositions, a maximum of twenty-five compositions per year. Other *a cappella* directors followed suit. According to a 1938 survey of seventy-five directors, 72 percent believed in limiting the repertoire of their choirs to from twelve to eighteen compositions yearly. Quite remarkably, few of Christiansen's selections came from what we commonly term the *a cappella* period. Works by Palestrina appeared only seven times in the programs of the St. Olaf Choir between the years 1912 and 1942. In 1926 Christiansen went to England where he became acquainted with the English madrigalists. But he used only one such piece in his programs over the same thirty-year period.[12] His programs were taken from the nineteenth-century Germans, the Russian liturgy, the seventeenth- and eighteenth-century Germans, and Christiansen's own arrangements.

The St. Olaf singers memorized their music in sectional rehearsals. No copies were permitted in full rehearsals or performances. The importance of memorization tended, itself, to discourage a large repertoire. A few members of the choir had pitch pipes, and at their performances, between pieces and during applause, the pitch of the next number was quietly passed around the choir. This stage trick was picked up by other *a cappella* choirs. The use of the baton was more widespread than among choral conductors today. Christiansen would have felt uncomfortable without such an implement, and this predilection was adopted by most of his followers. Many rehearsals were spent striving for intonation and balance. A former member reported a complete rehearsal spent in balancing just one chord![13] At the end of each year all singers in the choir resigned to be reauditioned at the beginning of the following year. Every factor was considered in the audition

from "breath control to personality." A so-designated straight-
ness of tone without vibrato in all vocal registers was considered
important.

Christiansen's ideal of a straight tone excited a controversy that
claimed the attention of all choir directors and to which no director could remain neutral. Opponents of the so-called straight tone
called Christiansen's ideal "flat and colorless." At the 1932 meeting of the Music Supervisors National Conference (MSNC), Christiansen suggested that "vibrato voices are the greatest menace we
have to contend with in our choral work," and later, "I have
nothing against

a vibrant, oscillating tone which may be very expressive of beauty, but
singers overdo it. They have a much larger tone than the violin and when
their voices wobble, flutter, and hover around the note, it is sometimes
impossible to even distinguish the intended pitch. . . . We must have
straight voices, not the dull untrained kind—although that is far more
preferable than the trained wobble —but the straight voice with developed color.[14]

The Chicago Singing Teachers Guild went on record as opposing
the straight tone. They believed its execution to cause permanent
harm to the voices "by establishing constricting tension in muscles
of the vocal organism and inhibiting spontaneous, natural im-
pulses."[15] But Jacob A. Evanson, the exceptionally successful director of the Flint, Michigan, A Cappella Choir and who credited
Christiansen as a profound influence, suggested that those who
criticized the straight tone did not understand it. Neil A. Kjos said
that "Christiansen was a violinist and naturally accepted an ordinary tremolo. He had a very good ear, almost absolute pitch. His
idea had been misinterpreted—every tone has a vibrato and Christiansen knew that. The straight tone was not void of vibrato."[16]

Richard Kegerreis believes that Christiansen's tonal concept was
influenced by the latter's association with the Thomanerchor of
Leipzig where it was the practice to use boy sopranos. In a review
of a New York performance of the St. Olaf Choir by Olin Downs,
the critic wrote that the women's voices had a "tone . . . so clear
and so impersonal in character that it suggested the voices of
boys."[17]

Whether the directors agreed concerning Christiansen's ideas
cannot detract from the considerable influence of the choir on

singing practices in the nation's schools and colleges. In 1925 Thaddeus P. Giddings talked about choral contests and observed that "voices with a tremolo should not sing in ensemble. These are never in tune. The St. Olaf Choir should be the ideal toward which vocal ensembles strive. The wonderful success of this organization is largely due to its perfect intonation."[18] In a survey of 135 college *a cappella* directors in the 1930s, a total of 55 listed Christiansen or the St. Olaf Choir as the greatest single influence in their work.[19] Christiansen extended his influence through the organization of two-week choir schools beginning in 1935 at Winona Lake, Indiana. Later there were two such sessions; one at Lake Forest, Illinois, and the other at Chambersburg, Pennsylvania. During the first four years of operation 851 students were taught the famous St. Olaf techniques. Of this number 506 were high school choral directors. One year twenty directors enrolled from Iowa alone. It had become known in that state that all choral directors from Iowa who had attended the school the previous year had won first divisions in contests the following year! In the over twenty-five years of its existence, more than nine thousand directors attended Christiansen's school including Richard P. Condie, director of the Mormon Tabernacle Choir who received his first conducting lesson at this school.[20]

In 1942 Christiansen retired and was succeeded by his son, Olaf, who maintained the quality of the choir that inspired and influenced so many.

WESTMINSTER CHOIR

A touring choir that became influential but that represented a different concept of singing tone was the Westminster Choir under the direction of John Finley Williamson. As a graduate of Otterbein College in 1912 and as a young choir director very much influenced by Christiansen and the St. Olaf Choir, Williamson at first instructed his singers in a tone quality modeled after that espoused by Christiansen. Later in the 1930s Mrs. J. Livingstone Taylor heard the choir and was sufficiently impressed that she contributed land and funds required to build a campus near Princeton, New Jersey.

There Williamson's ideas regarding choir tone gradually changed. He organized four choirs at the college: a chapel choir, an oratorio choir, a symphonic choir, and the Westminster Choir. The latter group maintained the *a cappella* ideal for many years. Williamson developed a "deep-throated" choral tone, giving a baritone quality to the tenor voices and an alto quality to the sopranos. This caused almost as much controversy in choral circles as Christiansen's straight tone. Many choral directors complained that the Westminster Choir used an excess of tremolo, making some pitches indistinguishable.

Williamson had unique ideas in relation to voice training. He refused to mention voice placement. He believed that "tight jaws" in singing were caused only by poor pronunciation or fear of the conductor. "Correct pronunciation was his solution to all rhythmic, phrasing, pitch, and tonal problems, but the final solution to pronunciation was an emotional relationship to the words." The setting of the correct mood was all-important.[21]

The only possible thing an individual can do is exactly the same thing he did as a child. If he is angry, the size of the cavity within the chest wall automatically changes; if he is joyous there is another change in the cavity. The thought, however, is not of changing the cavity but creating a mood. Creating a mood automatically makes the individual adjust the cavity to express that mood.[22]

But Kegerreis observes that it was Williamson's magnetic personality that made his rather strange sounding theories a success. Those who knew him and sang in his choirs were mesmerized by Williamson into doing what he wanted. He told stories, gesticulated, and postured until his choir caught the mood of the piece. His theoretical formulations were a product of the idiosyncratic methods he was able to use. He believed in bodily vitality from both singers and conductors and insisted that his students do push-ups and other daily exercises. A test in physical fitness remained an important element in the tryout system.

Though the Westminster Choir was not as influential as the St. Olaf group, a weekly radio broadcast in 1932–1933 presented thirty programs each Wednesday afternoon at 2:15. They acted as a complement to Walter Damrosch's radio concerts of the New York Philharmonic Orchestra. The broadcasts were important in stimulating interest in school choral activities as well as those in churches and colleges. The Westminster Choir continued a second season of broadcasts the following year, but then the weekly concerts were suspended. Other than the influence of the radio broadcasts, the principal focus of this choir was in the direction of church music. Most of the Westminster College graduates went into church work. The college did not add a music education program until 1961.

Another college choir to exert a strong influence on the high school *a cappella* movement was the Northwestern University Choir, directed by Peter C. Lutkin. Probably the first college *a cappella* choir in this country and certainly the first to persevere after its founding in 1906 and win a national reputation, the Northwestern University *A Cappella* Choir supplied well-trained *a cappella* choir directors to high schools and colleges. Lutkin came to Evanston to head the Northwestern Conservatory of Music in 1891. He immediately initiated efforts to encourage Northwestern University to incorporate the conservatory into the university as a music department. This was accomplished with some dispatch, and Lutkin became head of the music department and held a full professorship. In 1895 he developed a complete course of study, and the department became a school of music with Lutkin as dean. In 1928, he brought his well-trained choir to the MSNC convention and, along with the Flint, Michigan, *a cappella* high school choir, caused a sensation.

EARLY HIGH SCHOOL CHORAL PRACTICES

Vocal music and choral practice have been a part of high school activities since the beginnings of that institution. Not well organized, and often with uncertain purposes, the vocal activities could consist of casual auditorium singing, extracurricular glee clubs, or large groups for the purpose of singing oratorios. Casual singing classes could be found almost everywhere. The high school at Northampton, Massachusetts, offered a class in vocal music as early as 1837, and nearly all the girls in the school were reported to have taken the class.[23] There have been several reports of the inclusion of vocal music into various high schools in the country and several dating from the 1830s. But suffice it to say that no lists compiled today can be complete, and even if we had such an all-inclusive encyclopedia of "introductions," our purposes in this work would be no better served. It is reasonable to suppose that many high schools began to include vocal music quietly and without fanfare at what the school and community considered to be an advantageous moment. We have already seen the enthusiasm for music in the various private academies and select schools of the country. As these schools became public high schools, the various communities welcomed some form of music instruction. As the nation's schools moved through the nineteenth century and as more school systems reacted favorably to the request to include vocal music in the curriculum as a regularly established branch of instruction, the high schools moved in their own way to develop musical activities. They varied considerably between schools, and it would take the organizational efforts of the various national music teachers groups from the music division of the National Education Association to the Music Supervisors National Conference to develop a more common point of view.

In the hands of competent music teachers all evidence points to good instructional techniques and successful public performances. When such quality instruction was not in evidence, problems of interest, particularly among the boys, were noticed.

Edward Bailey Birge describes a required chorus sing in his own high school in Providence, Rhode Island, about 1887.

I well remember that when I was a pupil at Providence High School—there was but one then—we boys and girls of the Classical and English Departments, so-called, gathered once a week in the auditorium for music. There were no recitations in music, just singing, and the whole hour was very enjoyable, and I think profitable. But this was the entire musical opportunity in that large high school, and of all similar schools, generally speaking, everywhere.[24]

Such practices continued through the early years of this century. It was experiences like this that set such pedagogues as Will Earhart, Osbourne McConathy, and Frances Elliott Clark, among many others, to search for different avenues of music instruction among which was the music appreciation concept. The chorus was never abolished; it had been a part of school activities for too many years. But when the idea of appreciation became important, the chorus was merely used as a vehicle for the implementation of that concept.

By 1920 a survey of 359 schools in thirty-six states showed that required chorus was now favored by a minority of respondents.[25] But the evidence was not overwhelming as an elective chorus was offered by 180 schools and the required offering was found in 154 schools. A large majority of all the schools offered assembly singing. In most instances when chorus was required, it became little more than assembly singing with administrators interested in loyalty and school spirit rather than the aesthetics of music.[26]

As late as 1928 the Pennsylvania Secondary Schools Classification Directory required for "classification" one weekly period of general chorus throughout the year. The work was to include unison, two-part, three-part, and four-part songs under the supervision of a competent teacher."[27]

Perhaps it is even more remarkable that a few highly proficient teachers accomplished such unusual results with choruses of students who were obliged to participate. Alice Inskeep, of Cedar Rapids, Iowa, seated her mixed glee club in front of the auditorium and presented a program of unaccompanied singing as a part of the regular assembly singing in 1919. In 1890 Samuel W. Cole gave a performance of *The Creation* with the Dedham, Massachusetts, High School Chorus. They were assisted by a small orchestra, piano, and professional soloists. The following year this same group performed the *Messiah*. In 1893 Giddings directed a performance of *The Creation* with the entire student body of the Moline, Illinois, High School. Giddings was young and tackled such a difficult piece only through ignorance and lack of experience. His own tale has such charm that it bears repeating here in its entirety.

When I want to shock some of my musical friends I tell them that the first oratorio I ever heard I conducted and sang the tenor part. It was the "Creation" and it happened in the third year I was in Moline.

Now I had heard of the "Creation" but had the vaguest ideas as to *what* it was. To be sure I grew up twenty miles from Minneapolis, but it never occurred to me to go there and hear any music. I did not have the price.

When I asked for 200 copies of the "Creation" for the high school the only men of the Board of Education who knew anything about music laughed at the idea. The rest said let him try it. We did. We gave it entire. A piano and pipe organ furnished the accompaniment. Every pupil in the High School was in the chorus with the exception of two who had measles. One of the High School girls sang the soprano solos. One of the boys the bass. As mine was the only available tenor voice, I sang the tenor part. We very likely shattered some traditions, but we sang it two nights to crowded houses. As far as I have been able to learn this was the first oratorio performed by a High School in this country.

I went to the High School every morning for half an hour. Everyone sang as a matter of course. They all read music or tried to, and they got so they could sing difficult things at sight.[28]

Again in 1898 in Galion, Ohio, a performance of *The Creation* was given with the high school chorus which rehearsed one thirty-minute period per week. William H. Critzer was the director. Twenty-minute daily rehearsals were presided over by a member of the high school faculty. Two or three evening rehearsals were scheduled immediately preceding the performance. An orchestra of between eighteen to thirty-five was drawn from the student body, the grade school, "loyal alumni, and a few professionals." Professional soloists were hired. Critzer claimed that the entire student body was used. He tried out the singers by quartets before the performance. In succeeding years he presented performances of *Elijah, Messiah,* and *Judas Maccabaeus.*[29]

In 1911 the results of a survey of 659 high schools with 299 respondents revealed that 47 schools presented oratorios and that 151 schools had required chorus practice. What is perhaps even more interesting is that these feats were accomplished on an average weekly rehearsal time of forty-five minutes.[30] Oratorio performances increased in the 1910s and then decreased in the 1920s with the rise of glee clubs and a new interest in operetta performances. But with the rise of interest in *a cappella* singing toward the end of the 1920s and accompanied by the progressive educator's concern for individual differences, the concept of required choral practice was doomed.

Prior to 1930 there was every evidence of confusion in high school choral music. Some schools had glee clubs of various kinds, some given for credit, some not. The contest movement helped to stimulate interest in glee clubs, the first such event taking place on a statewide basis in Kansas in 1914. North Carolina followed suit in 1920, Michigan and Iowa in 1921, Montana in 1922, and Nebraska and Colorado in 1924.[31] Midwest contests that included five states were started in Kansas City in 1925. The contests encouraged the organization of glee clubs in the schools and gave them a new respectability. But the problem of literature based on philosophy of music education remained. Some glee clubs were used merely for purposes of entertainment, and light music with no serious purpose was performed. Other directors sought a better quality of music. But in a confused state, the high school choral supervisor watched the growing tide of instrumental music expand in a wave of popularity. A new standard was needed, and the impetus toward the realization of this standard was the development of the high school *a cappella* choir.

The 1928 meeting of the Music Supervisors National Conference was "one of the most significant events in the history of American high school choral music." Kegerreis expands upon this view.

Old high school choral traditions would slowly crumble. Assembly sings, extra-curricular glee clubs, hackneyed operetta productions, even major oratorio performances would no longer be accepted as proof of a superior high school choral program. Instead, high school choral directors would zealously dedicate themselves to the propagation of pure unaccompanied song.[32]

The president of the MSNC that year was George Oscar Bowen, a successful high school choir director. He was deeply concerned over the chaotic state of high school choral music. He set about to make the 1928 meeting a "singing conference." Arrangements were made for performances by thirteen choral groups. The only soloists who were to appear were vocal. Nine of the thirteen choral groups were high school. Vocal quartet contests were held for both male and mixed quartets.[33] *

Bowen concerned himself with the improvement of high school choir activities from the start of his administration. In 1926 he created the first Committee on Vocal Affairs, one of his first official duties. At the same time he, with the conference board, suggested a national high school chorus. But at that time such an idea seemed too expensive, and an In-and-About-Chicago Chorus was substituted. Undaunted, Bowen labored harder than ever for a national chorus. He had conducted the Southwest High School Chorus at the Southwestern Conference meeting in Tulsa where a chorus of five hundred appeared with the Southwest High School Orchestra.[34] And in the fall of 1927, Bowen worked personally on the project of a National High School Chorus. Early in October he picked Hollis Dann to conduct and R. Lee Osborn to organize the

---

* The mixed quartet contest was won by a group from Bowen's high school.

venture. Later Ernest G. Hesser, the chairman of the Committee on Vocal Affairs, was asked to assist in the selection of music and to help with the organization. The local supervisors were responsible for teaching the music to the students before the Chicago conference. Dann sent the supervisors seven different letters of instruction concerning the performance of the various selections. Dann held two open rehearsals daily, and the performance at Orchestra Hall climaxed an exciting convention.

PROGRAM

To Thee, O Country   Julius Eichberg
            Chorus and orchestra (sixty members
            of the Chicago Symphony Orchestra)

A Hope Carol   David Stanley Smith

The Sea Hath Its Pearls   Pinsuti
                Chorus—unaccompanied

The Sun Worshippers   Zuni Indian Melody
                        arr. Harvey Worthington Loomis

River, River   Chilean Folk Song
                                        arr. Clifford Page
            chorus of girls' voices and orchestra

All in the April Evening   High S. Rogerton
                chorus—unaccompanied

Mexican Serenade   George W. Chadwick
                chorus and orchestra

Were You There?   H. T. Burleigh
                chorus—unaccompanied

PART TWO

Sylvia   Oley Speaks
                piano accompaniment

Soldiers of the Captain   Spohr
            unaccompanied chorus of male voices

Spinning Chorus, from "Flying Dutchman"   Wagner
            chorus of girls' voices with orchestra

Listen to the Lambs   R. Nathaniel Dett
                chorus—unaccompanied

A Song of Victory   Percy Fletcher
                chorus and orchestra [35]

The concert was a resounding success. Edward Moore wrote in the Chicago *Daily Tribune* of April 21, 1928:

They were invariably on pitch, they always preserved a balance, they pronounced their words more plainly than an adult chorus of one-tenth their number; the sopranos were able to float up to a high B-flat without a squeal in a stageful. Even the boys could sing, and thereby another belief went crumbling into the dust. . . . In all cases they were alert, expressive, exact on attack and intonation, and in all cases they had this bewitching tone. Unless you have heard them sing you have no idea what enchantment lies in the human throat.[36]

Paul J. Weaver, editor of the *Music Supervisors Journal*, found the program selections somewhat disappointing but had high praise for the balance and blend of the ensemble.

Other choral groups sang during the conference week adding to the inspiration toward improved choral performance. Many sang *a cappella*. The Chicago Bach Choir, directed by William Boeppler, sang "Dir, dir Jehovah will ich singen," and the motet, "Jesu, Meine Freund." The three-hundred voice Nicholas Senn High School *A Cappella* Chorus, directed by Noble Cain, sang "Fierce Raged the Tempest," by Candlyn, "Hymn to Music," by Buck, and "Alleluia, Christ Is Risen," by Kopyloff. The Northwestern University *A Cappella* Choir, under the direction of Peter Lutkin, sang three Russian motets, four sixteenth-century Latin motets, two "American motets" by Lutkin, and two spirituals. There was much more.

The sum total was impressive, but the most important single performance came from a high school from Michigan. It was not a combined chorus of select individuals. It did not have an overwhelming number of singers. Yet its quality of performance was superior to anything that audiences had heard. The choir was directed by Jacob Evanson who was hired as an assistant to the executive and music organizer of the Community Music Association in 1924. Born on a small farm near Portland, North Dakota, Evanson practiced some piano and taught himself to play the flute. At the University of North Dakota, he was a liberal arts student majoring in sociology. He was active in all the musical organizations of the campus but took no formal music courses. Following graduation, Evanson studied flute with a member of the Minneapolis Symphony who offered him a job in a theatre orchestra. But he went to Flint instead. Though hired by a most active and vigorous Community Music Association, Evanson did most of his work in the high school. He taught choral music, harmony, and history of music. His first year's work found Evanson as director of the boys' glee club, the girls' glee club, the combined glee clubs, and an auditorium chorus. All were regularly scheduled classes and all received school credit.[37]

In 1926 the music department at the high school was enlarged. W. W. Norton brought three teachers from Minnesota—Neil Kjos, Olaf Christiansen, both graduates of St. Olaf College, and Walter Bloch, a graduate of the University of Minnesota. Norton came to Flint in 1921 as executive and music organizer of the Community Music Association. He had replaced George Oscar Bowen who successfully directed a community chorus, a community orchestra, and taught music at the high school.

The *a cappella* choir evolved from the combined glee clubs in 1927. Perhaps its organization was influenced by performances of the St. Olaf Choir, the Westminster Choir, and the Russian Symphonic Choir, all of which performed in Flint. In an interview with Jacob A. Evanson (with Kegerreis on August 16 and 17, 1963) the conductor reported that "he had noticed in rehearsals of the mixed chorus . . . that in individual spots in the music they sounded like the St. Olaf Choir. He reasoned that they could be trained to sound that way all the time and set about doing so."[38] Evanson reasoned that in 1926, the only medium that could "rival the great advances being made in the instrumental field of public school music" was the mixed chorus singing *a cappella*. He believed that only the great *a cappella* literature could compete with the symphonic masterpieces and "other great instrumental compositions being played by the school orchestra." The Flint *A Cappella* Choir was formed as a "solid" subject like geometry or Latin, to meet five hours a week and to be considered a prepared subject, receiving equal credit. He wrote in a program of the Flint Central High School in 1930 that the choir's primary objective was cultural, with a syllabus that included the best in that field. In 1928 and 1929, a special chorus was created for those who just missed selection for the *a cappella* choir. This group met "three times one week and twice the next alternating with gym work." It reviewed the fundamentals and studied and performed a standard opera or oratorio during the year, thus preparing them for the *a cappella* choir the following year.

The original choir roll listed ten first sopranos, ten second sopranos, eight first altos, nine second altos, eight first tenors, six second tenors, eleven baritones, and eleven basses. It was this combination of young people that was to make such an impression on the 1928 conference meeting of the MSNC.

On that eventful day, Thursday, April 19, 1928, it was not the large multi-voiced choirs that had been assembled for the conference that carried the day, not the college or university choirs that made the greatest impression, but a single high school *a cappella* choir from Flint, Michigan. A group with ordinary high school voices but molded by its director into a superb artistic unity—a musical tour de force that was recognized as possible of attainment by most American high schools if only the will and the special knowledge could be learned. Reviewers were delirious in their praise. Brown, in the *Musical Courier*, said:

For real choral singing there is no organization in America that is very much better than the Flint High School *A Cappella* Choir. At the . . . afternoon program there were tears in the eyes of many of the listeners. Diction? Superb. Shading and nuance? Likewise fine. Bach and the Russian number they sang were "amazing." No—there is no other word; we said "amazing."[39]

And on May 5, 1928, George Oscar Bowen wrote to Jacob A. Evanson regarding the appearance of the Flint *A Cappella* Choir:

I am sure I am conservatively expressing the sentiment of everyone who heard them in Chicago that it was about the finest piece of singing ever done by a high school group.[40]

One year later Bowen addressed the Southwestern Divisional Conference and asked rhetorically where one could go to hear an adult choir, excepting a few outstanding organizations, that could approach the "excellence in tone quality, fidelity to pitch and ready response to the demands of the conductor," as the Flint *A Cappella* Choir? Mabelle Glenn, the new conference president, wrote to Evanson that "all who heard the choir during the conference have gone back to their schools with higher ideals."

Neil A. Kjos reported that Evanson was a "careful meticulous worker who applied an instrumental technique to choral directing." He had developed a good ear and "spoke of experimenting with the choral sound, trying to make the choir 'sound like violins.'" He had studied books on voice production, such as Giddings's *Grade School Music*, Coward's *Choral Techniques and Interpretation*, and Hulbert's *Breathing for Voice Production*. The outstanding results he achieved were accomplished with ordinary high school singers. Duncan McKenzie, a voice teacher, reported in the 1929 *Proceedings of the Music Supervisors National Conference* that he

had the opportunity of testing individually all the tenors in the Flint High School Choir which sang at Chicago, and [he] found the voices individually no better than he had found in any of the high schools [he had] taught in. Most of them were youth's voices, a few were possible tenors, and only one had more or less a real tenor voice.

Evanson challenged his students to become better readers of music. He suggested that sight reading could be well mastered by a sixth grader, and that he expected his high school students to "be able to master the equivalent of hymn-tune reading in two weeks," or he could not give them a passing grade. By the end of the year he expected them to be able to read their parts to an eight-part motet at sight.[41] Evanson graded his students on their progress particularly in reading and expected work on assignments outside of school hours.

Evanson and the Flint *A Cappella* Choir pointed the way. It would now take more than skillful glee clubs for a school to demonstrate its superiority in vocal music. Even the performance of an oratorio would be unconvincing. A school would now require an *a cappella* choir if it were to rank with the best. More and more the *a cappella* choir directors came to know the best literature taken from masterpieces of the past and present. Evanson's programs in 1930 at the convention of the Music Supervisors National Conference featured works by Palestrina, Byrd, Gretchaninoff, Bach, Wilbye, Tallis, Lassus, Brahms, and Ralph Vaughn Williams.

So impressed was Percy Scholes who heard the performance that he personally extended a letter of invitation to the Flint choir for a "tour of the Old World." The choir worked hard to raise the money for such a venture, but their labors were not crowned with success. The winter of 1931 was a poor time for fund-raising.

Evanson left Flint at the end of the 1931 season. After a summer at Columbia, he went to Western Reserve the next fall. There he attempted to put into practice those ideas concerning a choral program "built around the literature." The program was not successful as the university gave "insufficient credit." He then went to Pittsburgh where he not only was able to develop his ideas in this regard, but came to believe that his concept of a strictly *a cappella* choir was limiting. "Too much great music was avoided merely because it had an accompaniment."[42]

The influence of the Flint choir was truly nationwide. The Virginia Federation of Music Clubs commented on the work of the Flint choir and challenged the members of the Virginia federation to give the children of Virginia the same advantages. The *Washington High School Annual* in Cedar Rapids, Iowa, drew attention to the Flint choir as well as that of St. Olaf's as fine choirs that set the standards for their new *a cappella* choir to emulate. An assistant superintendent wrote to the principal of the Flint Central High School requesting information concerning the values of *a cappella* singing in the schools. And when Jacob A. Evanson was asked to speak as a member of a symposium on "The Development and Training of A Cappella Choirs" at a sectional meeting of the Committee on Vocal Affairs at the 1932 meeting of the Music Supervisors National Conference, over five hundred people crowded into the ballrooms of the Hotel Statler to hear the discussion.

In the mid-1930s *a cappella* singing was at its height in the high schools of America. While many accepted the universality of the *a cappella* movement, this particular choral manifestation centered principally in the larger schools of the western and north-central states. At no time in the 1930s were there more than 50 percent of the nation's high schools with an *a cappella* choir. In a survey of eighty high schools in 1940, only 25 percent of the high schools surveyed in the northeastern states had *a cappella* choirs, 33 percent in the southern states, 52 percent in the midwestern states, and 63 percent in the western states. Of the schools with over one thousand students, 74 percent had such choirs while only 22 percent maintained such an organization if their school population was less than five hundred.

But even with such statistics Hollis Dann was to say in 1937 that the superior quality of an increasing number of choral organizations in the nation's high schools was "the outstanding choral achievement of the present decade."

Several factors contributed to the rise of *a cappella* singing in the schools, among which were the contest movement, the appearance of radio broadcasting, the desire of the choral directors to compete with mushrooming instrumental programs, the creation of the National High School Chorus, and, later, the effect of advertising by an industry that realized the potential for sales to high school *a cappella* choirs.

Choral directors were not as eager to embrace the contest as were their instrumental colleagues. Kegerreis suggests that perhaps there was too much disagreement as to what constitutes fine choral singing. Perhaps the contest was considered too undignified. But smaller schools were helped as the competition forced an improved repertory and higher standards of performance.

The National Broadcasting Company's "Music and American Youth" broadcasts were significant contributions to the stimulation of interest in high school *a cappella* singing. They were started in 1934 and were sponsored by the Music Supervisors National Conference. Until 1942 approximately twenty half-hour programs a year were broadcast in various American cities.

George Oscar Bowen admitted the success of the school instrumental movement in an address to the MSNC in 1932. He showed that this development of instrumental music had made possible the selling of the entire music program. "But at the same time," he confessed, "set us back a decade vocally, from which we are just now recovering."[43] And one year later Osbourne McConathy commented how the choral directors "stood abashed" while the instrumental people made such important strides in their area. But McConathy observed how the *a cappella* movement saved the day. "The young singers responded eagerly to the appeal of this subtle music which makes such exacting demands and offers such rich rewards."[44]

The National High School Chorus represented another influence in the *a cappella* movement. The first such organization much impressed the 1928 convention of the MSNC, and three years later the third National High School Chorus was formed to sing for the Department of Superintendence of the National Education Association. At that time all the selections were sung *a cappella* and were conducted by Hollis Dann. The last National High School Chorus was formed in 1932, and appropriately it was conducted by F.

Melius Christiansen, Charles M. Dennis, and Griffes J. Jones. Its sixteen selections were all performed without accompaniment.

Music publishers began realizing the possibilities of the *a cappella* movement in 1930 when G. Ricordi and Company began advertising in the *Music Supervisors Journal*. In May of that year the Oxford University Press advertised the *a cappella* selections that were sung at the Chicago conference by the Glenville High School Choral Club, the National High School Chorus, the Flint High School Choir, and the Chicago University Chapel Choir. In 1931 the *Journal* carried advertisements for *a cappella* choral music by nearly every publisher.

The ascendency of the *a cappella* choir enjoyed a "golden age" in the mid 1930s. Mrs. William Arms Fisher wrote in 1935 that

the problem of American audiences is not how to contact programs of *a cappella* singing, but nearing a stage of how to avoid them. When the supervisors of the public schools started to organize *a cappella* choirs, in junior and senior high schools, the real deluge began. Today a high school or college in an American city or town that does not maintain such a choir must suffer by virtue of comparison.[45]

But the *a cappella* ideal had certain limitations, and these limitations signaled the diminution of enthusiasm for the excesses of the *a cappella* ideal. There was a basic religious character of *a cappella* singing that, while proper in the St. Olaf Choir, was strained in the public high school. *A cappella* singing was justified in the high school only by some interesting distortions of philosophy. Discourses on the spiritual values of this form of choral singing emerged. Paul Klingstedt indicated in 1947 in an article in the *Proceedings* of the Music Teachers National Association that the "*a cappella* choir satisfies the spiritual urge of teenagers. I doubt if there is such a thing as religious education in the public schools. Still the religious urge is there."[46] Dykema and Gehrkens claimed that "Unaccompanied singing is . . . primarily a spiritual activity."

The defense was beginning to sound hollow. Harry Wilson gave the *a cappella* movement a smashing blow in 1941 when he said:

A cappella choirs, beautifully robed, became the fashion. Not too many conductors knew what the term meant; some of them could not even spell it. Accompanied singing was frowned upon; it was actually considered inferior. At times, even such selections as "The Hallelujah Chorus" from *Messiah* were performed unaccompanied.[47]

Other critics concerned themselves with the antiquarian nature of the literature performed by these groups, which excluded twentieth-century compositions. George J. Abbott writing the first article to appear in the *Music Supervisors Journal* attacking the *a cappella* choir wrote: "I think it is time we called a halt and evaluate this craze for *a cappella* singing which has swept the country." [48]

Other criticisms of the *a cappella* movement concerned themselves with the boring nature of the performances. Harry Carlson, director of the Chicago Swedish Choral Society, complained that in spite of the skill of the singers and their "mechanical dexterity and subtle tonal refinements," he left the concerts "without emotional exaltation and with a certain bored admiration for the skill displayed." [49] George Howerton believed that in so many instances the singers have "absolutely no understanding of the spirit of the music and no feeling for its meaning." All *a cappella* styles seemed to merge with the same "unvarying mode of expression, both vocal and facial." [50]

As complaints grew directors looked for alternative means of choral expression. The growing tendency at the end of the 1930s was to enlarge the choral idea with a gradual return to accompanied singing to be incorporated alongside the *a cappella* idea. The Music Education Research Council of the Music Educators National Conference (MENC) reported in 1937 that:

recently there has been a tendency to broaden the scope of the material used and to include not only more modern unaccompanied works, but also, material with special instrumental accompaniments, such as string quartet or woodwind ensembles. These accompaniments are less for the purpose of sustaining the choir in pitch and rhythm, as is the common use of the piano, than to add variety of tone color and comparatively independent musical effects. [51]

In the *Proceedings of the Music Educators National Conference* for the years 1930–1940, there were many articles on the subject of vocal music in the schools complaining of an overemphasis on unaccompanied music. Many came to believe that the use of piano or orchestral accompaniment would represent a richer vocal experience for the students and for the audiences. All admired the *a cappella* sound and what that ideal had done for the improvement and stimulation of choral singing in the schools, but they felt that a balance had to be achieved so that the "accompanied song would achieve its place in the musical sun" along with that of *a cappella* singing.

In 1945 the Music Education Curriculum Committee of the MENC stated its belief that *a cappella* groups should be maintained, but a "favorable balance should be struck between accompanied repertoire and that which is sung without accompaniment." The choral directors should not turn their backs on the great *a cappella* works of the past, but should, nonetheless, have "experience with some of the beautiful things in which the accompaniment is an important integral part of the composition."[52] Choral directors would now go their own way in matters concerning the selection of music.

A cappella literature has its own brand of classicism. No trend of our day or another will remove this great literature permanently from the repertories of choral groups. In the hands of choral directors who are themselves good and sensitively educated musicians, a balanced literature is likely to be taught, that which is accompanied taking place beside those compositions which require instrumental accompaniment.

Many high schools between 1930 and 1940 developed fine *a cappella* choirs. It is impossible to describe them all. Some of these school choirs exist only in the memories of those who still remember the warm glow of aesthetic delight when singing with such a group. Other choirs and their directors have been written about in monographs and local school histories, but because of the exigencies of time and space have been deprived of a place in this volume. It is hoped that the general trend is clear. Music education had become a powerful force in the public schools of the country. Though some schools struggled, rarely able to come to grips with the cultivation of the art, others blossomed, producing sensitive musicians who were able to continue their instruction in the nation's colleges, universities, and conservatories. The choirs of our high schools had won their place in the musical sun.

CHAPTER XVIII

Music Education and Rhythmic Movement

I N GENERAL, and as the introduction of instrumental music, the growth of rhythmic activities in the elementary school program was a result of the child-study movement. There were isolated examples of the informal use of rhythmic motion or movement in the schools before 1900. But at this time there were those who believed that physical activity was indeed harmful. Some thought that the mind could not function at its maximum capacity if the muscles were exercised! But physical education, of course, did enter the school curriculum, and it eventually came to be recognized that prolonged sitting at a school desk meant poor postural habits to say nothing of poor physical conditioning. Teachers began to realize that lessons could be learned more effectively if they could be separated by periods of rest or physical exercise. Some of these exercises assumed a dancelike character and hence are within the domain of our study.

In a graded course of instruction for the Chicago schools published in 1896 stress was given to the importance of the "wants and necessities of the body." The elimination of poor posture was considered important. In 1877 *A Graded Course of Instruction for Public Schools* also recommended physical exercises for the children and provided detailed instructions. In the lower grades it was suggested that this exercise be accomplished through marching. At times tempo indications were given and appropriate singing was suggested.

Only rarely was a dance activity accepted on its own merits. Most schools that did do so were of a progressive and experimental nature. One of the most notable of these schools was the famous laboratory school organized by John Dewey of Teachers College of Columbia University. Dance was taught there for its intrinsic values. The dance became part of the physical culture program simply because that department seemed to have necessary floor space. Physical education teachers were not necessarily in favor of dance as they felt that it had a more limited value as a physical culture activity. Nevertheless, by 1908 many physical educators saw the value of dance in their program. They came to believe that, if properly taught, dance trained a sense of rhythm and gave the body control, grace, and distinction. It invigorated both the body and the mind and promoted sociability. At the same time the folk dances and music of other nations helped to introduce the children to the lives and customs of other peoples.

The activities of the experimental schools operated by Teachers College of Columbia University under the direction of Thomas D. Wood exerted a strong influence for fifty years on dance in the schools. In the physical education departments of the Horace Mann and Speyer elementary schools, a program was developed in which dance was stressed. Wood advocated a system of gymnastics which he called the natural system. It was an outgrowth of the playground movement of the latter part of the nineteenth century. Perhaps for the first time the emphasis was not placed on formal drill but on the more modern concepts of free rhythmic movement. The dance activities included exercises in fundamental movements such as walking, running, skipping, hopping, jumping, sliding, and so forth. The folk dance was also a part of the program. The aim of this system was to encourage the physical well-being of the children, and it was not long before these various rhythmic activities were picked up and adopted by music educators to stimulate a rhythmic awareness among children.

The most elaborate of rhythmic training to appear in the twentieth century was the system of eurhythmics developed by Émile Jaques-Dalcroze around 1900. Developed in Europe, eurhythmics, as espoused by Jaques-Dalcroze, involved a complex system of expressing music through movement. The earliest mention of eurhythmics in the United States came between 1910 and 1920. Articles appeared describing personal visits to the Dalcroze School in Germany and noting the benefits derived from the system.[1]

Dalcroze eurhythmics were introduced to American educators during the first two decades of this century. The music educators were interested, but few schools used the system. A small number of colleges and private elementary schools added eurhythmics to the curriculum, the first being Bryn Mawr College in 1913. Two years later the New York School of Dalcroze Eurhythmics was founded.

Jaques-Dalcroze believed that within the child's body there was a mechanism that instinctively indicated the essential elements of rhythm to the child. Such an element was a sense of time. The heartbeat was the basic beat, but the heart could not be controlled. It was therefore of little value in realizing rhythm. The activity of breathing could be related to the rhythm of the measure or phrase. The regular gait furnished Jaques-Dalcroze with the perfect model of measure and the division of time into equal portions. Eurhythmics for children was based principally on marching. The child must be given repeated experiences in moving with music. He believed that a person was not completely musical if he could not respond physically to music. The consciousness of sound could only be acquired by a reiterated experience of the ear and voice. A musician must develop a consciousness of rhythm by repeated experiences of movement of the whole body. The idea of stepping the rhythm had been suggested by other music educators in the early 1900s, but it was Dalcroze who systematized and promoted the idea, and it is to him that the credit for this activity belongs.

Albert Gay tells us that the earliest major publication to recommend a modified eurhythmics approach was Zanzig's *Concord Teachers Guide* published in 1929. Zanzig recommended the use of action names for notes. In several instances he suggested the learning of Dalcroze movement for beats and notes. Various stepping activities were recommended throughout all six grades.[2] During the 1930s the device of stepping the tune became a fairly common activity in the lower grades. The textbook series, *The World of Music*, recommended that the child step the notes. Walking notes were associated with quarter notes and eighth notes were running notes.

The term *eurhythmics* was frequently used by music educators to refer to rhythmic movement in general. As eurhythmics was a system of teaching music through movement, so it was also a formal system that could be easily appreciated by the trained musician. Around 1930 the term *eurhythmics* seemed to have been well known. Gay tells us that interest was keen, and that the music educator was ready for such a system of teaching rhythm.[3]

Charles H. Farnsworth developed a program of eurhythmics at Teachers College, Columbia University, in the early years of the century. He taught rhythm through movement to children in the first grade. He believed in the imitation of the rhythmic motions of nature, the swaying of trees, the motions of water. Games like skipping rope and bouncing balls were used. Following the free movements he taught various steps of old dances, bowing, and certain military movements. Circles were to be described with the hand by the children and pulses either weak or strong would be so indicated. A large circle showed the strong beats and the small circles the weak. The circles were then transferred to the blackboard. When the child attained a certainty in the recognition in picturing of pulses, he would be asked to detect two- or three-part time to be identified in various rhythmic groups. In this way Farnsworth would attempt to teach not only the feeling for rhythm but the idea of rhythmic notation as well.

Jaques-Dalcroze believed in the values of eurhythmics in the life of man. The aim of this bodily activity of controlled physical expression was to develop a rapid and regular communication between the body and the brain. Such activities would lead toward a more perfect control of the body. Rhythmic gymnastics, believed Jaques-Dalcroze, would serve to educate the nerve centers of the body. It would "lessen the time lost between the conception of an act and its realization." He stressed the requirement of joy as it involved the physical discipline of movement by continuous practice and the regulation of so-called natural rhythms of the body. These rhythms would become automatic in "every degree of strength and suppleness, rapidity or slowness." The role of music, believed Jaques-Dalcroze, serves to regulate movement and inspires as well as stimulates the nerve functions. With this in mind it becomes the indispensable ally of gymnastics. But mere gymnastics were not enough. The body must also become an instrument of art.

The formal training in eurhythmics is divided into three branches: rhythmic movement; solfeggio, including ear training; and pianoforte improvisation. Only rhythmic movement has influenced American music education to any extent. The students would beat time, in the fashion of an orchestra conductor, ideally to the music improvised by the teacher. The children would simultaneously step the note values.

Efforts were made in the 1930s to introduce rhythmic activities into the public schools of America. Paul J. Weaver endorsed the Dalcroze system believing that rhythmic problems of the children would disappear with an appropriate rhythmic background. Russell V. Morgan indicated that eurhythmics in a modified form was bound to enter the classrooms. Karl Gehrkens prepared a report dealing with the newer practices and tendencies in music education. He, too, strongly supported a program of eurhythmics, believing that the music teachers of his day neglected, or approached merely through mathematical concepts, the rhythmic side of music teaching. Gehrkens pointed to the work of Jaques-Dalcroze as being the only system that had become well-known. Gehrkens was unwilling to accept all of the tenets advocated by Jaques Dalcroze, but he was enthusiastic about the almost unlimited possibilities of this type of work. He hoped that all supervisors would be trained in Dalcroze eurhythmics as a part of their preparation for teaching music in the public schools.

Initially the Dalcroze adherents defended the sanctity of the complete Dalcroze system. But by 1934 a gradual change appeared in this attitude. American educators were not about to accept the complete gospel of any system of music education. Gehrkens was enthusiastic about the ability of eurhythmics practice to stimulate listening and to "free the mind" through musical gymnastics. He was confident that this work would make Dalcroze immortal among the great educators of all time. But only a person with sufficient creative imagination, practical resourcefulness, and the ability to improvise interestingly should be entrusted to do this important work.[4]

Even by the late 1930s eurhythmics was still taught in only a few isolated public schools.[5] The course of study in music in the city of Pittsburgh for 1934 enthusiastically recommended a program of eurhythmics from the kindergarten through the sixth grade. But the course of study suggested strongly that only a trained person should teach the subject, and there appeared to be a strong belief that other types of rhythmic activity would be of little value. American educators were becoming more enthusiastic about eurhythmics. They would pay tribute to Jaques-Dalcroze, but would make the rhythmic activities fit the unique, eclectic American public school system.

Around the turn of the century a strong interest in the study of melody superseded the study of rhythm. Eleanor Smith in 1898 suggested that the child make certain observations regarding the rhythm of the piece by either recognizing its pulses or beating time.[6] Calvin Cady recommended that a student learn to swing the rhythm with a circular movement of the hand.[7] There was a feeling at this time that excessive movement of the body would interfere with singing. Movement was carefully controlled. The teacher would insist that each student should participate, and that all movements be exactly alike. Toward the end of the second decade of this century, an increase in the use of rhythmic movement can be perceived. A course of study in Nevada suggests the use of rhythmic activities in the second grade. A course of study in Missouri in the year 1919 shows that the idea of rhythm in music was as important as tonal considerations. A variety of activities, such as clapping, marching, tapping, and swinging of the arms, was suggested as a means for developing these rhythmic responses in children.

T. P. Giddings, that enthusiastic advocate of the sanctity of music reading in the public schools, decried the use of rhythmic play and games, marching, dancing, and singing. G. Stanley Hall was one of the first to advocate the teaching of music appreciation through the dance. He believed that music should be felt in order to be understood, and that this appreciation had to be accomplished through rhythmic movement. Music must get into the muscles, and he surmised that the child should be exposed to marchlike or dancelike music. Movement, Hall believed, was the ultimate means of expressing music.[8] As a major contributor toward the child-study movement, Hall's opinions were expressed to music educators in an address to the Music Section of the annual meeting of the National Educational Association in 1908. These views could not have helped but to influence the views of many music educators.

Thomas W. Surette expressed a point of view readily familiar to the modern music educator when he explained in 1916 that rhythm should be taught as other subjects—by imitation. "A child who has danced, or marched, or clapped his hands in exact time and rhythm with the notes can be taught later the time names of those notes without the slightest difficulty."[9] A child should not start by reading notes or attempting to interpret symbols believed Surette but should first develop a sense of rhythm. He believed that freedom and accuracy in rhythm can only be brought about by bodily movement.

In a point of view strongly reminiscent of the contemporary work of Carl Orff we find W. Otto Miessner discussing the need for rhythmic activities among children. The children should have experience in sensing rhythm through movement, believed Miessner, before the formal notation is presented.[10] Miessner suggested that the child retrace the development of the human race through the use of folk dances and singing games.

Between 1920 and 1930 American music educators had still not completely accepted the concept of rhythmic activity. Osbourne McConathy observed in a biennial survey of education, that eurhythmic activities was another phase of music study which "recently" had assumed important proportions. He pointed to the work of Jaques Dalcroze and said that eurhythmics had been introduced into a number of colleges and normal schools. "A few elementary schools, too, are experimenting with this system, but a far larger number are introducing less exacting rhythmic activities of various kinds which seem more practicable under our American school condition." McConathy pointed out that these activities were under the direction of the music teacher but also in many instances in cooperation with the physical education departments. As chairman of the National Committee on Music in Platoon or Work Study Playschools in 1927, Will Earhart reported the results of a questionnaire returned by 170 schools in twenty-one states. Earhart indicated that eurhythmics or rhythm practices was utilized in the first eight grades by between 34 and 62 percent of the respondents. The largest percentage of use occurred in grade two while the least percentage of use occurred in grade eight.[11]

Initially, the progressive educators saw the efficacy of rhythmic activities among children. Slowly the older music educators began to adjust to what appeared to be a significant trend. Hollis Dann attempted to update his series by publishing a *New Manual for Teachers*. In 1929 he talked about the "new education." Dann discussed the needs of childhood. He talked about tapping the creative instincts of children, suggesting that children work out their own reactions to music in the form of interpretive dances. He noted that these graceful and spontaneous interpretations would stimulate initiative and imagination "while providing a medium for rhythmic training and healthful exercises."[12] In 1912 Dann recommended only finger tapping while in 1929 he joined the movement advocating the expression of bodily action stimulated by the mood and movement of the music. Dann suggested the following activities during the first year: marching; listening; folk games; folk dances; rhythmic reaction through bodily movements; rhythm band; and rote songs. But after these preliminary statements the author failed to pursue or amplify these suggestions.

While psychologists such as Carl Seashore and Jacob Kwalwasser were suggesting that rhythmic skill was innate and not subject to improvement through teaching, another psychologist thought differently. James Mursell, a disciple of the progressivism and the child-study movement, postulated that rhythmic skills could indeed be learned. In his book *Principles of Musical Education*, Mursell discusses the essence of the rhythmic experience.[13] Listeners translate the rhythmic feel of the music into some sort of muscular action. The supreme illustration is the human tendency to march or to dance to music. Even the subtle aspects of rhythm in a piece of music are recorded in some form of muscular participation or accompaniment to the music. Mursell carries this idea further by suggesting that the larger muscles of the body respond to the slower rhythms while the feet can respond to the quicker rhythms. "Many a musician keeps time to music by incipient movements of the tongue, or by twitchings of the throat muscles."[14]

Mursell tells us that the rhythm of the meter and the rhythm of the melody are different and not necessarily related. A sense of satisfaction achieved by the listener while attending to the rhythm of the melody is not based upon his ability to appreciate or duplicate a uniform accuracy of timing.

What is more important was Mursell's feeling that a rhythmic sensitivity was indeed teachable, though he admitted at the same time that there are some who had little or no rhythmic sense! It was this teachability, however, that was to impress music educators and lead to a universal acceptance of rhythmic instruction as a part of the elementary music curriculum. Mursell pointed to Dalcroze as the best-known method for training the rhythmic sense. An even sense of timing could be practiced by tapping a finger against the musical score, a device Mursell borrowed from T. P. Giddings. Larger phrase sensitivity might be acquired through proper breathing and muscular coordination. Most important, the rhythmic process was not an unconscious response but a "high grade, voluntary, and educable" process. If the whole body responds to rhythm, it was then the responsibility of the music teacher to help the child to learn to use his body in this manner. Mursell mirrored Dalcroze when he said that rhythm depends upon muscular and organic coordinations, and "it is these coordinations which form the basis of executant technique."

Interest in rhythmic activities in the elementary school classrooms increased in the 1930s. Again, James Mursell was an important influence in the expansion of these activities. In the *Psychology of School Music Teaching*, which he coauthored with Mabelle Glenn, Mursell believed that a beat could be sensed through action. A child does not sense the beat by knowing the arithmetical number of pulses in a bar but by "catching the swing." Rhythm then is a motor experience and as such may be taught through movement. At this time Mursell and Glenn believed that tapping with the finger was insufficient because of the smallness of that reaction. "It is impossible to feel the sweep and swing of the rhythm in the small directive muscles of the finger." He believed that the large muscles such as the legs, arms, and trunk should be used. The authors believed that a free, unimpeded sweeping motion would be best with vigorous arm and body movements. The children were encouraged to develop highly coordinated movements with the entire body.

On the other hand, Lilla Belle Pitts, in her article on music education in the *35th Yearbook of the National Society for the Study of Education* in 1936, omitted the study of rhythm as a part of the musical experiences planned to meet the needs of a majority of the student body. In the same yearbook Mabelle Glenn did recommend that rhythm should be taught through movement. In the same yearbook Marguerite Hood strongly advocated the teaching of rhythm in her program for the rural schools. Gay points out that rhythmic activities at this time were nothing more than "mere" activities. They existed not for their own sake but for the general goals of music education.

The method books for the 1930s deal variously with the subject of rhythm education, though some books disapprove of this aspect of the music curriculum. A general overview of these volumes demonstrates an increasing interest in rhythmic activities. Alma Norton in *Teaching School Music* (1932) suggested that the children make some muscular movement that would correspond to the music.[15] She believed that the singer may move about freely while singing and would receive satisfaction from a fully integrated experience. By 1934 Karl Gehrkens's *Music in the Grade Schools* showed a marked interest in rhythmic activities. Such activities, believed Gehrkens, would lead to pleasure, dexterity, and grace and physical response to music rhythm. Gehrkens felt that the best way to train an individual in rhythm was through physical movement. In keeping with the new education Gehrkens believed that the aim in this kind of activity was not to teach the symbols of rhythm but to guide the child toward rhythmic responses.

The earlier concept that rhythm was an inborn sense faded from the educational scene. During this period rhythmic response became an area that could be improved with practice and would lead to a fuller appreciation of the art of music. Gehrkens believed that everyone who was normal had a "rhythmic germ in him" and that practically everyone had the possibility of becoming rhythmic. On the other hand, he suggested that this innate "rhythm germ" had to be developed through practice, and such practice involved free but organized muscular movements by the individual—movements that should be accomplished according to the music heard. In Clella Lester Perkins's book *How to Teach Music to Children*, published in 1936, the author presented definite procedures for the children to dramatize their songs.[16] The children were instructed where to put their arms, how to move them, whether to glide to the right or to the left, and when to flutter their fingers.

Rhythmic activity had come into its own. It would enter the elementary curriculum and occupy an important and dignified place to this day.

CHAPTER XIX

Some Newer Approaches from Abroad

THREE IMPORTANT music educators from abroad have influenced the direction of music education in the United States. They are Carl Orff, Zoltan Kodaly, and Shinichi Suzuki. None can be said to be entirely original in his concept, but each managed to focus international attention on his successful efforts. Carl Orff espoused the concept of creativity; Kodaly centered on the learning of rhythm and melodic ideas; and Suzuki initially confined his teaching to that of the violin and stressed rote instruction exclusively in the early stages.

THE ORFF SYSTEM OF MUSIC EDUCATION

Carl Orff investigated the common methods of music teaching in Germany in the early part of the century and determined that the children were exposed to defective instruction. The children, according to Orff, needed to experience music first. By removing it from the play atmosphere, music instruction had become a most serious business involved with fingerings, counting beats, reading clefs, and practicing. As a result, many children were expected to master instruments such as the piano or violin before they had experienced music. Orff believed this to be too conscious, too technical, and too mechanical. He felt that the typical eighteenth-century music studied by a child held no particular attraction for him.

Rhythm was usually forgotten, believed Orff, in spite of the warn-
ings of Jaques-Dalcroze.

Carl Orff was born in Munich on July 10, 1895. He studied at
the Munich Academy of Music. After a short period as a coach
and conductor in Munich, Mannheim, and Darmstadt, he returned
to Munich in 1920 to study under Heinrich Kaminski. In 1925 he
helped found the Gunter Schule where he taught until 1930. He
became impressed with the work of Jaques-Dalcroze and aimed
his teaching at the education of a lay public with an emphasis on
creative musicianship. His *Schulwerk* was published between
1930 and 1933 and was the product of his teaching experience.
Orff's educational activities and his professional work as a composer follow similar lines of approach. He was concerned about
the exaggerated expression of European opera at the end of the
century and wanted to reduce music to its elementary components
from which it was first created. His concern with the hiatus between modern art and the public prompted the composer to strive
for an artistic voice that at once broke with the romantic tradition
but which could nevertheless appeal to popular taste. His compositions, like his educational philosophy, demonstrated his predilection for rhythmic ordinality, with a sense of melody growing
from the rhythmic.

Orff's educational activities and ideas may be viewed in an historical context. The first twenty-five years of the century witnessed
a general neglect of music education in German-speaking coun-
tries of Europe. Only singing was taught and in many cases even
that as an elective. The reorganization of school music in Germany
dates from the 1920s. Leo Kestenberg was instrumental in promoting the creative forces of self-expression in an effort to enrich
the lives of the children. Music in Germany was to be elevated on a
level with traditional subjects, and Orff became interested at this
period. His concerns were in the mainstream of music education in
the twentieth century. He believed that early musical training
should be multifaceted and involve the whole body. Activities such
as dancing, clapping, stamping, and using instruments would be
combined to awaken the sense of rhythm and melody in the children. Creativity would enhance the child's self-expression and
would lead to the harmonious development of a total personality.

Carl Orff's *Music for Children* demonstrates his concepts of musical learning. Melodies in this book are pentatonic throughout. According to the author, the music based upon the five-note-scale technique represents a stage of development that corresponds closely to the mentality of children. Melody develops step by step: ony two tones are used at first, then a third is added, a fourth, and finally a fifth. The pentatonic tunes are accompanied by "burduns," or ostenati figurations. The typical cadential accompaniments seemed inappropriate for this work while the use of the ostenati led quite naturally to simple forms of polyphony. Ensemble instruments were constructed and used for this purpose and reflected the style of the music.

Orff believed in mallet-playing instruments and a variety of drums, cymbals, and accessories. Musical glasses were used and were tuned with different levels of water, while the glockenspiel was ordinarily played with wooden mallets and xylophones with rubber-headed mallets. The bass line of the burdun was ordinarily played by a stringed instrument, a viola da gamba or a cello, if possible. Otherwise a viola or violin was used. Orff recommended that a piano be ignored as he felt that the sound of the modern piano could not be successfully integrated into the ensemble. He embraced clavichords and spinets with some enthusiasm however. Although notation was not to be disregarded, children were encouraged to play from memory, thus guaranteeing a maximum of freedom. In this way the child may jot down any rhythmical pattern or melodic idea that occurred to him.

Orff's starting point was rhythm, which he regarded as the most basic of all the elements. It was not taught mechanically or mathematically but grew out of speech patterns. For the child, as for primitive man, speaking and singing, music and movement cannot be isolated. Speech patterns allowed a child to grasp each type of meter without difficulty, even up-beats or irregular bars. These rhythmical formulas could be experienced by moving the body and by using percussion instruments. These instruments provided accompaniments of a gradually increasing complexity.

The concept of melody was treated similarly. The simple intervals grew almost imperceptibly out of rhythm. The simplest of them all—the falling minor third—was introduced while other intervals were gradually incorporated, leading to a repertory of pentatonic tunes well suited for children. The composer pedagogue made every effort to keep children from imitating the overpowering examples of nonpentatonic music. The first volume of *Music for Children* is wholly pentatonic, while volumes two and three are devoted to major, volumes four and five to minor.

The children were expected to work in groups. They experienced the contrast between soli and chorus and between melody and accompaniment. The accompaniments were at first simple burduns or open fifths similar to the sound of bagpipes. Orff believed that these were particularly effective in pentatonic tunes, and they provided the necessary framework for melodic improvisation. These burduns developed into ostinato figures, opening the door to rhythmic variety.

Functional harmony appeared only after the introduction of melodies in major, but the commonplace dominant tonic relationships were carefully avoided. Consistent with the composer's feeling toward twentieth-century harmonic practices, the introduction of supertonic and submediant chords in parallel motion took precedence over the more traditional dominant relationships. When Orff introduced the minor mode to children, it was in relationship to other model melodies. Aeolian, Dorian, and Phrygian were used after rhythm and melody were introduced. Studies in form and improvisation were encouraged, and alternation between solo and chorus and the improvisation of a second section in ternary form resulted in a better understanding of formal principles in music and the beginning of a feeling for improvisation. Orff recommended the use of canons as the simplest and most natural introduction to imitation.

The melodies in Orff's music for children were fashioned by Orff himself. The texts were derived from nursery rhymes and singing games. These melodies were adaptations of traditional melodic patterns that were used as a basis for improvisation rather than a fixed body of melodic material to be used by the children.

Orff argued that the usual toy instruments could be harmful to the musical sensibilities of young children. To accommodate the child's need to play, he caused to be constructed some high-quality rhythmic and melodic instruments. The primary purpose of music education, believed Orff, was the development of a child's creative "faculty" that manifested itself in the ability to improvise. This type of creativity cannot be supplied ready-made using sophisticated materials. The child's creativity can only be developed by helping him to make his own music at his own level and by integrating his music making with other related activities of childhood.

The world of children involves speaking and singing, poetry and music, music and movement, playing and dancing. Governed by the play instinct, these activities are an indivisible prelude to the development of art and ritual. Orff believed that these activities closely paralleled the so-called primitive stages of our own civilization. Some nursery rhymes are known to date back to prehistoric times, and from this source comes the value of repetitive patterns and the pentatonic scale.

But Orff's system was not without its detractors. Janice M. Thresher, in an article in the *Music Educators Journal* of January 1964, expressed serious reservations concerning certain inconsistencies and difficulties of implementation inherent in the Orff method. As most music educators in the mid-twentieth century advocate varied types of musical activities, particularly in the elementary school, Thresher concerned herself with the *exclusive application* of the Orff method. She speculated that the teacher-training program necessary for the Orff method would be "staggering in terms of time, money, and personnel." Like other critics, she was also concerned about the excessive cost of the Orff instruments. His pedagogical music seemed unduly complex in spite of his concern with improvisation, and the written material required rehearsal and discussion by the children. Angel Company recordings were criticized as being almost too well done to reflect Orff's basic philosophy of improvisation. Thresher was also troubled by the comparative lack of listening activities for the children. They were busy making music, but no time was provided for listening to it.

Orff believed that the difficult art music of Western civilization should not be presented to children at an early age, but this philosophy is itself controversial. The extended use of the pentatonic scale does not reflect what the children hear outside of such a music class. There are modern music educators who find that children can receive a valuable aesthetic education through exposure to works of the great masters without alienating these children from music. In common with music educators of our time, Thresher believes that the Orff system of music education represents only one of many valid approaches.

THE HISTORICAL DEVELOPMENT OF THE KODALY SYSTEM

The Kodaly method of music education originated under conditions favorable to the goal of teaching all children to read and to write music. Such instruction began in the state-controlled schools of Hungary. These schools enjoyed a long heritage of strict academic training, and a structured music curriculum on a nation-wide scale was possible. Goals are established by the state, instructional materials are specified, and standards of achievement are defined at each grade level. Classes in vocal music in Hungary meet twice weekly for forty-five minute periods and are required through the eighth grade.

Instrumental music is not encouraged until children can read and write music at a particular level. The teaching of instrumental music in Hungary has its own organization and school system. These institutions are called music schools as opposed to the music primary schools. The classes in the music schools meet after school hours and are attended by the children for six years. The curriculum comprises private instrumental music lessons and simultaneous solfeggio classes. Music schools exist where especially selected children may receive a more intensive musical education. About 130 of these schools have been established since 1950.*

The principles and procedures espoused by Kodaly spread rapidly throughout the world. In 1958 at the conference of the International Society for Music Education, Jeno Adam introduced the Kodaly method. At successive meetings of the conference in 1961 and 1963 various Hungarian specialists on this subject lectured, and in 1964 Kodaly himself addressed the conference.

The ideas of Kodaly were brought to the United States by Europeans now living in this country and by Americans who went to Europe to study. Arpad Darazs, Katinka Daniel, Tibor Bachmann,

---

* That year Mrs. Marta Nemesszeghy established the first so-called singing primary school in Kecskemet, Kodaly's birthplace. The school was no different than any other in Hungary except that it had music every day in the week rather than the normal twice per week.

and Laszlo Halasz, among others, made American adaptations of the method. Jeno Adam, who worked closely with Kodaly, presented the method in the United States in writing for the first time. Mary Helen Richards published a series of songbooks and charts with American songs based on the principle of pictorial representation of the rhythmic and melodic patterns. Denise Bacon organized summer courses at the Dana School of Music in Wellesley, Massachusetts, and presented some of the leading Hungarian music educators as teachers and lecturers. In 1969, the Kodaly Musical Training Institute opened in September with Bacon as director. Her course included a certificate, a diploma, and summer courses both here and in Hungary.

One of the most serious problems in adopting the Kodaly method for use in American schools is the question of folk materials. The study of folk songs is vital in Kodaly's plan for music education, and each country that has adopted Kodaly's principles has had to gather and classify folk music of its own. Kodaly believed that every nationality has a wealth of folk music that can be used to teach the basic elements of musical structure. With its diversity of ethnic groups, the United States enjoys a rich pool of such music. Kodaly suggested that American music educators could use some of the forty thousand folk songs currently cataloged in the Library of Congress.

Kodaly believed that the music education curriculum should begin at as early an age as possible. Hungarian children begin their musical study in the government nursery schools, some at the age of two-and-one-half years. Kodaly noted that the development of a musical ear and discriminating taste would be enhanced if the children received the best possible instruction between the ages of three and seven. Like Carl Orff, Kodaly believed that the individual child reenacts the musical development of his race in order to develop a high level of musicianship.

A carefully planned and systematically developed sequence of musical concepts and experiences must be part of the instruction. Rhythmic and melodic concepts, key signatures, meter signatures, and other theoretical aspects of music reading are integrated into a carefully organized instructional regimen. Kodaly and Orff both believed that young children should respond naturally to singing and rhythmic movement. Singing games are an important and appropriate method for teaching music in the elementary grades. Children walk and clap in rhythm with the beat. Under the Kodaly plan, musical taste and aesthetic sensitivity would be developed by the time of adolescence. An understanding of a child's natural heritage in music was important not only of the folk song literature but also of the musical classics.

Reading and writing musical notation are primary goals in the Kodaly system. To determine the best method of teaching music reading, Kodaly examined all of the existing systems and adopted that of John Curwen, an English musician and pedagogue of the nineteenth century. The plan was based on the tonic sol-fa arrangement, which used the principle of movable Do. The syllables were abbreviated by their initial letters, and their rhythmic values were notated by Curwen with punctuation marks. Kodaly adopted the initial letters that stood for the syllable names of pitches but used other aids for teaching rhythmic notation. His plan used standard notation for note values introduced to the children in rhythmic and melodic motives. Abstracted from the musical context and repeated many times, the motives are recognized by the child first as sounds and then as symbols using colored sticks. Sometimes the children themselves stand either alone or with linked arms to express the various rhythmic motives. Large body motions are used at first, followed by hand signals and eventually staff notation. The syllable names and functions of pitches are introduced to the children in a definite order that is strictly followed: sol-mi, la-sol-mi, la-sol-mi-do, la-sol-mi-re-do, fa and ti. Kodaly wrote dozens of exercises using the rather restricted range of two, three, four or five tones. When the children had acquired the full use of the diatonic range and the chromatic syllables fi, si and ta, they then used the sol-fa syllables to learn the principles of modulation.

The basic mode of instruction in Kodaly's method is singing. Kodaly believed that the voice was the most immediate and personal way of expressing oneself in music. By the use of vocal music the ear could be trained to distinguish intervals and to keep the children in tune. As in the Dalcroze method, this training preceded that of instrumental study. The students were expected to use their voices as carefully as possible. Pure tone and accurate intonation were sought.

The knowledge of rhythmic symbols began with an imitation of the teacher. Soon the students clapped the rhythm of the song or exercise and observed the "rests" with appropriate silences. In Hungary pictorial representations were used to show durations of tones as well as rests. Once the basic pulse was established, quarter note values were learned through singing and hearing, by isolating them in songs, and by representing them by the means of the time name ta and by line notation of the standard quarter note or a stem without notehead. Eighth notes were written in pairs as two stems joined by a ligature. The rhythm patterns were reinforced through pictures and body movements, while half notes were represented by the time name ta-da, dotted half notes by ta-a-a, and whole notes by ta-a-a-a.

Ear-training exercises involved recognizing intervals and distinguishing relationships among scale tones. Children sang silently in their minds in an effort to develop a sense of inner hearing. The first instrument to which a child was exposed was the xylophone with removable bars. Only the bars sol and mi would be used initially while others would be added as those corresponding scale degrees were introduced. Somewhat later the recorder was added. The child would then learn the names of absolute pitches and the corresponding names of lines and spaces on the treble staff.

Kodaly was deeply concerned over the neglect of Hungarian music. In the early years of this century, the influence of German romanticism manifested itself in many parts of Europe, but nationalism as evidenced in Eastern Europe and in France had become a strong and viable alternative to the German cultural blitzkrieg. Hungary had its own music, an art form that went back a thousand years. Musicians sought to preserve this ancient treasure.

Kodaly was numbered among the preservationists, and by 1923 the composer sensed the educational possibilities of using the nation's musical heritage. Kodaly heard a boys' choir singing the *Psalmus Hungarious*. Two years later he heard a group of girl students from a teacher-training college who were learning some music which they in turn planned to teach the children. Kodaly was appalled at the shallow, trivial tunes. At that time he committed himself to establishing the folk song as the basis of music education in the schools of Hungary.

Kodaly devoted himself to arrangements and compositions of

suitable works for school children. On April 2, 1925, performances of *The Straw Guy* and *See the Gipsy* by the Wesselenyi Street Choir created a sensation. In time the composer began to influence English school music; in 1925 Hubert Foss visited Budapest and offered to publish English editions of the works of Kodaly and Bartok by the Oxford University Press.

Kodaly's work gradually reached the United States, and those American music teachers breaking away from progressivism embraced it. To await the "proper" growth period before note reading should be attempted was uncomfortable to teachers who worshipped at the shrine of method and whose self-image as a teacher required a central position in the learning process.

Kodaly's methods return to reading as an important aspect of music teaching. Appreciation is not lost, and teachers concerned with the welfare of children will create the same sensitive educational atmosphere of good feeling that is essential to a "progressive" classroom. The work of Orff and Kodaly should complement one another. A careful balancing of the two approaches should result in a combination of the creative elements of music with a strong conceptual approach as encouraged by Kodaly's emphasis on reading. The American music teacher could find a place for both Orff and Kodaly in the instruction of music.

THE SUZUKI CONTRIBUTION TO INSTRUMENTAL TEACHING

Shinichi Suzuki demonstrated his love for children through the sharing of the violin. He realized that a child learns his mother tongue easily through early and repetitive efforts. He reasoned that children could be taught music at an early age in a similar manner and promptly began to test these ideas with classes of children. His successful experiences in teaching children to play the violin by rote testify to the efficacy of his ideas. His primary goal was to teach young people music, and as a violinist he saw the potential of the violin to achieve this purpose. As the size of these instruments could be made especially small, he was able to teach thousands of children from the age of two to play.

The basic principles of the Suzuki program are "listening, proper techniques, motivation, and reinforcement." Playing by rote will improve a child's musical ear. He will be able to devote his undivided attention to the problems of acquiring a good technical foundation, to learn to play without music, and to be highly motivated to perform the music he has heard so often.

Young children start with four basic technical aspects of violin playing: holding the violin, holding the bow, placing the left hand and fingers, and moving the bow. They learn to hold the violin without support from the left hand and practice muscle-building exercises as they move the bow back and forth in the air. Tapes are placed in the proper places on the violin and the bow to guide the children in acquiring the correct technique. The skills, isolated but learned concurrently, can be learned easily without the hindrance of music reading.

As motivation is important in all learning, Suzuki stresses this in talks with parents. So that the children may learn by example within the home, parents are instructed on the instrument. Initially the child accompanies his parent to the lesson and will normally wish to participate. Realizing the importance of parental attitudes, Suzuki admonishes the parents to compliment the child to encourage his or her progress.

Lessons divide into three sections, focusing on the current piece, some earlier pieces for review, and some preview of new materials. The review pieces are used to promote higher standards, where better intonation, improved tone quality, and emphasis on posture is pursued. Étude material is avoided in the beginning stages, but the children develop technique by repeating sections of the pieces to be learned. The students have a common repertory and hear other children play the pieces they are studying or will study. The group lessons reinforce the social aspects of the experience.

The Suzuki method encourages students to remain in one key for some time in order to develop an accurate sense of pitch. The keys of A major, D major, and G major are similiar enough in their technical application to reinforce one another. The first of Suzuki's books stresses preparation. The child prepares for everything he does such as posture, string changes, and finger placement. The children are encouraged to play strongly for a full tone from the very beginning. Suzuki demonstrates a full, strong sound for the children and asks them to imitate this tone. In Japan the note-reading process is not begun until the child can play the Vivaldi A minor Violin Concerto, but in the United States many violin teachers following the Suzuki concept teach reading earlier. But by the time reading is introduced, the children treat this activity independently and are not concerned with the concurrent introduction of the beginning elements of technique. Suzuki's methods should not be new to America's music educators. Children in the elementary classrooms in this country have been learning songs by rote since the inception of public school music in the nineteenth century. But never have we had a systematic attempt to teach instrumental music by this system. In fact, most instrumental teachers distrusted rote playing, believing it to injure the normal development of an instrumentalist or musician. The musically literate world has recognized the sanctity of the printed page since the time of Beethoven, and any pedagogical system placing its emphasis elsewhere was immediately suspect. The first reform period of the early eighteenth century in this country concerned itself with the "evil" predilection of the populace to improvise on the psalm tunes. The barricades were raised between those followers of the popular art forms and those devotees of "serious" music that required the reading of notes as an initiation rite. Suzuki succeeded in healing this schism and has bestowed the rote concept with a new dignity.

American music educators may now make a virtue of playing by ear when sensitivity to tone and tonality may be more easily discerned. Note reading can follow the pattern of language learning—first the speaking knowledge, then the symbolization.

CHAPTER XX

An Acceptance of Diversity

1950-1970

THE 1950s showed many manifestations of the progressive movement. Children were seen as individuals, and many school systems introduced flexible curricula with the expectation that students would elect courses and experiences commensurate with their interests and abilities. Music education could prosper under such an approach, and that it did so in certain areas under good instruction cannot be doubted. A teacher shortage became acute as the rising birthrate disturbed all predictions of needed fa cilities and teachers. The ranks of the traditionally underpaid teachers became depleted as many able teachers deserted the profession for more lucrative occupations.

In the 1950s it was accepted that the classroom teacher would have to assist in the instruction of elementary music. Elaborate programs were outlined in the music series books to help the classroom teacher continue instruction initiated by the music specialist. If the classroom teacher could not sing adequately, a record was provided. But as music is ultimately an art requiring a high degree of skill, not only for its execution but also for its teaching, the results achieved in this fashion were modest.

In the 1940s and into the 1950s the prevailing philosophy was that learning was best accomplished if taken from ordinary life. The curriculum often centered around integrated units or "problems" courses. In this way could the various areas of study be related, a plan of study now termed "interdisciplinary." The influence of the progressives was strong, and the voices of those critical of the theories of John Dewey were muted.

With the launching of Sputnik a reaction against the progressive philosophy followed quickly. America had not produced a sufficient quantity of engineers and scientists. Too many high school students were passing their years in easy courses. Their high school diplomas were suspect. It is not surprising that the American public again blamed its schools, and this time the blame was placed clearly at the steps of the then-prevailing philosophy—progressivism. In its accustomed manner, American education responded to the needs and emotions of the time, and science instruction received an immediate infusion of both interest and money. There were threats to existing music programs, but hindsight shows those intimidations mild compared with the educational upheavals of the 1970s. The philosophical differences of opinion were then softened by a general augmentation of financial support for educational programs.

But certain aspects of progressivism had acted as an embarrassment to music educators at this time. The skillful management of a "progressive" classroom, whether under the tutelage of Pestalozzi or the modern euphemism "open school," requires special skills on the part of the teacher. When measurable learning did not take place, an inferior teacher could use the activity itself to camouflage an educationally ineffective game. For music education to hold a respectable place in the educational hierarchy, it had to assume the mantle of an academic discipline.

As music as a part of the curriculum was challenged, it became evident to the leaders of the profession that those reasons given for the inclusion of music as a regular course of study were tenuous. If music were to survive as a school subject, the many ancillary reasons for its support so often put forth by music educators would have to be replaced by a careful philosophy based upon the recognition that our children were entitled to instruction in a viable art form. Instruction in music would need to assume a new dignity. The music education profession would have no time for disputes over method. The debate over learning by rote or by reading became of secondary importance to the survival of the art as a school subject. As our educational philosophies often mirror society's expectations, it became incumbent upon the leaders of music education to suggest that music be treated as an academic discipline. Yet, the profession accepted the idea of academic values in music with some misgivings. As attitudes and feeling for an art form are important to its understanding, the mere reiteration of information about music was treated with skepticism.

The Music Educators National Conference (MENC) played an important role in the communication of ideas that the profession felt responded to the needs of American society. In the early 1950s the MENC promoted a study of music in American education. The program was established in the administration of President Marguerite V. Hood and continued under President Ralph E. Rush. Committees deliberated and results were disseminated through the *Music Educators Journal*. The vast amount of material, however, called for the publication of a source book, *Music in American Education: Music Education Source Book Number Two*. The aim of this volume was to stimulate contributions from a wide selection of music educators to obtain disparate views on a number of problems in the profession. The first and major part of this study dealt with the music education curriculum, followed by a consideration of the professional and public relations responsibilities of the music educator. The study attempted to show the various aspects of music for childhood as well as the nature of instrumental music in the schools. The scope of the book represented a considerable expansion over the previous work of the conference. Edited by Hazel Nohavec Morgan, the book, in its extensive approach, depth of detail, and quality of writing, reflected a general improvement over earlier publications of the conference.[1]

Marguerite V. Hood had high hopes that such a publication would stimulate an improvement in music teaching in America. She told the nation's music teachers that doing an "increasingly good job" at improving America's musicality was not enough. One of the responsibilities of the profession would be to "assume leadership and to take the initiative in making plans and setting standards."[2] She admonished the profession to take initiatives rather than react to problems. Hood told the profession to prepare itself for the role of leader, to become knowledgeable about the general problems of education, to be able to discuss music intelligently with professional musicians, and, finally, to understand general culture and what it can mean to music educators. It was a call to action.

In 1954, under the title of "Music in American Life," ten commissions were organized by MENC in an effort to improve the range of activities of the conference. The commissions included the following: Basic Concepts in Music Education; Standards of Music Literature and Performance; Music in General School Administration; Music in Preschool, Kindergarten, and Elementary School; Music in Junior High School; Music in Senior High School; Music in Higher Education; Music in the Community; Music in Media and Mass Communications; and Accreditation and Certification. The stated purposes of the commissions were to study the various areas of music education that concerned the profession. Publications and special sessions at meetings focused attention on problems in the hope of providing solutions. As a result of these activities, a number of publications emerged that were destined to have considerable importance during the next decade.

Among these publications were *Basic Concepts in Music Education*, volume I of the *Fifty-sixth Yearbook of the National Society for the Study of Education*; *Music for Fours and Fives*; *Music in Everyday Living and Learning*; *Singing in the Schools*; *Music Teachers and Public Relations*; *Art in a Changing America*; and *Music Education in a Changing World*.

Basic Concepts in Music Education was the most significant publication during this period. Its interdisciplinary approach brought together the fields of psychology, sociology, philosophy, and aesthetics. The writing was highly creative, representing the profession of music education in its most mature form. Music educators had for too long been preoccupied with the daily aspects of teaching. The practical activities now required a stronger psychological and philosophical rationale on which judgments and methodology could be based. The book attempted to bring theory and practice closer together.

Art in a Changing America represented a personal statement of the committee chairman, Max Kaplan. He concerned himself with the arts in American education and arts as a totality within the framework of American society. He discussed the arts as they were affected by societal influences. Looking at social change, leisure, and art, he noted that the rapid change in society could not help but affect the arts to the point that teacher training should include blends of social psychology, sociology, and social sciences. Kaplan looked to the research techniques of the social sciences—such as the analysis of small groups, sociometric patterns, and interpersonal relations—to effect a practical improvement of music education. His emphasis on the social sciences, with the thought of developing different attitudes on the part of America's music teachers, opened new areas of research in music education.

Among the problems investigated by the profession in the late 1950s was the quality of music performance. At the same time, the profession debated "balance" versus diversity in the music education curriculum. Teachers were to take more interest in music in the general education program. A sensitivity to the idea of individuality expressed itself in many statements concerning an institutionalized failure to meet the needs of all students. Music educators were admonished through articles in the *Music Educators Journal* to note the growing importance in American society of science, which would take an ever-increasing role in the school curriculum.[3]

The threat of Soviet scientific superiority, exemplified by the launching of Sputnik, strongly influenced American curricular development, which in turn affected education. As schools reemphasized the sciences, school administrators were invited to publish articles in the *Music Educators Journal* concerning the values of music in the schools. Music educators needed that assurance and the public had to be reminded again that human values could best be attained through the arts. At the convention of the American Society of School Administrators in 1959, concern was expressed about the creative arts in American education. This group passed a resolution firmly supporting the arts in the schools of America. With this confirmation the crisis as perceived by the music education profession seemed to subside.[4]

But much good came in response to this threat. The older arguments in defense of music education now seemed hollow and no longer serviceable. The argument that music could promote democratic living, health, profitable leisure, and improved human relations now seemed counterproductive and could only relegate the study of music to the curricular sidelines.

Bennett Reimer expressed this concern in an article in the *Music Educators Journal* of 1957 when he observed that a discussion of the values of music to our society must contain something unique to the art, not something that was equally applicable to any other field.[5] He advocated enlightened human choices in terms of world goals rather than a stance that simply pitted art against technological advance.

The Russian threat made its mark. The American public put a new premium on the education of the capable student, and in the late 1950s our national survival appeared to rest on scientific and technical competition with the Soviet Union, a viewpoint still part of our national consciousness. During the first half of the century the academically talented student was underprivileged. The prevailing belief was that this child could learn without much assistance. The traditional American disdain and fear of the intellectual also figured in this outlook.

The National Education Association, aided by the Carnegie Foundation of New York, organized a project to propose more suitable programs for gifted students. In 1958 it issued *The Identity and Education of the Academically Talented Student in American Education.*[6]

The music education profession soon responded to the challenge, and in June 1960 a three-member committee consisting of William C. Hartshorn, Wiley L. Housewright, and Eleanor Tipton made a report later published as *Music for the Academically Talented Student in the Secondary School.* It was a guide for the development of a music program for the upper 20 percent of students attending American secondary schools. It attempted to define the intellectual difference that would require a special program. Greater depth and breadth of content would be required, with the learner free to develop insights, to see relationships, and to establish independent values.[7]

As a direct by-product of this movement, interest was renewed in the importance of the general music class. In 1962 this emphasis on the nonperforming student was advanced at the national conference by President Allen P. Britton who announced the theme of the conference as "The Study of Music as an Academic Discipline." But the profession did not totally embrace this idea.

Hartshorn attempted to clarify the issues in a speech before the 1962 meeting. The concept of music as an academic discipline would not weaken performance but would strengthen it. Performance would be used for learning, with a better balance achieved between the applied and the historical and theoretical.[8]

As an outgrowth of these forces, a movement emerged aimed at studying music as part of the humanities with particular emphasis on the related arts. Those opposed feared that music would lose its value as an art if the intellectual aspects were studied too deeply. The profession was divided and many began to turn in an oblique direction that appeared a compromise between the two positions. The stage was set to look at the study of music in aesthetic terms.

Aesthetics is a branch of philosophy and hence acceptable to both those interested in the academic nature of music study and those concerned that an excessively academic approach would undermine music as an art. Aesthetics gave music teachers reasons for teaching music but not necessarily reasons to change methods. The reaction against the mere acquisition of facts about music was an important outgrowth of this inquiry.

The profession could look to aesthetics as unique to the arts and yet "academic" in nature. The music educator could have the best of both worlds! But this approach would only provide additional rationale for the study of music in the schools. Little change was evident in the daily methodology of the public school classroom. The earlier references to the aesthetic experience in this decade spoke of music "in the spiritual life of man."[9] Little attempt was made to define the aesthetic experience beyond such generalities with the exception of Bennett Reimer who challenged music educators to put aside their nonmusical objectives and look to aesthetic qualities. He cited the writings of Langer, Dewey, and Jung for support.[10]

The 1962 conference signaled a growing interest in aesthetics, which embraced three themes: the attempts to define the aesthetic qualities of music; the descriptions of the aesthetic experience; and the identification of the aesthetic experience.[11] Suzanne Langer's concept of form as a symbolic communication was much in evidence in the writings of this time, as music seemed a special form of symbolic language that could express the forms of life experience. If this was important in the life of man, it was hence important in education.

E. Thayer Gaston reported that aesthetic sensitivity was one of the senses. It was important for life enrichment. Man has always learned the music of his culture "and still finds it essential to his life."[12] Because of man's need for time and rhythm, children must have music for their normal development.

George L. Duerksen believed that aesthetic sensitivity meant a receptiveness to many different facets of the aesthetic experience. He referred his readers to the sensuous quality of sound and urged sensitivity to the expression of the composer and performer as well as a sensitivity to what was communicated by the music.[13] And Bennett Reimer responded again in mid-decade to the educational needs involved in an aesthetic awareness. He spoke of "perception" and "response." "To experience music without perceiving its nature is a superficial experience." The professional could help develop and refine the individual's perceptions.[14] Reimer advocated the development of concepts and knowledge that pertain directly to music. Students should analyze the content of the music, then perform or actively participate. There was some agreement that little could be done to affect the "feelingful reaction" to the aesthetic event. A clear distinction was attempted between a knowledge of music and a love for it. The former was possible and well within the domain of the schools, while the latter could be hoped for but not universally accomplished.

The academic emphasis of the 1960s led again to an "interdisciplinary" approach, to the integration of knowledge. The increasingly colorful series books dealt with the relationships between the historical, artistic, and scientific subjects along with that of the musical.

The experimentalism of Dewey returning as creativity became important in the education of children. Music educators realized that the essence of musicality was the creative impulse using the raw materials of music itself. Similar to the philosophical tenets of Carl Orff, the creative approach would acquaint the student with the technical and aesthetic aspects of music as well as with the fundamentals of music as an art form.

From June 17 through June 28, 1963, an important seminar was held at Yale University. Attending were thirty-one representatives of our nation's schools and colleges in addition to representatives of the music profession. An extended discussion of the school music curriculum led to the determination that those offerings that had previously been part of the music curriculum were inadequate.

The report of the conference pointed to the failure of music education to develop "the creativity, originality, and individuality needed to deal with the rapid cultural development of the society." Musicality was said to be the prime objective of formal school programs. Musical understanding could best be achieved through knowledge of the structure of music. Structure was said to include melody, harmony, rhythm, and form. The seminar suggested activities that would lead to the goals of performance, listening, ear training, rhythmic movement, and composing with emphasis placed on the individual student.[15] These suggestions underscored those procedures that had been favored by Orff, by Kodaly, and earlier by Jaques-Dalcroze.

An influential book appeared in 1960 by Jerome Bruner called *The Process of Education*.[16] The book synthesized ideas from a 1959 conference sponsored by the National Academy of Sciences which was attended by scientists, scholars, and educators. Aimed at improving teaching of sciences in the schools, the conference coined the oft-repeated statement that "any subject can be taught in some intellectually honest form to any child at any stage of development." The idea grew that children were more musically able than had been otherwise believed. The profession was admonished to examine the structure of music and base its educative process on this structure. Many believed that skills of musical composition could be taught at an earlier age than had commonly been the practice. Bruner's interest in the spiral curriculum was examined in many articles of the *Music Educators Journal*, with their authors imperfectly aware of the older growth and development theories that had been propounded by James Mursell a generation before. It was now believed that young listeners could hear complex music and, even with an imperfect understanding, appreciate it at various levels of sophistication. The "discovery method" was appropriate for the development of independence in the musical experience.

New ideas influenced the training of teachers. The Seminar on Comprehensive Musicianship advocated that potential music teachers be able to teach the theoretical and historical studies and relate them to performance.[17] There appeared to be a subtle shift toward the middle of the decade toward an emphasis on "musicality" rather than on a purely academic or aesthetic view.

In 1967 a symposium was convened at Tanglewood by MENC in cooperation with the Theodore Presser Foundation, the Berkshire Music Center, and the Boston University School of Fine and Applied Arts. Scientists, labor leaders, musicians, sociologists, educators, and representatives of corporations, foundations, and government attended the conference to discuss "Music in American Society."

The assemblage noted a need to revise elementary music instruction so that the substance and structure of music could be emphasized. The time-honored curriculum of singing, playing, reading, creating, and moving was to be retained, but a study of structure and substance of music would lead to an awareness of music as an art form. The music specialist, and not the classroom teacher, should be entrusted with this responsibility. The existing polyglot in the general music classes of the junior high schools was to be replaced by a curriculum that would stimulate the intellectual and the emotive aspects of music.

The contemporary literature of a society almost two-thirds of the way through the twentieth century would receive more attention. In addition, the musical contributions of Asia and Africa would be recognized. No longer would it be possible to look exclusively toward Europe. The American ideal of a pluralistic society demanded a recognition of the musical and artistic contributions of all peoples of the world.

The 1967 Tanglewood symposium called on the profession:

• to clarify and define music in the society and in education
• to explore the mutual concerns and possible means of cooperation with the social institutions responsible for the development of music within the society
• to prepare statements and publications that would clarify objectives and programs in music education and that would assist administrators, supervisors, and teachers.

Toward the end of the 1960s it became increasingly apparent that there was too much divergence between "school music" and what the children listened to outside school. It became necessary to examine the dichotomy between the music taught in the schools and the societies' music. The country's struggle for racial equality could not overlook the Afro-American contributions to America's music. As schools became desegregated, the curricula began to reflect the cultural diversity of the school populations. Music educators now began to teach jazz. As David P. McAllester said,

The popular music of our youth embodies high art and a content, both cultural and aesthetic, that must inevitably receive serious attention from the entire musical community. I include blues, jazz, folk music, . . . and

. . . rock. Financially, and in the size of its audiences, it is the dominant music of our era. . . . It should be a stirring thing for anyone concerned with the arts to see the social and aesthetic force of this music. . . . An analysis of rhythm, cadence, fugue, of variation, when made with music that our students instantly respond to, ensures that it is an analysis they will be interested in and will remember.[18]

A growing recognition of the importance of music in society went hand in hand with a growing involvement by the federal government in the arts. The year 1963 marked the building of Lincoln Center for the Performing Arts. Interest in the arts by the Kennedy administration and later by the Johnson administration acted as a catalyst in focusing the attention of the profession on its social responsibility.

In 1961, Secretary of Labor Arthur Goldberg intervened in the Metropolitan Opera strike. A year later the appointment of August Heckscher as special consultant to the president on the state of the arts and humanities was a symbol of the importance of the arts in American society. Kennedy's appointment of an Advisory Panel on the Arts reinforced the commitment.

In 1965 the National Foundation on the Arts and Humanities Act was passed by Congress. And the same year the National Endowment for the Arts supported research and the improvement of education in the arts. That same year the Elementary and Secondary Education Act passed with its enormous potential for the development of music education. The profession was now cognizant of its role in perpetuating the cultural heritage of the country. School children were to receive an education in those values that had proved their worth in our culture.

CHAPTER XXI

Conclusion

T HE STUDY of the forces that influence an art and its instruction is a continuous process. While the attraction of music is universal, sophisticated understanding of it requires instruction. The more subtle forms of the art are often lost when not learned formally. In New England, during the age of the singing school, many people in that relatively homogeneous society elected to take music instruction. But for instruction to be universal in a pluralistic society it is necessary to teach the art in the public schools.

In the mid-nineteenth century, as the curricula of the schools began to expand, instruction in music was included along with art, geography, science, and, later, manual training. Music was the interloper then as well as now. It has always required a defense. It is axiomatic that mankind can survive without the arts although it is equally clear that endurance is the least common denominator in a society that expects more from itself than mere survival. A sense of human grace requires ultimately the recognition of the importance of the arts.

In an historical sense, it is difficult to evaluate teaching methodology and make significant generalizations about its efficacy or universality. Americans developed an education not altogether concerned with doctrine or strict methodology. Its eclecticism was brought about in part by diversity and by a need to adapt to a new environment. Instruction with this disparity of method did not always succeed. Results varied from the time of the introduction of music into the public schools in the third decade of the nineteenth century to the present day with the expansion of music education into the areas of instrumental music, music appreciation, *a cappella* choral music, and that coalescence of older ideas—the Orff and Kodaly approaches to creativity and music reading.

But our society has deemed that instruction in music is important. The art is too complex to be left to chance. It is the function of culture to transmit to the young those qualities that seem important to the elders or tastemakers of that society. The more complex the society, the more schooling is necessary to produce a functioning member of that society. Thus, schooling in the Western world must be long and formalized. If our art music is deemed worthy of perpetuation, our schools become the natural instrument for its accomplishment.

The music education profession should not be ignorant of its past efforts and accomplishments. It is important to be able to separate sound ideas from those that have been found wanting. Without an historical framework educators are sentenced to lifetimes of errant travel, "flying Dutchmen" of the curricular processes, attempting various approaches to solve our educational problems once and for all.

Education in the United States has often been recognized by articulate contemporaries in each generation as being in a less than healthy condition. From the first reform in music education in the early eighteenth century, our erstwhile reformers confidently predicted educational salvation if only the "present practices" were put aside. The people seemed destined to be deprived of their art, and the public schools were recommended as places where European musical culture could and should be preserved.

No sooner had music entered the curricula of the public schools than a concern arose regarding method. How important was it that children learn to read notes? Then as now, American educators could not find a universally acceptable answer.

The arts have always found acceptance difficult in America. It should not be surprising that this country's suspicion of the artist should manifest itself in a jaundiced view of the arts as a subject to be taught in the public schools. In a country that prides itself on its egalitarian democracy, the practice of "classical" music or the refined arts smacks of the aristocracy, a class to which America has never admitted.

The introduction of the arts into the public schools required a rationalization. Not often accepted on their own terms, the arts were introduced and defended for ancillary reasons. But the defenders of some of the early introductions argued well and spoke convincingly. Some spoke of the musical advantages the churches would reap if music were taught in the schools. What an exciting discovery to see that children could be taught music at a time when it was widely perceived that children had no such capability.

The history of music education in the United States has shown that the educational climate in America reflected other sociological and political events. Educators lead society only with difficulty, if at all. It is more usual for the schools to reflect those ideas already endorsed by the society they serve. Music continues to be taught in the schools, most often under duress with a continuous need to defend and rationalize its existence. It is most difficult to evaluate the quality of this instruction, and certainly beyond the intention of this study. But each year a percentage of American people attend concerts and collect records, showing a predilection for music that requires some previous exposure. It is reasonable to assume that without instruction in the schools, the number of Americans showing an awareness of art music would be substantially reduced.

Music is defined variously for different people, but it is apparent that the need for music is all but universal. The arguments about musical taste will continue, and these discussions will take place in the schools as well as our concert halls. But that music in some form will continue to be taught cannot be doubted, and a principal place for this instruction will most likely be the public schools. The public will again look toward its schools to ensure the intellectual and cultural continuity that a sophisticated society requires. Reflecting the economic problems of the 1970s and 1980s, the entire educational establishment has taken to the barricades. It is difficult to discuss educational methodology when survival is at stake. While the future of the profession is impossible to predict, it may be reasonably said that the teaching of music (or any of the arts) will always be an undertaking laced with nobility.

Notes

CHAPTER I

1. Waldo S. Pratt, *Music of the Pilgrims* (Boston: Oliver Ditson Co., 1921), p. 6.
2. Ibid., p. 16.
3. Gilbert Chase, *America's Music* (New York: McGraw-Hill Book Co., 1955), p. 17.
4. Pratt, *Music of the Pilgrims*, p. 8.
5. Ibid., p. 10.
6. Ibid., p. 13.
7. Gustav Reese, *Music in the Renaissance* (New York: W. W. Norton Co., 1959), p. 796.
8. Percy Scholes, *The Puritans and Music in England and New England* (London: Oxford University Press, 1934).
9. Ibid., p. 51.
10. In 1539 a German printer sent a press to Mexico to be operated by an Italian. There over 200 imprints were produced eighty-one years before New England was colonized. Samuel Eliot Morison, *The Intellectual Life of Colonial New England* (New York: New York University Press, 1956), p. 113.
11. Thomas Prince brought out this edition.
12. For an interesting discussion of the possibility that an edition of the *Bay Psalm Book* previous to the ninth edition contained music see Irving Lowens, *Music and Musicians in Early America* (New York: W. W. Norton and Co., 1964).
13. This edition was printed in Boston by B. Green and J. Allen, for Michael Perry, under the West End of the Town House, 1698.
14. Irving Lowens, *Music and Musicians in Early America* (New York: W. W. Norton and Co., 1964), p. 34.
15. Scholes, *Puritans and Music*, p. 69.
16. Samuel Sewell, *Diary* (New York: Macy-Masius, 1927), p. 506.
17. W. S. B. Mathews, ed., *A Hundred Years of Music in America* (Chicago: G. L. Howe, 1889), p. 11.
18. See J. Spencer Curwen, *Studies in Music Worship*, first series (London: J. Curwen and Sons, 1888).
19. Scholes, *Puritans and Music*, p. 264.
20. John Cotton, *Singing of Psalms: a Gospel Ordinance* (London: 1647), p. 62.
21. Walter L. Woodfill, *Musicians in English Society from Elizabeth to Charles I* (Princeton, N.J.: Princeton University Press, 1953), p. 157.
22. Chase, *America's Music*, p. 15.
23. Thomas Symmes, *The Reasonableness of Regular Singing, or Singing by Note* (Boston: B. Green for Samuel Garrish, 1720).
24. Ibid.
25. Mathews, *A Hundred Years of Music*, p. 17.

CHAPTER II

1. Later published in three parts, cantos, medius, and basses, the treble part published only in the 1st, 2nd, and 4th editions. J. H. Butler, "John Tufts, Aurora Unaware," *Music Educators Journal* 35 (January 1969): 46.

2. Frank Metcalf, *American Writers and Compilers of Sacred Music* (New York: The Abingdon Press, 1925), p. 16.

3. Ibid.

4. Clifford K. Seboley, *Harvard Graduates, 1690–1755* (Boston: Massachusetts Historical Society, 1933–1965), V, p. 413.

5. Justin Walker, ed., *The Memorial Society of Boston* (Boston: Tichner, 1880, 1881), II, p. 317.

6. Thomas Walter, *Grounds and Rules of Musick Explained* (Boston: J. Franklin for S. Garrish, 1721), p. 2.

7. Ibid., p. 4.

8. Ibid., p. 5.

9. Metcalf, *American Writers*, p. 19.

10. Ibid.

11. Ibid., p. 21.

12. Thomas Walter, *The Sweet Psalmist of Israel* (Boston: J. Franklin for S. Garrish, 1722).

13. Walter L. Woodfill, *Musicians in English Society from Elizabeth to Charles I* (Princeton, N.J.: Princeton University Press, 1953), p. 144.

14. Ibid., p. 151.

15. Ibid.

16. Ibid., p. 152.

17. Timothy Dwight, *Travels in New England and New York*, as quoted in June Mussey, *Yankee Life By Those Who Lived It* (New York: Alfred A. Knopf, 1947), p. 140.

18. John, V. D. S. and Caroline R. Merrill, *Sketches of Historic Bennington* (Cambridge: Riverside Press, 1911), p. 57.

19. *Notes on Bennington History*, compiled from various sources, principally the Day Papers, III, University of Vermont Library (1926), 171; and *Bennington Banner*, April 12, 1866, in *Notes on Bennington History*, p. 171.

20. Silas Leroy Blake, *The Later History of the First Church of Christ* (New London: Day Publishing Co., 1900), p. 229.

21. S. P. Cheney, "Moses Cheney," *The Vermont Historical Gazeteer*, ed. Abby Maria Hemenway (Burlington, Vt.: The Author, 1871), 1:419.

22. Ibid., p. 420.

23. Moses Cheney, "Letter to Friend Mason," *Musical Visitor*, Vol. 2, No. 17 (December 1, 1841), 132–133, and No. 18 (January 1, 1842), 139–140. Boston: Published by an Association of Gentlemen, Kidder & Wright, Printers, 1841–1842.

24. Ibid.

25. Ibid., p. 139.

26. Joseph Tenny, *The Gamut or Scale of Music* (Windsor, VT.: 1795).

27. Cheney to Mason, p. 139.

28. George Pullen Jackson, *White Spirituals in the Southern Uplands* (New York: Dover Publications, Inc., 1965), pp. 4, 8; Allen P. Britton, *Theoretical Introductions in American Tune Books to 1800* (Ph.D. diss., University of Michigan, 1949), p. 205; Alan C. Buechner, *Yankee Singing Schools and the Golden*

Age of Choral Music in New England, 1760–1800 (Ed.D. diss., Harvard University, 1960), p. 253; and Hamilton C. MacDougall, *Early New England Psalmody, 1620–1820* (Brattleboro, N.H.: Stephen Daye Press, 1940), p. 39.

29. Cheney to Mason, December 11, 1841, p. 132.

30. Ibid.

31. Ibid.

32. Henry Swan Dana, *History of Woodstock, Vermont* (Boston: Houghton Mifflin Co., 1889), pp. 220–21.

33. Ibid., p. 222.

34. Ibid., from a story told to Dana by Job Richmond.

35. William Tans'ur, *A New Musical Grammar* (London: Jacob Robinson, 1746); and "New Introduction to the Grounds of Music" and *American Chorister* (Boston: Ecles and Gill, 1770).

36. J. Murray Barbour, *The Church Music of William Billings*, p. 43, quoted in Robert Murrell Stevenson, *Protestant Church Music in America* (New York: W. W. Norton and Co., 1966), p. 60.

37. Charles Seeger, "Contrapuntal Style in the Three-Voice Shape-Note Hymns," *Musical Quarterly*, 26, no. 4 (October 1940), 483.

38. Irving Lowens, "The Origins of the American Fuging Tune," *Journal of the American Musicological Society*, 6 (Spring 1953), 51.

39. Simon Jocelyn and Amos Doolittle, *Chorister's Companion* (New Haven: T. and S. Green, 1782), p. 1.

40. Harriet Beecher Stowe, *Poganuc People* (Boston: Houghton Mifflin Co., 1884), p. 73; and Frederick Holbrook, "Address at the Congregationalist's Jubilee," *Annals of Brattleboro*, ed. Mary R. Cabot (Brattleboro, Vt.: E. L. Hildreth & Co., 1921), p. 337.

41. Reverend E. H. Sears, "History of the Oxford Singing School," *Dwight's Journal of Music*, 18, no. 15 (January 12, 1861), 331.

42. Hiel Hollister, *Pawlet for One Hundred Years* (Albany: J. Munsell, 1867), p. 70.

43. Asahel Benham, *Federal Harmony* (Middletown: Moses H. Woodward, 1795), p. 13.

CHAPTER III

1. Jacob Kimball, *Rural Harmony* (Boston: Thomas and Andrews, 1793).

2. Thomas Walter, *Grounds and Rules of Musick Explained* (Boston: J. Franklin for S. Garrish, 1721), p. 15.

3. Andrew Law, ed., *The Musical Magazine* (Cheshire: W. Law, 1792), pp. 2–3.

4. Andrew Adgate, *Rudiments of Music*, 3rd ed. (Philadelphia: John M'Culloch), quoted in Allen P. Britton, "Theoretical Introductions in American Tune Books to 1800" (Ph.D. diss., University of Michigan, 1949), p. 196.

5. Britton, "Theoretical Introductions," p. 200.

6. Walter, *Grounds and Rules*, p. 18.

7. W. L. Already, *A Supplement to the New Version of the Psalms* (London, 1708).

8. Jeremiah Ingalls, *Christian Harmony* (Exeter, N.H.: Henry Ranlet, 1805).

9. Ibid.

10. Asahel Benham, *Federal Harmony* (Middletown: Moses H. Woodward, 1795).

11. Thomas Atwill, *New York and Vermont Collection of Sacred Harmony*,

2d ed. (Albany: The Author, 1804); and Joel Harmon, *The Columbian Sacred Minstrel* (Northampton: A. Wright, 1809), pp. XIII, XI.

12. Britton, "Theoretical Introductions," p. 240.

13. See Gram with Holyoke and Holden, *Massachusetts Compiler*, p. XXIX.

14. Britton, "Theoretical Introductions," p. 211.

15. Samuel Sewell, *Diary* (New York: Macy-Masius, 1927), I, p. 351 and II, p. 151.

16. Stephen Jenks, *Delights of Harmony* (New Haven: Printed and Engraved for the Purchaser, 1805).

17. Samuel Holyoke, *The Columbian Repository* (Exeter, N.H.: Henry Ranlet, 1802).

18. Solomon Howe, *Farmer's Evening Entertainment* (Northampton: A. Wright, 1804).

19. Andrew Law, *Select Harmony* (New Haven: Thomas and Samuel Green, 1779).

20. John W. Moore, *The Vocal and Instrumental Self-Instructor* (Bellows Falls, Vt.: The Author, 1843).

21. Law, *Select Harmony*.

22. Eric Blom, ed., *Groves Dictionary of Music and Musicians*, 5th ed., vol. III (New York: St. Martin's Press, Inc., 1955), p. 366.

23. For an excellent detailed study of ornamentation, see Hans Engelke, *A Study of Ornaments in American Tune Books* (Ann Arbor, Mich.: University Microfilms, 1960).

24. Thomas Atwill, *The New York and Vermont Collection*.

25. Tans'ur's information was taken from Robert Barber's *The Psalm Singer's Choice Companion* (1727) and Aaron Williams's *Universal Psalmist*, both important British sources. Information is rare even in British sources.

26. Holyoke, *Columbian Repository*, p. XI.

27. William Billings, *Continental Harmony* (Boston: Thomas and Andrews, 1794), p. xxi.

28. William Tans'ur, *A New Musical Grammar*, 3d ed. (London: Robert Brown for James Hodges, 1756), p. 29.

29. Holyoke, *Columbian Repository*.

30. *Uranian Instruction* (Philadelphia: Young and McCulloch, 1787), p. 10.

31. William Billings, *Singing Master's Assistant: or Key to Practical Music*, 3d ed. (Boston: Draper and Folsom, 1778), p. 11.

32. Stephen Jenks, *Harmony of Zion* (Dedham: The Author, 1818), p. vi; Daniel Read, *Sacred Harmony* (Boston: C. Cambridge, 1790), p. 12; and Simon Jocelyn, *Chorister's Companion*, 2d ed. (New Haven: The Author, 1788), p. 16.

33. Andrew Law, *Harmonic Companion* (Philadelphia: The Author, 1807).

34. Holyoke, *Columbian Repository*, p. xxiv.

35. Oliver Holden, *Union Harmony*, 2d ed. (Boston: Thomas and Andrews, 1796).

36. Jocelyn, *Chorister's Companion*, p. 15.

37. Daniel Read, *New Haven Collection of Sacred Music* (Dedham: Daniel Mann, 1818), p. xi.

38. Jacob Kimball, *Rural Harmony* (Boston: Thomas and Andrews, 1793), p. viii.

39. Billings, *Singing Master's Assistant*; and Daniel Read, *American Singing Book* (New Haven: The Author, 1785).

40. Billings, *Singing Master's Assistant*, p. 7.

41. Solomon Howe, *Worshipper's Assistant* (Northampton: A. Wright, 1799), p. 4.

42. Simon Jocelyn and Amos Doolittle, *Chorister's Companion* (New Haven: T. and S. Green, 1782), p. 11.

43. Daniel Bayley, *A New and Compleat Introduction to the Grounds and Rules of Music* (Newburyport: D. Bayley, 1764), p. 20.

44. James Lyon, *Urania* (Philadelphia, 1761), p. x.

45. Ibid. The *turned shake* can be traced to Purcell's posthumous work of 1696. The table of ornaments from Purcell can be found in Adolph Beyschlag, *Die Ornamentik der Musik*, 2d ed. (Leipzig: Breitkopf and Hartel, 1953). John Walsh reproduced almost all of Purcell's ornaments in his *Harpsichord Master* of 1712. The illustrations for the *turned shake* were passed from Walsh to James Lyon. See Engelke, *A Study of Ornaments*, p. 92.

46. Christopher Simpson, *Division Violist or an Introduction to the Playing Upon a Ground* (London: William Gadbid, 1659).

47. Jocelyn and Doolittle, *Chorister's Companion*, p. 11; and Holyoke, *Columbian Repository*, p. xxiii.

48. Daniel Read, *Columbian Harmonist*, no. 1 (New Haven: The Author, 1793), p. 6.

49. Kimball, *Rural Harmony*, p. viii.

50. Billings, *Singing Master's Assistant*, p. 11.

51. Engelke, *A Study of Ornaments*, p. 138; and Billings, *Singing Master's Assistant*, p. 11.

52. Albert Henry Smyth, *The Writings of Benjamin Franklin*, vol. IV, ed. Carl Van Doren (New York: Macmillan Co., 1905–1907), p. 373.

53. Oliver Loessel, *The Use of Character Notes and other Unorthodox Notations in Teaching the Reading of Music in Northern United States During the Nineteenth Century* (Ann Arbor: University of Michigan, Dissertation, 1959), p. 100.

54. Nathaniel Gould, *History of Church Music in America (1853)*, p. 55, as quoted in George Pullen Jackson, "Buckwheat Notes," *Musical Quarterly*, 19, no. 3 (July 1933), 395.

55. See Jackson for an extended discussion of this area, "Buckwheat Notes."

56. Frank Metcalf, *American Writers and Compilers of Sacred Music* (New York: The Abingdon Press, 1925), p. 72.

57. Richard Crawford, *Andrew Law, American Psalmodist* (Evanston, Ill.: Northwestern University Press, 1968), p. 7.

58. Elias Mann included 110 major tunes and 52 minor in his *Massachusetts Collection* (1807); Daniel Read included 29 major tunes and 18 minor in his *American Singing Book* (4th ed., 1793), quoted in Robert Stevenson, *Protestant Church Music in America* (New York: W. W. Norton and Co., 1966), p. 75.

59. Daniel Wilfred McCormick, "Oliver Holden, Composer and Anthologist," (Ph.D. Diss., Union Theological Seminary, 1963), from *Dissertation Abstracts*, vol. 24, 1963–64, p. 2172.

60. Samuel Gilman, *Memoirs of a New England Village Choir with Occasional Reflections* (Boston: Crosby and Nichols Co., 1828), p. 76.

61. H. Earl Johnson, "Early New England Periodicals Devoted to Music," *Musical Quarterly*, 26, no. 2 (April 1940), 157. Brown was a schoolmaster, singing teacher, and compiler of the *Bridgewater Collection*. He was leader of the Old Colony Musical Society, of Plymouth County, Massachusetts, which was the official sponsor of the *Old Colony Collection*, that was issued in two volumes from

1814–1818. The publication was the first American collection devoted to oratorio music. See Donald Nitz, *Community Musical Societies in Massachusetts to 1840* (Ann Arbor: University Microfilms, 1964); also Donald Nitz, "The Norfolk Musical Society 1814–1820; an Episode in the History of Choral Music in New England," *Journal of Research in Music Education*, vol. 16 (1968), 319–28.

62. From "Essays on Music," The Universal Asylum, and Columbian Magazine, Philadelphia, 4 (March 1790), 181, quoted in Britton, p. 392.

63. For an extended study see Stevenson, *Protestant Church Music.*

64. George Pullen Jackson, *White Spirituals in the Southern Uplands* (New York: Dover Publications, Inc., 1965), p. 21.

CHAPTER IV

1. S. Alexander Rippa, *Education in a Free Society* (New York: David McKay, 1967), p. 15.

2. Samuel Eliot Morison, *The Intellectual Life of Colonial New England* (New York: New York University Press, 1956), p. 63.

3. Norman Arthur Benson, *The Itinerant Dancing and Music Masters of Eighteenth Century America* (Ph.D. diss., University of Minnesota, 1963), p. 22.

4. John Peyton Little, "History of Richmond," *Southern Literary Messenger* XVII (October 1851), 234–36, quoted in Ivan W. Olson, *The Roots and Development of Public School Music in Richmond, Virginia 1782–1907* (Ph.D. diss., University of Michigan, 1964), p. 11.

5. Morison, *The Intellectual Life*, p. 64.

6. Rippa, *Education*, p. 42.

7. Morison, *The Intellectual Life*, p. 67–70. Morison believes that the "Old Deluder Satan" Act was much more than a device to perpetuate Puritanism and quotes the 1648 revision of the act which states "for the better trayning up of youth of this towne, that through God's blessinge they may be fitted for publique service hereafter, either in church or commonweale."

8. William H. Kilpatrick, *The Dutch Schools of New Netherland . . .* (1912), p. 229; quoted in Morison, *The Intellectual Life*, p. 83.

9. Morison, *The Intellectual Life*, p. 70.

10. Ibid., p. 96.

11. Ibid., p. 37.

12. Donald O. Schneider, *Education in Colonial American Colleges, and the Occupations and Political Offices of their Alumni* (Ph.D. diss., George Peabody College for Teachers, 1965).

13. Morison, *The Intellectual Life*, p. 42.

14. Benson, *The Itinerant Dancing*, p. 34.

15. Ibid., p. 42.

16. Ibid., p. 65.

17. *The Journal and Letters of Philip Fithian, 1773–1774: A Plantation Tutor in the Old Dominion*, new ed. (Williamsburg, VA.: Colonial Williamsburg, Inc., 1957), quoted in Benson, *The Itinerant Dancing*, p. 74.

18. Ibid., p. 44. His inventory included a fiddle and harpsichord along with the following music: two sets of Pasquali's Overtures; ten books of Handel Songs; four large sets of Italian songs; six sonatas by Schickard; four books of "Symphonies" [sic] to Handel's Oratorios; *Musical Entertainment*; Lampe's Songs; *Apollo's Feast*, by Handel; Lessons by Nares; Concertos by Avison; six Concerti by Burgess; six Concerti by Hasse; four small books by Stanley; six sonatas by Degeardino; Lampe's *Thorough Bass*; eight Sonatas by Alberti; five

Concerti by Ramesa; two Concerti by Avison; six Concerti by Hepten in seven parts; one Concerto by Avison in seven parts; twelve English Songs by Pasquali; one large book of songs by Palma; Songs in Acis and Galatea, by Handel; Lessons by Alcock; Songs by Grannom; one volume of Felton's Concertos; eight concerti by Avison; Felton's Lessons; Corelli Sonatas in manuscript score; Corelli Sonata no. 13; Leveridge Songs; Songs by Hasse; Catches by Purcell and Blow; Ballads by Grannom; an unbound book of Italian Songs, five large books of concerti and manuscripts; *Harlequin Rangers*; and other loose music.

19. *Pennsylvania Gazette*, July 12, August 2, 1744, quoted in Oscar Sonneck, *Francis Hopkinson and James Lyon* (New York: Da Capo Press, 1967 [original date of publication, 1905]), p. 16.

20. Benson, *The Itinerant Dancing*, p. 128.

21. Marquis de Chastellux, *Travels in North America in the Years 1780, 1781, 1782* (London: G. G. J. and J. Robinson, 1787), II, pp. 187–88, quoted in Benson, p. 127; and Edmund Burke, *An Account of the European Settlements in America* (Dublin: Peter Wilson, 1762), II, p. 251.

22. Printed by John Watts in 1729 and 1731 and containing the popular songs of the day.

23. The city's first theatre production took place in 1703. Later, in 1735, a theatre was built with the cost borne by private subscription. For an extended discussion, see Oscar Sonneck, *Early Opera in America* (New York: G. Schirmer, 1915).

24. Sonneck, *Francis Hopkinson*, p. 17.

25. Quoted in ibid., p. 13.

26. Benson, *The Itinerant Dancing*, p. 237.

27. *Federal Gazette* and *Philadelphia Evening Post*, February 20, 26, 28, 1789.

28. Benson, *The Itinerant Dancing*, p. 211.

29. Ibid., p. 214.

30. Joseph P. Sims, *The Philadelphia Assemblies 1748–49* (Philadelphia: George H. Buchanan, 1947), quoted in ibid., p. 215.

31. Marquis de Chastellux, pp. 315–16; Benson, *The Itinerant Dancing*, p. 216.

32. William Priest, *Travels in the United States of America* (London: J. Johnson, 1802).

CHAPTER V

1. William Boyd, *The History of Western Education* (London: Adam and Charles Black, 1952), p. 281.

2. Ibid., p. 296, quoting Rousseau, *Émile*, book 4, p. 304.

3. Heinrich Pestalozzi, *How Gertrude Teaches Her Children*, ed. Ebenezer Cooks, trans. Lucy Holland and Francis Turner (London: Sonnenschein, 1894), p. 35.

4. Edward H. Reisner, *The Evolution of the Common School* (New York: Macmillan Co., 1930), p. 206.

5. Boyd, *Western Education*, p. 323.

6. Heinrich Pestalozzi, "The Method, a Report by Pestalozzi," in *How Gertrude Teaches*, p. 316.

7. Ibid., p. 143.

8. Heinrich Pestalozzi, *Letters on Early Education Addressed to J. P. Greaves Esq., from Pestalozzi* (London: Sherwood, Gilbert and Piper, 1827), p. 128.

9. Pestalozzi, "Rede An Sein Haus and seinem 74. geburtsgage, den 12 *Jänner*

1818, Samtliche Werke, X, 535, cited in Howard Ellis, *The Influence of Pesta-lozzianism on Instruction in Music* (Ph.D. diss., University of Michigan, 1957), p. 22.

10. Michael Traugott Pfeiffer and Hans Georg Nageli, *Gesangbildungslehre nach Pestalozzischen Grundsatzen* (Zurich: H. G. Nageli, 1810). The *Gesang-bildungslehre* was not the only Pestalozzian text to emerge early in the nineteenth century in Germany. In fact, there were many such texts, some more accurately Pestalozzian than others. But the *Gesangbildungslehre* made its influence felt not only in Germany but also in America, coming to the attention of William C. Woodbridge and Lowell Mason. The detailed description is therefore more ger-mane to our purposes than the study of several other German texts would be.

11. Pestalozzi, *Letters*, p. 114.

12. Will S. Monroe, *History of the Pestalozzian Movement in the United States* (New York: Arno Press and the *New York Times*, [originally, Syracuse, N.Y.: G. W. Bardeen Publishers, 1907]), p. 72.

13. Ibid., p. 52.

14. Joseph Neef, *Sketch of a Plan and Method of Education founded on the Analysis of the human faculties and natural reason, fitted for the offspring of a free people and of all rational beings* (Philadelphia: The Author, 1808).

15. Ibid., p. 137.

16. *Transactions of the Fourth Annual Meeting of the Western Literary Insti-tute, and College of Professional Teachers, held in Cincinnati, October 1834* (Cincinnati: Josiah Drake, 1834), p. 241.

17. See Robert W. John, "Elam Ives and the Pestalozzian Theory of Music Ed-ucation," *Journal of Research in Music Education*, 8 (1960), 45–50.

18. William C. Woodbridge, "On Vocal Music as a Branch of Common Edu-cation," *American Annals of Education and Instruction*, 3 (1833), 200.

19. Elam Ives, *Manual of Instruction in the Art of Singing* (Philadelphia: American Sunday School Union, 1831), p. 3.

20. Quoted in Ellis, *The Influence*, p. 146.

21. Lowell Mason, *Normal Singer* (New York: Mason Brothers, 1856), p. ii.

22. Ellis, *The Influence*, p. 147.

23. Augusta Peabody, *The Child's Book for the Use of Schools and Families* (Boston: Richardson, Lord, and Holbrook, 1830).

CHAPTER VI

1. Edgar W. Knight, *Education in the United States* (Boston: Ginn and Co., 1929), p. 156.

2. Sidney L. Jackson, *America's Struggle for Free Schools* (New York: Russell and Russell, 1965), p. 12.

3. Knight, *Education*, p. 154.

4. From a story told by Mason to Thayer and published in the latter's article, "Lowell Mason," *Dwight's Journal of Music*, 39 (November 22, 1879), 186–87; and 39 (December 6, 1879), 195–96.

5. From Lowell Mason, *An Address on Church Music, delivered July 8, 1851, in Boston* (New York: Mason and Law, 1851).

6. *Juvenile Psalmist; or The Child's Introduction to Sacred Music.* Prepared at the request of the "Boston Sabbath School Union" (Boston: Richardson, Lord, and Holbrook, 1829).

7. Lowell Mason, *The Boston Handel and Haydn Society Collection of Church Music* (Boston: Richardson, Lord, and Holbrook, 1831).

8. Lowell Mason, *Manual of the Boston Academy of Music, for Instruction in the Elements of Vocal Music on the System of Pestalozzi*. (Boston: Carter, Hendee and Co., 1834.)

9. Ibid., chapter I.

10. Ibid.

11. Ibid.

12. *Anleitung zum Gesang-Unterrichte in Schulen*, or Guide to the Study of Singing in Schools (Stuttgart: J. B. Metzler schen Buchhandlung, 1826).

13. See Howard Ellis, *The Influence of Pestalozzianism on Instruction in Music* (Ph.D. diss., University of Michigan, 1957), p. 173ff for an extended study.

14. Mason, *Manual*.

15. See Thayer, "Lowell Mason"; Samuel A. Eliot, "Music in America," *North American Review*, 52 (April 1841), 330–31, reported in Arthur Lawndes Rich, *Lowell Mason* (Chapel Hill: The University of North Carolina Press, 1946); Henry Barnard, ed., "Educational Labors of Lowell Mason," *American Journal of Education*, IV, 141; and M. B. Scanlon, "Pioneer Music Masters," *Music Educators Journal*, XXV, 20.

16. Thayer, "Lowell Mason"; and Theodore F. Seward, "Dr. Lowell Mason," *The New York Musical Gazette*, VI (September 1872), 129–30.

17. Eliot, "Music in America," 320–38.

18. Thayer described Webb as "a fine English musician, long his friend [Mason's] and coadjutor." Thayer, "Lowell Mason" (December 6, 1879), 195.

19. Frank Damrosch, "Music in the Public Schools," *The American History and Encyclopedia of Music*, VII (Toledo, Ohio: The Squire Cooley Co., 1910), p. 21.

20. J. Baxter Upham, "Vocal Music as a Branch of Education in Our Common Schools," American Institute of Instruction, *Papers and Proceedings* (1973), p. 162, quoted in Rich, *Lowell Mason*, p. 17.

21. Eliot, "Music in America," 332.

22. Quoted in Edward Bailey Birge, *History of Public School Music in the United States* (Boston: Oliver Ditson Co., 1928), pp. 49–50.

23. Groves Dictionary American Supplement, p. 334.

24. Boston Academy of Music, *Annual Reports*, VII (1839), 12–13.

25. Samuel L. Fluecker, "Why Lowell Mason Left the Boston Schools," *Music Educators Journal*, XXII, no. 4 (February 1936), p. 20.

26. Ibid.

27. Ibid., p. 24.

28. Ibid., p. 23.

29. Richard Lee James, *A Survey of Teacher Training Programs in Music from the Early Musical Convention to the Introduction of the Four Year Curricula* (Ph.D. diss., University of Maryland, 1968), p. 21.

30. *Boston Musical Gazette*, 1838; quoted in ibid., p. 27.

31. George F. Root, *The Story of a Musical Life* (Cincinnati: The John Church Co., 1891), p. 29.

32. "Woodbury and Baker's Class," *American Journal of Music and Musical Visitor*, 4 (August 26, 1845), 107.

33. "Western Musical Conventions," *New York Musical Review and Gazette*, 7 (July 26, 1856), 232.

34. John Sullivan Dwight, "Editorial," *Dwight's Journal of Music* I (August 14, 1852), 150.

35. Ibid.

36. Henry S. Perkins, "The Musical Convention: Its utility and its abuse," *Official Report of the Eleventh Annual Meeting of the Music Teachers National Association* (Indianapolis, Ind.: M.T.N.A., 1887), 209.

37. Western Vermont Musical Association, *Records*, 1858.

38. Burlington, Vt. *Free Press*, January 5, 1859.

39. Burlington, Vt. *Free Press*, October 29, 1859.

40. Lowell Mason, *Hallelujah* (Boston: Oliver Ditson and Co., 1854).

41. Ivan Walter Olson, Jr., *The Roots of Public School Music in Richmond, Virginia, 1782–1907* (Ph.D. diss., University of Michigan, 1964), p. 24.

42. John Peyton Little, "History of Richmond," *Southern Literary Messenger*, XVII (October 1851), 132, quoted in Ivan Olson, "Music and Germans in Nineteenth Century Richmond," *Journal of Research in Music Education*, no. 1 (Spring 1960), 28.

CHAPTER VII

1. John Peyton Little, "History of Richmond," *Southern Literary Messenger*, XVII (October 1851), 234–36, quoted in Ivan Olson, "Music and Germans in Nineteenth Century Richmond," *Journal of Research in Music Education*, no. 1 (Spring 1960), 28.

2. C. Van Woodward, *Origins of the New South, 1877–1913* (Baton Rouge: Louisiana State University Press, 1951); also *A History of the South*, vol. 9, ed. Wendell Holmes Stephenson and E. Merton Coulter (1959), p. 61.

3. S. Alexander Rippa, *Education in a Free Society* (New York: David McKay, 1967), p. 138.

4. William Dabney, *Universal Education in the South*, I (Chapel Hill: University of North Carolina Press, 1936), p. 302.

5. Edgar W. Knight, *Education in the United States* (Boston: Ginn and Co., 1929), p. 466.

6. Johann Friedrich Herbart, *Brief Encyclopedia of Practical Philosophy*, trans. Robert Ulrich in Robert Ulrich, ed., *Three Thousand Years of Educational Wisdom: Selections from Great Documents*, 2d ed. (Cambridge: Harvard University Press, 1965), p. 511.

7. Johann Fredrich Herbert, *The Science of Education: Its General Principle Deduced from Its Aims*, trans. Henry M. and Emmie Felkin (Boston: D. C. Heath and Co., 1895), p. 126.

8. Rippa, *Education*, p. 180.

9. A. Theodore Tellstrom, *Music in American Education, Past and Present* (New York: Holt, Rinehart, and Winston, 1971), pp. 59 and 79.

10. Rippa, *Education*, p. 172.

11. Herbert Spencer, *Education: Intellectual, Moral, and Physical* (New York: D. Appleton and Co., 1897), p. 115.

12. Ibid., p. 61.

13. Ibid., p. 78.

14. Ibid., p. 76.

15. Ibid., p. 74.

16. Ibid., p. 72.

17. Ibid., p. 109.

CHAPTER VIII

1. Edward H. Reisner, *The Evolution of the Common School* (New York: Macmillan Co., 1930), p. 316.

2. Gordon E. Fouts, "Music Instruction in the Education of American Youth: The Early Academies," *Journal of Research in Music Education*, XX (Winter 1972), 471.

3. John Poor, *A Collection of Psalms and Hymns Affixed for the Use of the Young Ladies Academy of Philadelphia* (Philadelphia: John McCulloch, 1794).

4. Benjamin Rush, "Thoughts Upon Female Education, Accommodated to the Present State of Society, Manners, and Government, in the United States of America," *The New England Quarterly Magazine*, vol. 1 (April–May–June, 1802), 146–53; quoted in Fouts, "Music Instruction," 473.

5. Harriet Webster Marr, *The Old New England Academies Founded before 1826* (New York: Comet Press Books, 1959), p. 220.

6. Arthur F. Stone, *The Vermont of Today* (New York: Lewis Historical Publishing Co., 1929), p. 372.

7. Samuel Colcord Bartlett, "The History of Education in New Hampshire," in *New England States*, ed. William T. Davis (Boston: D. H. Hurd and Co., 1897), p. 1611.

8. Earlier books on teaching include Christopher Doch, *Schulordnung* (Germantown: Christopher Saur, 1770); Joseph Neef, *Sketch of a Plan and Method of Education founded on an Analysis of the Human Faculties, and Natural Reason, suitable for Offspring of a Free People, and for all Rational Beings . . .* (Philadelphia: The Author, 1813); and Joseph Neef, *The Method of Instructing Children Rationally, in the Arts of Writing and Reading . . .* (Philadelphia: The Author, 1813).

9. Arthur D. Wright and George E. Gardner, *Hall's Lectures on School Keeping* (Hanover, N.H.: The Dartmouth Press, 1929), p. 11.

10. Andover Seminary, *Circular*, 1830.

11. Samuel Read Hall, *Lectures to Female Teachers on School-Keeping* (Boston: Richardson, Lord, and Holbrook, 1832), p. 62.

12. Ibid., p. 64.

13. Ibid., p. 73.

14. Wright and Gardner, *Hall's Lectures*, p. 30.

15. Samuel Read Hall, *The Instructor's Manual: or Lectures on School-Keeping* (Boston: J. P. Jewett and Co., 1852), p. 2.

16. St. Johnsbury *Caledonian*, July 11, 1857.

17. Bakersfield North Academy, *Catalog*, November 1854.

18. Samuel Swift, *History of the Town of Middlebury* [Vermont] (Middlebury, Vt.: A. H. Copeland, 1859), p. 395.

19. Ibid., p. 393.

20. Emma Willard, *An Address to the Public; Particularly to the Members of the Legislature of New York Proposing a Plan for Improving Female Education* (Middlebury, Vt.: J. W. Copeland, 1819), p. 39.

21. Lizzie S. Converse, *In Memoriam of the Rev. John Kendrick Converse* (Philadelphia: J. B. Lippincott and Co., 1881), p. 78.

22. Burlington Female Seminary, *Catalog*, 1838.

23. Burlington Female Seminary, *Catalog*, 1850–1851.

24. Essex Academy, *Catalog*, 1870.

25. Barre Academy, *Catalog*, 1868.

26. Z. K. Pangborn, "Vermont Academies," *The Teacher's Voice*, I (March 1854), 129.

27. State of Vermont, *School Report*, 1848, p. 9.

28. Ivan Walter Olson, Jr., *The Roots and Development of Public School Mu-*

sic in Richmond, Virginia, 1782–1907 (Ph.D. diss., University of Michigan, 1964), p. 17.

29. Ibid., p. 30.

CHAPTER IX

1. National Education Association, Music Education Department, "Minutes," (1886) p. 563.

2. *The Vermont School Journal and Family Visitor*, D. L. Milliken, ed. (February 1866), 14.

3. Vermont Teachers Association, *Proceedings*, 1854.

4. State of Vermont, *Journal of the House of Representatives* (Middlebury: Register Book and Job Office, 1856), p. 559.

5. State of Vermont, *Journal of the Senate* (October 1856), p. 353.

6. State of Vermont, *Report of the Secretary* (1857), p. 9.

7. Vermont State Board of Education, *Report of the Secretary* (1857), p. 8.

8. City of Burlington, *School Report* (1869).

9. Henry Swan Dana, *History of Woodstock* (Boston: Houghton, Mifflin and Co., 1889), p. 130.

10. Town of Burlington, Vt., *Report of the Burlington Superintendent* (February 1, 1863).

11. George Gary Bush, *History of Education in Vermont* (Washington: Government Printing Office, 1900), p. 32.

12. Vermont Teachers Association, *Proceedings*, 1857.

13. *Vermont Chronicle*, August 1858; from newspaper clipping in possession of the Bailey Library at the University of Vermont.

14. Vermont Board of Education, *Report of the Secretary* (1862), p. 101.

15. T. J. Holmes, "Vocal Music in the Common Schools," Vermont Board of Education, *Report of the Secretary* (1862), p. 102.

16. Ibid., p. 103.

17. "Vocal Music in the Public Schools," *The Vermont School Journal*, 6 (April 1864), 83.

18. Vermont Board of Education, *Report of the Secretary*, p. 113.

19. Walter Aiken, "Music in the Cincinnati Schools," *Journal of Proceedings of the Seventeenth Annual Meeting to the Music Supervisors National Conferences* (Tulsa, 1924), p. 49.

20. Ibid.

21. Ibid.

22. Ibid.

23. Ibid., p. 47.

24. Calvin E. Stowe, *Report to the Ohio Legislature*, quoted in ibid., p. 49.

25. Common Schools of Cincinnati, *Fiftieth Annual Report*, p. 76; in Charles L. Gary, "History of Music Education in the Cincinnati Public Schools," *Journal of Research in Music Education*, 2, no. 1 (Spring 1954), p. 14.

26. *Minutes of the Board of Trustees and Visitors of Common Schools*, Cincinnati, Ohio, February 26, 1855, vol. 6; quoted in Gary, "History," p. 13.

27. *Minutes of the Board of Trustees and Visitors of Common Schools*, vol. 7, p. 199.

28. Aiken, "Music," p. 53.

29. Minutes of the Columbus Board of Education, August 19, 1854, vol. I, p. 156; in Miriam B. Kapfer, "Early Public School Music in Columbus, Ohio," *Journal of Research in Music Education*, 15 (1967), 192.

30. Kapfer, "Early Public School Music," p. 197.

31. Asa D. Lord, "First Annual Report of the Superintendent, July, 1848," *The Public School Advocate*, I (July 1851), 100–104; quoted in ibid., p. 195.

32. *Ohio State Journal*, March 28, 1851.

33. *Ohio State Journal*, December 23, 1852.

34. Poletiah W. Huntington, "Old-Time Music of Columbus," *The Old Northwest Geneological Quarterly*, 8 (April 1905), 136–140; quoted in Kapfer, "Early Public School Music," p. 198.

35. *Ohio State Journal*, December 23, 1852.

36. Oscar G. Sonneck, *Early Concert Life in America (1731–1800)* (New York: Musurgia Publications, 1949), pp. 45–46.

37. James L. Fisher, *The Origin and Development of Public School Music in Baltimore to 1870* (Ph.D. diss., University of Maryland, 1970), p. 18.

38. Lubov Keefer, *Baltimore's Music* (Baltimore: J. H. Furst Co., 1962), p. 66.

39. Fisher, *Public School Music in Baltimore*, p. 223.

40. *Fifteenth Annual Report of the Commissioners of Public Schools to the Mayor and City Council, 1843*, quoted in ibid., p. 61.

41. Fisher, *Public School Music in Baltimore*, p. 64.

42. "Proceedings of the Musical Convention Assembled in Boston, August 16, 1838," *Boston Musical Gazette*, I (February 1839), p. 169; discussed in ibid., p. 65.

43. William A. Tarbutton, *Music for the Public Schools; Selected and Arranged* (Baltimore: Board of Commissioners of Public Schools, John Woods, Printer, 1846).

44. Fisher, *Public School Music in Baltimore*, p. 84.

45. *Thirty-First Annual Report of the Commissioners of Public Schools, to the Mayor and City Council* (Baltimore: Bull and Tuttle, 1860), p. 260; in ibid., p. 86.

46. *Forty-Fourth Annual Report of Commissioners of Public Schools, to the Mayor and City Council of Baltimore, for the Year Ending December 31, 1872* (Baltimore: King Brothers, 1880), p. xxvii, in Fisher, *Public School Music in Baltimore*, p. 88.

47. *Thirty-First Annual Report*, pp. 27–28.

48. *Baltimore Sun*, May 10, 1851.

49. *Thirty-Eighth Annual Report of the School Commissioners . . . 1866*, p. 287; quoted in Fisher, *Public School Music in Baltimore*.

50. *Baltimore Sun*, December 30, 1870.

51. *Report of the Committee on Music from the Forty-Eighth Annual Report of the Commissioners of the Public Schools* (1876), p. viii.

CHAPTER X

1. Robert W. John, *A History of School Vocal Instruction Books in the United States* (Ph.D. diss., University of Michigan, 1953), p. 43.

2. Ralph Baldwin, "Evolution of Public School Music in the United States, A Symposium," *Music Teachers National Association Proceedings* (hereafter *MTNA Proceedings*) (1922), p. 169.

3. Quoted in John, *School Vocal Instruction*, p. 47.

4. Joseph Bird, "To Teachers of Music," pamphlet (1850), p. 14.

5. *Twenty-First Annual Report of the Board of Trustees of the Public Schools of Washington* (1868), p. 28, quoted in John, *School Vocal Instruction*, p. 86.

6. George B. Loomis, *First Steps in Music* (Indianapolis: The Author, 1868).

7. Loomis, *First Steps*, vol. 3 (New York: Iveson, Blake, Taylor, 1871), p. 2; quoted in John, *School Vocal Instruction*, p. 90.

8. John, *School Vocal Instruction*, p. 93.

9. L. W. Mason, *National Music Course*; quoted in Edward Bailey Birge, *History of Public School Music in the United States* (Boston: Oliver Ditson Co., 1928), p. 100.

10. Luther Whiting Mason, *Second Music Reader* (Boston: Ginn, Heath and Co., 1870), p. iii.

11. Osbourne McConathy, "From Lowell Mason to the Civil War, a Period of Pioneering," From Evolution of Public School Music in the United States, *MTNA Proceedings* (1922), p. 161.

12. Quoted in Walter R. Jones, *An Analysis of Public School Music Textbooks Before 1900* (Ph.D. diss., University of Pittsburgh, 1954).

13. *MTNA Proceedings* (1922), p. 161. The remarks were signed by Carl Bergmann, Alfred Jaell, Carl Zerrahn, C. Plagman, and Henry Band.

14. Upham was chairman of the Boston School Board's Committee on Music during this period. *Dwight's Journal of Music* (April 13, 1867), reported by the Reverend R. C. Waterston, p. 11.

15. Ibid.

16. J. Baxter Upham, "Music in the Boston Public Schools," *Dwight's Journal of Music* (February 22, 1873), 387.

17. Ibid.

18. National Education Association, *Journal of Proceedings and Addresses* (1886), p. 593.

19. Ibid., pp. 594, 596, 597.

20. Jones, *Public School Music Textbooks*, p. 135.

21. Ibid., p. 112.

22. W. S. B. Mathews, "Summer School in the Natural Course of Public School Music," *Music*, 8 (September 1895), 522.

23. Richard Lee James, *A Survey of Teacher Training Programs in Music from the Early Musical Convention to the Introduction of the Four Year Curricula* (Ph.D. diss., University of Maryland, 1968), p. 70.

24. W. S. B. Mathews, "Letter to a Future School Music Supervisor," *Music*, 20 (November 1901), 457–58.

CHAPTER XI

1. H. G. Good, *A History of American Education* (New York: Macmillan Co., 1956), p. 214.

2. Daniel Putnum, *A History of the Michigan State Normal School* (Ypsilanti, Mich.: Scharf Tag, Label and Box Company, 1899), p. 251; quoted in Richard Lee James, *A Survey of Teacher Training Programs in Music from the Early Musical Convention to the Introduction of the Four-Year Curricula* (Ph.D. diss., University of Maryland, 1968), p. 76.

3. *Catalogue of the South Missouri State Normal School Located at Warrensburg, Johnson County, for the Academic Year 1873–74* (Jefferson City, Mo.: Regan and Carter, Public Printers, 1874), p. 15; quoted in James, *A Survey*, p. 78.

4. *Catalogue of the Michigan State Normal School, 1868–69* (Ypsilanti, Mich.: 1869), p. 29.

5. James, *A Survey*, p. 79.

6. Kansas State Normal School, Emporia, Kansas, 1869–1870, *Catalogue* (Emporia, Kansas: Emporia News Book and Job Office, 1870), p. 14; quoted in James, *A Survey*, p. 79.

7. George B. Loomis, "Music in Normal Schools," *Addresses and Proceedings of the American Normal School and National Teachers Associations* (Washington, D.C.: American Normal Schools and National Teachers Associations, 1871), pp. 65–71.

8. Frank A. Beach, "Music in the Normal Schools," *Addresses and Proceedings of the National Education Association* (Ann Arbor, Mich.: National Education Association, 1916), pp. 587–92.

9. *Catalogue and Circular of the Pennsylvania State Normal School of the Fifth District, Mansfield, Tioga County, Pennsylvania, for the Year 1871–72* (Elmira, N.Y.: Advertiser Association Steam Job Printing House, 1872), p. 39.

10. Ibid.

11. Putnam, *Michigan State Normal School*, p. 252.

12. *Forty-Seventh Annual Report of the Superintendent of Public Instruction of the State of Michigan* (Lansing, Mich.: W. S. George and Company, 1884), pp. 76–77.

13. Beach, "Music in the Normal Schools," pp. 587–92.

14. "A Day at North Reading, Mass.," *Dwight's Journal of Music*, 11 (July 4, 1857), 111–12.

15. *New York Musical Review and Gazette* (June 27, 1857), 199.

16. Quoted in James, *A Survey*, pp. 43–44.

17. A. W. T. "The Normal Music School at North-Reading," *Dwight's Journal of Music*, 11 (July 25, 1857), 133–34.

18. *New York Musical Review and Gazette*, VIII (June 1857), 199; quoted in James, *A Survey*, p. 45.

19. "The Normal Music Schools," *The Musical Independent*, 2 (May 1870), 71.

20. See Christine M. Ayars, *Contributions to the Art of Music in America by the Industries of Boston, 1640–1936* (New York: H. W. Wilson Company, 1937).

21. "What Ginn and Co. Have Done to Further School Music," *Music Supervisors Journal*, 1 (September 1914), 15.

22. Hosea E. Holt, "Educational Science in Teaching," *Official Report of the Eleventh Annual Meeting of the Music Teachers National Association* (Indianapolis: Music Teachers National Association, 1887), p. 220.

23. "Summer Schools," *Music*, 20 (August–September, 1901), 274.

24. *Music*, 6 (July 1894), quoted in James, *A Survey*, p. 201.

25. Robert Foresman, *Outline of Study for the Modern Music Series* (New York: Silver Burdette and Company), p. 7.

26. Julia Ettie Crane, "Normal School Music," *Music Review* 3 (February 1894), 227.

27. Julia Ettie Crane, *Music Teachers' Manual*, 3rd ed., (Potsdam, N.Y.: Courier and Freeman, p. 7.

28. Julia Ettie Crane, *Music Teachers' Manual*, 7th ed., (Potsdam, N.Y.: Courier and Freeman, pp. 4–8.

29. Will Earhart, *Music in Public Schools*, U.S. Bureau of Education, Circular of Information, 1914, no. 33 (Washington, D.C.: Government Printing Office, 1914), pp. 72–81.

30. Iowa State Teachers College, *Catalogue and Circular*, 1910–1911 (Cedar Falls, Iowa: Bulletin of the Iowa State Teachers College, Vol. XI, No. 1), pp. 63–64; quoted in James, p. 225.

31. Karl W. Gehrkens, "Report of the Committee on Training Courses for Supervision," *Journal of Proceedings of the Fourteenth Annual Meeting of the Music Supervisors National Conference* (St. Joseph, Mo.: Music Supervisors National Conference, 1921), pp. 216–231.

CHAPTER XII

1. William James, *Principles of Psychology* (New York: Henry Holt & Co., 1890).

2. G. Stanley Hall, "The Contents of Children's Minds Upon Entering School," *The Princeton Review*, XI (May 1883), 249–72.

3. G. Stanley Hall, *Adolescence: Its Psychology and Its Relations to Physiology, Anthropology, Sociology, Sex, Crime, Religion and Education*, 2 vols. (New York: D. Appleton and Co., 1904).

4. G. Stanley Hall, "The Psychology of Music and the Light it Throws Upon Musical Education," *Journal of Proceedings and Addresses of the National Education Association, 1908*, p. 853.

5. G. Stanley Hall, "The Ideal School as Based on Child Study," *The Forum*, XXXII (September 1901), 24–39.

6. John Dewey, *Democracy in Education: An Introduction to the Philosophy of Education* (New York: Macmillan Co., 1916), p. 383.

7. John Dewey, "Interest in Relation to the Training of the Will," 2nd supp. to *1st Yearbook of the National Herbart Society* (Bloomington, Ill.: Pantagraph, 1896), pp. 204–46.

8. Dr. Rush, "Editorial," *The Annals of Education and Instruction*, 1 (February 1831), 64–65.

CHAPTER XIII

1. Will Earhart, "Report of the Conference Committee on High School Music," *School Music*, XIII (January 1912), 25.

2. Percy Scholes, *Music Appreciation, Its History and Techniques* (New York: M. Witmark and Sons, 1935); quoted in Richard Lee Dunham, *Music Appreciation in the Public Schools of the United States, 1897–1930* (Ph.D. diss., University of Michigan, 1961), pp. 1–2.

3. Thomas Whitney Surette, "Musical Appreciation for the General Public," *Music Teachers National Association Proceedings* (hereafter *MTNA Proceedings*) (1906), pp. 109–110.

4. Ibid., p. 111.

5. W. S. B. Mathews, *How to Understand Music*, vol. 2 (Philadelphia: Theodore Presser, 1888), p. 5.

6. Ibid., p. 46.

7. Henry Krehbiel, *How to Listen to Music* (New York: Charles Scribner's Sons, 1897).

8. Ibid., p. 3.

9. Ibid., p. 61.

10. Mary L. Regal, "The Study of the Appreciation of Music in the High School of Springfield, Mass.," National Education Association, *Journal of Proceedings and Addresses* (hereafter *NEA Journal*) (1910), p. 804.

11. Mary L. Regal, "Report to the NEA," p. 804; quoted in Dunham, *Music Appreciation in Public Schools*, p. 18.

12. Ibid., p. 805.

13. Ibid., p. 806.

14. Will Earhart, "The Critical Study of Music in the High Schools," *School Music Monthly*, 5 (January 1905), 11.

15. Ibid., p. 12.

16. Dunham, *Music Appreciation in Public Schools*, p. 27.

17. See Leonard B. McWhood, "Music in College and Secondary School," *MTNA Proceedings*, p. 73; and "Music in the Chelsea School, 1906–1907," *School Music Monthly*, 7 (November 1906), 12.

18. McWhood, "Music in College," p. 73.

19. McWhood, "Music in the Chelsea School," p. 10.

20. Osbourne McConathy, "Music in the High School," *NEA Journal* (1908), p. 815

21. Ibid.

22. George Oscar Bowen, "Music Education in Secondary Schools," *MTNA Proceedings* (1908), pp. 176–177.

23. Alice C. Clement, "The Cultivation of Musical Taste in Public Schools," *School Music Monthly*, 7 (September 1906), 22.

24. William H. Critzer, "Chorus Work in High Schools," *MTNA Proceedings* (1908), p. 179.

25. Ada M. Fleming, "Music in the High School — Needs of the Hour Plan," *School Music*, 8 (January 1908), 24.

26. Edward Bailey Birge, "Music Appreciation in the Public Schools," *MTNA Proceedings* (1909), p. 144.

27. Thomas Whitney Surette and Daniel Gregory Mason, *The Appreciation of Music* (New York: H. W. Gray and Co., 1907).

28. Dunham, *Music Appreciation in Public Schools*, p. 43.

29. See Edward Dickenson, *The New Musical Education* (New York: The Aeolian Co., 1908), pp. 67–74.

30. Dunham, *Music Appreciation in Public Schools*, p. 44.

31. Scholes, *Music Appreciation*, pp. 272–73.

32. Daniel Gregory Mason, *A Guide to Music* (New York: Baker and Taylor Co., 1909), p. 15.

33. Fleming, "Music in High School," p. 28.

34. George Coleman Gow, "The Pros and Cons of the Mechanical Player," *MTNIA Proceedings* (1910), pp. 83–84.

35. John G. Thompson, "The Automatic Player in Schools," *NEA Journal* (1910), pp. 809.

36. Leo Rich Lewis, "Mechanical Inventions as an Aid to the Teaching of Music," *NEA Journal* (1910), 607.

37. Frank A. Beach, "Observations and Reflections," *School Music*, 13 (November 1912), 8.

CHAPTER XIV

1. Clark does not tell us what Professor Venzie's specialty was. See Frances Elliott Clark, "School Music in 1836, 1886, 1911, and 1936," National Education Association, *Journal of Proceedings and Addresses* (hereafter *NEA Journal*) (1924), p. 606.

2. See Eugene M. Stoddard, *Frances Elliott Clark: Her Life and Contributions to Music Education* (Ph.D. diss., Brigham Young University, 1968).

3. Clark, "School Music," p. 607.

4. Stoddard, *Frances Elliott Clark*, p. 65.

5. Paper in the personal files of Frances Elliott Clark, reported in ibid., p. 177.

6. Frances Elliott Clark, "The Lady from Indiana," manuscript, personal files of Frances Elliott Clark, quoted in ibid., p. 74.

7. Ibid., p. 79.

8. Ibid., p. 82.

9. From an interview with John Clark, Jr., quoted in ibid., p. 82.

10. Ann Shaw Faulkner, *What We Hear in Music* (Camden, N.J.: The Victor Talking Machine Co., 1913), pp. 274–75; quoted in Richard Lee Dunham, *Music Appreciation in the United States* (Ph.D. diss., University of Michigan, 1961), p. 80.

11. *Music Appreciation With the Victrola for Children* (Camden, N.J.: The Victor Talking Machine Co., 1923), pp. 66–67.

12. Statement of Frances Elliott Clark at a Traveling Men's Meeting in Philadelphia, September, 1924, from the personal files of Frances Elliott Clark, quoted in Stoddard, p. 120.

13. Frank A. Beach, "The Introduction of Music into Schools Which at Present Have Little or None," *Journal of Proceedings of the Music Supervisors National Conference for 1917* (hereafter *Proceedings MSNC*), p. 144.

14. Alice Keith, "Music Appreciation Materials," *Proceedings MSNC for 1929*, p. 143.

15. Statement of Frances Elliott Clark at the Southern Music Supervisors Conference in Tulsa, Oklahoma, March 3, 1927, from the personal files of Frances Elliott Clark, quoted in Stoddard, p. 135.

16. Percy Scholes, *The Complete Book of Great Musicians* (London: Oxford University Press, 1920) and *The Listeners Guide to Music* (London: Oxford University Press, 1933).

17. "Music and Radio," *Proceedings MSNC for 1928*, p. 59.

18. Radio Corporation of America, *Teachers Manual for RCA Educational Hour* (New York: Radio Corporation of America, 1928), p. 34; quoted in Dunham, *Music Appreciation in the United States*, p. 175.

19. Ibid., p. 176.

20. "Stimulating Music Appreciation through Radio," *Proceedings MSNC for 1930*, p. 95.

21. "Radio in the Pacific Coast States," *Proceedings MSNC for 1929*, p. 426.

22. "Radio in Music Education," *Proceedings MSNC for 1929*, pp. 425–26.

23. C. M. Tremaine, "The Music Memory Contest," *Proceedings MSNC for 1918*, pp. 99–107.

24. "Music in the Dallas Schools Describing the Music Memory Contest," *The Musical Courier* 82 (February 10, 1921), 30; quoted in Dunham, *Music Appreciation in United States*, p. 183.

25. Ibid.

26. The National Bureau for the Advancement of Music, *Some Results of the Music Memory Contest* (New York, 1924), p. 3.

27. Dunham, *Music Appreciation in United States*, p. 187.

28. Sudie L. Williams, "The Advantages and Dangers of the Music Memory Contest," *Proceedings MSNC for 1923*, pp. 125–28.

29. Thomas H. Briggs, "Music Memory Contests," *School Music*, 25 (September–October, 1925), 10.

30. The National Bureau for the Advancement of Music, *Adaptations of the Music Memory Contest* (New York, 1928), p. 5; quoted in Dunham, *Music Appreciation in United States*, p. 191.

31. Dunham, *Music Appreciation in United States*, p. 191.

32. Ibid., p. 192.

33. Ibid., p. 193.

CHAPTER XV

1. William D. Fitch, "Backgrounds in the Development of Instrumental Music in the Public Schools," *Instrumentalist*, 12 (August 1958), 80.

2. Ibid.

3. H. Earl Johnson, *Musical Interludes in Boston 1795–1830* (New York: AMS Press, 1943), p. 283.

4. For an excellent study of the teaching of instruments in classes, see Charles Edmond Sollinger, *The Musical Men and the Professors—A History of String Class Methods in the U. S. 1800–1911* (Ph.D. diss., University of Michigan, 1970).

5. James L. Howell, *New Class Book*, (Cotton Plant, Ark.: The Author, 1859), p. 6.

6. Sollinger, *Musical Men*, p. 47.

7. Lewis A. Benjamin, Sr., *The Musical Academy* (New York: The Author, 1851).

8. Benjamin, *Musical Academy*, p. 3, quoted in Sollinger, *Musical Men*, pp. 50–51.

9. Sollinger, *Musical Men*, p. 57.

10. Frank T. Benjamin, *Free Violin School* (Philadelphia: Frank T. Benjamin, 1891).

11. Sollinger, *Musical Men*, p. 80.

12. Ibid., p. 77.

13. Albert Mitchell, *The Class Method for the Violin* (Boston: Oliver Ditson Co., 1918).

CHAPTER XVI

1. For an interesting discussion of the early history of bands in the United States, see Emil H. Holz, *The National School Band Tournament of 1923 and Its Bands* (Ph.D. diss., University of Michigan, 1960).

2. Ibid., p. 19.

3. Letter from J. Otto Miessner dated December 9, 1959, quoted in ibid., p. 25.

4. "Report of the High School Music Committee," *Journal of Proceedings of the Music Supervisors National Conference* (hereafter *Proceedings MSNC*) *for 1912*, p. 60.

5. *Proceedings MSNC for 1916.*

6. *Proceedings MSNC for 1919.*

7. Jay W. Fay, "Report of the Committee on Instrumental Music," *Proceedings MSNC for 1923*, pp. 234–36.

8. Edgar B. Gordon, "The Band as a School and Community Asset," *Proceedings MSNC for 1923*.

9. Walter Damrosch, *My Musical Life* (New York: Charles Scribner's Sons, 1923), p. 243.

10. Ibid., p. 255.

11. Rossiter Johnson, *A History of the World's Columbian Exposition*, vol. I. Narrative (New York: D. Appleton and Co., 1897), pp. 437–38.

12. Holz, *The National School*, p. 47.

13. C. C. Birchard, "Competitive Tests of School Singing in New England," *Music*, 12 (July 1897), 388–93.

14. Frank Beach, "Music Competitions," *Music Teachers National Association Proceedings* (hereafter *MTNA Proceedings*) (1925), p. 240.

15. Ronald J. Neil, *The Development of the Competition Festival in Music Education* (Ph.D. diss., George Peabody College for Teachers, 1944), p. 10.

16. Holz calls attention to a publication entitled *State and National High School and Grammar School Band Contests* (New York: National Bureau for the Advancement of Music, 1925), p. 15; a document which stated that band events had been included in the music contests at Emporia for the past ten years.

17. *Proceedings MSNC for 1922*, p. 199.

18. Kleffman, letter, in Holz, *National School Band Tournament*, p. 62.

19. Emil Holz, "The School Band Contest in America," *Journal of Research in Music Education*, 10 (1962), 7.

20. J. W. Wainwright, "The Educational Relation of the National School Band Contest on the Fostoria Schools and Community," *Proceedings MSNC for 1924*, pp. 242–43.

21. *Fostoria Daily Review*, June 11, 1923; quoted in Holz, *National School Band Tournament*, p. 221.

22. Interview of Emil Holz with John Hayfield, Fostoria, Ohio, February 12, 1960; reported in ibid., p. 264.

23. Interview between Emil Holz and McQueston, Detroit, Michigan, March 23, 1960; reported in ibid., p. 264.

24. Carl D. Greenleaf, "The Instrument Manufacturers and Local Bands," *MTNA Proceedings* (1930), p. 173.

25. Sousa voted against the inclusion of the alto clarinet "on the grounds that the only American qualified to teach it had been dead for years," from a recorded interview with Joseph E. Maddy, November 5, 1959. Also see Joseph E. Maddy, "The Battle of Band Instrumentation," *Music Educators Journal*, 44 (September–October 1957).

26. Ibid.

CHAPTER XVII

1. Richard Kegerreis, *History of the High School A Cappella Choir* (Ph.D. diss., University of Michigan, 1964), p. 63.

2. "Music: The Musical Art Society," *New York Daily Tribune*, March 4, 1894, p. 4; quoted in ibid.

3. "The Musical Art Society's Concert," *New York Daily Tribune*, April 23, 1894; quoted in ibid., p. 65.

4. Edward T. Rice, "A Tribute to Frank Damrosch," *The Musical Quarterly*, 25 (April 1939), 128–34.

5. *New York Times*, November 10, 1930, p. 21.

6. Olin Downs, "The English Singers," *New York Times*, November 8, 1925, p. 29.

7. See Leola Nelson Bergmann, *Music Master of the Middle West: The Story of F. Melius Christiansen and the St. Olaf Choir* (Minneapolis: University of Minnesota Press, 1944), pp. 31–64.

8. Kegerreis, *A Cappella Choir*, p. 88.

9. H. F. P., "St. Olaf Choir Sets New Choral Record," *Musical America*, 32 (May 8, 1920), 45.

10. *New York Times*, November 13, 1926, section 9, p. 14.

11. Eugene E. Simpson, *A History of the St. Olaf Choir* (Minneapolis: Augsburg Publishing House, 1921), p. 123.

12. Kegerreis, *A Cappella Choir*, p. 98.

13. Ibid., p. 102.

14. F. Melius Christiansen, "Ensemble Singing," *Journal of Proceedings of the Music Supervisors National Conference* (hereafter *Proceedings MSNC*) *for 1932*, p. 122.

15. Broadside of the Chicago Singing Teachers Guild, c. 1938; cited by Kegerreis, *A Cappella Choir*, p. 105.

16. Interview between Kegerreis and Neil A. Kjos, September 26, 1963, reported in Kegerreis, *A Cappella Choir*, p. 106.

17. Olin Downs, "The St. Olaf Choir," *New York Times*, February 9, 1927, p. 17.

18. Thaddeus P. Giddings, "Contests," *Music Supervisors Journal*, 12 (October 1925), 50.

19. Wilfred C. Bain, *The Status and Function of A Cappella Choirs in Colleges and Universities in the United States* (Ph.D. diss., New York University, 1938), p. 6.

20. Interview Kegerreis and Kjos; reported in Kegerreis, *A Cappella Choir*, p. 108.

21. Ibid., p. 123.

22. John Finley Williamson, "Training the Individual Voice," *Music Teachers National Association Proceedings* (hereafter *MTNA Proceedings*) (1930), p. 54.

23. Alexander James Inglis, *The Rise of the High School in Massachusetts* (New York: Teachers College, Columbia University, 1911), p. 147; in Kegerreis, *A Cappella Choir*, p. 147.

24. E. B. Birge, "The High School in Music Education," *MTNA Proceedings* (1920), p. 55.

25. Osbourne McConathy, *Present Status of Music Instruction in Colleges and High Schools, 1919–1920*, U.S. Bureau of Education, bulletin no. 9 (Washington: U.S. Government Printing Office, 1922), p. 46.

26. Kegerreis refers to a 1931 text on extracurricular activities which suggests that the singers participating in such assemblies be seated according to voice parts in order to facilitate the singing in parts. See Elbert K. Fretwell, *Extra-Curricular Activities in Secondary Schools* (Cambridge: Riverside Press, 1931), p. 249; cited in Kegerreis, *A Cappella Choir*, p. 155.

27. See George L. Lindsey, "Fundamental Values of Vocal Music in the Modern High School," *Proceedings MSNC for 1931*, p. 78.

28. T. P. Giddings, "Early Events in the Professional Life of One T. P. Giddings," *Music Supervisors Journal*, 13 (February 1927), 15.

29. William H. Critzer, "Chorus Work in the High School," *MTNA Proceedings* (1908), pp. 179–82.

30. Ralph L. Baldwin and Osbourne McConathy, "Report Concerning the Present Status of Music in High Schools of New England, New York, and New Jersey," *MTNA Proceedings* (1911), p. 219.

31. "Report of the National Research Council of Music Education—The Music Competition Festival," *Proceedings MSNC for 1930*, p. 262.

32. Kegerreis, *A Cappella Choir*, p. 1.

33. "National High School Chorus," *Proceedings MSNC for 1928*, p. 313.

34. "Program: Southwestern Conference," *Music Supervisors Journal*, 13 (March 1927), 63–64.

35. "Program," 1928, *Proceedings MSNC for 1928*, pp. 32–33.

36. Edward Moore, "New Idea of Beauty of Choral Tone Given by 300 Young Voices," *Chicago Daily Tribune*, April 21, 1928, p. 17; quoted in Kegerreis, *A Cappella Choir*, p. 5.

37. "Tenth Annual Report of the Flint Community Music Association, 1926–1927," Flint, Michigan, p. 2; cited in Kegerreis, *A Cappella Choir*, p. 172.

38. Kegerreis, *A Cappella Choir*, p. 174.

39. Brown, "A Resumé," *Musical Courier*, 96 (May 3, 1928), 22.

40. Kegerreis, *A Cappella Choir*, p. 10.

41. Evanson, "Classroom Choral Technique," *Proceedings MSNC for 1932*, p. 142.

42. Kegerreis, *A Cappella Choir*, p. 196.

43. George Oscar Bowen, "Senior High School Choral Music," *Proceedings MSNC for 1932*, p. 126.

44. Osbourne McConathy, "Is High School Music Making Progress?" *Proceedings MSNC for 1933*, p. 46.

45. Mrs. William Arms Fisher, "America Becomes Choral Conscious," *MTNA Proceedings* (1935), p. 320.

46. Paul Klingstedt, "The School Music Program and Its Effects on Teen-Age Singers," *MTNA Proceedings* (1947), p. 247.

47. Harry Robert Wilson, *Music in the High School* (New York: Silver Burdett, 1941), p. 93.

48. George J. Abbott, "Loudlie Sing Cuckoo," *Music Supervisors Journal*, 20 (May 1934), 46.

49. Harry Carlson, "The Interest in Youth in Oratorio," *Proceedings MSNC for 1936*, p. 182.

50. George Howerton, "Music Education through the Choral Experience," *Proceedings of the Music Educators National Conference* (1939–40), p. 331.

51. Music Educators Research Council, "Music in the Senior High School," *Proceedings of the Music Educators National Conference* (1937), p. 59.

52. Hazel R. Nohavec, ed., *Music Education Curriculum Committee Reports*, 1945 (Chicago: Music Educators National Conference, 1946), p. 31.

CHAPTER XVIII

1. See, for example, C. M. Hook, "American Music Student and the Situation in Berlin," *Musician Magazine* (January 1911), 441–42.

2. Augustus D. Zanzig, *The Concord Teachers Guide* (Boston: E. C. Shirmer Music Co., 1929), pp. 4–49.

3. Albert Gay, *Rhythmic Movement in Music Education in the Elementary School, 1900–1940* (Ph.D. diss., University of Michigan, 1966).

4. Carl W. Gehrkens, *Music in Grade School* (Boston: C. C. Birchard Co., 1934), pp. 109–10.

5. N. Trimingham, "Trends in Vocal Music in Elementary School," *Yearbook of the Music Educators National Conference* (1938), p. 295.

6. Eleanor Smith, "A Primer of Vocal Music," *The Modern Music Series* (New York: Silver Burdett and Co., 1898), p. 4.

7. Calvin Brainerd Cady, *Music-Education* (Chicago: Clayton F. Summy Co., 1902), p. 18.

8. G. Stanley Hall, *Educational Problems*, vol. I (New York: D. Appleton and Co., 1911), p. 117.

9. Thomas W. Surette, "Public School Music," *Atlantic*, 113 (December 16, 1916), 820.

10. W. Otto Miessner, "The Need of Correlation Between the Private and Public School Music Teacher," *Music Teachers National Association Proceedings* (1913), p. 155.

11. Will Earhart, Chairman, "Music in Platoon Schools," *Report of a National Committee on Music in Platoon or Work Study Playschools*, City School leaflet no. 27, U.S. Bureau of Education (July 1927), p. 3; reported in Gay, *Rhythmic Movement*, p. 98.

12. Hollis Dann, *New Manual for Teachers* (New York: American Book Co., 1929), pp. 3–7.

13. James Mursell, *Principles of Musical Education* (New York: Macmillan Co., 1927).

14. Ibid., pp. 46–47.

15. Alma M. Norton, *Teaching School Music* (Los Angeles: C. C. Crawford, 1932), p. 39.

16. Clella Lester Perkins, *How to Teach Music to Children* (Chicago: Hall and MacCreery Co., 1936), p. 42.

CHAPTER XX

1. James E. Houlihan, *The Music Educators National Conference in American Education* (Ph.D. diss., Boston University, 1961), p. 180.

2. Marguerite V. Hood, "Music in American Education," *Music Educators Journal*, 38 (February–March 1952), 17.

3. Maureen Dorthea Hooper, *Major Concerns of Music Education: Content Analysis of the Music Educators Journal, 1957–1967* (Ph.D. diss., University of Southern California, 1967), p. 48.

4. Ibid., p. 53.

5. Bennett Reimer, "What Music Cannot Do," *Music Educators Journal*, 46 (September–October 1959), 40–45.

6. *The Identity and Education of the Academically Talented Student in American Education*, National Education Association, aided by the Carnegie Foundation, National Project on the Academically Talented Student (Washington, D.C., 1958).

7. William C. Hartshorn, *Music for the Academically Talented Student in the Secondary School*, National Project on the Academically Talented Student (Washington, D.C.: National Education Association, 1960).

8. William C. Hartshorn, "The Study of Music as an Academic Discipline," *Music Educators Journal*, 49 (January 1963), 25–28.

9. Hooper, *Major Concerns*, p. 66.

10. Bennett Reimer, "What Music Can Do," *Music Educators Journal*, 46 (September–October 1959), 29–32.

11. Hooper, *Major Concerns*, p. 68.

12. E. Thayer Gaston, "Aesthetic Experiences in Music," *Music Educators Journal*, 49 (June–July 1963), 25–64.

13. **George L. Duerksen, "On Teaching Aesthetic Sensitivity,"** *Music Educators Journal*, 50 (January 1964), 85–86.

14. Bennett Reimer, "The Development of Aesthetic Sensitivity," *Music Educators Journal*, 51 (January 1965), 33–36.

15. Claude V. Palisca, *Music in Our Schools: A Search for Improvement*. Report of the Yale Seminar on Music Education, Office of Education, U.S. Department of Health, Education, and Welfare (Washington, D.C., 1964).

16. Jerome Bruner, *The Process of Education* (Cambridge: Harvard University Press, 1960).

17. The Foundation for College Education in Music, the Contemporary Music Project (Ford Foundation, September 1965).

18. David P. McAllester, *The Substance of Things Hoped For*, Documentary Report of the Tanglewood Symposium, ed. Robert A. Choate (Washington, D.C.: Music Educators National Conference, 1968).

Index

Index